PALESTINE

AND THE PALESTINIANS

1876-1983

PAMELA ANN SMITH

ST. MARTIN'S PRESS
New York

Library of Congress Cataloging in Publication Data

Smith, Pamela Ann.
    Palestine and the Palestinians, 1876-1983.

    Bibliography: p.
    Includes index.
    1. Palestine – History – 1799-1917. 2. Palestine –
History – 1917-1948. 3. Palestinian Arabs. I. Title.
DS125.S63   1984   956.94   84-13433
ISBN 0-312-59487-9
ISBN 0-312-59488-7 (pbk)

To my parents, and the families
of those who died at Tel Zaatar, Sabra and Chatilla

CONTENTS

Contents

MAPS AND TABLES

Maps

Tables

ACKNOWLEDGEMENTS

Palestinians from many walks of life proved ready and willing to answer my interminable questions, either about Palestine or about their own personal experiences. Some also played a crucial role in helping me to gain access to others who were more reticent to speak. They include Ibrahim Ibrahim, Walid and Rasha Khalidy, Yusif and Rosemary Sayigh, Antoine and Rosemary Said Zahlan, Mazin and Yusif Bandaq, Rashid Hamid, Mahmoud al-Ghul, Muhammad Zuhdi Nashashibi, Hikmat Nashashibi and Burhan Dajani; leaders of the resistance, notably the late Ghassan Kanafani, Bassam Abu Sharif, Nabil Shaath, Shafiq al-Hout and Salah Khalaf (Abou Iyad); as well as scores of others who prefer to remain anonymous, but whose openness to a foreigner and, in many cases, endless hospitality paid tribute to their ideal of living in a state based on mutual tolerance. Bassam Shaka, Muhammad Milhelm and Rashid Shawa kindly allowed me to interview them in London. Others knowledgeable about Palestinian affairs helped to enlighten my background in Arab politics, notably Lutfi al-Kholy, Muhammad Sid Ahmad, Muhammad Hassanain Haikal, Elias Saba, Halim Barakat, Lakhdar Brahimi and Simha Flapan.

In England a special note of thanks must go to Albert Hourani at Oxford. His confidence provided the encouragement and inspiration I needed to begin a daunting project at a time when my disillusionment with academic life was at its highest. His single-minded concern over a number of years and his willingness to help correct an obtuse manuscript is appreciated more than he knows. The late Malcolm Kerr graciously agreed to supervise my graduate work at the University of California, Los Angeles, and his untimely death in Beirut, like that of so many others, has left both a personal and professional void that will be difficult to fill. Thanks must also go to Lou Cantori and Afaf Lutfi el Sayed Marsot at UCLA, who helped to nurture my interest in Arab affairs; to Michael Gilsenan, whose anecdotes about the *abadiyyat* of north Lebanon and the working-class poor of Cairo helped me to keep my sense of perspective; and to Bassim Musallam, whose love of Arab poetry, politics and history first kindled my interest in the Palestinians.

Conversations with a number of close friends about the Palestinians and about other victims of oppression sustained me through the isolation of trying to write at night and on weekends. They include Marian Weil, Cindy Horan, Felicity Edholm, Barbara Smith and my sister, Lyn. Joanne Omang kept her faith in the project over many years and provided invaluable encouragement despite my long stays abroad. May Seikaly and Sarah Graham-Brown read parts of the manuscript and graciously agreed to help compile the references and bibliography.

While none of those who helped or contributed to this project can be held responsible for, or would necessarily agree with, the opinions expressed in this study, their unselfish interest and concern made the project come to life and helped to see it though completion. A final note of thanks is due to my publisher, David Croom, who offered to accept the work when the subject was still unpopular in the West and who waited patiently for the final text.

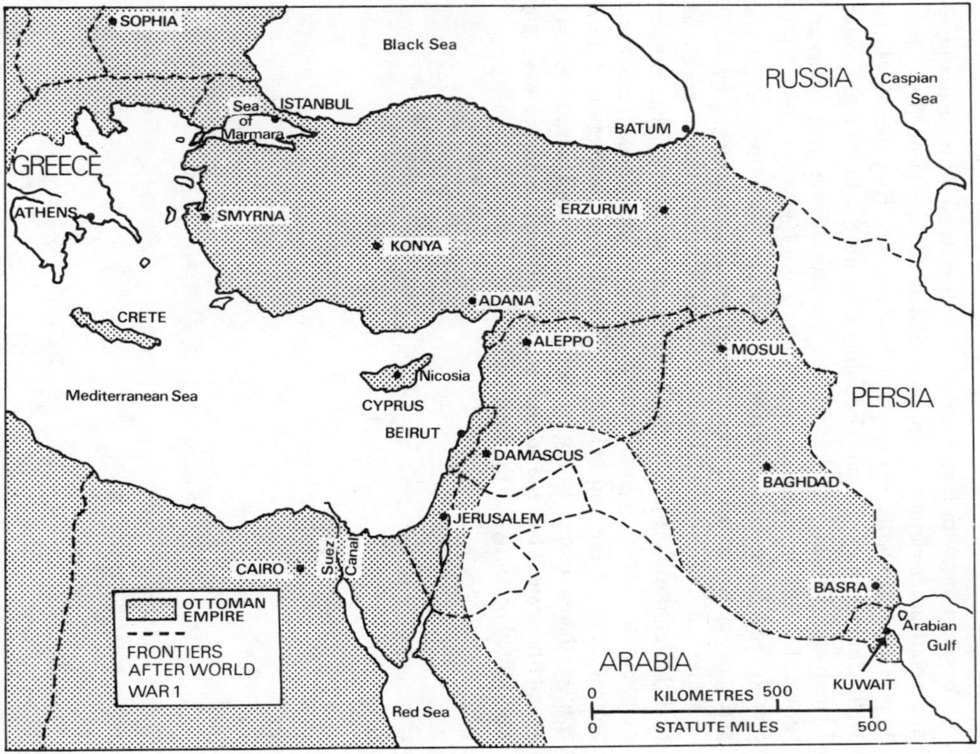

Map 1. The Ottoman Empire, 1876

INTRODUCTION

My interest in the Middle East dates back to the time of the 1967 war, when I was working as a journalist editing international news in New York. Nasser had just resigned, yet the Cairene crowds in their millions were pouring into the streets in a demonstration of love and affection that took many world leaders by surprise. Who was this man, so reviled by Britain and the United States, that had become not only the hero of Egypt and the Arab world, but of the Third World as well? And who were these Egyptians, whose affection had not been daunted by one of the worst defeats a country could suffer? Alas, as almost all the despatches from Cairo were tossed into the waste-basket in favour of those from Tel Aviv, I had to return to academic life to find out.

After completing an MA degree in Middle Eastern studies at Harvard University, I found myself facing the task of proposing a doctoral thesis topic to the political science department at the University of California, Los Angeles. Nasser had departed from the scene and the Palestinians had taken his place in the limelight. However my decision to focus on them reflected less my interest in the guerrillas and in the politics of the PLO as such than in the ways in which peasant societies react to profound social and economic change and, in the case of the Palestinians, to exile.

Until the word Palestine was erased from the map in 1948, the country had contained a population that was overwhelmingly agricultural, using traditional modes of production. Twenty years later this population had come to include one of the most dynamic and enterprising communities in the Arab world. Behind the guerrillas stood massed ranks of engineers, doctors, civil servants, businessmen and professors, many of whom played a major role in the development of Lebanon, Jordan, Saudi Arabia and the Gulf states and who were also occupied in channelling 'petrodollars' to the United States and Europe before the word had been invented.

How had such a society, given its long years in exile after 1948, managed not only to survive but also to make that intangible leap into the modern world when other, less oppressed, societies still found themselves enmeshed in tradition, poverty and exploitation? Even more importantly, how had the Palestinians maintained their sense of collective identity, despite the pressures wrenching their society apart, and transformed this identity into a movement for national liberation that seemed to grow from strength to strength despite the overwhelming odds?

Later, as my research developed, it became clear that this assertion of a national identity raised significant questions about the maintenance, or lack of maintenance, of traditional loyalties within a society that was spread across wide geographical areas and undergoing a dramatic change in its class structure. Did the Palestine Liberation Organisation, and the various movements which formed it, embody a new revolutionary spirit born out of these changes in the class structure, or did it simply make manifest a sense of national consciousness that had existed unchanged throughout the years of exile? Could the existing PLO leadership remain in power given the rise of a younger, more militant, generation?

The initial research for this study was conducted in Beirut before the civil war. Unfortunately nothing in my academic training had prepared me for the situation I found. Given the lack of documentary material, national archives and studies of Palestinian society, the immediate problem was to identify the Palestinians, where they were, and under what conditions they had lived since 1948. For this task, journalism, rather than social science, was of more use, and I began to amass an extensive series of informal, unstructured interviews with Palestinians from all walks of life: the peasant immigrant without legal papers, the shy academic who preferred to speak of his own scholarly work, the proud businessman who spoke of his people's accomplishments amid great adversity, the mother who had lost a son to the struggle, the student who hoped to fill the ranks of the guerrilla intellectuals after graduation.

These interviews provided the bedrock of many of the impressions contained in this work. Later, when I had returned to the United States and, in 1974, began working in London, they were supplemented by more structured discussions held with Palestinians whom I interviewed in the Middle East, Europe and the United States either for this study or for the magazines to which I have contributed since the mid-1970s. The task of analysing the material and of presenting a historical framework that would allow some comparative observations to be made over time was greatly helped by the articles and books which began appearing in the 1970s from the Institute of Palestine Studies and the PLO's own

Research Centre in Beirut, as well as by the more recent studies of Palestinian society that have been published in the United States, Britain and France.

Throughout I have attempted to build up a picture of Palestinian society — and the changes which have occurred within it — using the evidence that is available rather than imposing a model from 'above'. The difficult conditions in which many Palestinians live and the loss or destruction of valuable archives make it virtually impossible to avoid generalisations that may be subject to revision later as more information comes to light.

That having been said, it should also be noted that the theoretical frameworks available to students of Third World societies provide little help in sorting out a mass of data that is often conflicting and subject to manifold interpretations. The 'liberal' tradition prevalent in American social science, with its artificial divisions between tradition and modernity, conflict theory, structures and functions, too often suffers from an ethnocentricism that makes it inappropriate for the Third World. In the case of Palestinian society, where even the definition and identification of a 'Palestinian', 'refugee' or 'exile' has been subject to intense polemical debate, theoretical approaches drawn from this tradition often carry implicit biases which confuse, rather than clarify, the issues involved.

However other problems arise if one tries to use a Marxist approach exclusively. Aside from the difficulty of applying concepts like class to a pre-capitalist society, the sheer paucity of research on countries like Lebanon, Jordan, Saudi Arabia or Kuwait almost invariably means that one must draw on comparative Marxist analyses derived from the study of societies whose social formations and political economy may be quite different. The end result all too often is a revision, or critique, of Marxist theory rather than a study of the society in question.

Here I have simply tried to use what C. Wright Mills called 'the sociological imagination',[1] and to avoid the pitfalls of an abstract empiricism on the one hand and grand theorising on the other. Hopefully such an approach will help to enlighten us a little more about the ways in which, as Peter Worsley has written, 'everyday personal lives are connected to the major structures and movements of our time'.[2]

Part One

HISTORICAL PERSPECTIVE

1 PALESTINE UNDER THE OTTOMANS

The area historically known as Palestine contains some of the most varied topography in the world. From the summit of the Jebel Jarmaq almost 4,000 feet high in the hills of Galilee the country stretches south some 350 miles to the Negev desert and the Dead Sea, 1,300 feet below sea level. The long coastal plain has a Mediterranean climate, but snow is not uncommon in the winter in the central hills and in Jerusalem. Further east the terrain drops sharply to the Jordan river valley where both the heat and humidity give it a tropical fertility. In contrast, the Negev and Plain of Gaza receive less than ten inches of rain a year, making cultivation precarious without irrigation.

From time immemorial Palestine has been a crossroads between three continents. The Megiddo pass in the north, from which the word Armageddon is derived, and the valleys around it have seen waves of invasions, including that of the Crusaders under Richard I. Napoleon sought to reach the Euphrates through the pass in 1799, but was forced to turn back after three months. To the south the country forms the only passable land bridge between Asia and Africa. Semitic tribes originally established in the deserts to the north and east of Palestine settled in the country in the fourth millenium BC *en route* to the Nile, while the ancient Aegean peoples known as the Philistines are thought to have arrived from Egypt around 2000 BC.

The Hebrew tribes of the Old Testament established the kingdoms of Judah and of Israel in Palestine in the middle of the second millenium BC after their exodus from Egypt, but they were taken captive by the Assyrians and then deported to Babylon eight hundred years later. The Babylonians were defeated by Alexander the Great whose successors, the Ptolemys, ruled Palestine from the Hellenic city of Alexandria in Egypt. They in turn were succeeded by the Romans who conquered the country shortly before the birth of Christ. In the seventh century AD Palestine was again conquered by nomadic tribes from the east: the Bedouin of the Arabian Peninsula who arrived carrying the banner of Islam and the sacred words of the Prophet Muhammad.

Ottoman rule in Palestine dates back to the reign of Sultan Selim I (1512-20). His armies had wrested control of the land from the

Mamlukes, the caste of educated slaves who ruled Palestine, southern Syria and Egypt after their defeat of the Mongols in the middle of the thirteenth century AD. Although the Sultan's successor, Sulaiman the Magnificent (1520-66), fortified the walls of Jerusalem and made it a garrison for his imperial troops, Ottoman rule in Palestine was considerably weakened in the seventeenth and eighteenth centuries and the country was again subjected to an invasion from Egypt during the reign of Muhammad 'Ali in the first part of the nineteenth century.

By the late 1870s, when the Ottomans under Sultan Abdul Hamid II (1876-1909) sought to restore their authority, the Palestinian countryside was divided into a number of districts and areas, many of which were under the control of local sheikhs and amirs. In the coastal towns and especially Jerusalem the patchwork quilt of different cultures, religions and ways of life spawned by the endless waves of invasion had produced a network of anarchic *bonhomie* where Maghribi mystics, Armenian craftsmen, Talmudic scholars, British mercenaries, Turkish gendarmerie and Greek Orthodox traders lived side by side with the merchants, landowners and religious elite who made up the upper echelon of Sunni Muslim society.

By the end of the century both countryside and city had changed dramatically: as the Ottoman Empire declined, the race to carve up its dominions had gathered pace and Palestine, the land of three great religions, was caught in a web of intrigue which stretched to London, Paris, Rome, St Petersburg and Istanbul. It was to culminate in Britain's occupation of Palestine in 1917. However, before examining the impact of this latest invasion we need to look more closely at the country as it existed on the eve of Sultan Abdul Hamid's accession and at the way in which his reforms affected the economic and social life of the population.

Sheikhal Rule and Clan Warfare

Although Palestine was nominally under the control of the Ottomans at the time of the Sultan's accession in 1876, actual authority lay in the hands of the country's great tribal clans (*'ashair*), each of which was headed by a sheikh appointed by the most powerful households (*'ailah*) within the clan.[1] They were distinguished by their skill at war, their wealth or their aristocratic lineage, and each consisted of a large network of kin bound by blood ties. The clans in turn were united into one of two larger tribal confederations, either the Qais or the Yaman.

Table 1.1: Tribes and Clans in Palestine, c. 1875

Area or Region	Name	Main Residence
Bir al-Saba; Gaza	al-Azazaneh; al-Khanajarah; al-Tarabin (family of Bani al-Sittah); al-Tayaha; al-Jabarat	–
Jaffa, coastal areas	Arab al-Jaramanah; Abu Kishk	–
Acre, environs	Arab al-Hawassi (al-Hinadi)	–
al-Faraghah Valley	al-Mas'udi; al-Fa'ur	–
Baisan Valley	Arab al-Ghazawiyyah	–
Hebron, environs	Dar al-'Umru	Durrah
	Dar al-'Izzi	Bait Jibrin
	Dar al-Laham	–
Janin and Nablus, environs	Dar al-Jarrar	Khanur
	Dar al-Tuqan	–
	Dar Abd al-Hadi	'Arrabah
Haifa, coastal areas	Dar Madi	
Jerusalem:		
Bani Malik area	Dar Abu Ghush	al-'Ainab
Bani Hasan area	Dar al-Shaikhah	al-Malikah
al-Dadiyya area	Dar al-'Arifat	Abu Dabbas
	al-Qur'an	al-Birah
	al-Zabadanah (Dar al-Khatib)	Bait Aksa
	al-Dabawanah	Dair Dabwan
Bir Hamar area	Dar al-'Aql	Fa'lin
Banu 'Amir, Wadi al-'Arar area	Banu Harith	Ra's Kawkir
	al-'Uwisat	al-Burj
Bani Zaid, Bani Marrah area	al-Baraghuthah	Dair 'Usanah
Banu Sa'ab	al-Jaiyussi	Kawr
al-Sha'rawiyat area	al-Barqawi	Shufah
Jama'in, Jura 'Umar	Dar al-Qasim	Bait Wajn
	Dar al-Riyan	Majdal Yaba
Mashariq al-Baitawi	Dar al-Haj Muhammad	Bait Furik
	Banu Shamas	Baita

Source: 'Umar Salih al-Barghouthi and D. Khalil Tawtah, *Tarikh Filistin (History of Palestine)* (Jerusalem, 1922), pp. 265-8; Muhammad 'Izzah Darwazah, *Al-'Arab wa-l-'Urubah (The Arabs and Arabism)* (Damascus, 1960), cited in Nabil Badran, *Al-Ta'lim wa-l-tahdith fi-l-mujtama' al-'arabiyyi al-filistiniyyi (Education and Modernisation in Palestinian Arab Society)* (Beirut, 1969), pp. 29-30.

A member of either confederation was bound to avenge any wrong committed against a fellow member by adherents of the opposing group.[2] Neighbouring villages, controlled by different sheikhs, often belonged to opposing factions, while some towns, such as al-Birah, Tayibah, Dair al-Jarir and Jerusalem contained both Qaisis and Yamanis.[3] Christians and Muslims could belong to either of the confederations and all members of one faction shared the spoils of war as well as the obligations of revenge and mutual defence.

Although some historians have attributed the violence which erupted in Palestine in the middle of the nineteenth century to the persistence of the clans and tribes, conflict was not inherent in the system. In normal times a pattern of arbitration and reconciliation limited the amount of violence that could occur, while at the same time ensuring that each member of the clan was physically protected and provided for during periods of great insecurity or impoverishment. In those areas where the system was preserved in its original form, agriculture and trade throve due to the absence of conscription, forced labour and excessive taxation. In addition, the local sheikhs enforced the common law, the Shari'ah al-Khalil, or 'Law of Abraham'. Unlike the more orthodox Shari'ah Muhammadiyyah, which was propagated and interpreted by an urban elite consisting of *muftis* and *qadis* appointed by the Sultan, the Shari'ah al-Khalil reflected local custom and tradition.[4]

When the countryside was free of warfare, the sheikhs and their kin could amass considerable wealth. Ihsan al-Nimr, a descendant of one of the most powerful families in the Nablus area, has described the position of his own clan in the middle of the nineteenth century:

> Their possessions were of great variety, reflecting their princely status (*al-imara*) and honour ('*izzah*). They owned soap factories, bathhouses, vegetable gardens, pottery works, mills, bakeries, olive and sesame presses, shops and the best land ... They bequeathed their possessions to their own households and their descendants and their kinfolk followed their example. They said that so far as their property extended, so also did their kinfolk, and through their leadership (*qiyadah*) the family of al-Nimr preserved their domain, a tenure they held for more than three centuries.[5]

Other families in the country had become so powerful that they were able to ensure that the post of Ottoman governor (*wali*) for their area was chosen from among their own ranks. In the Nablus area, for example, the post of governor was held by either the Abdul Hadis or the Tuqans from 1840 to 1860; an Abdul Hadi even served for a while as the Ottoman governor of the city of Gaza.[6]

The sheikhs' power and wealth were derived from their right to collect the taxes and to keep the peace locally. A Palestinian historian has described the process as follows:

> Each year a governor, the wali ash-Sham, came [from Istanbul] to Damascus and gave to every shaikh of the surrounding districts a suit of shaikh's robes — a robe of honour — and his orders; that is, the commands of the government. The shaikhs then guaranteed the taxes [which] were allotted according to the size of the villages, the largest paying 500 zalat, while others gave 200, 150, or what not. A similar official came to Jerusalem for the same purpose.[7]

While on paper the process entailed a direct chain of command from Ottoman governor to sheikh to peasant, the conditions prevailing in the countryside often dictated otherwise. This was particularly true in Palestine in the middle of the nineteenth century, after the retreat of Ibrahim Pasha and his Egyptian forces, when the Ottomans found themselves preoccupied with revolts in their Balkan provinces and with Tsarist Russia's attempts to occupy the Crimea. Law and order disintegrated at the same time that the Porte's need for funds and soldiers escalated rapidly. In an effort to obtain more funds, the Ottoman authorities made the tax concessions, known as *iltizam*, subject to annual renewal, depending on a sheikh's ability to raise the troops he needed to extract the sums from the peasantry and to ensure that law and order prevailed in the district.

This 'divide-and-rule' policy, which pitted the sheikhs against each other and encouraged tribal and clan conflict, was also exacerbated by the rivalry which existed between the clans, as for example between the Abdul Hadis and the Tuqans in the Tulkarm, Nablus and Janin districts and between the sheikhs of Hebron and Bait Jibrin in the south. In 1850 the conflict erupted in a civil war which gradually engulfed almost the whole of Palestine and which lasted, intermittently, until 1874.

The Rise of Private Property

The decline of the tribal system and the transformation of the clans into smaller landowning families on the one hand and impoverished peasantry on the other began with the enactment of a new Land Law in 1858. Prior to the implementation of the Law, the right to gather the taxes on the land was decided directly by the Sublime Porte — the administrative headquarters in Istanbul. A tax concession (*iltizam*) was superimposed over every source of revenue: urban commerce, the guilds and built-up land as well as that which was cultivated with crops. With the exception of a few estates composed primarily of orchards, vineyards and vegetable gardens in or near the towns which had been allowed to retain their freehold status from the time of the Islamic conquests, or which were subsequently given by the Sultan as *mulk* — i.e. as freehold — to those who had served the Empire, the actual ownership of the land remained in the hands of the state.

The person who received the tax concession, the *multazim*, was obliged to make sure the lands were cultivated and the taxes on its revenue delivered to the state Treasury, in return for which he was allowed to keep a portion of the collections in lieu of a salary to help defray his expenses. Failure to cultivate the land, or to turn over the taxes, led to the confiscation of the land and its return to the state for re-appointment to another *multazim*.[8] The actual cultivation of the land was carried out by villagers who apportioned a share each year to their members depending on how many oxen the villager owned and how much land he could reasonably expect to plough and sow. The *multazim* himself only appeared on the scene at the time of harvest, when the taxes due to the Treasury were assessed.[9]

This system of parcelling out the land, which was known as *musha'* (from the Arabic word meaning 'to circulate'), was prominent in almost the whole of Palestine at the beginning of the nineteenth century. Its prevalence helps to explain why the country, even in periods of great turmoil, remained an important agricultural area: as one part of the country became uninhabitable because of increasing raids by the Bedouin or the lack of security in general, the peasantry would simply move to another area (usually the hills) where they easily found other land to sow. And while the state officially held title to the land, any produce gained from it belonged to those who had brought it under the plough. As the cultivation was carried out by the peasantry on a communal basis, the ownership of the land, in effect, was held collectively by the peasantry.

Under the terms of the Land Law of 1858 and the Land Registration Act passed that same year, the right to collect the taxes was made virtually hereditary within the family of the *multazim*. The registration of land and the issuance of title deeds gave the *multazims* the right to dispose of their property freely, whether through the transfer of their land or its designation as *waqf* (see below). Finally, although the right of the state to confiscate land which was left uncultivated remained, enforcement of the procedure was so weakened that a landlord had simply to turn the earth on his holding once every three years – and then only superficially – to avoid its confiscation.[10]

Amendments to the Land Law in successive years further defined and elaborated these decrees. In 1867 foreigners obtained the right to own land and two years later the Majallah Code allowed state, or *miri*, land to be converted into *mulk*, i.e. from 'leasehold' to 'freehold'. In addition, those who brought grazing, or *mewat*, land under the plough were granted the right to a title deed as well, providing they paid the taxes due on the land.[11] The reduction of the peasantry to sharecroppers was thus extended to the Bedouin who were deprived of their grazing rights and subjected to expulsion or to the authority of the landlord in whose name the land was registered.

Although the Land Law and its amendments were not uniformly enforced throughout the countryside, the changes it introduced encouraged the rise of private property to the extent that many of the country's most influential families had become enormously wealthy landlords by the 1870s. The Abdul Hadis who, as we have seen, exercised control over much of the area around Nablus were reported in 1875 to have owned 17 villages and 60,000 *dunums* of land, or about 5,400 hectares (13,350 acres); the Jaiyussis, whose main residence was at Kur near Banu Sa'ab, owned 24 villages. The Barghouthis owned even more, 39 villages in all in the area around Bani Zaid and Bani Marrah.[12] In the south of Palestine the Taji family (also known as the al-Faroukis) owned an estimated 50,000 *dunums* of land around Ramlah; the Tayans of Jaffa some 40,000 *dunums* and the Shawa family of Gaza as much as 100,000 *dunums*.[13] A Jewish family, the Bergheims, was said to own 20,000 *dunums*, and possibly much more, in and around the village of Abu Shusha.[14]

With the growth of the large landed estates the collective solidarity of the clans diminished. The families who held the tax concessions and received the right to pass land down to their heirs became wealthy at the expense of their poorer kinsmen who lost their right to share in the benefits which would otherwise have been shared by the clan as a whole. This pattern of increasing social differentiation in the countryside was further compounded by the tendency of the poorer peasantry and of the Bedouin to avoid registering their lands altogether, or to register them in the name of a local sheikh or family, to avoid taxation and conscription (see Chapter 2). When in the early part of the twentieth century the landlords gained the right to sell their land as well, those with title deeds benefited at the expense of those who relied on the traditional rights of cultivation rather than ownership of the land as guaranteed by the possession of a registered title.

The introduction of private property also led to the decline of subsistence farming and to the introduction of cash crops and production for export. The cultivation of hard wheat (*durra*), originally produced in the Syrian province of the Hauran, became increasingly prevalent in Galilee and in other parts of northern Palestine from where it was exported to the European ports of Trieste and Marseilles via Acre and Haifa.[15] In other parts of the hill country the cultivation of olives and of sesame seeds also expanded considerably. Produce from these crops was exported in the form of oil to Europe and as soap and tahina to Egypt and other parts of the Middle East and North Africa.[16]

The most sweeping change, however, occurred in the cultivation of citrus fruits. Huge plantations (*biyyarat*) were established in the coastal plain and by 1890 some 200,000 cases of oranges and lemons were being exported each year from the port of Jaffa. By 1913 this figure had risen eightfold, to 1.6 million cases.[17]

Such capital-intensive agriculture provided far greater profits than did the traditional crops of grain, legumes and livestock. Those families, particularly in the interior, which had access neither to suitable land for cash crops nor to the capital needed to develop products for export, were reduced to the level of small producers at best and, in some cases, to a standard of living not far removed from that of the sharecroppers. The old clan system which had ensured solidarity within one's kin disintegrated and, as we shall see, was replaced by one in which social relations were increasingly dictated by the market and by Palestine's integration into the world economy.

European Settlement

The Land Law of 1858 was only one of a series of reforms enacted in the middle of the nineteenth century which dramatically changed the economic and social foundations of Ottoman rule in Palestine. Other decrees, known collectively as the *Tanzimat* reforms, introduced a modern system of education that included the establishment of a university, military and medical colleges and institutions of foreign languages as well as courses in secular subjects such as finance, commercial law, engineering and science.[18] Decrees affecting the status of the Christian and Jewish minorities removed the poll tax to which they had been subject and gave them the right to sit in the newly established administrative councils (*majlis-i idara*) set up in the provinces and in the parliament established in Istanbul in 1876. Non-Muslims were also allowed to take part as judges, lawyers and clients in a system of new mixed courts which were allowed to adjudicate criminal as well as commercial law.[19]

Still other reforms introduced Western principles of business, including the right to establish shareholding companies, to repatriate profits and to allow foreign contractors to enter into legal and binding contracts in the Ottoman Empire.[20] By the end of the century, as the Empire declined still further and began to amass extremely large foreign debts, whole sectors of economic activity — banking, transport and communications, public utilities and mining — had been turned over, *carte blanche*, to European interests in an effort to stave off bankruptcy and to preserve the last vestiges of Ottoman rule in Palestine and in the other provinces which had not yet been lost to European encroachment.

The *Tanzimat* decrees were also accompanied, in the last two decades of the century, by a series of measures aimed at encouraging immigrants to settle on the land and to open it to cultivation. At first the immigrants came mainly from those areas of the Empire which had been lost to Russia or to the Europeans: Bosnians fleeing the Hapsburgs, Circassian refugees from the Caucausus and Maghribis who had lost their struggle against the French conquest of North Africa. Later their numbers were gradually supplemented by non-Muslims who came from outside the Empire as well. While in Palestine these included some from Christian countries, such as the German Templars and American Protestants, the main response came from the Jewish communities of Russia and Eastern Europe where a series of pogroms and severe oppression had created a new spirit of resistance that was to culminate in the formation of the Zionist movement. By the year 1900 some 5,000 Jewish agricultural settlers had arrived in Palestine and were settled in some 19 colonies covering a total of 275,000 *dunums* of land.[21]

The opening of the country to foreign trade and to settlement from Europe and Russia led to a massive rise in the price of land and to a wave of speculation that was to continue until the end of the British Mandate in 1948. While many of the Arab estates which were sold to the Jewish settlers between 1882 and 1920 were sold by absentee landowners living in the neighbouring Arab countries, Palestinians from the landed families often made considerable profits either by selling small plots of their own or by acting as brokers (*simsar*) for the sale of land by others.[22] In the next chapter we will look in greater detail at how this speculation, the rise of private property in general and the increased European settlement affected Palestinian society and led to the emergence not only of a wealthy landowning class but also of a new rural proletariat consisting of landless tenants, sharecroppers and impoverished small farmers.

2 THE TRANSFORMATION OF PALESTINIAN SOCIETY, 1876-1917

The period from 1876 to 1917, the date of General Allenby's arrival in Jerusalem, was not a long one; yet these three decades witnessed profound political and social changes which left an indelible mark on Palestinian society. Outside the country the European *détente*, which had resulted in a combined effort to guarantee the integrity of the Ottoman Empire, was crumbling; Britain and France struggled for control of North Africa and the Red Sea while at home the Sublime Porte in Istanbul was preoccupied with revolts in the Balkans and Tsarist expansion on its northern borders. In 1909, 33 years after he had come to power, Sultan Abdul Hamid was overthrown by a group of army officers and intellectuals who were collectively known as the Committee of Union and Progress or, more informally, as the 'Young Turks'.[1] The deposition was universally welcomed: the Committee, shortly after its triumphant entry into Istanbul a year earlier, had promised to restore the constitution, suspended in 1877, and to guarantee the rights of all citizens regardless of race, creed or sex. Parliament was reconvened, and delegates from all parts of the Empire, including Palestine, took their seats whereupon they began demanding even more drastic reforms.[2]

Even at the moment of victory the Young Turks were besieged on all sides. In 1908 Bulgaria had declared her independence, Austria had formally annexed Bosnia-Herzegovina and Crete had proclaimed its unity with Greece. Three years later Italy, which was seeking to establish a foothold in North Africa alongside the British and French, declared war on the Empire. In 1912 this resulted in the loss of Tripolitania and the Dodecanese.[3] Later that year, in October, the Balkan states declared war on what was left of the Empire.[4] The Young Turks, faced with a combined military operation that threatened to remove the last vestige of Ottoman rule in Europe and North Africa, suspended the constitution, initiated one-party rule and, in 1913, shortly before entering the First World War on the side of Germany, set up a military dictatorship under the control of three infamous pashas — Enver, Talaat and Jemal.[5] Throughout the Arab provinces their combined policies of forced conscription, exorbitant taxation and the ruthless confiscation of land, animals and buildings to serve the Ottoman armies robbed them, and

17

the Empire, of any support they still enjoyed among the native population. And, as we shall see, it was during this period that the first wave
of emigration from Palestine in modern times occurred.

The physical disintegration of the Empire was accompanied by
unprecedented ideological turmoil throughout the Arab world.[6] The
Young Turks, having failed in their programme of democratic reforms,
initiated a policy of pan-Turkish solidarity in 1914, seeing this as the
only way to preserve their own legitimacy in the face of the ethnic
nationalisms sweeping the provinces in Europe. (Although the idea
of a pan-Islamic resurgence had been suggested as an alternative, the
revolts of the Sufi brotherhoods — particularly of the Mahdiyyah in
the Sudan and the Sanussis in Libya, the uprisings of the Wahhabis in
Arabia and the writings of the Salafiyyah reformers in Cairo rapidly
destroyed any notion of Islamic unity.)

The decision to rally the Turkish elements, in Central Asia as well
as in Anatolia and the Balkans, left the Arabs feeling even more
oppressed and isolated than ever. For Palestine, as well as Syria, Lebanon, Mesopotamia and Arabia, the choice now lay solely between the
quest for autonomy, within the confines of a reformed Empire, or the
pursuit of total independence and the establishment of a unified Arab
nation. The extent and manner in which these nascent ideologies found
expression in Palestine preceding the First World War were conditioned
by the unique economic and social changes the country experienced,
and it is to a study of how these changes affected social relations in
Palestine that we now turn.

Palestine at the end of the nineteenth century still consisted of
a large peasantry dominated by a ruling elite drawn mainly from the
cities and provincial towns. However, whereas throughout much of
the period preceding the *Tanzimat* reforms this elite consisted of the
tribal sheikhs who presided over the various clans (*'ashair*), by the time
of the First World War they had been replaced by a heterogeneous
ruling class composed of two distinct factions: the intellectual aristocracy (*ashraf*) and the large landed families (*'ailah*) within the clans
which gradually amassed influence and material wealth and wrested
power away from the sheikhs.

The *Ashraf*

Little has been written about the *ashraf*, yet these 'men of the pen'
played a crucial role in both the economy and politics of Palestine.

Part of their influence derived from the fact that Islam traditionally refused to recognise, at least in theory, a division between the temporal and the spiritual realms of existence; that is, between the earthly pursuit of gain and the preparation of one's soul for the hereafter. Another factor was that the Ottomans, unlike the earlier dynasties such as the Umayyads and the Abbasids which ruled the Muslim world after the initial Islamic conquests, were never fully recognised by the Muslim World as the rightful heirs of the first Caliphs; hence the use of the term 'Sultan', rather than 'Caliph', to describe the Ottoman ruler, the former term expressing merely his *de facto* control of the realm rather than a lawful right to succession. Throughout the long centuries of rule from Istanbul the general populace, in Palestine as elsewhere in the Arab world, continued to give formal obeisance to the secular authorities while reserving its true allegiance for the upholders of the Koran and of the indivisible unity of the faithful, namely the *ashraf*.

Members of the *ashraf* (singular = *sharif*) were distinguished by birth; most traced their ancestry to, or claimed to be descended from, either the Prophet Muhammad or the great military commanders who had led the early Islamic conquests in the seventh century AD. As such they enjoyed certain privileges: they paid no taxes and were exempt from military service, as well as from prosecution under criminal law. They could be tried only by their leader, the *naqib*, and if necessary were imprisoned in the *naqib*'s house rather than in state prisons.[7]

Their material wealth was derived from their control of the *awqaf* (singular = *waqf*), the charitable estates and foundations set up in perpetuity under Islamic law. The Tamimis, for example, had been given *waqf* and other huge tracts of fertile land in southern Palestine by 'Umar ibn al-Khattab, the second Caliph, in the seventh century at the time of the Islamic conquests. Another family, the Daudis of Jerusalem (later known as the Dajanis), were entrusted with the control of the *waqf* of Nabi Daud about the same time. While a portion of the revenues derived from *waqf* land was enjoined for the upkeep of mosques, schools and public gardens as well as for distribution to the poor, revenues obtained from immovable property built on *waqf* land (*wirku*), or from the tithes (*'ushr*) payable on its agricultural produce, were generally kept by the *ashraf* to defray the expenses they incurred in the course of their duties.[8]

Under the Ottomans the *ashraf* were recognised as a corporate body, organised in guilds, with the power to designate their own members, the visual symbol of which was the wearing of the green turban. While in theory the highest religious positions in the country could be held by any Muslim, however low-born, in Palestine virtually all the *muftis*, *qadis* and *imams* were chosen by the sharifian families. The Khatibs, for example, derived their prestige and influence from their control of the post of Imam at the venerable Al-Aqsa Mosque in Jerusalem, a position they held until the 1930s. The Nusaibahs had been given the care of the keys to the city of Jerusalem by 'Umar ibn al-Khattab about the time the Tamimis had received their lands in southern Palestine, and they held this position until the end of the Ottoman era. Another family, the Dajanis of Jaffa, although not originally of sharifian origin, had been promoted by the Ottoman governor, Muhammad Agha Abu Nabut, after Napolean's retreat. Thereafter the position of Mufti of Jaffa was reserved for the Dajanis, who often controlled the post of chief Qadi and mayor as well.[9]

Although at times, such as in Acre in the early nineteenth century during the reign of Jazzar Pasha, the *ashraf* were more powerful than their rivals, the *iqta'iyyin* or feudal lords (to the extent, for example, that the *ashraf* could force the lords to avoid an excessive display of wealth), their power had begun to decline in the countryside. They responded by forming alliances with some of the largest families in Jerusalem, such as the Hussainis, Khalidis, Nashashibis and Jarallahs, as well as with the Alamis, who were originally from Gaza. Eventually these families also claimed some of the privileges of the *ashraf* and, in many cases, became virtually indistinguishable from their predecessors in terms of their position within Palestinian society.[10]

Both elements of this new ruling class profited from the land system in Palestine. The insecurity and disorder which occurred during the civil war led to a considerable increase in the amount of land registered as *awqaf*, and so too to an increase in the lands and property available to the *ashraf* and their allies. The conversion of land to *awqaf* ensured that it could not be confiscated by the Ottoman authorities for lack of cultivation or for failure to pay the tribute demanded by the Sultan's military governors.[11]

Furthermore, because of the prevailing system of inheritance in Palestine, which ordained the parcelling of land to all the heirs and consequently led to the fragmentation of estates within the space of a few generations, the *ashraf* and their allies benefited from the tendency to register land as *awqaf* to escape the harsh laws of succession.[12] As a result the *ashraf* and the leading families of Jerusalem often enjoyed a level of prosperity which was higher, at least in the nineteenth century, than that enjoyed by their counterparts in Cairo, Damascus, Baghdad, Mecca and Medina, where the laws of succession were different and where there was less incentive to turn valuable agricultural or urban land into *awqaf*.

Equally important were the *Tanzimat* reforms and the centralisation of authority under Sultan Abdul Hamid II which, however oppressive, nevertheless provided new means by which the *ashraf* could exploit their holdings and expand their wealth and influence. This occurred in several ways. First of all, the new schools and governmental departments were staffed by the sons of the sharifian families or by the sons of the landed families whose education and qualifications had been certified by the *ashraf*. By recruiting civil servants and army officers from amongst their kin or related families, the *ashraf* were effectively able to monopolise the advancement and promotion of Palestinians within the Ottoman administration.[13]

Second, the fact that the holding of religious offices within the Empire became hereditary in the latter part of Ottoman rule meant that certain of the *ashraf* were able not only to dominate the religious hierarchy but also to ensure that the control of the *awqaf* remained within their own households.[14] As we shall see later, the prestige which was attached to the holding of government office, whether in the religious institutions and courts or in the secular administration, enabled many of the sons of these families to regain their privileges and material wealth after the creation of the state of Israel in 1948.

Third, the restoration of order and the expansion of cultivation which occurred under Sultan Abdul Hamid increased the revenues from the *awqaf* and so too that of the *ashraf*. This enabled the *ashraf* and their allies to purchase uncultivated land, which they could often obtain at an unusually low price as well, through their positions in the Ottoman bureaucracy and their access to the courts. (The judges, or *qadis*, who adjudicated disputes concerning the ownership and cultivation of land were, as we have seen, drawn from the ranks of the *ashraf*.) In addition, their authority to determine which lands were suitable for such purchases, the price they were worth and the amount to be offered for sale, increased both their influence among those eager to buy land and their ability to earn substantial sums of money from such certifications.[15]

Fourth, the changes in the manner in which the harvest was assessed, and in the amount due in payment of the tithes (*'ushr*), enabled them to obtain a larger amount of produce, in advance of the harvest, from their own holdings and that of the *awqaf*. With these payments in kind they were able to engage in trade and to amass wealth both by providing an outlet for the agricultural surplus and the money needed by the peasantry to finance next year's crop.[16]

Last but not least, many of the *ashraf*, after the changes in the Land Law, were often able to obtain sizeable estates by the simple tactic of registering the land communally cultivated by the peasantry as their own. The peasantry, which was already overburdened with debt, was often left with no choice: registration in the name of a *sharif* was the only way in which a peasant could escape the high taxes. After the Young Turks began forcibly to conscript large numbers of the peasantry into the army, even more land was registered in the name of the *ashraf* or of the local sheikh (see below). In addition to relieving the peasant of the crushing burden of taxes, such a move also enabled him to ensure that his sons would not be registered for military service.[17]

The Landed Families

In contrast to the *ashraf*, whose position in society was ordained by birth, the large landed families and clans ruled the countryside by virtue of the strength of their kinship ties and blood affiliations. The ability to rally sizeable numbers of the clan ensured not only that the land was cultivated and the produce kept for its members' use but also that its land and property were kept safe from marauding Bedouin and rival claimants. As we have seen, their power over their extended network of kin enabled the sheikhs to ensure that members of their households were appointed as governor at times when Ottoman rule in Palestine was relatively weak.

At the beginning of the nineteenth century Palestine was divided into *muqata'at* (provinces), *nahiyah* (regions) and villages. In each division a sheikh, or *amir*, presided over the local inhabitants who were related, or affiliated, to them.[18] The sheikh was generally chosen by the members of the village, household or clan, and in turn was assigned rights to the land by the Ottoman *wali* or his subordinates. However after the civil war and the implementation of the *Tanzimat* reforms, the ruling sheikhs, as we have seen, obtained a hereditary right to the tax concessions (*iltizam*) and then the right to dispose of their land freely. (Only later, in the last stages of Ottoman rule, was this right revoked in favour of a system whereby the tax concessions which became available were sold at auction to the highest bidder.) The net result was that certain households within the various families and clans, i.e. those which possessed the tax concessions at the time that they became hereditary, became more powerful than others within the clan.

The sheikhs with these hereditary rights in turn came to resemble a distinctive class, whose interests conflicted with the sheikhs who did not own tax concessions and land as well as with the peasantry, even though they were members of the same clan.

The disparity between those sheikhs who owned *iltizam* and those who did not was further compounded by the changes which occurred in the administration of the Empire. Those households which were allied to the *ashraf* and had access to state positions in the civil service or army or to higher education in the new technical colleges and training institutes in Istanbul gradually gained ascendancy over those which did not. As these positions were reserved for the sons of the more powerful families, i.e. those with land, the poorer relations gradually found themselves further excluded from power and influence (*wajahah*), to the extent that some lived in conditions not unlike those of the peasantry. While marriage into one of the more powerful clans or to a member of the *ashraf* sometimes provided an escape route for the poorer sheikhs, others were banned from pursuing such a path since many of the larger landowning clans, such as the Barghouthis, the Jaiyussis and the Abdul Hadis, forbade their members to marry outside the clan.[19]

At the same time, however, the position of the sheikhs and of the clan system as a whole was endangered by the changes occurring within the Empire. As the *ashraf* were able to use their positions in the cities to gain access to land and markets, the sheikhs lost their exclusive control of agricultural production and the distribution of goods to the internal market. Similarly, although the restoration of security under Sultan Abdul Hamid enabled some of them to open new lands to cultivation and to expand their holdings, it also deprived them of their greatest collective asset; namely, their power to preserve the peace. As the peasantry found it less and less necessary to rely on them for the maintenance of order, the sheikhs found themselves increasingly unable to maintain the allegiance of their kin and the services which they provided. The alliances with the Bedouin also disintegrated and this in turn affected the ability of the sheikhs to control the lucrative internal caravan trade. In a few cases, such as where the sheikhs had been empowered to protect the route of the annual pilgrimage to Mecca, the result was a considerable loss in the payments they received from the Ottoman Treasury as well.

Thus by the beginning of the First World War the collective power of the sheikhs had declined dramatically in favour of a new system dominated by the *ashraf* and large landowning families within the clans.

Although the sheikhs retained their titles, and often their prestige among the peasantry, despite their loss of material wealth, power and influence passed to the leaders of the great households such as the Abdul Hadis, the Tuqans and the Shawas (as well as the Barghouthis and Jaiyussis), who were able to use their lands, position and kin to amass financial benefits and to expand their political influence (*za'amah*) in order to survive and compete in a society in which the accumulation and investment of capital was becoming increasingly important.

Finally, it should be noted that while in theory the accumulation of surplus capital in private hands, and the increasing concentration of it within a few large landowning families, should have enabled the latter to invest in new industries serving the local market, few actually did so. The Tuqans used part of the vast sums they obtained from their tax concessions in central Palestine to expand the Nablus soap industry; others, in the period after 1900, set up small food-processing plants, flour mills and brickworks.[20] Large sums were also invested in the expansion of citrus cultivation. Yet neither this activity nor the expansion of the few processing industries in Palestine actually led to the development of an indigenous industrial sector, or of a nationalist bourgeoisie.[21] The surplus capital that accumulated in the hands of the large landed families was primarily diverted either into land speculation or into an intense form of conspicuous consumption which included the purchase of expensive dowries and the support of a vastly increased body of retainers — agents, bodyguards, middlemen — as well as the construction and furnishing of luxurious urban residences.

This kind of ostentatious display became even more predominant after the Young Turk revolution and the introduction of parliamentary and local elections, as each of the landed families sought to impress upon its kin, and rival claimants, its superiority in terms of wealth in a bid to maintain, or expand, its political influence and control of the ballot box. While in part this reflected their growing awareness that the nature of the game had changed, and that blood ties had to be lubricated with cash payments and other forms of largesse to maintain the allegiance of their followers, it also reflected their unwillingness, and inability, to compete successfully with the Christian merchants who benefited from the excessively low tariffs imposed on imported goods (see below). The landed families also failed to gain access to those economic activities, such as the construction of roads and railways, the distribution of water and electricity, banking and the export of cash crops such as silk, tobacco and salt, which were highly profitable but which were reserved by the Porte for foreign companies or for those subjects, primarily the Christians, who were favoured by the foreign embassies.

The Urban Merchants

Throughout most of the period of Ottoman rule control of foreign commerce, as distinct from internal trade and local, small-scale commerce, was largely in the hands of non-Muslim minorities: Greeks, Italians, Armenians, Jews and other indigenous residents who benefited from the Capitulations, the series of extra-territorial privileges granted by the Sultans to the European powers.[22] Although originally the concessions had been allowed only to foreign consuls and their local agents, by the seventeenth century local merchants, both Christians and Jews, were able to obtain licences, known as *berats*, from the European embassies and consulates which allowed them to escape the import duties and taxes normally imposed on goods of foreign origin.[23] Under pressure from the European powers the Porte extended these privileges so that by the 1870s virtually all the remaining restrictions imposed on the local non-Muslim merchants were removed. Among the most important was the ban on engaging in internal trade, a prohibition which the Porte had ordered to protect the local market. As one historian has noted, the non-Muslim merchants 'thus enjoyed the best of both worlds — legal equality with the Ottoman citizens, and continued legal and economic privileges under the capitulations'.[24]

Yet these privileges alone cannot explain the rapid expansion of this class during the period from 1876 to 1914. Rather it was the combination of the overall growth of the population of the country, from both immigration and births, and the increasing prosperity which provided the context in which the urban merchants could use these privileges to flourish. By the time of the First World War they formed a nascent commercial bourgeoisie, albeit one of the comprador kind, which, had it not been for the oppression of the Young Turks and the defeat in the war, might have successfully challenged the dominant power of the *ashraf* and of the landed families and opened the economy to even greater capitalist activity.

The growth in population occurred partly as a result of the restoration of order after the accession of Sultan Abdul Hamid and partly as a result of the immigration of Christians and Jews. Although the statistical evidence available for the period is rudimentary, reliable estimates show that the total population grew from less than half a million in 1895 to almost 700,000 by 1914, an increase of almost 40 per cent in less than twenty years.[25] Part of this was due to Jewish immigration, which increased greatly after the formal establishment of the Zionist movement at the first Zionist Congress in Basle in 1897. Between that year and 1914 the Jewish population in Palestine doubled from some 50,000 to almost 100,000.[26] The majority, between 50,000 and 60,000, lived in Jerusalem or its environs. About 12,500 were located in Safad, in Galilee, and another 12,000 in Jaffa and the newly established neighbouring colony of Tel Aviv.[27] In addition to Jewish immigration, there was also a sizeable influx of Christian missionaries, laymen and teachers; from an estimated 10 per cent of the population in the earlier part of the century, the Christian proportion of the total population rose to 16 per cent by 1914.[28]

Immigration, together with the high natural increase among the indigenous Muslim population, led to another development which benefited the merchants; namely, the rapid growth of Jerusalem and of the cities located along the coast. Jerusalem grew from 35,000 inhabitants in 1880 to 80,000 in 1915. The population of Jaffa quadrupled during the same period, rising from 10,000 to 40,000; Haifa, a small town at the time of Sultan Abdul Hamid's accession, also experienced a fourfold increase in its population, from 5,000 in 1880 to 20,000 in 1915.[29]

Urbanisation, and the rising land prices that went with it, benefited the Christian merchants in particular, since they traditionally were located in these cities, close to the foreign consulates and their foreign protectors, as well as to the ports and international trading centres.[30] Thus, while the Muslim landed families invested in urban, as well as rural, land and obtained a rising share of profits from land speculation and rents, the Christian merchants benefited from the demand for housing, building materials and services as well as from the increase in land prices and rents.

The influx of settlers and of pilgrims also led to an increase in tourism and the demand for hotels, hostels and other temporary accommodation. By 1914 some 40,000 new visitors were arriving annually, mainly through the port of Jaffa which became a centre of the boom in hotel construction. But other cities, notably Jerusalem and Haifa, also benefited from the influx, and witnessed a significant increase in services which catered to the tourists as well as in the construction of hotels and hospices.[31]

By far the largest increase in wealth accruing to the Christian merchants, however, came from their almost exclusive access to Western imported goods at a time when the demand for these goods was rising dramatically among all sectors of the population as a result of the general expansion in trade, agriculture and investment. The value of imports through the three main ports of Gaza, Jaffa and Haifa rose almost six-fold, from a modest total of £240,000 sterling in 1886 to £1,310,000 by 1913.[32] In addition to Western clothing and luxury goods — the printed silks and English cutlery — Palestine began importing a vast range of basic goods that were formerly produced locally. White flour for bread-making replaced the native hard wheat which was reserved almost solely for the manufacture of noodles and macaroni. Kerosene, which could be imported at only one-third the cost of local olive oil, replaced the latter as a fuel for lamps and stoves. The iron ard, a plough made from imported metal, spread from the Jewish and German settlements to more general use in Arab agriculture.[33] The introduction of commercialised farming methods on the citrus plantations in turn required substantial imports of irrigation machinery and packaging materials.[34]

Graced with their newly established access to the inland markets, the urban Christian merchants found it possible to compete with the *ashraf* and with Muslim traders for control of the inland trade. Their position was enhanced still more by the excessively low tariffs imposed on imported goods, which amounted to 11 per cent *ad valorem* or less, or about a quarter of the duties which exporters from the Ottoman provinces had to pay in Europe.[35]

Finally, the expansion of transport and communications in the latter part of Sultan Abdul Hamid's reign also added to the possibilities open to the urban merchants. Virtually all the materials, fuel and rolling stock needed for the railways were imported; once completed the railways reduced the cost of freight and transport significantly, thereby enabling the urban merchants to penetrate the interior markets even more.[36]

Aside from the wealth obtained from the import of foreign goods, the urban Christian communities in general also benefited from the rise in secular education and the new opportunities this provided for employment in foreign firms. While the expansion of foreign banks, trade bureaux, shipping companies, printing works, customs posts and commercial agencies in the coastal cities increased the demand for skilled labour and professional services within the Christian community in general, the granting of important concessions to European companies, or to their local affiliates, by the Porte in Istanbul opened up yet another important channel of profitable economic activity for Christian (and Jewish) merchants. In addition to the contracts for the management of the railways and ports, foreign companies obtained monopolies in certain areas over the production and export of tobacco, the generation of electricity and the supply and distribution of water as well as certain important oil and mineral rights.[37]

While most of the concessions were located in the larger provinces of the Empire, such as Syria and Mesopotamia, the importance of Palestine as a growing financial and communications centre and the existence of potentially profitable resources in the country led to the granting of a number of rights and licences to foreign firms, or to their local agents, in the country. The Imperial Ottoman Bank, which was founded in the early 1860s by French and British interests, opened offices in Palestine as well as in every other major city in the Empire. It enjoyed an exclusive right to issue banknotes and played an important role in raising loans for the Ottoman Treasury. Later other foreign banks established local branches or representative offices in Palestine, among them Crédit Lyonnais, the Banque de Salonique and the Damascus-based Deutsche Palestina |Bank. (The British-based Anglo-Palestine Bank was founded by Zionist interests, as was the Jewish Colonial Trust.) Christian merchants in Palestine also obtained special rights to other important activities such as public transport, the provision of electricity and water in Jerusalem, land reclamation in the north and rights to exploit deposits of salt and potash.[38]

The growth of foreign trade and the increase in the size and wealth of the Christian merchants also led to the formation of a small but important 'petite bourgeoisie' among the Christians in Palestine which consisted on the one hand of shopowners, distributors and retailers and on the other of a nascent intelligentsia composed of teachers, journalists, lawyers and civil servants. The predominance of Christians in the retail trade stemmed not only from their access to the importers and wholesalers but also to their location in the cities which experienced the most rapid growth and increase in disposable incomes. Similarly, members of the intelligentsia, who profited from their secular, scientific education and access to positions in the privately owned educational institutions as well as in the foreign-owned firms, were often able to have an impact that belied their small numbers. Many taught not only the sons and daughters of their Christian colleagues but also influential members of the Muslim establishment such as the Hussainis and the Alamis. Still other important avenues of influence open to the intelligentsia stemmed from the rapid proliferation of Arabic newspapers, books and journals in the decade preceding the war. Some, like the Jaffa daily *Filistin* (*Palestine*) and *al-Karmil* (*Carmel*) of Haifa, both of which were owned by Christians, played an extremely active role in organising the struggle against Zionism as well as in developing modern ideas of Arab nationalism.[39] Their campaigns were actively supported by the majority of the Christian merchants who were opposed to the Zionists, not least because they feared that the new Jewish immigrants, with their access to foreign capital, would provide greater competition in those sectors of the economy in which the Christians were most active.

The Artisans and Craftsmen

Unlike the urban merchants who expanded and grew because of the increase in foreign trade, the rising dependence on imports from the West adversely affected the artisans and craftsmen who drew their living from providing goods to both the urban and rural populations. But the impact was not uniform. Few peasants had access to cash and traditional, locally made articles remained in widespread demand in the countryside. In contrast, the increasing use of money as a medium of exchange, the rise in disposable income and the easy availability of imported goods in the cities led to a decline in the consumption of locally made goods among the urban population.

Aside from the differences between the urban and rural areas, the various crafts were also affected differently by the flood of imports. Cotton weaving, for example, continued to flourish in Gaza and Majdal, primarily because of the easy access to export markets, while wool knitting and weaving declined because of the fall in demand for the Bedouin cloaks (*a'bayah*) traditionally worn in the rural areas. The low tariffs imposed on imported silk cloth, which in some cases meant that it could be sold at a quarter of the cost of locally made fabric, also accentuated the decline in silk weaving, a process that had already begun in the second half of the nineteenth century.[40]

Although detailed information on the crafts, and their guilds, is still lacking, certain trends are noticeable in the period just prior to the war. The most pronounced was the steadily increasing impoverishment of the artisans who lived and worked in the inland towns and villages. In part this reflected the growing impoverishment of the peasantry, on whom they relied for most of their custom. Another important factor was the considerable rise in prices for their raw materials, most of which were bought locally, and the inflation which affected the country as a whole. This, combined with the competition provided by the influx of cheap foreign goods, forced many to give up their trade and to seek work elsewhere, or to emigrate to the cities, a process which accelerated greatly in the first years of British rule.[41]

A second important trend concerned the growing disparity between the free craftsmen and those who still worked within the framework of the traditional guild system. As was the case elsewhere in the Ottoman Empire, most of the urban guilds in Palestine were under the control and patronage of leading members of the *ashraf*, who were responsible for the collection of taxes, the regulation of standards and prices (which was carried out by a *muhtasib*, or 'keeper of the accounts' appointed by the *ashraf*), the certification of apprentices and the arbitration of any disputes which occurred between the guilds and the government.[42]

Where the guild, or market, was located on *waqf* land, or in *waqf* buildings, the *ashraf* had even more influence, such as in the allocation of workshops, the choice of members and the determination of rents. However, by the end of the nineteenth century, when the guild system was declining due to the competition of foreign goods and the loss of skilled craftsmen to other work, or to the cities, the *ashraf* began to lose their exclusive control over the guilds. The guilds in turn gradually lost their ability to control the prices of their goods. However they still retained the right to certify apprentices and to provide workshops in the markets, a practice which made it difficult for craftsmen to escape their influence. The *ashraf* also discouraged any innovations, social or technological, within the guilds: such actions, they felt, would diminish their control of the guilds, and of craft production in general.[43]

Despite this, the new markets created by foreign immigration in the larger towns gradually enabled some craftsmen to move away from the inland towns and villages and from the traditional markets, or *suqs*, located in the larger cities. The official abolition of the guild system by the Young Turks in 1912, while not universally enforced, nevertheless made it possible for craftsmen to take up work legally in new neighbourhoods, outside the guilds. Some began to adapt their work to changing styles and demand. Others attached themselves to the bourgeoisie or to the foreign communities and established workshops employing other craftsmen as paid labour.[44]

The introduction of capitalist innovations, both for production and for marketing, was particularly prevalent in the Christian towns, such as Ramallah and Bethlehem, and in the Christian quarters of Jerusalem. In these areas the production of locally made goods from sea shells and olive wood, such as religious articles, *objets d'art* and holy candles, could be combined with access to foreign markets and to the creation of an internal market amongst both the indigenous Christians and the Christian tourists visiting from abroad.[45]

Elesewhere independent workshops sprang up outside the towns and their owners competed with the traditional craftsmen still located in the urban quarters. Hebron, for example, became a centre of independent craftsmen working outside the city walls and specialising in glass production; unlike the urban guilds in the city, they produced glass for 'export' to the larger cities rather than for local consumption.[46] In still other cases groups of craftsmen migrated to the coastal cities and set up workshops and small factories catering to the new markets, producing articles such as educational books for the foreign-owned schools, wines and alcoholic beverages.[47]

Thus while many of the traditional guilds remained, the introduction of foreign goods, the spread of money payments and the altered demand in the larger cities undermined their exclusive control over local production. And although demand in the rural areas for many traditional, locally produced goods remained strong, the gradual impoverishment of the peasantry (see below), and of the craftsmen, together with the introduction of wage labour in the cities, led to the decline of traditional skills within the crafts. While the 'working class' as such was still very small – too small to support any effective trade unions for example – the basis had been laid for what was to be a dramatic rise in their numbers after the First World War. Even more importantly, the growth of independent crafts and the creation of new markets among the immigrants paved the way for the secularisation of the workplace. At the same time, new groups of skilled workers, freed from their traditional reliance on the *ashraf* and the guilds, were rapidly drawn into the Westernised sectors of production and distribution, and this trend increased greatly after the establishment of British rule and the enormous increase in Jewish immigration in the 1920s and 1930s.

The Peasantry

Despite the growth of the coastal cities, the overwhelming majority of the population of Palestine continued to live in the inland towns and villages. The first post-war census, taken in 1922, put the percentage living in the countryside at 81 per cent, but if we make allowance for the high level of emigration from Jerusalem and the coastal areas during the war, a more accurate figure might be about 75 per cent.

Most of the rural population made their living from the land, either as peasants or as Bedouin, although a few, in the last years of the Empire, had begun to engage in small-scale trade, providing animals and produce to the inland towns as well as to those in neighbouring Syria and Trans-Jordan. The large landowners and *ashraf* tended by and large to live in the cities, away from their estates, and their increasingly ostentatious way of life further accentuated the perennial social division between the *fellahin*, or peasantry, and the *madaniyyin*, the urban dwellers and townsmen who enjoyed a more settled way of life.

What made this division one which even today sharply parallels the class divisions within Palestinian society and, if anything, one which is even more acutely perceived than class, was not so much the increasing wealth of the cities and larger towns but the simultaneous proletarianisation of the peasantry, a process which was to reach its peak during the 1930s under the British. The rise of private, hereditary property concentrated in the hands of a few large families was a major factor. But two others were also important: namely, the increasingly high burden of taxation and the heavy conscription inflicted on the peasantry, particularly after Turkey's declaration of war on the European Allies in 1914.

The change in the Land Laws, beginning with the Land Code of 1858, and the consequent gradual erosion of the peasantry's communal rights to the land and its produce, was paralleled by a change in the method in which the peasantry traditionally financed the tools and seeds needed to plant the year's crops. Whereas in the past it had been customary for the *multazim*, or landowner, through the village sheikh, to lend the necessary supplies in kind in advance in return for the right to a portion of the harvest, the loss of their lands and livestock, combined with the increasing use of money payments, left the *fellahin* dependent on the urban money-lenders. These in turn became more and more reluctant to lend to the peasantry given their lack of land, or animals, as security.[48] As a result, the peasant had to pay an exorbitant rate of interest, in the form of produce, to the money-lender or rely on the landowner (who was often the money-lender as well) to provide not only tools, animals and seeds but also the food he needed to maintain his family until the harvest.[49] Although in the past the *multazims* had often attempted to charge a relatively high proportion of the crop in return for these services, the village sheikh was often able to mediate and modify the demands in return for the provision of other services to the *multazim*. The landowners, unlike the *multazims*, had little such constraint, particularly since their interest in the land focused less on its value to produce crops than on its potential worth for speculation and eventual sale.

Similarly, the role of the village sheikh changed. Instead of acting as a mediator, he became a virtual employee of the large absentee landowner, and often an ally of the money-lender as well. In return for receiving payment from the landowner, he enforced the code of kin solidarity.[50] As more and more landowners themselves became money-lenders (especially after the rapid accumulation of surplus capital in the hands of the landed families), the sheikh's independence was reduced still further, and the oppression experienced by the peasants increased. From 1880 on, the accounts of European visitors to Palestine are replete with tales of peasants being forcibly removed from the land because of their indebtedness.[51] Even the Bedouin were not immune: the Banu Hawarith were forced to mortgage part of their land to a Christian merchant family from Jaffa, the Tayans, who later sold it to the Jewish National Fund.[52]

By the end of the century the rapid escalation in land prices and the increase in the demand for land as a result of Jewish immigration gave the large landowners a further incentive to displace the peasantry, or simply to sell land without regard to the traditional pasturing rights of the Bedouin or the fact that generations of peasants had tilled it as their own. By 1914 the amount of land owned by the Jewish National Fund and other Zionist institutions in Palestine had risen to a total of 420,700 *dunums* (38,000 hectares, or 94,000 acres) compared with only 25,000 *dunums* in 1882. The number of Jewish settlements rose to 47, compared with only 5 in Palestine thirty years earlier.[53] As a result evictions became commonplace in the coastal districts and in parts of the Galilee where the Jewish holdings were concentrated. The sale of the Sursock lands in the Plain of Esdraelon alone resulted in the ultimate displacement of some 8,000 peasants and loss of 22 villages.[54] And while some of the peasants themselves sold their lands to the immigrants, the overwhelming majority of sales, particularly after 1900, represented purchases by the Zionists from either those Arab landowners living outside Palestine, or those who were resident in the country.[55]

In addition to the indebtedness caused by the need to rely on the landowner for the provision of all the basic means of production, the peasantry also faced a rapidly rising rate of taxation from the state, particularly after the Young Turk revolution and the onset of preparations for war. Along with the *'ushr*, or tithe, which amounted to about one-tenth of the crop, the peasant was obliged to pay a tax, the *wirku*, on the buildings situated on land he cultivated. Finally, those peasants who owned their own animals paid yet another tax, the *ghanim*.

Although the *'ushr* was officially limited to 12.5 per cent in 1897, by the early 1900s rates as high as 30 or even 50 per cent were being forcibly collected. The rate at which the *wirku* was assessed also rose; it ranged between 20 and 30 per cent of the value of the built-up property. Aside from the higher rates of taxation, the amount assessed was increasingly calculated on the value of the gross, rather than the net, proceeds of the harvest. This meant that the costs which the peasant incurred as part of the process of production were not deducted from his taxes.[56] The fact that the owners of the large estates were often able to bribe the tax collector or civil servants to reduce their own liability further added to the exorbitant rates, as the state, desperate for money, arbitrarily extracted the sums needed from those it was most able to coerce.

A final blow came when the Young Turks began demanding the payment of taxes in cash, rather than in kind, on certain crops such as grapes and hay. Already in debt to pay the landlord, the peasant was forced to turn to the money-lender, or landlord, to raise the funds to pay the tax collector as well as to finance his crops. Given the usurious rates charged for cash loans, which varied from 40 to 50 per cent on average, large numbers of peasants were forced to sell their communal plots or to register them in the name of the landlord in order to reduce their own liability for the taxes. Others simply lost their land — either to the landowner or the state — for failure to pay their debts.[57]

Such sweeping changes in land ownership and in the financial state of the peasantry led to equally dramatic changes in the traditional social relations of the countryside. The concentration of wealth in the hands of the landlords and the urban money-lenders, in addition to draining the surplus product from the rural areas, severely strained the village solidarity on which the peasant depended. The collective work of ploughing, sowing and harvesting gave way to the fragmentation of work and the division of labour along class lines. At the bottom of the social scale were the hired labourers, the *harathin*, who worked on a seasonal basis, usually as ploughmen, but also occasionally as cultivators in the orchards.[58] Next came the sharecroppers, who, in theory if not always in practice, retained the right to a share of the produce. Aside from their increasing indebtedness, they had been adversely affected by the intense fragmentation of *musha'* land that the new system encouraged, as more and more of their land was concentrated in the hands of the largest landowners. By 1909 the *fellah* on average held less than one-half a *dunum* of land (about 450 square metres) per family, a figure which was considerably below the amount needed to provide subsistence. The situation was particularly acute in the hill country, where arable land was in short supply, and it was not uncommon for sharecroppers in these areas to find themselves in a position where their debts were never paid in their lifetime, but instead were passed down from one generation to the next, until the end of the Ottoman Empire.[59]

Further up the scale were the small landowners and sharecroppers who managed to extend their holdings to include a privately owned family garden or plot on which to grow their own crops. These plots (*hawakir*) often provided enough vegetables, olives or fruit to raise the peasant's standard of living above subsistence level. Although in most cases these plots were simply wasteland brought under cultivation by peasants, or small parcels purchased by those who had managed to earn some cash by working in the city, a few were quite large. For example, it was not uncommon in the last years of the Empire that the village sheikh owned a sizeable plot given to him by the landlord in return for his services (see below).[60]

The fragmentation of the land and the penetration of money into the countryside forced many more tenants and sharecroppers to seek paid work on the new settlers' farms, in the citrus plantations, or as manual labourers in the cities. One Zionist immigrant noted in his diary in 1910 that:

> Hundreds of Arabs are gathering in the wide market square, near the workers' hostel; they have been waiting here since dawn. They are the seasonal workers. Among them are a number of full-time Arab workers, who live on the settler's farm and go straight to the orange grove. There are about 1500 of them altogether every day.[61]

Within the village, this reliance on wages to finance part of the family's earnings led to a further weakening of communal ties, which were already strained by the rise of small property holders and the division of the village into those that supported, and those that opposed, the new alliance between the village sheikh and the landowner. The custom of working collectively disappeared and was replaced by one in which those peasants who were working for wages outside the village often refused to perform the tasks needed by the village to maintain its joint holdings and to ensure the collective security of the village against outside threats.[62]

Access to wage labour also created conflicting cultural outlooks within the village: while the day labourers in the plantations or in the Jewish settlements were exposed to the attractions of a Western way of life, their kin who remained in the villages turned increasingly to their own traditions to compensate for the disintegration of communal ties. The veneration of local saints' tombs took on a new meaning, as did the annual religious festivals and local fairs which were often the only time the villagers met others from neighbouring communities.[63] Similarly, the growing conflict of interest between the agricultural tenants and the landowner, and between the peasantry as a whole and the *ashraf*, led to divisions within the village between those who still maintained their respect and allegiance for the traditional elite and those who increasingly turned their attention to the local religious figures and holy men who shared their problems and their way of life. As we shall see later, this division was to play a crucial role in the development of the national struggle against the British in the mid-1930s.

The declaration of war in November 1914 ushered in yet another wave of oppression for the peasantry, one that was to threaten them not only with a loss of their livelihoods and traditional social ties but also with the physical destruction of the countryside as well. Tens of thousands of peasants, their ranks still decimated by the loss of their kin during the Crimean war sixty years earlier, were called up as conscripts, and most of these were sent to distant fronts. Food and livestock were commandeered, trees were cut down for fuel and whole villages quartered off for troops. As one observer noted: 'The work of months often proved more effective than the neglect of centuries in destroying the agricultural foundations of village life. Nearly all the improvements of the previous fifty years were swept away.'[64] The foreign population in the cities began to leave: the European consulates were closed; most of the missionaries and teachers left, emptying the great schools and hospitals established by France, Italy and the other European powers. The Greek and Armenian patriarchs, together with their staffs, were deported to Damascus; the Anglican bishop was forced to take refuge in British-occupied Egypt. Many of the Jewish immigrants who had retained their Russian, Romanian or Polish nationality returned to their native lands, while others fled to Egypt.[65]

Within the indigenous population there were fewer ways of escape. Some of the wealthier urban merchants sought refuge with their kin who had opened importing and exporting businesses in Europe or the Americas. Several hundred Christian villagers from Bethlehem, Ramallah and the neighbouring areas made their way to the United States where their relatives had earlier settled to market the religious articles made in their native towns. A few took advantage of contacts made with the Lebanese and Syrian communities already existing in places like Boston, New York, Santiago, Sao Paulo and Buenos Aires to leave, either permanently or temporarily.[66] But these were the exceptions. The majority of peasants, whether Christian or Muslim, had no option but to remain on their lands. Many registered their plots in the name of the sheikh to avoid conscription, but those who escaped this fate often succumbed to starvation and to the endemic diseases which multiplied as a result of the appalling wartime conditions.[67] As the land went untilled, the few animals left were slaughtered for food. Ronald Storrs, who was appointed military governor of Jerusalem shortly after the British army entered Jerusalem in December 1917, reported his shock at a sight which greeted him a few weeks later:

My nightmare anxiety was the scarcity of food amounting almost to famine. One morning in January, I became aware of a crying and screaming beneath my office window. I looked out on a crowd of veiled Arab women, some of whom tore their garments apart to reveal the bones almost piercing their skin ... The fellah were a shivering bundle of rags.[68]

So great was the devastation that it was not until the early part of 1919 that the military administration could turn its attention away from the immediate problems of feeding, clothing and heating the population to the urgent task of setting up a new government.[69] But by then the peasantry, as well as the urban dwellers, were no longer in any mood to rejoice at the final downfall of their Turkish overlords. For they had discovered that one brutal occupation had ended, only to be replaced by another. Although it was more humane at first, it was certainly more alien and, in the end, even more destructive.

3 THE BRITISH MANDATE, 1922-1948

The fall of Jerusalem in December 1917 marked the end of nearly 1,300 years of Islamic rule in Palestine. Yet the British troops, led by the Commander-in-Chief of the Egyptian Expeditionary Force, General Edmund Allenby, were welcomed with much celebration and rejoicing. In addition to ending the war and tyranny of the Young Turks, the allied victory was expected to result in the imminent declaration of independence for the Arab provinces. In Palestine, it was thought that the country, together with Syria, Mesopotamia and the Arabian Peninsula, would soon be united in a single state headed by the Hashimite Sharif Hussain of Mecca.

Although few in Palestine had heard of the letters exchanged between Hussain and the British High Commissioner in Egypt, Sir Henry McMahon, in which the British had promised to recognise Arab independence save for 'the two districts of Mersina and Alexandretta and portions of Syria lying to the west of the districts of Damascus, Homs, Hama and Aleppo' (i.e. present-day Lebanon and the Syrian coastal districts), many Arabs, in Palestine and elsewhere, had volunteered to serve in the Arab revolt led by the Sharif's son Faisal and assisted by the British.[1] Allenby's proclamation to the people of Palestine, read on his official entry into Jerusalem, 11 December 1917, was tailored to fit British pledges made to the Arabs prior to the revolt. He declared:

> Since your city is regarded with affection by the adherents of three of the great religions of mankind, and its soil has been consecrated by the prayers and pilgrimages of devout people of these three religions for many centuries, therefore do I make known to you that every sacred building, monument, holy spot, shrine, traditional site, endowment, pious bequest or customary place of prayer ... will be maintained and protected according to the existing customs and beliefs of those to whom [these] faiths they are sacred.[2]

Yet as is so often the case where affairs of state are concerned, the reassurances offered on one specific matter, the sanctity of the Holy Places, belied an intent to wreak great change elsewhere. In the case

38

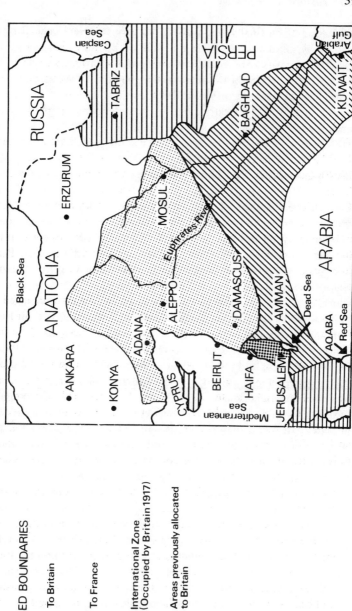

Map 2. The Sykes-Picot Agreement, 1916

39

PROPOSED BOUNDARIES

To Britain

To France

International Zone
(Occupied by Britain 1917)

Areas previously allocated
to Britain

of Palestine the final result was no less than the replacement of one people by another and of Turkish rule by British occupation for the next thirty years. Arab independence, and the promises made to support it, were helpful in winning the war, but the 'pipedreams of backward peoples', as one official called them, could have no place in the more sober discussions carried out by the statesmen of imperial Europe once the war was won.[3]

British Colonialism and Zionist Settlement

Even before the final allied victory and the signature of the armistice on 11 November 1918, the British Cabinet had become concerned that the growing success of the Arab revolt and the promises outlined in the Hussain-McMahon correspondence would damage British interests in Palestine, whose control it now saw as vital to the protection of the Suez Canal and to the new imperial air, sea and land routes which extended from the Mediterranean across the Mesopotamian oilfields to India.[4] To protect these interests, it was vital that an understanding be reached with the French, as well as with Britain's other major wartime ally, Russia. Accordingly the British Foreign Minister, Sir Edward Grey, told the French ambassador in London, Paul Cambon, of the agreements outlined in the correspondence with Hussain and suggested that representatives of the three powers meet to discuss the future disposition of the Ottoman territories.[5] Seven months later, in May 1916 — less than a year after promising Hussain that the Arab lands would be granted independence — the French representative, Georges Picot, and Sir Mark Sykes, Secretary of the War Cabinet in London, signed the 'Tripartite Agreement for the Partition of the Ottoman Empire', more commonly known as the Sykes-Picot Agreement.

Under its terms, Russia was to receive the right to occupy Istanbul, both shores of the Bosporus and parts of Turkish Armenia in return for giving up her claim to Jerusalem and other parts of Palestine. France was to receive a free hand in the greater part of the Levant, i.e. in Lebanon and Syria east to Mosul. Both powers agreed to recognise British claims to Iraq and Trans-Jordan. Palestine, the area of greatest contention, was to be separated from Syria and placed under an international administration whose ultimate fate would be decided at the peace conference where representatives of the United States and of the other European Allies would also be present.[6] The peoples affected were to be allowed no voice in determining their future, and for this reason the terms of the treaty were kept secret until the end of the war.

Rumours of the agreement however began circulating in Palestine, and the Turks lost no time in conveying its contents to Sharif Hussain once it had been published by the Bolsheviks after the downfall of the Tsar. Requesting an explanation, Hussain was presented this time with a declaration signed by both the French and the British. Once again they promised full independence to the Arabs:

> The end that France and Great Britain have in pursuing in the East the war unloosed by German ambition is the complete and definite freeing of the peoples so long oppressed by the Turks and the establishment of national Governments and Administrations deriving their authority from the initiative and free choice of the indigenous populations.

> France and Great Britain have agreed to encourage and assist the establishment of indigenous Governments and Administrations in Syria and Mesopotamia ... and in the territories whose liberation they seek.[7]

Allied duplicity seemed to know no bounds, and Lord Balfour's subsequent comment to the Cabinet, that 'the Powers have made no statement of fact which is not admittedly wrong, and no declaration of policy which, at least in the letter, they have not always intended to violate', while made in reference to Palestine, might equally have applied to the whole of the Arab territories liberated from Turkish rule.[8]

Yet British and French betrayal of their promises to the Arabs was not the end of the story. Despite the success of the Arab revolt, which Allenby later described as 'invaluable' to the British cause, the Allies found need to enlist the support of still other sympathisers in the last year of the war.[9] The months of September to November 1917 were particularly difficult. As David Lloyd George, then Prime Minister, described the situation to Parliament twenty years later:

> It was one of the darkest periods of the war. At the time the French Army had mutinied, the Italian Army was on the eve of collapse, and America had hardly started preparing in earnest. We came to the conclusion that it was vital that we should have the sympathies of the Jewish community.[10]

Debate has raged ever since about why Lloyd George's government singled out the Jews for special attention: the explanations range from the cynical to the benign. The need to obtain financial assistance from men like Lord Rothschild, an ardent Zionist; Britain's interest in preventing the French from using their close alliance with the Latin Church to establish French claims to the Holy Places; the need to enlist sympathy among Jews in the United States to ensure American support for the allied war effort; the desire to create a 'fifth column' among the Jewish communities in Germany and in occupied Eastern Europe; all these reasons were later cited for Lloyd George's subsequent support of Zionist aims in Palestine. But whatever the reason, the British government saw fit to throw in its lot with the Zionists, rather than with those among British Jewry who argued that Judaism was a religion, not a nationality, and that such a move could endanger their co-religionists elsewhere in Europe. In a letter written to Lord Rothschild on 2 November 1917 and approved by the War Cabinet, Lord Balfour — then Foreign Secretary — wrote:

> His Majesty's Government view with favour the establishment in Palestine of a national home for the Jewish people, and will use their best endeavours to facilitate the achievement of this object, it being clearly understood that nothing shall be done which may prejudice the civil and religious rights of existing non-Jewish communities in Palestine or the rights and political status enjoyed by Jews in any other country.[11]

Despite Britain's efforts to portray the document as a moral obligation incumbent on all civilised peoples (an argument which had a highly favourable effect in Wilsonian America), it has been more aptly described as 'the promise by one nation to a second of the country of a third'.[12] Winston Churchill himself firmly squashed any such pious rhetoric. He said:

> The Balfour Declaration must . . . not be regarded as a promise given from sentimental motives; it was a practical measure taken in the interests of a common cause at a moment when that cause could afford to neglect no factor of material or moral assistance.[13]

Immediately after its proclamation, leaflets containing the Declaration were dropped by air on German and Austrian towns; others were widely distributed in the areas of Poland and Eastern Europe which had large Jewish concentrations.[14] The Declaration was widely publicised in the American press and circulated by hand in Tsarist Russia (where, to Whitehall's dismay, it had to compete with Bolshevik pamphlets also eagerly read by the Jewish populace). Yet it was only officially published in Palestine in 1920, after the war had ended and Britain's hold on the country was ensured.[15]

By then it was too late. Despite the efforts of some Cabinet ministers to place the entire range of secret treaties on the negotiating table prior to the Paris Peace Conference, and the strenuous efforts of other officials, particularly in Cairo and in Palestine, to bring about a *rapprochement* between the Zionists and the Arabs, severe anti-Zionist riots broke out in Jerusalem and elsewhere in Palestine in 1920 and 1921.[16] The hopes of the Palestinian Arabs that the troubles, together with intense diplomatic action aimed at changing public opinion in Britain, might prevent the installation of a British protectorate in Palestine and the fulfilment of the Balfour Declaration were in vain. On 24 July 1922 the Council of the League of Nations approved the British Mandate for Palestine and Trans-Jordan which included the provisions of the Balfour Declaration as well as specific clauses granting the Jewish Agency a direct role in setting up the 'national home'. Other Mandates were established for Iraq (to Britain), Syria and Lebanon (to France). Although the Powers for years attempted to deny criticism that the mandate system was little more than a legal fiction aimed at sanctifying the imposition of colonial rule from the Mediterranean to the Gulf, Britain's own White Paper of 1922, in which it set out its own interpretation of the Mandate for Palestine and Trans-Jordan, made it eminently clear that rather than holding the country 'in trust', Britain intended to rule the country without any regard to the expressed desires of the native population.[17]

The Creation of the Yishuv

Even before the Mandate had been approved, Britain had taken steps to set up its own civilian government in Palestine and to begin implementing the provisions of the Balfour Declaration. Four months after the proclamation of the Declaration, in March 1918, a Zionist Commission headed by Dr Chaim Weizmann (later the first President of Israel) arrived in Palestine with the express aim of creating *faits accomplis* that would produce an atmosphere favourable to Zionist claims on Palestine at the forthcoming Paris Peace Conference.[18] The twelve Zionist schools were re-opened and their number increased to forty to facilitate Zionist demands that Hebrew should be recognised alongside Arabic as a language of instruction.[19] Blue and white flags bearing the Star of David were distributed to the Jewish population and the Zionist national anthem was ordered to be sung in mixed gatherings. The most flagrant abuse of all in Arab eyes was the attempt made by Weizmann, with Storrs' assistance, to demolish part of the approaches to the Wailing Wall, which the Muslims regarded as sacred property. This, it seemed, was a clear violation of Allenby's promise. Its actual implementation was prevented only after Storrs had second thoughts and withdrew his assistance.[20]

Complaints by military officers in Palestine, who were attempting to rule the country according to the Laws and Usages of War which stated that the *status quo* must be maintained, went unheeded. Instead of the Zionist Commission being abolished, as they asked, it was the military administration itself which was dissolved.[21] On 1 July 1920, two years before the League had even agreed that a British Mandate should be established in Palestine, a permanent civilian government headed by Sir Herbert Samuel, a former Minister in the War Cabinet, was installed in Palestine.

Samuel's unenviable task was to implement the conflicting terms of the Balfour Declaration (which was then being written into the terms of the proposed Mandate); namely, to create in Palestine the political and economic conditions needed to secure the establishment of the Jewish National Home, while at the same time safeguarding the rights of the Arab majority. Less than two months after his arrival, on 26 August, the first quota for Jewish immigration was announced: 16,500 immigrants were to be allowed into Palestine during the next year.[22] Following the publication of the 1922 White Paper and the approval of the Mandate by the League of Nations, the annual quotas were fixed according to the 'economic absorptive capacity' of the country. Despite violent disputes both within the British government and within Palestine about how many immigrants could be absorbed without damage to the rights of the indigenous Palestinians, the number of Jews admitted between 1922 and 1939 amounted to an average of 17,140 a year.[23] By the end of 1939 the Jewish population in Palestine had risen to 445,457, nearly 30 per cent of the total population of 1,501,698.[24]

To accommodate the immigrants, the Jewish National Fund, which was established in 1901 in the wake of the First Zionist Congress in Basle, the Keren Hayesod (Palestine Foundation Fund), the Palestine Land Development Company and other Zionist organisations began buying up yet more land in Palestine, primarily from absentee land-lords.[25] Between 1921 and 1925, 200,000 *dunums* (18,000 hectares) of fertile land near Nazareth were acquired by the Keren Hayesod from the Sursock holdings.[26] In 1929 the Jewish National Fund bought another large tract of land, which originally belonged to the al-Hawarith tribe, from the Tayans of Beirut.[27] Additional tracts were subsequently obtained from an estate comprising 400,000 *dunums* (36,000 hectares) in the Beisan area of the Jordan Valley (which was originally part of Sultan Abdul Hamid's personal domain but which had been leased to its Arab tenants) and from another large concession, originally held by the Salams of Beirut, in the Huleh area of northern Palestine.[28] Smaller plots, including the villages situated on them, were purchased in the Tulkarm area, on the coastal plain between Haifa and Acre and in several districts of Galilee, as well as elsewhere throughout the country.[29] Between 1920 and 1939 more than 846,000 *dunums* (76,150 hectares) were purchased by Jewish organisations and individuals. Together with the land acquired before the First World War, this brought the total amount of Jewish-owned land in Palestine to 1,496,000 *dunums* (134,775 hectares), about 5 per cent of the total land area.[30]

Aside from the immediate impact of Jewish immigration and land purchases, the first decades of the Mandate also witnessed the beginning of what was to become a massive influx of Jewish capital. Unlike the first and second *aliyahs*, which had consisted primarily of poverty-stricken emigrants fleeing the pogroms of Russia and Central Europe, and the third wave, which began in 1924 and which consisted of small traders and craftsmen mainly from Poland, the fourth wave of Jewish immigration into Palestine in the 1930s consisted largely of refugees fleeing the growing repression in Germany.[31] Having previously sought to assimilate into what, in the 1920s, was regarded as one of the most advanced societies in Western Europe, this new wave differed from its predecessors not only in terms of its greater commitment to Western cultural and social values but also in terms of its capitalist orientation and sizeable wealth. Rather than seek to develop communities based on the land and on the collective sharing of labour, the new immigrants flooded into the emergent urban areas located along the coast, where they invested in urban real estate, capital-intensive citrus groves and industry.

Altogether the amount of capital brought into the country by Jewish immigrants from 1920 to 1935 is estimated to have amounted to more than £P80 million (Palestinian pounds).[32] (The magnitude of such a sum at that time can be gauged by the fact that the entire government budget for Palestine in the early years of the Mandate was only about £P2 million a year; altogether it could not have exceeded £P30 million between 1922 and 1935.[33]) Expressed another way, while the number of immigrants arriving with at least £1,000 sterling in 1930 amounted to only 178, or about 4 per cent of the total, the number had increased to 6,309 five years later, a figure which represented 10 per cent of the immigrants coming to Palestine that year.[34]

The colonisation of the land, and the injection of massive amounts of capital, was accompanied by an increasing colonisation of the labour market as well. As early as 1904, at the start of the second *aliyah*, there had been demands by Zionists that only Jewish labour should be employed on Jewish farms. In part this demand reflected the different orientation of the immigrants: unlike their predecessors who had arrived in Palestine seeking only to live and die in the land of their forefathers, the immigrants who arrived from Poland and Central Europe in the first decade of the century were imbued with the socialist ideals then finding expression in the coffee houses and working men's clubs of Central Europe. Many became members of Poale Zion, the party founded in Austria-Hungary which aimed to represent the Jewish worker and to ally socialist principles to Zionism. These new pioneers attacked the policies of Rothschild and the Palestine Colonisation Association (PCA) which they saw as simple capitalist exploitation based on the use of cheap Arab labour employed in large plantation-like colonies. By the end of the decade they were successful in ensuring that all land bought by the Jewish National Fund, in contrast to that owned by the PCA, would be granted to settlers on leasehold only on condition that Jewish labour be employed exclusively.[35]

With the enormous increase in immigration during the first fifteen years of the Mandate, and especially after 1930, it became imperative in the view of the Jewish Agency (which replaced the Zionist Organisation in 1929) that this policy be extended to all operations funded by the Agency. In part this reflected the way in which the immigration quotas were allocated; namely, on the basis of labour certificates provided to the Agency by the Mandatory power. This made it imperative for the Agency, in theory if not always in practice, to show that work was available for the immigrants.[36] But the major reason for extending the policy of employing Jewish labour exclusively lay in the desire to create the economic basis for a separate community and, eventually, a separate state.

In 1920, the first year of the Mandate, the Palestine Workers' Fund, which had been set up by Poale Zion in 1912, was taken over by the newly formed Histradrut, the General Confederation of Jewish Workers in Palestine. Unlike most trade unions, it acted as an employer, as well as a representative of the employed, developing infant Jewish industries as well as forgoing strikes where these were seen to be inimical to the expansion of Zionism and of the Jewish economy in general. The 'conquest of labour', which started in the building sector, soon spread to other sectors: transport, distribution and trade. In 1931 it was decided that the share of Jewish labour to be employed on public works projects funded by the government would be determined by the amount of taxes paid by the Jewish community (rather than by their percentage within the work-force as a whole), thus further increasing the scope for the employment of Jewish labour.[37]

The massive influx of capital in the 1930s encouraged this trend still further. Even greater numbers of Jewish workers, and new immigrant labourers, were needed in the workshops, factories and urban industries set up by the wealthy arrivals from Germany and Central Europe. By 1935 a form of economic apartheid existed in almost all the larger coastal cities, as well as in many of the agricultural settlements. Segregated residential and industrial districts existed in Tel Aviv-Jaffa, Haifa and Safad; in some areas the boycott of Arab labour even extended to the boycott of Arab farm products: dairy foods, vegetables and grains.[38] The general strike proclaimed by the Arabs in 1936 ironically helped to complete the process: the *Yishuv* – the Jewish community in Palestine – could survive economically on its own. By 1939 the leaders of the Jewish Agency were ready to embark on the next stage in the plan to secure an independent state: namely, the attempt to partition Palestine territorially and to effect the transfer of Arab residents out of those areas to be included in a Zionist state.[39]

British Policy and the Palestinian Arabs

From the beginning of the Mandate, British policy towards the indigenous Arab community in Palestine was marked by a refusal to recognise its national existence, either in Palestine or as part of a larger pan-Arab state. The Arabs invariably were described as 'the non-Jewish communities' (the Balfour Declaration) or simply as 'the other sections of the population' (the Mandate). Where it was necessary to distinguish between them and the immigrants, the use of the terms 'Muslim', 'Christian' or 'Jew' was adopted, as for example in the official annual reports. The fiction that Palestine was inhabited only by a small number of people, or by disparate religious sects, was encouraged; in this context it would be easier to add to one, i.e. the Jewish community, without such action being seen internationally as a denial of the rights of another. However what was especially provocative as far as the Arabs were concerned was the decision to give the Jewish Agency a special role in formulating Mandatory policy while the Arabs were denied any representation at all, save through their religious leaders. Although they still constituted the overwhelming majority of the population, they might well not have existed at all as far as their legal and civil rights were concerned.[40]

This reduction of the body politic to virtual juridical oblivion was accompanied by the re-drawing of the country's political and territorial borders in such a way that the Arabs of Palestine became a community separated from their compatriots living in the neighbouring areas. Trans-Jordan, a new country created by the British out of the wastes of the Arabian desert after the consolidation of Ibn Saud's hold in the remainder of the Peninsula, was placed under a separate administration, distinct from Palestine.[41] The Amir Abdullah, one of the leaders of the Arab revolt and the son of the Sharif Hussain of Mecca, was installed on the throne of Trans-Jordan with the aid of the British army. His brother, Faisal, who had been forcibly removed by the French from Damascus in 1920, was installed as King of Iraq. With the two main leaders of the Hashimite dynasty, and their domains, now subject to British protection, the British controlled a broad sweep of Arab territory stretching from Palestine and the Jordan Valley through to the Arabian Gulf. (The Sharif Hussain himself was to receive no such compensation after his expulsion from Mecca by the Saudis; rescued by a British warship from the beach of Aqaba, he was transported to British-controlled Cyprus where he died in 1931.)

The French occupation of Damascus in 1920 was followed by the further division of geographical Syria into four separate autonomous provinces: Lebanon, Damascus/Aleppo, Latakia and the Jebel Druze. Customs barriers were erected and the Syrian currency was drawn into the franc zone, thereby necessitating a complete re-orientation of the country's financial and commercial ties with Palestine.[42] The traditional trade routes, which linked Galilee and the hill country, the Huleh and the Jordan Valley with Damascus, Homs, Hama and Aleppo, were severed. Imports from the port of Beirut destined for Palestine became liable to duties imposed by both the French and the British. The announcement of new regulations governing citizenship and nationality left many Palestinians and Syrians living abroad stateless. Henceforth an Arab living in Jerusalem required both a passport and a French visa to visit his cousin in Beirut or Damascus.[43] The Druze community of northern Palestine was separated from its kin in the

Jebel Haruan; the semi-settled tribesmen and women who lived around Nablus, Hebron and Jerusalem and who possessed lands on both sides of the Jordan Valley found themselves paying taxes to two different governments. Their merchant colleagues in the cities found it difficult to carry on the lucrative trade that connected Palestine with the annual pilgrimage route that ran from Damascus south to Mecca and Medina. (The more mobile Bedouin of the Jordan Valley managed to escape the customs duties and took advantage of the restricted trade to open up new smuggling routes across the borders, plying livestock and dairy products to Aleppo in return for grain.[44]) Meanwhile any new immigrant who had lived in Palestine for two years could become a citizen simply by applying to the High Commissioner.[45]

With borders re-drawn in such a way, and with the neighbouring lands under separate European administrations, the Arabs of Palestine found themselves to be a distinct community within the Arab world as a whole, yet lacking the benefits that the creation of a separate national existence in Palestine might have provided. So it is not surprising that even before the creation of the state of Israel and the dispersion of the Arab population the quest for legal and international recognition of their national rights and of their distinct identity became a dominant theme in the struggle by the Palestinian Arabs to regain their land.

The division of the Arab territories into separate states ruled by one or the other of the European powers and the creation of Palestine as a distinct political unit were followed by the drafting of new legislation aimed at developing the economy and society of Palestine along capitalist lines. British civil servants in the first decade of the Mandate introduced sweeping new laws concerning taxation, land registration, the adjudication of disputes, currency, fiscal policy and trade. An immediate priority was the expansion of the country's transport and communications systems to facilitate Jewish immigration and to serve the interests of the expanding British Empire. An ultra-modern port, at the time the biggest in the Middle East, was built at Haifa. Significantly, it included a huge refinery and export terminal for oil pumped from the British-control fields in nothern Iraq.

The fishing port at Jaffa was expanded to handle local imports and exports and in 1936 work began on the construction of a large new port at Tel Aviv. Modern airports were constructed at Haifa and Lydda (Lod) and Palestine was linked by air to both London and Delhi. New railroads connected Haifa with Syria, Trans-Jordan and Saudi Arabia. Heavy metalled roads capable of carrying army vehicles and troop transports as well as heavy lorries were laid from Jerusalem to Hebron, Beersheba, Jaffa, Jericho and Nablus. An international road system linked Jerusalem and the Mediterranean coast with the Arabian Gulf via Trans-Jordan and Syria.

The establishment of new lines of communication further enhanced Palestine's role as 'the geographical centre of the British Empire'.[46] Overland mail routes were opened between Palestine, Iraq, Egypt, Sudan and Turkey; an air-mail route operated from Lydda to London. Cable and telephone facilities were opened in the larger cities and provided services to most parts of the Arab world as well as to Britain and the United States. New broadcasting stations, for both military and civilian use, were opened in Jerusalem, Ramallah and Lydda.[47]

The development of a modern system of transport and communications led to a vast increase in international trade not only with Britain and other parts of Europe but also with Iraq, the Gulf states and India. The value of imports, mainly industrial machinery, consumer goods and foodstuffs, rose more than threefold between 1923 and 1935, from £P4.9 million to £P17.9 million.[48] Although Britain and her overseas possessions benefited greatly from the opening of the market in Palestine, the country's unique international status, and specifically Article 18 of the Mandate which forbade the imposition of tariffs against any member of the League of Nations, meant that other suppliers also took advantage of the increased demand engendered by the Jewish immigration into the country. For example, Germany, Poland, Romania and other Eastern European countries sent goods worth more than £P4.8 million to Palestine in 1935. Altogether they accounted for about a quarter of Palestine's total imports in the years from 1934 to 1937, slightly more than the average for Britain and its overseas possessions. Syria and Egypt accounted for another 10 to 13 per cent in the mid-1930s, while the United States sent goods worth £P1.5 million in 1935, about 8.5 per cent of the total merchandise imported by Palestine that year.[49]

The European exporting countries found that Palestine played a role in sustaining their economies at a time when world-wide depression, and the consequent erection of impenetrable tariff barriers within the industrial countries, had led to mass unemployment and wide-scale bankruptcy. But for Palestine itself the result was disastrous: the flood of Western consumer goods, often sold at prices below cost, not only destroyed the possibility of developing local industry but also led to a huge imbalance in the country's trade. From £P4.1 million in 1922, the annual deficit rose to a frightening £P13.3 million by 1935.[50]

The magnitude and permanence of such a financial drain was made possible only by the huge influx of Jewish capital which, while covering the trade deficit, effectively transferred the country's resources from the Arab to the Jewish sector and further broadened the gulf between the two sectors.

However the effect of colonialism on the Arab economy of Palestine was even more dramatic in the way in which it affected the country's exports. Until the completion of the oil refinery in Haifa in 1939 when petroleum products dominated, the country was almost totally dependent on the export of citrus fruits to Britain. The export of oranges, lemons and grapefruit rose from just over 1.5 million cases in 1914 to 10.8 million cases in 1937, a rise which reflected the conversion of Palestinian agriculture from the production of subsistence crops — wheat, barley and olives — to cash crops capable of producing high export earnings. By the mid-1930s, citrus exports accounted for nearly 80 per cent of the country's total export revenue. (The British market alone took two-thirds of the total citrus crop.)[51] A fall in world prices, as happened during the depression of the 1930s, a bad harvest or the closure of the British market, as occurred during the Second World War, meant that Arab agricultural exports stagnated, and export revenues declined sharply.

The Emergence of Class Society, 1922-36

The segregation of the economy into an Arab and a Jewish sector and the reduction of the Arab population to the status of second-class citizens were paralleled on the one hand by the increasing proletarianisation of the peasantry and on the other by the enrichment, relative to other members of the community, of the Arab landowners and urban merchants. However, unlike the pre-war period, the virtual destruction of the indigenous economy and the growing concentration of the means of production within the Zionist community led to the fragmentation of the Arab bourgeoisie and to extreme factionalism within the traditional ruling class. British colonial policy, in addition to encouraging divisions between Arab and Jew, also exacerbated class antagonisms within the Arab community. In 1936 the latent conflicts became manifest and Palestine found itself engulfed in civil war and revolution.

The Proletarianisation of the Peasantry

The lot of the peasant, already harsh under the Ottomans, became virtually intolerable under the British. Aside from the attempts to commercialise agriculture, and to make Palestine a source of cash crop exports, the government's encouragement of Zionist settlement without regard for its effect on the indigenous society led to the growing impoverishment of the peasantry, which even as late as 1936 still made up more than two-thirds of the total Arab population in Palestine. Although by 1935 Jewish organisations and individuals owned only about 5 per cent of the country's total land area, their holdings included 1 million *dunums*, or nearly 12 per cent, of the total *arable* land.[52] The remainder, amounting to about 8 million *dunums*, suddenly had to provide crops for export in addition to supporting an Arab population that had grown from 668,258 in 1922 to 952,955 at the end of 1935.[53] Yet the division of arable land between the two communities meant that while each Jewish resident in 1935 had, on average, 28.1 *dunums* of arable land, there were only 9.4 *dunums* for each Arab.[54] Given that the minimum amount of land (without irrigation) needed to sustain a family of six was calculated to range from 100 to 130 *dunums*, it is obvious that while the Jewish agricultural settlers had both adequate land and capital, the Arab peasantry lacked the space it needed relative to its growing population.[55]

In fact the pressure on the land within the Arab community was even greater than these somewhat artificial figures imply, since a large part of the land available to the Arab community was concentrated in a few large land-holdings held by a small handful of families or as *waqf*. It is not surprising then that as early as 1930 a committee commissioned by the Palestine government revealed that within the 104 villages surveyed 28 per cent of the households were without access to any land at all. Of the remainder, who either owned land or cultivated it as tenants, only two in five had more than one *feddan* of land (about 120 *dunums*), or enough to support their families.[56] Surveys commissioned elsewhere in the country showed a similar pattern.

Even for those who had access to land, changes in the method of taxation and in the way the taxes were assessed led to increasing indebtedness, often to the point where the smallholder was obliged to sell his land or to register it in the name of a large landowner, or urban merchant, in order to pay off the debt. Shortly after the start of the Mandate the government abolished the tax concessions (*iltizam*) set up by the Ottomans and the peasant became liable to pay tax directly to the government, in cash rather than in kind. Although the tithe (*'ushr*) was officially fixed at 12.5 per cent, and later reduced to 10 per cent, it became payable on the gross proceeds of the harvest, rather than on net income. Having lost the ability to deduct the costs of production from his revenue, the peasant found himself paying taxes that averaged 25 to 50 per cent of his income, even though he was already making well below the amount of money needed for subsistence.[57] The decision of the government in 1928 to commute the tithes to a fixed annual payment based on the amount of tax paid during the previous four years added to his woe. For while the price of wheat and other grains – the main crops cultivated by the peasantry – had risen to record heights in the mid-1920s as a result of Syrian demand, they had plummeted dramatically during the world depression. Even greater falls occurred in the early 1930s after the conclusion of a new trade agreement with Syria which flooded Palestine with cheap Syrian wheat.[58]

Despite government measures in the early 1930s to reduce the rate at which the tithe was set, the fact that it remained payable not only on the gross product but also on valuations that were often one-third or more above the prevailing market prices made it virtually impossible for the peasant to escape from the burden of debt and to avoid passing it down to his heirs.[59] When, in addition, the small owners or tenants were obliged to pay usurious rates of interest to the landowners (who in many cases also enjoyed a monopoly on the lending of money) the situation became oppressive in the extreme.[60] In 1930 C.F. Strickland, a member of the Indian Civil Service sent by the British government to study the condition of the peasantry and to advise on the setting up of co-operatives in Arab villages, reported that: 'No small percentage of the cultivators are entirely insolvent and neither co-operative credit nor any form of state loans can place them on a solvent footing if the whole . . . claim of their creditors is to be paid.'[61]

After 1930 the condition of the peasantry worsened still further, despite efforts by the government to provide credit and to prevent the wholesale eviction of tenants from their land. Land prices rose to unprecedented levels as a result of the massive emigration of Jews from Germany and Eastern Europe, particularly in the period from 1933 to 1939.[62] The enormous influx of capital led to an excessively high rate of inflation at a time when agricultural wages were severely depressed.[63] Even more importantly, the increasingly effective boycott of Arab labour, and of Arab agricultural products, coupled with the evictions which resulted from the increased sale of land to the Jewish National Fund, reduced still further the number of peasants who could lease or rent land or work on it as day labourers.[64] By 1936 the problem of the displaced peasantry had become a national one which, as we shall see, was to have an enormous impact on the growth of the struggle for independence.

The Rise of Wage Labour

For the displaced peasantry unable to obtain land in the countryside, the only available alternative was to find work in the mushrooming cities of the coast. Many families sent a son there to earn cash while other relatives remained in the village attempting to till what remained of the family plot. As a result cities like Haifa, Jaffa and even Gaza grew immensely in the late 1920s and early 1930s, and indeed throughout the Mandate.[65] The peasants were concentrated in the numerous shanty towns which sprang up on the outskirts of the cities where they lived in appalling conditions. Nevill Barbour reported that in Haifa alone in 1935 there were over 11,000 Arab workers living in hovels made out of old petrol-tins, without any water supply or the most rudimentary sanitary conditions. Similar conditions prevailed in Jaffa and, to a lesser extent, in Gaza, Ramlah, Lydda and Janin. Some of the migrants were forced to sleep in the open, in caves or on building sites, where the contrast between their misery and the spectacle of the 'handsome new boulevards erected in the more desirable parts of the towns by and for the immigrant population' could not escape notice and bitter comment.[66] Others found themselves forcibly barred by Zionist pickets from finding work, or subject to physical threats and abuse should they attempt to seek work in Jewish-owned enterprises.[67]

Aside from the fact that government policy allocated a larger share of government jobs to the Jewish sector than their numbers warranted (see above), the wage rates paid by both public and private employers clearly discriminated against the Arab. Wages in unskilled government employment – as guards, dockers, labourers and porters – averaged 100 *mils* a day or less (equivalent to £P2.50–£P3.00 a month) for Arab workers compared to 200 or 300 *mils* a day for unskilled Jewish workers.[68] Since many government contracts for the provision of supplies and equipment, the construction of roads, bridges and military buildings and the maintenance of existing installations were awarded to Jewish firms who refused to employ Arab labour at all, the situation was even worse than the wage scale alone would indicate. Furthermore, the Arab worker, unlike his Jewish counterpart, was often obliged to work up to 16 hours a day, received no social security benefits and enjoyed no job security whatsoever.[69] It is not surprising, therefore, that the displaced peasants and workers in the urban areas provided much of the support for the violent demonstrations of 1929 and 1933. By 1935 many were beginning to take up arms in a bid to win independence and to halt Zionist immigration and colonisation.

Side by side with the influx of landless peasantry into the cities came those craftsmen and skilled workers whose traditional occupations had been ravaged by the decline of the Arab economy and the flood of cheap imports from Europe. Those who had managed to continue their trades in the countryside (see Chapter 2) found themselves faced with the dilemma of either travelling to the cities, where they might hope to continue selling goods to their local villagers, or of seeing their custom decline (at the same time that the prices of their raw materials were rising considerably) to the point where their own livelihood was threatened. Some were able to take advantage of the new cash economy which prevailed in the cities to set up small garages, repair shops or metal-working plants which catered to the immigrants or the government. A few even managed to employ workers of their own and thus became part of the growing petite bourgeoisie.[70] But these were the exceptions. Most of the craftsmen and the skilled workers had no choice but to join the expanded pool of surplus labour and to seek unskilled work in the cities. By 1931 the number of skilled Arab workers employed in small-scale manufacturing or in the traditional crafts had fallen to less than 19,000, a figure which represented only about 9 per cent of the labour force.[71]

Those who remained in employment often saw their wages decline dramatically. For example the daily wage of a worker in the woollen industry fell from an average in 1919 of 250 to 600 *mils* to only 80 to 130 *mils* by 1930. A worker in the soap industry who in 1919 could hope to earn from 250 to 500 *mils* a day depending on his skill would have been lucky to earn 120 *mils* a day, including overtime, by 1930.[72] In certain areas, such as Haifa or Jaffa where the influx from the countryside was particularly high, wages were even lower than the national average. A government survey of 1,000 workers in Jaffa carried out in November 1936 revealed that 935 made less than £P6 a month. More than half (570) earned less than £P2.75 a month, and even if we add the higher paid, 98 per cent of the total still earned less than £P10 a month.[73] Since the minimum cost of living in Jaffa at that time, according to government estimates, amounted to £P11.5 a month per household, it appears that the overwhelming majority of the workers and their families in Jaffa lived below subsistence level, even allowing for the fact that wives and children were often employed, at appallingly low wages, as domestic servants, street vendors and porters.[74]

The Growth of the Bourgeoisie

Ironically, by the mid-1930s Palestine had become one of the most prosperous economies in the Middle East, thanks to the combination of cheap labour, surplus capital and a modern infrastructure. The burgeoning economic opportunities spawned the growth of a class of importers and exporters, middlemen, wholesalers, commission agents, brokers and small manufacturers who benefited from the increase in foreign trade, the commercialisation of agriculture, the sale of land and the rise in urban rents. However, unlike the pre-Mandate period, this new 'bourgeoisie' was no longer confined primarily to the urban Christian elements, but drew new recruits from all strata of Muslim society: from the craftsmen and urban landlords as well as from the poorer branches of the more aristocratic families. In 1931 an estimated 12 per cent of the Christian, and 8 per cent of the Muslim, population made their living from trade. If we add to this the number of Arab Palestinians who engaged in finance, construction and the service industries such as shipping, tourism and retailing, the relative size and growth of this embryonic class becomes more readily apparent.[75]

While the Jewish sector predominated in the import of heavy machinery, textiles and building materials, the Arabs — both Christians and Muslims — specialised in the import and export of agricultural produce as well as in the wholesale and retail sectors of the foodstuffs trade.[76] The value of wheat imports, primarily from Syria, rose from £P16,000 in 1927 to £P448,000 in 1933. Imports of wheat flour also increased considerably during the 1920s and early 1930s. By 1936 they were worth £P353,000 a year. High increases were also recorded for barley, whose imported value rose from £P5,000 in 1928 to £P167,000 in 1936.[77]

Virtually all this trade was handled by Arab merchants and most combined it with their already extensive activity in the internal trade of foodstuffs. The trade in imports made up for the lack of supplies when harvests were poor at home; it also provided an exceptionally high margin of profit since both wheat and barley could be imported from Syria free of duty.[78] In addition, the merchants could enhance their profits by withholding supplies, whether of imported or local origin, until the market price was right.[79]

Mandatory economic policies encouraged the expansion of other food imports as well: sheep, goats and other livestock; fresh fruits and fish; rice and eggs. Certain semi-manufactured goods produced in the neighbouring Arab countries, such as leather goods, shoes, textiles and cement, were also imported in large quantities.[80] Each activity, like the grain trade, provided opportunities for the commercial bourgeoisie to expand and to add to its wealth: given the ready demand in Palestine and the excess of disposable capital, the risks were small.

Other forms of trade more common to the United States and Europe also made their appearance in Palestine during the first half of the Mandate. Both franchising and commission sales, through manufacturers' representatives or local agents, became common. While some of the agents dealt in foodstuffs and agricultural produce, the majority usually traded in consumer goods and luxury items imported from the West or in commercial or industrial goods ordered on contract by government buyers.[81] The foreign manufacturer benefited by avoiding the costs of setting up a foreign branch and only paid the agent for what he actually sold. The local representative or salesman did not need to invest a great deal of capital in the venture, as did the bigger traders, and by relying on orders was able to keep his inventory and storage costs to a minimum.

The servicing of the citrus crop also provided opportunities for entrepreneurial talent among the Arab population in Palestine. Although the bulk of the output came from estates owned by large land-owners (see below), the huge growth in exports during the first fifteen years of the Mandate spawned a number of related activities in shipping and transport, manufacturing, marketing and packaging. In Haifa and Jaffa some family firms, like those owned by the Majdalanis, the Badrans and Sahyouns, opened factories to produce the tiles, pipes and blocks needed to irrigate the new plantations; others specialised in the import of wood for packing crates, in providing commercial intelligence on the industry or in the supply of labour at harvest time.[82]

Finally it needs to be mentioned that since the merchants and the newer sectors of the bourgeoisie tended to be concentrated in the coastal cities where they had easy access to the ports, diplomatic consulates and foreign agencies, they profited more than the rest of the population from the enormous increase in urban property values and rents that occurred as a result of Jewish immigration and the unmet need for sufficient housing. For example the price of a *dunum* of Arab land near the Jewish settlement of Rishon-le-Zion (south of Tel Aviv) rose from eight shillings to as much as £P25 by 1931.[83] While this was unusually high, increases of three- or fourfold for land situated along the coast were not uncommon in the decade from 1925 to 1935 (see below). With their windfall profits, the urban bourgeoisie purchased larger, but cheaper, plots of arable land in the interior or, more commonly, invested their money abroad.

The Fragmentation of the Ruling Class

For the *ashraf* and large landed families in Palestine British rule represented a mixed blessing. Both profited from the expansion of trade, the demand for land and the huge growth of the coastal cities and towns. However the *ashraf*, unlike the *iqta'iyyin*, whose wealth derived from their own family holdings, were adversely affected by the confiscation of *waqf* lands, the creation of a secular administration outside their control and the imposition of British officials and Western-trained staff in positions formerly dominated by their members. The degree to which these losses were overcome by the benefits which accrued to them as landowners, or as advisers to the government, varied from family to family and, indeed, from individual to individual within the same family.

The landed families who had expanded their holdings during the late Ottoman era (see above) were the main beneficiaries of the huge rise in the cost of cultivated land in Palestine. Statistics produced by the Mandatory government show that the average price of land sold to the immigrants reached £P13.6 a *feddan* in the period from 1930 to 1938, compared with only £P6.9 a *feddan* in the period 1921 to 1929. In the three years from 1933 to 1936 alone land worth more than £P4.2 million was sold by Arab landowners to Jewish organisations and individuals.[84] Even allowing for the fact that an estimated two-thirds of all the land sold during the Mandate was purchased from absentee Arab landowners in Beirut, Damascus and other countries outside Palestine, the landowning families in Palestine still reaped substantial gains from the land sales, particularly during the period up to 1936 when the largest amount of land changed hands.[85]

Aside from the profits accruing directly to the landowners, the demand for land also led to the formation of a sub-class composed of brokers, lawyers, surveyors, accountants and estate agents affiliated to the landowners, or who were drawn directly from the landowning families themselves. Because the members of these families, particularly the younger sons, had access to posts in the secular administration and to education abroad, they were well placed to facilitate the sale of land, and many used their positions to do so before the issue became controversial. As early as 1925 the extent of both land sales and brokerage (*samsarah*) among the landowning families was so great the editor of the nationalist daily, *al-Karmil*, was moved to write bitterly:

The British Government should not be blamed for their refusal to heed our demands. We are to be blamed since we charged with the running of our affairs, the untrustworthy, the sellers, the brokers and the office-seekers, whom the British despise and the people . . . belittle.[86]

By 1933 even the German consul in Jerusalem, who was avidly courting Arab leaders, had become cynical. There were those amongst the Arabs, he said, 'who in daylight were crying out against Jewish immigration and in the darkness of the night were selling land to the Jews'.[87]

With their profits the landed families increasingly turned to the cultivation of capital-intensive cash crops: olives, sesame, dairy products and vegetables as well as citrus. The amount of Arab land devoted to orchards rose from 332,000 *dunums* in 1921 to more than 832,000 by 1942.[88] Vegetable production rose tenfold between 1920 and 1938; the production of cattle and poultry for meat, eggs and milk increased 60 per cent by 1936.[89]

The greatest change occurred in the cultivation of citrus fruits — oranges, grapefruit and lemons. Not only was there an important new market for the crop in Europe, and the capital needed to bring new lands into intensive cultivation, but the cultivation of citrus on large plantations reduced the need for labour while at the same time guaranteeing lucrative returns on investment. Given that the average cost of bringing a *dunum* of land up to the fruit-bearing stage ranged from £P75 to £P125 (depending on whether the cost of the land itself was included), it was an activity only the rich could afford.[90] However the Arab grower, like his Jewish counterpart, stood to gain not only from the high export value of the crop but also from the government subsidies and artificially low taxes imposed on citrus.[91]

As a result, the amount of Arab-owned land devoted to citrus cultivation rose from 22,000 *dunums* in 1922 to 144,000 *dunums* in 1937.[92] Most of the holdings were concentrated in the hands of a few landowners: of the 700 to 1,000 Arab growers in 1937, for example, less than 12 per cent owned 47 per cent of the land.[93] In addition, some 270 growers exported their crop themselves, thereby reaping the added value which occurred in the trade, as well as in the cultivation, of citrus fruit.[94] Given that the net income, after subtracting the cost of maintenance, shipping and transport, came to about £P5 a *dunum*, this meant that the top 12 per cent together earned about £P338,400 in the 1937/8 season alone, even before their profits from trading were obtained.[95]

The concentration of wealth in this segment of Palestinian Arab society was particularly glaring when contrasted with the state of the peasantry. And, since many of the owners of the citrus plantations also extorted exorbitant rates of interest for loans to the peasants, or in the form of land rent, they increasingly became the targets of the peasants' wrath.[96] During the 1936-9 revolt, the plantation owners were often subjected to abuse and physical violence, especially since they were also seen as directly responsible for the eviction of tenant farmers as a result of their having sold land to the Jews.

Unlike the large landowners, the *ashraf* remained dependent on the government for the maintenance of their position within society, and specifically for control of the property and landed estates dedicated as *waqf* (see above). The replacement of Ottoman rule by a power that was both foreign and non-Islamic posed an immediate challenge to their claim to represent the Arab community in matters both secular and spiritual. A confrontation was not long in coming. Storrs recorded that during the Easter troubles which broke out in Jerusalem in 1920, the mayor of the city, an elderly and venerated member of one of the most prominent sharifian families in Palestine, Musa Pasha Kazim al-Hussaini, had declared himself the leader and spokesman of the opposition to the British Mandate. He recalled that:

> I had met him one afternoon marching before a rabble to demonstrate against the Zionist offices, and bade him take them and himself home lest trouble should arise. The same evening I warned him that he must make his choice between politics and the Mayoralty . . . He became first intractable and then defiant, and I informed the Administration that I proposed to dismiss and replace him forthwith.[97]

Having rejected suggestions by the military authorities that an Englishman be appointed in his place (a move which might have firmly united the Palestinian leadership to oppose British rule), Storrs then proceeded to mount a classic divide-and-rule tactic by offering the post to Hussaini's chief rival within the Jerusalem aristocracy, Raghib Bey al-Nashashibi, who accepted on the spot. On the other hand, less than a year later, when the Mufti of Jerusalem, Kamal Effendi al-Hussaini, a cousin of Musa Kazim, died unexpectedly, his half-brother, Hajj Amin al-Hussaini, was appointed in his place against the wishes of the Nashashibis.[98] The division of the country's leading families was thus ensured, for the two most important Muslim posts in the country were now in the hands of rival claimants. This rivalry, and the subsequent division of the *ashraf*, continued throughout the Mandate and, as we shall see, lasted even after the creation of the state of Israel and the dispersion of the majority of the Arab population.

Equally as important was the decision taken by the military government in 1921 to create a new Supreme Muslim Shari'ah Council (SMC), and to appoint Hajj Amin as its President in March 1922. The Council was stripped of any power to represent the Muslim community in matters other than those affecting the personal status of Muslims in Palestine but in return was given a free hand to manage the affairs of the *awqaf* and to appoint all the religious officials in the country: the *muftis* in the districts outside Jerusalem, the *qadis* (judges) of the Shari'ah courts, the *imams* and *khatibs* (clerks) as well as the administrators and teachers of charitable institutions such as schools, hospitals and orphanages.[99]

Hajj Amin, who remained as permanent head of the Council until his removal from the post by order of the High Commissioner in the wake of severe rioting in 1937, was thus personally placed in a position in which he could exercise pre-eminent control over Muslim affairs in Palestine, an activity that had formerly been exercised by the collective authority of the *ashraf* as a whole. The degree to which his position, and that of the mayors, remained dependent on retaining the goodwill of the British Mandatory officials was demonstrated not only by the circumstances of his ultimate removal but also by the fact that the members of the Council, and their staffs, received their salaries directly from the government. Furthermore, appointments to the Shari'ah courts also were made subject to the final approval of the Mandatory government. Finally, the tithes due on *waqf* land and property were paid directly to the government, rather than to the Council, who received a fixed income from the government (the tithes minus a collection charge). When the government decided unilaterally to commute the tithes payable on *waqf* land and to reduce the rate at which they were assessed during the 1930s, the Council's income fell dramatically. It was restored only in 1934 after Hajj Amin and the Council agreed to a further reduction in their powers.[100]

In other words, the *ashraf*, unlike the landowners, not only became dependent on the goodwill of the government to maintain their traditional right to the highest religious positions in the land, and to the income which they obtained through their control of the *waqf*, they lost their collective solidarity and ultimate ability to decide the allocation of the country's leading religious posts. The result was that the *ashraf* divided once again into *majlisiyyin* and *mu'aridin*, i.e. into those who supported the Council and, indirectly, the supremacy of the Hussainis, and those who were opposed to it and to the Hussaini clan. The situation was not unlike that which prevailed in the middle of the nineteenth century, when the country was divided into Qaisis and Yamanis, or at the end of Ottoman rule when the leading families were divided between those who supported the Ottoman Parliament and those who opposed it in favour of Arab autonomy. What was different this time was that the majority of the peasants were no longer exclusively bound to preserve and follow these anachronistic tribal divisions. For them, they were irrelevant, and they preferred to organise themselves around their hostility to the Zionists and to the British, if necessary without, or in opposition to, their traditional leaders.

Finally, it must also be noted that the matter was made still worse by the readiness of the leading landowning families to ally themselves with one or other of the leading rivals: the Hussainis or the Nashashibis. In so far as neither opposed British rule directly, but instead concentrated their wrath on their opponents within their own community, the landowners could aspire to a leading position within Palestinian Arab society without seeing their own ability to accrue material benefit from British occupation put at risk. Thus, for example, until the 1936 revolt, the Tajis, the Shawas, the Tuqans, the Barghouthis and the Dajanis (of Jerusalem), as well as the mayors of Jaffa, Ramlah, Nablus, Hebron and other cities, tended by and large to support the opposition. Hajj Amin and the Hussainis obtained broad support from sections of the Tamimis, the Alamis, the Jaiyussis, the provincial *muftis*, *imams* and *qadis* (most of whom were appointed by Hajj Amin in his capacity as head of the Supreme Muslim Shari'ah Council), the village sheikhs and the Muslim officials who administered the *awqaf* properties and estates.[101]

By the early 1930s the division had become so entrenched that when the Hussainis began a campaign to stop the payment of land taxes to the government — a move which was opposed by many of the large landowners — the Nashashibis countered by insisting that all government officials resign their posts, ostensibly as a protest against the failure of the British to grant the Arabs a legislative assembly and representative institutions. Such a plan, if successful, would have directly undercut the pre-eminent role of the Hussainis in the Council and in the administration of the courts and the *awqaf*, and as a result Hajj Amin was forced to drop his campaign against taxation.

Arab Revolt and Civil War, 1936-9

The Revolt

While the notables of Jerusalem argued, the country simmered with discontent. The rise of Hitler in Germany and the passage of the Nuremberg laws depriving Jews of their citizenship made even more desperate the plight of those seeking a safe haven from persecution. As one by one the doors of entry were tightened in the United States, Britain and France, Palestine seemed the only escape.[102] Illegal immigration increased relentlessly, and few in the United States and Europe — least of all the trade unionists who encouraged the restrictive legislation — seemed mindful of the consequences their actions caused elsewhere, whether in Germany, Poland or Palestine. By 1935 unemployment among both Jews and Arabs in Palestine was escalating, as the world recession at last found its way to the eastern Mediterranean. There was very little work available in the construction trades and the citrus crop was badly affected by *khamsin* winds. The crop that was harvested had to be sold at a loss due to the dramatic fall in world prices as a result of the depression.

The deterioration in the economic situation was matched by rising social discontent. In January Arabs being evicted from land bought by Jews attacked the police with stones. They were answered with gunshots, and one Arab was killed.[103] In August a group of peasants attacked a number of Jews who were ploughing land the peasants claimed as their own.[104] The result was another Arab death. In October a shipment of cement cases destined for Tel Aviv was opened at Jaffa port and was found to contain hundreds of pistols, revolvers, bayonets and several hundred thousand rounds of ammunition.[105] On 26 October Arab workers at the port of Jaffa went on strike, only to find their jobs filled by a rush of Jewish immigrants.[106] In November an obscure band of religious patriots emerged from the hills of Galilee to declare war on British imperialism and to demand the expulsion of the foreigner. Police cornered the band near Janin, killing four of its members. One of them was the venerated Sheikh 'Izzaddin Qassam, who had rebelled against the *'ulama* of Jerusalem and rallied the Islamic faithful to his cause while carrying on social work among the poor and destitute of Haifa.[107]

Meanwhile, in the cities and towns of the coast, young Arab workers and students read in the Arab press of the anti-British riots and demonstrations taking place in Egypt and of the radical demands made by the nationalists in Syria, where a general strike against the French occupation was in progress. Hopes that the British might make concessions in Palestine, as they had in Egypt that year (and as the French subsequently did in Syria), were finally dashed in February and March 1936 when both the House of Commons and the House of Lords firmly refused to respond to the Arab call for elections, a legislative assembly, the ending of immigration and a halt to the eviction of Arab peasants from their lands.

In the middle of April rioting broke out in many parts of the country, leaving several Arabs and a score of Jews dead or fatally wounded.[108] On the 17th the government declared a country-wide curfew and a state of emergency. Three days later local committees which had been formed in Nablus, Jerusalem, Jaffa, Tulkarm and elsewhere responded by calling a general strike. Within hours the country was brought to a standstill. The Arab revolt, which was to last three years and which, in its way, was as significant for the future of the Middle East as was the Spanish Civil War for Europe, had begun.

By the summer of 1937 hundreds of armed bands, equipped with weaponry captured from the British or with First World War rifles smuggled in from Syria or Lebanon, roamed the hills of Palestine. Telephone and telegraph communications were cut, the oil pipeline from Iraq to Haifa was severed, police stations attacked, rail lines blown up, roads mined and bridges destroyed. For more than 18 months the interior of the country remained in rebel hands. One senior policeman later told Nicholas Bethell: 'Their bombs were efficient, their landmines blew us off the road, their barricades stopped our patrols and in the end we had to withdraw from the countryside.' Another administrator, Hugh Foot (later Lord Caradon and the author of United Nations Resolution 242), recalled that 'All ordinary administration ceased. Every morning I looked through a long list of disorders and destruction.'[109]

By the autumn of 1938 the rebels were enforcing their collective writ throughout much of Palestine and enacting measures which reflected their social consciousness, as well as their will to national independence. A moratorium on debts to landowners was declared; urban creditors − mostly merchants and landowners − were forbidden to enter villages under rebel control; and the owners of citrus plantations were 'taxed' to support the uprising. The sale of land to Jews was forbidden, and those found guilty of such transgressions, or of acting as brokers for land sales, were liable to trial, and even execution, in rebel courts.

In the towns and villages, the victorious rebels cancelled rents, forbade the wearing of the hated Turkish head-dress, the *tarbush*, worn by the urban elite (a measure which also helped to prevent the rebels from being recognised by their *kuffiyahs*) and confiscated property left by those who had fled abroad.[110] In January 1939 Sir Harold MacMichael, the High Commissioner, wrote to the Colonial Secretary, Malcolm MacDonald:

Something like a social revolution on a small scale is beginning. The influence of the landlord-politician is on the wane. He had done nothing but talk (and pay): others have taken the risks, and these others are disposed to take a line of their own.[111]

George Antonius, the dispassionate historian of Arab nationalism who served as General Secretary to several Palestinian delegations, wrote at the time:

Far from being engineered by the leaders, the revolt is in a very marked way a challenge to their authority and an indictment of their methods. The rebel chiefs lay the blame for the present plight of the peasantry on those Arab landowners who have sold their land, and they accuse the leaders of culpable neglect for failing to prevent the sales ... Their anger and violence are as much directed against Arab landowners and brokers who have facilitated the sales as against the policy of the mandatory power under whose aegis the transactions have taken place.[112]

Yet, in the end, the rebels, despite their determination, their ability to endure collective punishment on a scale seldom practised by the 'democracies' of the West, and their superior numbers, were defeated. Thousands were killed, while those that survived were rounded up and hanged, imprisoned or exiled.[113] Palestine was successfully 'reconquered', and the population completely disarmed. The opportunity to prevent the creation of a separate Zionist state, let alone to achieve national independence, was lost. Within a decade the Palestinians would find themselves forcibly uprooted and their country a name only they, and the historians, would remember.

Civil War and Class Conflict

Since 1939 debate has raged within the Palestinian community about the causes of the defeat. There is no doubt that the rebels were up against one of the most formidable opponents of their time: the British, facing the prospect of war with Nazi Germany, were determined at all costs to prevent the loss of their vital communications routes in the Middle East, and to preserve access to the oil reserves of the Gulf. By 1937. the British Treasury had doubled its expenditure on defence and security in Palestine to £P1,920,000 (compared to £P843,000 in 1935). Some 20,000 troops and several hundred Air Force personnel were stationed in the country.[114]

Furthermore, the extremists in the Jewish Agency showed that if the British government was unable to defeat the rebels on its own, they were more than ready, and capable, of lending a helping hand. Like their counterparts, the French settlers in Algeria, they engaged in a campaign of terror against the villagers and urban population that was supported and led by men like Orde Wingate, the ardently pro-Zionist British officer who helped Moshe Dayan and other Zionists set up the 'special night squads', mixed Jewish and British units secretly trained in the kind of counter-insurgency tactics that later became so notorious in Malaysia and Vietnam.[115] No doubt any liberation movement, let alone one which was so ill equipped, would have found itself fighting a long war of attrition at best under such circumstances. However given that geographically Palestine lacked the kind of territorial reserves a guerrilla army needs for logistical support, such a war of long duration was bound to benefit the enemy.

Yet arguments such as these, however important, cannot entirely explain why the rebellion failed. The lack of unity within the Palestinian community, and the failure of the leadership to support a national struggle when it compromised their own positions within society, were also major factors in the defeat. A few illustrations will suffice to demonstrate this point and to indicate the degree to which internal conflict, bordering on civil war, as well as rebellion against the British and the Zionists, characterised the revolt.

Firstly, at the time of the general strike, in the spring of 1936, the leaders of the Palestinian community, then grouped together in the Arab Higher Committee (AHC), refused repeated calls by the local committees to call out government workers in support of the national stoppage. While such a move would have ensured that the strike affected the vital sectors of the administration, as well as the economy, the head of the AHC, Hajj Amin al-Hussaini, and his supporters also knew it would have led to the loss of their positions within the Supreme Muslim Shari'ah Council and to the loss of their control over the ranks of salaried officials employed by the Council in Jerusalem and elsewhere. In addition, the tithes received from the government would also have ceased, thereby removing the Mufti's financial control of the Palestinian national movement.

The Nashashibis, while supporting the proposed strike by government workers as one way to do away with their hated rivals, nevertheless refused to support a strike by mayors and municipal officials, namely by those they counted as supporters of their own faction within the ruling class. In the end the government workers remained on the job for almost the entire duration of the general strike, and this included, in addition to the members of the Supreme Council, the mayors, municipal officials and workers in such important sectors as the railways, telecommunications and posts, ports and oil refineries.[116]

Secondly, once the strike threatened to extend into the critical period of the autumn when the citrus crop was due to be harvested, the leaders of the national movement acted to ensure that the revolt did not threaten their vital interests. The powerful landowners on the Higher Committee, such as 'Auni Bey Abdul Hadi and Ya'qub al-Ghusain, supported by Hajj Amin and Raghib Bey al-Nashashibi, issued an appeal urging that the strike be called off despite the fact that no concessions regarding Arab demands had been obtained. Given the fact that the Higher Committee had taken the precaution beforehand of ensuring that the appeal was supported by the neighbouring Arab leaders of Trans-Jordan, Saudi Arabia and Iraq (which meant, among other things, that any plan to raise strike funds from Arabs living outside Palestine to replace those withdrawn by the Higher Committee would be made more difficult), the peasantry was left with little alternative but to comply.[117]

Thirdly, when the peasantry and urban workers began to realise that non-violent protest was futile and began to plan an armed uprising, the leaders again intervened in an effort to prevent it from taking place or, if possible, to limit its scope and effectiveness. When, for example, several members of the local committees approached Hajj Amin for support, he admonished them instead for the demonstrations against the government they had already organised. Such actions, he warned, would cost the Arabs the support they enjoyed in London. He urged them to embark on a peaceful campaign aimed at winning political support in other Muslim countries, or at a minimum to postpone their revolt until circumstances were more favourable.

On another occasion he pressed them to forgo attacks they planned to make against police stations, army camps and other British military installations and to concentrate their attacks on the Jewish settlements instead.[118] Only after several of the more radical sheikhs and religious leaders in the villages around Haifa and Jerusalem had already declared a *jihad* against the British and challenged his commitment to the Islamic cause did he actively take part in the revolt.[119] Aside from Hajj Amin, a similar attitude prevailed among the other leaders, many of whom actively resisted the leaders of the revolt. The Nashashibis, for example, refused to support an armed struggle on the grounds that the arms might be directed against themselves.[120]

Finally, once the revolt had indeed taken on the aspects of a revolutionary struggle against the feudal elite, as well as against the British, the Nashashibis and large landowners, supported by some of the wealthier merchants and village notables who had lost their positions to the rebels, organised their own counter-revolutionary squads which attacked guerrilla strongholds in the countryside.[121] In some areas supporters of the Nashashibis handed information to the British which led to the capture and arrest of rebel commanders.[122]

Collaboration of this kind demonstrated the extent to which the nature of the struggle changed during the long course of the revolt and the degree to which the majority of the Arab population, which consisted for the most part of the peasantry, the workers and the urban 'lumpen-proletariat', were openly opposed by their own leaders; that is, by the landowners and those sections of the urban aristocracy who stood to lose as much from a revolution within their own community as from a continuation of British rule. The Palestinian ruling class, rather than engaging in a national struggle for independence, chose instead to defend its own interests as a class above all. Rather than cede their place of leadership to the insurgents among their compatriots, they chose either exile or counter-revolution. The rebels, fighting the British and the Zionists, could not successfully wage class warfare at the same time, and were forced to postpone the struggle until the end of the Second World War. By then it was too late to prevent the final collapse.

Partition, Defeat and Exile, 1939-48

The outbreak of war in Europe dramatically altered the situation in Palestine. Zionist leaders, despite their misgivings over Britain's curtailment of immigration and the retreat from the Balfour Declaration implied in the 1939 White Paper (see below), threw their weight behind the Allies in an effort to secure the defeat of Nazi Germany. Units of the Haganah, the underground Jewish army, volunteered to serve alongside British forces in Palestine and helped to organise commando raids into enemy territory and to prepare for resistance in the case of an Axis occupation of Palestine itself. The Jewish units (which were still illegal) were secretly armed, trained and deployed at strategic sites around the country.[123]

While the military authorities, both in Britain and in Palestine, encouraged such a policy, the civil administration feared that the leaders of the Jewish Agency, who disavowed any association with the Haganah in public but fostered its growth in private, would use the Jewish troops against Britain to obtain independence once the hostilities had ended in Europe. Such fears were totally justified.

David Ben-Gurion, Weizmann's successor as head of the Jewish Agency and later Prime Minister of Israel, wrote at the time that

> the Jews will create a strong army, equipped with the best weapons, and the Arabs will not be able to face it; the Jews . . . not satisfied with their narrow boundaries, will spread into undeveloped areas, and cause troubles to the British.[124]

Jewish discontent with the policies of the British government had been growing since July 1937 when the Peel Commission, which had been set up to investigate the causes of the Arab revolt, recommended limiting Jewish immigration into Palestine to no more than 12,000 a year and called, for the first time, for the partition of the country into three separate states: one for the Jews, another for the Arabs and a third – consisting of Jerusalem, Bethlehem and the mixed towns of Tiberias, Safad, Nazareth and Acre – to be placed under direct British rule.[125] Although the plan was dropped after fierce resistance, the idea of limiting Jewish immigration was revived in the 1939 White Paper, which called for the admission of no more than 75,000 immigrants during the next five years.[126]

Jewish leaders, mindful not only of the pressing need to find a refuge for those being persecuted in Germany but also of the effect such a limitation would have on their anticipated post-war struggle to create a Jewish state in Palestine, launched a massive public relations campaign in Europe and in the United States aimed at defeating the policy. More extreme groups, like the Stern Gang and the Irgun Zwei Leumi – later headed by Menahim Begin – began to prepare a campaign of terror against British targets, both civilian and military, in Palestine. Three years later, as the persecution and imprisonment of Jews had spread to other countries in Europe occupied by Nazi Germany, and as the reports of the horrors of the concentration camps began to filter outside Germany, a conference of American Zionists met in New York and called for a complete end to all controls on immigration, the granting of authority to the Jewish Agency to develop the uncultivated lands in Palestine and the establishment of a 'Jewish Commonwealth' in the whole of Palestine.[127]

The statement, later named the 'Biltmore Programme' (after the hotel in which the conference was held), marked a turning point in the history of Zionist relations with the West. Henceforth the United States, which had entered the world war six months earlier, would become the prime focal point of Zionist attention in the attempt to secure a Jewish state in Palestine. Britain, which had begun to favour Arab demands for a revision of its policies towards the Zionists in an effort to secure its vital military bases and oil supply lines in Egypt, Jordan, Iraq and the Persian Gulf, would be relegated to second place until the war's end, when the Jewish struggle for independence could be conducted openly.

For the Arab community in Palestine the outbreak of war in Europe coincided with severe political repression at home. The British government, anxious to avoid any repeat of the conflict which had engulfed the country during the three years of the revolt, banned virtually all forms of political activity and refused to allow leaders of the nationalist movement to return from exile. British officials took over direct control of the *awqaf* funds which financed the movement and initiated a new system of police and military tribunals which were given extensive powers to search homes, seize suspects and detain them without trial for unlimited periods.[128]

Economically, however, the war years brought prosperity to many sections of the population which had suffered severely during the general strike and revolt. The peasantry obtained high prices for its agricultural produce while the workers obtained significant rises in their wages. The merchants benefited as well, primarily by obtaining lucrative government contracts involving military construction, the import of goods and the supply of labour. Even though wartime inflation diminished some of these gains and exacerbated the severe shortage of housing and consumer goods, many of the most impoverished sections of Palestinian society experienced an increase in their standard of living for the first time in decades.

However these benefits ended suddenly once peace was concluded in Europe in 1945. Even before the war had drawn to a close Britain had signalled its intention to renege on the promises made in the 1939 White Paper. Under pressure from the Cabinet and influential pro-Zionist politicians in both the Conservative and Labour parties as well as public opinion in the West, which was outraged by the revelations of the extent of the Nazi atrocities, it had begun to prepare once again for the partition of Palestine into two separate states, one for the Jews and another for the Arabs.

Representations by US Congressmen favourable to the Jewish

position and by President Truman directly urging a complete relaxation of any limitation on immigration and the immediate declaration of a Jewish state also contributed to the change in policy, which became focused on the need to provide a refuge for the hundreds of thousands of stateless Jews in Europe.[129] The victory of the Labour Party in the British elections held in the summer of 1945, two months after VE day, also worked in the Zionists' favour, giving them strong support among both the parliamentary leadership and in the party as a whole.

In November the new Foreign Minister, Ernest Bevin, announced that a joint Anglo-American Committee of Inquiry would be established to look at the question of Jewish immigration into Palestine and the problems of Jewish refugees in Europe. The Committee's Report, published in the spring of 1946, called for the immediate granting of 100,000 immigration certificates to refugees in Europe and the admission of still others as suitable conditions developed in Palestine. In addition it called for the lifting of restrictions on land sales to the Jews and the continuation of British rule.[130]

No doubt the Committee hoped that concessions such as these might induce the Jewish Agency to co-operate in the suppression of Jewish terrorism which at the time was threatening to engulf Britain in a conflict far worse than the one it had experienced during the Arab revolt and which had come at a time when Britain's morale and military might were at a low ebb.[131] A failure to enlist the Agency's co-operation would also have led to the appalling prospect of British troops having to fire on Jewish resisters when the horrors of the concentration camps were still fresh in the public mind.[132] Whitehall was not prepared to do this. Given Arab determination to avoid any further Jewish immigration and land sales, such a policy inevitably meant that the White Paper, and the hope it had held out to the Arab community of creating a unified and independent Palestine, was confined to the dustbin of history.

Partition was now inevitable and in February 1947 Britain, faced with the impossible task of trying to reconcile the opposing pressures from Jews and Arabs, announced its intention to turn the matter over to the United Nations. In November the UN General Assembly, meeting in New York, called for an end to the British Mandate by the following August. Two independent states, one Jewish and one Arab, were to be established in the country; Jerusalem was to be placed under an international administration. For the Arabs the UN role meant that the dismemberment of their community had been endorsed by the representatives of the world's most powerful countries. For the Jews it marked a historic victory against overwhelming odds. For both Arab and Jew in Palestine, it meant war was inevitable.

Given the state of Jewish preparedness and the extent of Arab division, the outcome, although unexpected at the time, was inevitable. On 15 May 1948, after a fierce campaign which had led to the dispersal of hundreds of thousands of Arabs from those portions of the country designated for inclusion in the Jewish entity, the state of Israel was declared. A few hours earlier the last British troops, accompanied by the High Commissioner, Sir Alan Cunningham, had sailed ignominiously out of Haifa port.

After thirty years of occupation, the Palestinian Arab nationalists had inadvertently achieved one of their main goals; but just as the ending of Turkish rule had brought only more travail in its wake, so too did the ending of the British Mandate. Although Britain had withdrawn militarily and politically, it had left behind new settlers whose leaders, anxious to secure a home for their own refugees, were determined not only to occupy the country but also to expel the indigenous inhabitants from their lands and livelihoods.

Map 3. Palestine – the UN Partition Plan, 1947*

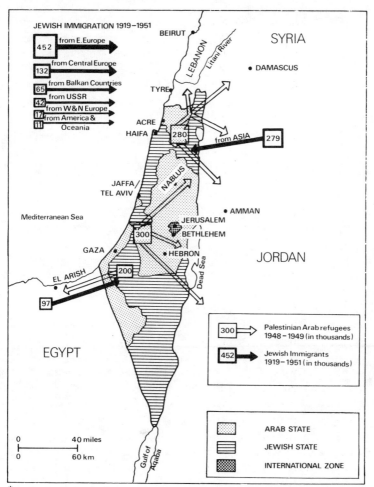

JEWISH IMMIGRATION 1919–1951

452	from E. Europe
132	from Central Europe
65	from Balkan Countries
42	from USSR
17	from W & N Europe
11	from America & Oceania

BEIRUT

SYRIA

LEBANON

Litani River

• DAMASCUS

TYRE

from ASIA | 279 |

ACRE
HAIFA | 280 |

JAFFA / TEL AVIV

NABLUS

Mediterranean Sea

• AMMAN

JERUSALEM
BETHLEHEM

| 300 |

GAZA

• HEBRON

JORDAN

EL ARISH | 200 |

| 97 |

Dead Sea

EGYPT

| 300 | ➡ | Palestinian Arab refugees 1948–1949 (in thousands) |
| 452 | ➡ | Jewish Immigrants 1919–1951 (in thousands) |

| 0 | 40 miles |
| 0 | 60 km |

Gulf of Aqaba

▢	ARAB STATE
▤	JEWISH STATE
▩	INTERNATIONAL ZONE

* Immigration/Emigration figures compiled from The New Cambridge Modern History, vol. XIV, Cambridge (UK), 1970.

Part Two

THE PALESTINIAN DIASPORA, 1948-1983

4 THE DECLINE OF THE RULING FAMILIES, 1948-1967

The dispersal of the Palestinians and the loss of a large part of the country to the Zionists led to radical economic and social change even in those parts of Palestine – the West Bank and Gaza – that remained under Arab control. The influx of hundreds of thousands of refugees undermined the traditional patterns of social organisation and control and threatened to produce a revolution within Palestinian society itself. However, although the creation of the state of Israel had catastrophic effects on a large part of the peasantry and working class and led to the enforced exile of sections of the bourgeoisie and upper class as well, it actually benefited certain elements of the sharifian and large landowning families who retained their estates in the Arab-occupied sectors of Palestine. The flood of refugees depressed wage rates to levels not experienced since the mid-1930s and provided a vast pool of skilled and unskilled labour desperate to find work even at starvation wages. At the same time the existence of this huge new labour market provided an unparalleled incentive to local landowners and capitalists in the West Bank and Gaza to open new lands to cultivation, to engage in foreign trade and to develop indigenous industries capable of providing for the needs of the expanded population.

The cessation of direct British rule and its replacement in the Arab sector by the monarchies of Egypt and Jordan also provided new hope to the *ashraf* who, for the first time since the demise of the Ottomans, looked forward to the restoration of their privileged positions within an Islamic hierarchy that would, they thought, give them access to high positions in government service and restore their control of the religious institutions. However in the longer term the partition of Palestine and the loss of hegemony by the Palestinian ruling class paved the way for the emergence of new classes and the assumption of political power by men not committed to the traditional social framework.

This chapter looks at the position of the *ashraf* and large landowning families in Arab-occupied Palestine and in Jordan until their decline after the 1967 war when their claim to political leadership was challenged by the Palestine Liberation Organisation and the armed

77

cadres of the various Palestinian guerrilla movements. However, to understand the full impact of the creation of the state of Israel and the annexation of the West Bank by Jordan on the class structure in general and the ruling families in particular, we need to look more closely at the internecine conflict which erupted within the Palestinian leadership during the Second World War.

The Defeat of the National Movement, 1943-8

The Istiqlal and the Hussainis, 1943-5

In the summer of 1942 few in Palestine, whether Arab or Jew, were hopeful that their national goals would be achieved. Indeed it appeared that neither community would obtain an independent state and that instead it would be the Germans who would gain Palestine, replacing the British as occupiers. Field Marshal Erwin Rommel had completed his blitz across North Africa in May; by the end of June he had reached El Alamein, only 150 miles from Cairo and less than 500 miles by road from Jaffa and Tel Aviv. To the north the main German army had advanced across the Ukraine, reaching Rostov in July. From there it was expected to turn south across the Caucasus mountains to join the German forces coming from the Sahara. A giant pincer seemed set to close not only on Palestine but also on Turkey, Iran and the whole of the Arab world.[1] By October, however, it was clear that Montgomery's victory that month over Rommel at the battle of El Alamein had not only freed North Africa from the spectre of Nazi occupation but had also changed the tide of the war. Throughout the Middle East an allied victory appeared more likely than ever before, a prospect that was confirmed when the Russians defeated the Germans at Stalingrad later that year.

By early 1943 both the Arab and Jewish communities in Palestine were sufficiently confident of a British victory to begin plans for renewing their struggle to gain concessions once the war had ended. The Jewish community, vastly reinforced in arms and moral determination, launched a fierce political campaign in Britain and the United States to achieve greater and greater sympathy as the news of the Nazi holocaust filtered through to the radios and newspapers of the West. The Arabs, embittered by Zionist designs on their country and concerned about the increased support which the Jewish Agency was receiving in the United States, threw off their political apathy and began once again to agitate for the removal of restrictions on political activity and for the creation of a unified national movement. Aside from the need to counter Zionist claims to Palestine, they hoped to have their voice heard in any discussions held among the Allies about the future disposition of Palestine and of the occupied Arab lands. Fears that the British Prime Minister, Winston Churchill, still favoured the partition scheme recommended by the Peel Commission and that Britain might renege on the promises outlined in the 1939 White Paper once the war had ended added to the sense of urgency.

Within the Arab community the only group among the landowners and *ashraf* that was not discredited or in exile consisted for the most part of members of the Istiqlal (Independence) Party which had been formed at the end of the First World War by a number of young urban intellectuals from the Arab landowning classes of Palestine, Syria and Iraq.[2] Originally supporters of Faisal's government in Damascus, many had fled after his fall to neighbouring Trans-Jordan were they came into conflict with the Amir Abdullah and were expelled in the late 1920s.[3] In 1932 Palestinian members of the Istiqlal set up a separate branch in the country which advocated an end to British rule, pan-Arab unity and social reform.[4]

Although it was composed of members of the landowning nobility, such as 'Auni Bey Abdul Hadi and Rashid al-Hajj Ibrahim, a member of a leading family in Haifa, the party also drew extensive support from the younger sons of the upper class and from the new middle-class professionals who had been trained in Western schools either in Palestine or abroad. Certain sections of the Christian community were also attracted by its secular ideology. However, shortly after its establishment in Palestine profound differences emerged within the party concerning the inter-Arab dynastic quarrels between the Hashimites and Saudis; by 1936, when the revolt broke out, it had virtually ceased to function as a collective unit.[5] Despite this, individuals from the party played prominent roles in the national committees set up at the start of the general strike and a few participated actively in the revolt. 'Auni Abdul Hadi, together with Ahmad Hilmi Pasha Abdul Baqi — a leading financier and former Ottoman general who had joined the party shortly after its foundation — were named to the first Arab Higher Committee formed in April 1936, the former serving as the Committee's general secretary and the latter as its treasurer.[6] When the British decided to deport the members of the Committee in 1937, 'Auni Bey Abdul Hadi, who was outside the country at the time, was excluded from re-entry; Ahmad Hilmi Pasha and another Istiqlalist, Rashid al-Hajj Ibrahim, were deported to the Seychelles Islands in the Indian Ocean where they remained for the next eighteen months.

Although the Istiqlal had originally urged collaboration with Italy and Germany in the late 1920s as a way to fight British occupation of their own country, Britain's adherence during the war to the terms of the White Paper, its support for Arab unity and its announced intention to curtail the terrorist activities launched by the Irgun and other underground Zionist groups in Palestine, together with their dislike for Hitler, led the former Istiqlal leaders to adopt a distinctly pro-British policy. As early as 1939 both 'Auni Abdul Hadi and Ahmad Hilmi had urged the Higher Committee to recognise the change in British policy and to accept the White Paper.[7] They therefore found themselves in a more favourable situation *vis-à-vis* the Mandatory government than the Mufti and his supporters and were allowed to return to Palestine earlier than the other exiles.

In 1939 the former leaders of the Istiqlal detained by British troops were freed from internment to attend the London Conference at St James's to discuss Britain's proposals for the future of Palestine. By the early 1940s they had returned to the country, unlike their rivals among the Hussaini faction who remained in exile or in detention. Ahmad Hilmi, who had founded the Arab National Bank in 1930, returned to his position as chairman, and both Abdul Hadi and al-Hajj Ibrahim were drawn into it as members of the Board.[8] They lost little time in trying to re-establish their political influence and shortly after their arrival purchased the widely read Arabic newspaper, *Filistin* (*Palestine*). This gave them, and the party, a national platform from which to air their views.[9] The party's financial resources were also bolstered by the huge war profits placed on deposit in the bank which it used to invest in land, industry and trade. Ahmad Hilmi's establishment of the Arab National Fund in August 1943 added still more to the party's power and prestige.

By the end of the war the Fund had invested substantial sums in the purchase of Arab lands from the indebted peasantry and had encouraged others to convert their land to *waqf* property with the proceeds allocated to the Fund. With the abolition of the Supreme Muslim Council and the removal of its control over *waqf* land after the deportation of Hajj Amin al-Hussaini in 1937, the Arab National Fund became the only institution in the country capable of preventing the sale of land to the Zionists and as such earned considerable support among the peasantry as well as among the emergent bourgeoisie.[10] Voluntary subscriptions to the Fund poured in from all parts of Palestine and by the summer of 1944 it had opened up offices in all the Arab towns and in most of the larger villages as well.[11]

The growing popular success of the Istiqlal leaders and of the Fund posed a direct threat to the hopes of the Hussainis, who had assumed that they would be able to regain control of the national leadership once the war had ended and their leaders were allowed to return to Palestine. In this they received a sympathetic ear from other clans within the Jerusalem nobility, who, however much they disagreed with Hussaini's conduct during the 1936-9 revolt, nevertheless felt threatened by the Istiqlal's ability to transcend class divisions and to challenge the existing power structure within the Arab community.[12] In November 1943 the Hussainis, together with their supporters from among the mayors and village headmen – the *mukhtars* – boycotted a national conference called by the former Istiqlal leaders aimed at setting up a unified national leadership to choose a delegate to the forthcoming Arab unity talks in Cairo (see below). They were joined in the boycott by members of the Reform Party and the Congress of Arab Youth, whose leaders – Dr Hussain Fakhri al-Khalidi and Ya'qub al-Ghusain (a wealthy landowner from Ramlah) – had been deported from Palestine in 1937.[13]

Six months later, in April 1944, the Hussainis were ready to re-establish the Palestine Arab Party, which originally had been set up by Hajj Amin and his supporters in 1935. At a meeting in Jerusalem delegates from most of the larger towns in Palestine formed a central committee and national executive chaired by Tawfiq Salih al-Hussaini, a cousin of the Mufti. Party offices were opened in Jerusalem, Jaffa, Haifa and Nablus. The Jaffa daily, *Al-Difa'* (*Defence*), though not officially owned by the party, served as its mouthpiece. Funds were provided by the Arab Bank, the institution set up by Abdul Hamid Shoman in Jerusalem in 1930, and by voluntary contributions donated by Palestinians and various Muslim organisations outside the country. The fact that the party also retained the support of the Futuwwah, the paramilitary youth group which had been set up in the mid-1930s by the Mufti, also worked in its favour, particularly since the Istiqlal had no similar body of armed support.[14]

However the party continued to be hampered by the fact that its two main leaders, the Mufti and Jamal Hussaini, were still in exile, and by the loss of the *awqaf* funds after the government took over the administration of the estates in 1937 at the time of the revolt. The fact that the Mufti had taken refuge in Nazi Germany, after fleeing from the British in Iraq and Iran, and was engaged in spreading anti-British propaganda in Berlin, also weakened the party. His supporters at home, while arguing that his presence in Germany stemmed less from

his support of the Nazis than from his hatred of the British, nevertheless found it inopportune to advocate their loyalty to the Mufti openly
as long as the war continued and an allied victory was in sight. Despite
this, they were able to hold several public meetings in which they called
for the return of the Hussainis. The funeral of Amin al-Tamimi, who
had died in detention in Southern Rhodesia in October 1944, and the
anniversary of the Balfour Declaration the next month were occasions
which were used to great effect to enlist public sympathy while evading
the severe political restrictions imposed by the British in Palestine.[15]

The Struggle for Leadership, 1945-7

The end of the war in Europe opened up a new era in Palestinian
politics and in the Middle East in general. From VE day until 7 November
1947, when the United Nations decided to partition Palestine, Arab
activity both inside and outside Palestine centred on the need to
defeat the Zionists' attempts to reinstate mass immigration and to
partition Palestine between the Jews and the Arabs.

The lack of unity within the Palestinian ruling class threatened
to weaken these efforts and to deflect the struggle from its primary
aim. For this reason, the Arab states, prior to their meeting in
Alexandria in October 1944, decided to appoint a delegation, headed
by the Syrian Prime Minister, Jamil Mardam, to visit Palestine and to
obtain the consent of the major parties for the sending of a joint
representative to the talks. Mardam proved unsuccessful in his attempt
to rally the Hussainis and the former Istiqlal leaders and instead
appointed Musa Alami (a British-trained lawyer who had served as
Secretary to the High Commissioner and as Crown Counsel to the
Mandatory government) as representative.[16] The failure within the
Palestinian ruling class to agree on the choice of a representative was
an indication of just how divergent were the views of the Palestinian
leadership and how determined the Hussainis were to avoid participating in any movement which they themselves did not control.

The choice of Alami (who had retained a reputation as an independent) further aggravated the tension within the Palestinian ruling class.
At the Alexandria meeting he was promised funds to set up a land
development scheme in Palestine and to establish Arab information
offices in London, Washington and Jerusalem, a facility that gave him
a uniquely influential role in representing Palestinian views in the
allied capitals.[17] The first task brought him into conflict with the
Istiqlalists and the Board of Directors of the Arab National Fund who
hoped to retain control over the land issue; the second aroused the ire

of the Hussainis and the Palestine Arab Party members who felt that the Arab states had undercut their own claim to represent the Palestinians abroad as the leaders of the national movement.

A second attempt by Jamil Mardam in November 1945 to re-establish a unified movement met with only temporary success. The second Arab Higher Committee formed through Mardam's mediation quickly came under the control of the Hussainis, prompting the withdrawal of the other parties and of Musa Alami as well. The formation of a third Committee, this time at the urging of Jamal Hussaini (who had returned to Palestine in early 1946 after his release from detention in Southern Rhodesia) produced another split. While Hussaini and the Palestine Arab Party retained control of the Committee, the Istiqlal, joined by the other parties and by the League of National Liberation and the Arab Workers' Society, formed a separate group called the Arab National Front.[18] Only in June 1946, after a wave of terror launched by the underground Zionist groups in Palestine and after President Truman had endorsed the recommendations of the Anglo-American Committee of Inquiry (which, among other things, called for the immediate immigration of 100,000 Jews into Palestine and a lifting of restrictions on the sale of land to the Jews) did the Arab states, now formed into the Arab League, succeed in unifying the Hussainis and the opposition parties in Palestine, and this occurred largely due to the acquiescence of the opposition to Hussaini control.

At the instigation of the League a Fourth Higher Committee (also known as the Arab Higher Executive) was formed which included members of both the Third Higher Committee and the Arab National Front. Jamal Hussaini was elected Vice-President, the chairmanship being reserved for Hajj Amin who had been allowed to settle in Egypt the previous month but who was still officially banned from entry into Palestine. Although Ahmad Hilmi Pasha, the head of the Arab National Fund, and Dr Hussain al-Khalidi of the Reform Party were also included, the expansion of the Committee in January 1947 (just prior to the London Conference on Palestine) to include four other members of the Palestine Arab Party confirmed the victory of the Hussaini faction which from then on became the undisputed leader of the Palestinian national movement. The loss of the representatives from the emergent bourgeoisie, not to mention the lack of representation for the peasantry, reaffirmed the dominance of the traditional ruling-class elements. Aside from 'Izza Darwazah and Emile Ghouri, both loyal supporters of the Mufti and Ahmad Hilmi Pasha, the Committee was composed entirely of members of the large landowning families and *ashraf*. While some of these came from leading provincial families, the Committee itself was dominated by members of the same Jerusalem families who had served as the country's leaders since Ottoman days.[19]

Israeli Occupation and the Defeat of the Mufti, 1947-8

Britain's decision in February 1947 to turn the question of Palestine over to the United Nations, followed by the announcement in September that year that it intended to terminate the Mandate and to withdraw from Palestine, transformed the situation in Palestine. Preparations for military conflict could no longer be avoided. While the Hussainis called for volunteers, the Arab League states held a series of conferences to decide their strategy in the event that the United Nations decided to accept the recommendations of the Anglo-American Committee of Inquiry or, worse, partition between the Zionists and the Palestinian Arabs. In October 1947 representatives of the seven League states — Egypt, Trans-Jordan, Syria, Iraq, Saudi Arabia, Yemen and the Lebanon — decided to set up a military commission, headed by an Iraqi general, Ismail Safwat, to consider the deployment of Arab League troops along Palestine's borders.

In December, after the UN resolution in favour of partition and the subsequent outbreak of fighting in Palestine, the heads of state of the seven countries agreed to set up an army of volunteers, the Jaish al-Inqadh (Rescue Forces), which was composed of 2,500 men from the Arab League and 500 Palestinians. Weapons for the forces were to be supplied by the League and they were to be placed under the command of General Safwat and the Military Commission, which was to arrange for them to be trained in Syria. In February 1948 the League set up a committee of Arab Chiefs of Staff to decide on military strategy in Palestine.[20] Two months later the Political Committee of the League drew up an invasion plan for the regular armies of Egypt, Trans-Jordan, Iraq and Lebanon. In May, just before the date set for British withdrawal, the League agreed to appoint another Iraqi, Brigadier Nur al-Din Mahmoud, as Commander-in-Chief of all Arab forces in Palestine, including the volunteers.[21]

The Arab League preparations were strongly opposed by the Mufti and by the Arab Higher Committee who feared that they would wrest control of the resistance movement from the Palestinians in general and from the Committee in particular. In October 1947 the Mufti had denounced the proposal to deploy Arab League troops along the borders. With four of the seven states — Iraq, Trans-Jordan, Egypt and

Yemen — bound to Britain by military treaties, he feared that the League would support Britain should it decide in favour of partition.[22] The decision to recruit volunteers was also rejected: the Mufti sought to retain control over the funds and training of those fighting in Palestine and regarded the Jaish al-Inqadh as a rival to his own volunteer force, the Jaish al-Jihad al-Muqaddas (the Forces of Sacred Struggle), which was commanded by Abdul Qadir al-Hussaini, the son of the former Mayor of Jerusalem, Musa Pasha Kazim al-Hussaini. (At one point, in March 1948, the two groups nearly came to blows. The following months, in the crucial battle for Jerusalem in April, during which Abdul Qadir was killed, the Arab volunteers led by a Syrian, Fawzi al-Qawuqji, refused to come to the aid of the Palestinian irregulars fighting under Hussaini's command.[23])

Earlier, in February, the League's refusal to provide a loan to the Arab Higher Committee to cover its administrative and relief expenses and its rejection of demands by the Mufti to establish a Palestinian government-in-exile and to appoint Palestinians as military governors in the country had tended to confirm the Mufti's view that the Arab League states were interested less in helping the Palestinians to defend the country than in ensuring that the Arab states themselves retained control over the resistance and, ultimately, over the future fate of Palestine as a whole.[24] Only Egypt, which by then was engaged in a bitter struggle to amend its 1936 treaty with Britain and to obtain the evacuation of British troops from the Suez Canal Zone, came to the rescue of the Mufti and the Arab Higher Committee. It provided rifles to the Committee and allowed volunteers from Egypt, mainly from the Muslim Brethren, to serve in the Mufti's forces in Palestine.[25] Along with Saudi Arabia and Syria, Egypt also argued the Mufti's point of view within the meetings of the League but this stemmed less from Cairo's support of his role in Palestine than from King Farouk's determination to oppose King Abdullah's plans to accept partition and to occupy Jerusalem and Central Palestine (see below).

Despite Egypt's military aid and diplomatic support, the Mufti's forces suffered heavy losses in Palestine. The defeat of Abdul Qadir al-Hussaini's troops at Kastel, outside Jerusalem, in March removed the Hussainis' traditional base of support and led to a mass exodus of the capital's leading families. The Mufti himself, still banned from Palestine, left Egypt and fled to the Lebanon where he was joined by other members of the Arab Higher Committee. After the coastal towns and large parts of the Galilee fell into Jewish hands, still other Committee members took refuge in Trans-Jordan, Syria and Egypt.

By 15 May, the day the state of Israel was declared and the Arab armies marched into Palestine, not a single member of the Committee remained in the country.[26]

The entry of the regular Arab armies from Lebanon, Syria, Iraq, Trans-Jordan and Egypt appeared at first sight to offer the Hussainis and the Committee new hope. A defeat of the Zionists was widely expected in the Arab world and Palestinians of all persuasions thought that the earlier victories scored by the Haganah in the coastal areas and in Galilee would be overturned. Unfortunately the Arab intervention concealed sharp differences among the League members. King Abdullah had refused to take part in the action unless he was made Commander-in-Chief of the Arab forces. Although he obtained the formal acquiescence of the other League states to his request, in the actual fighting each state operated on its own.[27]

Abdullah's troops marched into central Palestine and quickly besieged East Jerusalem. The move was aimed both at regaining the Holy City and at depriving the Mufti's forces of any chance of restoring their control in those portions of the country which Abdullah sought, with Britain's backing, to include in his own kingdom.[28] The League, despite its formal acceptance of Abdullah's demands when he was made Commander-in-Chief, responded by agreeing on 9 July (the day before the expiration of the first ceasefire) to set up an Administrative Council for Palestine chaired by Ahmad Hilmi Pasha, the Treasurer of the Arab Higher Committee.[29]

At the end of September, after both Britain and the United States had accepted the recommendations of the UN mediator, Count Bernadotte, calling for the merger of what remained of Arab Palestine with Trans-Jordan, the League authorised the Council to proclaim the establishment of a Palestinian government. A Cabinet, including all the factions within the ruling class in Palestine (both inside and outside the Arab Higher Committee), was announced on 22 September. Ahmad Hilmi, named as Prime Minister, informed the Arab League that the new government, which was to be based in Gaza, would be democratic and based on a constitution.

On 1 October the Arab Higher Committee called a Congress of Palestinian Arabs at Gaza which proceeded to set up a National Assembly. Representatives were chosen from the Arab Higher Committee, the mayors, the local councils, national committees, Bedouin tribes and professional trade unions. The Assembly proclaimed Hajj Amin as President and announced the declaration of independence and the creation of a sovereign Palestinian state stretching from Syria and

Lebanon in the north to Egypt in the south. The western border was to end at the Mediterranean Sea and the eastern at Trans-Jordan.[30]

Although it was clear that the new All-Palestine government – as it came to be known – could not enforce its sovereignty in the Zionist-held areas, it did exercise authority in those parts of southern Palestine occupied by Egypt, the Mufti's primary supporter in the Arab League. However its reign was to last only a few weeks. In mid-October the Haganah launched a fierce campaign in the southern areas and succeeded in dislodging the Egyptian forces from their main bases and splitting the Egyptian army in three. The Arab Legion, ordered by King Abdullah to replace the retreating units, disarmed both the Mufti's supporters and the Egyptian *feda'iyyin* who remained, then occupied Hebron and Bethlehem.[31] In November and December the Israelis completed their occupation of the Negev, cutting Arab Palestine in two. Egyptian authority in Palestine was reduced to only a tiny portion of land along the coast at Gaza.

With the defeat of Egypt and its subsequent agreement to enter into armistice negotiations with the Israelis, the Mufti's long dominance of the Palestinian national movement came to an end and the Arab Higher Committee ceased to function. Although the All-Palestine government remained, it existed in name only despite the issuance of occasional statements from its headquarters in Cairo, and in 1959 its offices were closed by President Nasser. Power to represent the Palestinians had long ago passed to the Arab states and their leaders and most of these, as we shall see, were far more concerned about their relationships with their neighbours and their own internal stability than with the restoration of Palestinian rights to their land.

The Ruling Families under Jordanian Rule, 1948-67

The entry of the Jordanian army into Palestine in May 1948 marked the partial fulfilment of an ambition which King Abdullah had voiced as early as 1937. It entailed the partition of Palestine into two distinct units - one for the Jews and another for the Arabs – and the merger of Palestine with Trans-Jordan under Abdullah's rule.[32] However successive negotiations with the British and with the Jewish Agency failed to obtain their acquiescence in carrying out the plan. Eventually, in the spring of 1948, as the British despaired of creating a wider union of the Arab states that would remain pro-British and as the Zionists prepared for an all-out war to occupy the area granted to the Jews in the UN Partition Plan, it was agreed that Abdullah would be allowed to occupy central Palestine as part of a plan to annex the area. In return he agreed not to dislodge the Zionists from the areas designated for inclusion in the Jewish state nor from those parts of West Jerusalem already occupied by the Haganah.[33]

The British, in addition to sanctioning the partition of Palestine and the absorption of central Palestine by Abdullah, agreed in March 1948 to come to the King's aid should he be attacked and promised to increase their annual subsidy to the Arab Legion, which was commanded and supplied by Britain directly. Their pledges were renewed after Abdullah had succeeded in occupying the whole of central Palestine (except for the areas under Iraqi control around Janin) as well as those parts of southern Palestine vacated by the Egyptians and not designated for inclusion in the Jewish state.[34] The Arab Legion, under the command of General John Glubb, proceeded to disarm the remnants of the Palestinian guerrillas loyal to the Hussainis and other units of the Jaish al-Jihad al-Muqaddas which had sought to carry on their resistance in scattered outposts in Gaza and the West Bank as well as in the Arab quarters of Jerusalem, Bethlehem and Hebron.[35]

Under the terms of the armistice agreement concluded between the Israelis and Trans-Jordan at Rhodes in early April 1949, King Abdullah, in addition to ceding disputed territory in the border areas and in Jerusalem to the Israelis, agreed to prevent all 'land, sea or air military or para-military forces ... including non-regular forces' from committing 'any warlike or hostile act against the military or para-military forces' of Israel.[36] It was also agreed that the Iraqi forces still occupying parts of central Palestine around Janin and Tulkarm would withdraw and their place be taken by the Arab Legion. On 26 April 1949 the official name of the enlarged country was changed to the Hashimite Kingdom of Jordan, the King having decided to drop the word 'Palestine' both from the name of the country and from the list of his own titles as King. In December 1949 Palestinians resident in the Jordanian-controlled areas, as well as in Jordan itself, were declared Jordanian citizens.[37] Finally, on 24 April 1950, in his Speech from the Throne, King Abdullah announced the formal annexation of central Palestine; a decree confirming this was issued the same day, and all official communiqués henceforth referred to the area as the 'West Bank' (of the Hashimite Kingdom of Jordan).[38]

Partition was now complete, and with the gradual pacification of the remaining resistance forces the struggle for Palestinian independence passed to the political stage with the drama taking place outside Palestine itself. During the next decade Amman, not Jerusalem, served as the focal point for the expression of Palestinian aspirations. But it was a one-sided battle. With Abdullah and his successors, backed by virtually all the Western powers, intent on preserving the *status quo*, the remnants of the Palestinian nobility faced a crucial choice: either to accept Abdullah's annexation and the peace and economic opportunities it made possible, or to confront the monarchy and its supporters in Britain and the USA. In the end they chose the first option and in the process lost the support of their own people, who looked increasingly to more militant leaders elsewhere in the Arab world to continue the struggle to end the Israeli occupation and to obtain an independent state.

The Restoration of the Pro-Abdullah Faction

Abdullah's attempts over the years to create a clientele in Palestine favourable to partition and to the annexation of central Palestine by Jordan came to a successful conclusion in the autumn of 1948 when his military triumphs were followed by a rallying of his supporters in the West Bank. In October 1948 he summoned a 'National Congress' of those ruling-class elements favourable to the Hashimite throne and to British rule. Headed by Sheikh Sulaiman al-Taji al-Faruqi, a member of the traditional elite from one of the country's wealthiest families and a supporter of the National Defence Party in the mid-1930s, the Congress met in Amman and proceeded to issue resolutions repudiating the claims of the All-Palestine government established at Gaza a few days earlier. It also called on King Abdullah to bring the Arab-occupied areas of Palestine under his protection.[39]

The Congress, which could hardly be seen to be representative of Palestinian opinion since it was held on Jordanian, rather than Palestinian, soil and since its participants were appointed directly by the King, nevertheless gave Abdullah an excuse to prevent the entry of his enemies among the Hussaini camp and to ban the activities of the All-Palestine government in those parts of Palestine under the control of the Arab Legion. In addition, it provided him with vitally needed time to organise a broader appeal to his supporters.

In December 1948, having succeeded in expanding his control of the Arab sector of Jerusalem and of the area around Bethlehem, Ramallah and Hebron, Abdullah convened a larger conference of Palestinian Arabs in Jericho attended by former mayors, government officials, businessmen and lawyers as well as landowners and tribal leaders from the West Bank.[40] Sheikh Muhammad 'Ali al-Ja'abari, the Mayor of Hebron and a supporter of the Hashimites since the 1930s, was appointed by the King as President of the conference. Another former mayor, Ahmad Khalil of Haifa, and members of the Nashashibi, Dajani and Tuqan clans helped to organise the conference while the Arab Legion, under Glubb's directions, provided transport and subsidies to those willing to attend.[41] A seven-point resolution, largely drawn up by Abdullah's political and military advisers, was passed and then ratified by the Jordanian Cabinet and Parliament within a fortnight.[42] Among its most important provisions were a call for 'the unity of Palestine and Transjordan' and a declaration proclaiming 'Abdullah King of all Palestine'.[43] Although the Congress also stated that it believed 'in the unity of Palestine' and regarded 'any solution that does not comply with this' as 'not . . . a final solution', the resolution was regarded by the King as approval of his plan to open negotiations with Israel and to annex Arab Palestine.

On 11 December Abdullah sent a message to Eliahu Sasson, a member of the Jewish Agency's Arab Affairs Department, insisting that the decisions of the conference be respected. Two days later Sasson indicated Israel's willingness to do so, provided Abdullah declared a lasting truce and exerted 'his efforts' to enforce the removal of the Egyptian troops from Jerusalem and Hebron and of the Iraqis from the border areas in central Palestine, a demand, as we have seen, that Abdullah was eager to implement.[44] Later that month one of his leading supporters among the Palestinians, 'Azmi al-Nashashibi, was appointed Deputy Military Governor-General (under 'Umar Matar) of central Palestine, with his headquarters at Palestine.[45] Among his tasks were the co-ordination of efforts with the Arab Legion to pacify the resistance and to begin the work of sealing the border between Israel and the Arab-occupied parts of the country.

Finally, on 20 December King Abdullah appointed Sheikh Husamuddin Jarallah, a member of a sharifian family from Jerusalem allied with the Nashashibis and who had served on the Supreme Muslim Council in the 1920s, as the new Mufti of Jerusalem, replacing Hajj Amin.[46] The pro-Abdullah faction within the Palestinian ruling class had now achieved that goal that had so eluded them in the 1930s, namely the removal of Hajj Amin from both the highest religious post in the land and from the leadership of the national movement.

A final blow to the Hussainis, if one was needed, came in the next few weeks as scores of his followers and other members of the All-Palestine government in Gaza switched allegiances and transferred their loyalty to Abdullah. Among them were four members of the Cabinet of Ministers established at Gaza: Ahmad Hilmi Pasha, 'Awni Abdul Hadi, Dr Hussain Fakhri al-Khalidi and 'Ali Hasanah, as well as the Secretary of the Cabinet, Anwar Nusaibah.[47] For almost the next two decades these men, together with others from the Tuqans, Dajanis, Khatibs, Nimrs, Barghouthis and Jaiyussis, dominated what remained of Palestinian politics and, as we shall see, a large part of its economic activity as well.

The Economic Benefits

The annexation of the West Bank in 1950 completely transformed the economy and society of Jordan. The population more than doubled with the influx of refugees and of those living in the areas occupied by Jordan. By 1955 it totalled more than 1,450,000. Of these some 610,000 — about two-thirds of the total — were either refugees from Israeli-occupied Palestine or Palestinians resident in the West Bank who had not been displaced by the 1948 conflict.[48] Even though the annexation of the West Bank had also added a total of about 532,500 acres of cultivable land to Jordan (bringing the total up to an estimated 2,132,500 acres), the pressure on the land became acute. In the West Bank the influx of refugees raised the number of persons per square kilometre of arable land from 200 to 580; in the East Bank the figure rose from 80 to 107.[49]

The effect on the cities and towns of both banks was equally dramatic: Amman, a city of less than 40,000 in the early 1940s, saw its population rise threefold in 1950 to 120,000; by 1960 it had reached 220,000, an increase of more than 550 per cent in less than twenty years. The other major towns of Trans-Jordan — Salt, Zarqa, Irbid and Ajloun — which together had a population of less than 75,000 in 1943, became major cities in their own right.[50] In the West Bank the urban areas of East Jerusalem, Ramallah, Jericho, Nablus, Tulkarm and elsewhere also experienced a huge increase in their population; in some cases, like Jericho, the refugees even outnumbered the original inhabitants by as many as eight to one.[51]

This combination of a shortage of land and rapid urbanisation provided unparalleled opportunities for the large landowners in the West Bank. Some of them, as mentioned earlier, had bought land in the area of central Palestine during the days of the Mandate with the profits they had accumulated from the cultivation and export of citrus crops. Others had expanded their family holdings as a result of the indebtedness of the peasantry under the British or through the registration of titles formerly held by the lesser members of their clans. After the Second World War still others had invested the profits they had made from supplying the British and from the construction boom in farm land in the West Bank or in Jordan, particularly along the Jordan Valley and in the Yarmouk river area.[52]

After 1948 there were not only sufficient funds for investment in land but, more importantly, great incentives to invest. Unlike the 1940s, when the drain of labour to the cities and to the coast had led to a huge rise in wage rates for agricultural workers, the cost of farm labour had dropped to unprecedentedly low levels due to the influx of the hundreds of thousands of landless refugees. Furthermore, in an effort to encourage agricultural output, the government introduced a new income tax law in 1951 exempting all income derived from agricultural land and the sale of its produce. This, plus the dramatic rise in food prices due to the vastly increased demand, provided a unique opportunity for making exceptional profits. Farming, even on unirrigated land, became a lucrative business for those with land and the capital to bring it into cultivation.

By the mid-1950s, the rising demand for produce in Saudi Arabia and in the neighbouring countries of the Gulf added still more possibilities and as a result the production of traditional crops rose dramatically. The amount of acreage devoted to the cultivation of wheat, for example, rose from 153,000 acres in 1949 to 280,000 in 1957; for barley the figures were 51,000 and 93,000 acres respectively. Combined with the higher yields made possible by the introduction of new techniques, production rose almost as dramatically, despite the use of less fertile land. Wheat production rose from 139,000 metric tons in 1949 to 220,000 tons in 1957; the barley crop increased from 56,000 to 81,000 tons over the same period. For other crops like sesame, chick peas, lentils and broad beans, the increases were even more remarkable. The production of sesame seed rose from less than 1,000 tons in 1947 to 4,000 tons in 1957; for chick peas the figures were 1,000 and 4,000 tons respectively.[53] And, as production and profits increased, so did investment in modern equipment. The number of tractors in Jordan, for example, rose from 350 in 1954 to 1,552 in 1964; by the end of 1966 the number was 2,068, nearly six times as many as in 1954.[54]

While the nature of the land in the West Bank and the traditional patterns of cultivation led at first to a concentration on dry farming crops such as wheat, barley and other grains, the gradual introduction of both terracing and irrigation on the larger estates owned by Palestinians on both sides of the Jordan Valley led to a rise in the production of cash crops such as citrus fruits, early vegetables, olives, figs and dairy products which were exported to other parts of Jordan (especially

Amman), Syria, Lebanon, Iraq and the Gulf states.[55] However, the ability to invest either in modern machinery or in the cultivation of cash crops was limited to those with both large estates and the capital needed to finance such development. Although official figures on land tenure for the period of Jordanian rule are generally unavailable, the indications are that the numbers of landowners who were able to profit from the new agricultural situation and to expand their holdings were fairly large. One study, for example, estimated that in 1964 a total of 647 landowners in Jordan (including the West Bank) each owned land totalling more than 250 acres; together they owned as much as 68,728 peasants whose holdings averaged less than 25 acres each.

By the time of the June 1967 war there were 666 holdings which totalled 250 acres or more, including 245 of 500 acres or more and 67 of at least 1,250 acres. Twenty-two private holdings averaged 2,500 acres or more.[56] While there is no indication of how many Palestinians were among the large landowners, other studies conducted in the mid-1950s indicate that even though the number of small-holdings on the West Bank was higher than elsewhere in Palestine before the 1948 war, large estates existed in several areas of the West Bank, such as around Jerusalem, Nablus and Hebron. In the Jerusalem district, 36.9 per cent of the land was divided into units of more than 250 acres in size; in Hebron the figure was 17.4 per cent and in Nablus 16.2 per cent.[57]

Capital to invest in agriculture was available to the large landowners who had profited from the Second World War and invested their funds abroad. Again, although exact figures are not available, Palestinian sources suggest that a substantial part of the £10 million in sterling balances held by Palestinians in London at the end of the Second World War was invested in agricultural development in the West Bank and in the Jordan Valley after the 1948 war, as well as in urban real estate in Amman and other East Bank cities.[58] Other funds became available in 1953 when Israel released part of the deposits held by Palestinians in Arab banks which came under Israeli rule in 1948.[59]

Another important source of capital arose when the government of Jordan established an agricultural mortgage programme in 1950. By the end of 1954 it had granted a total of more than JD3 million (Jordanian dinars) ($8.5 million) in loans mainly to those large land-owners who supported the monarch. The amount of land in the West Bank that was mortgaged reached a total of 28,000 *dunums* (2,550 hectares), or about 1.3 per cent of the total land area. In some places, such as the area around Jericho where the combination of inexpensive labour, proximity to markets and access to cultivable land was particularly attractive, the figure reached as much as 3.3 per cent at the end of 1954.[60] The fact that the JD3 million granted in mortgages during this five-year period went to less than four hundred borrowers indicates the extent to which the mortgage scheme concentrated capital for agricultural development in the hands of the large landowners and increased the growing disparity between them and the smallholders who had access neither to capital for development nor the financial resources to employ either skilled or unskilled labour on their lands, however low the wage rates.[61]

Aside from their ability to marshal both capital and labour, the large landowners also benefited from their access to markets, both at home and abroad, and from their domination of trade between the West and East banks. At first this took the more traditional form of using various Bedouin tribes as agents and transporters of agricultural produce. The Nimrs, for example, in addition to their substantial landholdings in the Nablus area, continued to enjoy close relationships with relatives and tribesmen in the Balqa area of the East Bank, a situation which gave them a privileged position in the early days of Jordanian control of the West Bank when the trade patterns shifted suddenly to encompass Amman, Syria, Lebanon and the Gulf states rather than concentrating on the supply of goods to and from the Mediterranean ports and Red Sea areas.[62]

Similarly, certain families in Hebron and some of the Christian tribes which dominated the central area of the Jordan Valley enjoyed close ties with the Majali clan of Trans-Jordan and through these ties had access to officials at the highest levels of administration in Amman as well as to the Royal Court and the army. Matters concerning export licences, border passes and access to transport posed few problems as a result.[63] Still other sheikal landlords, primarily from the Tawarneh, Tamimiyya, Tarabin, Azazimah and Jibarat tribes of southern Palestine, engaged in trade between the two banks, transporting livestock and agricultural produce from their lands located on both sides of the border. There was also an extremely lucrative trade in hashish, involving the smuggling of supplies grown in Lebanon and Syria across Palestine and the Sinai desert to customers in Egypt.[64]

Later, as production from the newly reclaimed land became more reliable and yields improved, the large landowners of the West Bank began to maket the goods themselves (much as they had done with citrus fruits in the days of the Mandate) or formed alliances with the large merchant families on the East Bank to dominate the export trade.

The extent of the opportunities which existed in this sphere is demonstrated by the fact that the value of cash crop exports from Jordan rose astronomically in the first decade of Jordanian rule. For example, while exports of fresh (mostly early) vegetables were worth only JD63,000 ($176,000) in 1949, by 1957 they were valued at JD1,442,000 ($4,038,000); for fresh fruit exports (apples, melons and berries as well as citrus), the figures were JF31,000 ($86,000) in 1949 and JD827,000 ($2,316,000) in 1957; raw wool exports, although small in volume compared to other products, were worth JD72,700 ($204,000) in 1957 compared to only JD4,000 ($11,200) in 1949.[65]

One of the most successful ventures concerned the trade of olive oil from the estates owned by the Tuqans in the Nablus area. By establishing an incorporated company and using their access to the relevant ministries in Amman they were successfully able to prevent the import of other edible oils and the export of olives and olive oil abroad at the time of harvest. This guaranteed them and the other large producers and merchants with whom they were allied a high price for their product at the market. They were also able to buy the crop from smaller producers at drastically reduced wholesale prices, thereby obtaining huge profits. In addition, the Tuqans invested in storage and warehousing facilities to enable them to hold back the crop until the price reached its maximum. In this way they soon obtained an edge over other producers and traders who were forced to sell shortly after harvest.[66]

The Jarrars, who owned huge olive groves in the area around Janin and who were allied with the Tuqans, invested capital in deciduous fruit trees which they planted between their olive trees. In this way they were able to expand their longer-term investment in a highly profitable cash crop while at the same time gaining profits from the export of fruit to the East Bank.[67]

The Abdul Hadis, in another variant of the theme, began to cultivate and trade olive tree seedlings in the 1960s about the same time Palestinians who were working in the Gulf states began to seek ways to invest in the olive crop back home. At one of their nurseries they produced some 65,000 specially selected seedlings using the latest techniques in grafting.[68] Other landowners, including the Tuqans, increased the value of their produce by expanding soap-making facilities and by opening up new markets for soap made from olive oil in Syria, Lebanon and the Gulf as well as in the more traditional outlets of Egypt and Trans-Jordan. Still others with capital to invest began to cultivate cash crops like melons, tomatoes and vegetables which they then exported to

Amman. A few invested in grain mills and in factories to produce maca-roni, paper and textiles, thereby adding to the value of the agricultural crops produced on their estates.[69] The sheikhs of the southern tribes, in addition to cultivating the state lands handed over to them by the Crown and transporting goods to the East Bank, dominated the supply of skins and hides to Amman. Some opened up new tanneries and leather goods workshops in Hebron; from there they exported the finished product to the East Bank, Egypt, Saudi Arabia and the Gulf states.[70]

These efforts by the large landowners to dominate the supply of certain goods to specific markets in the West and East banks and to increase their exports abroad received added encouragement in 1950 when the government in Amman decided to set up an inspectorate headquartered in the Jordanian capital charged with regulating imports and exports to and from the West Bank. This reduced the ability of the smaller producers and manufacturers in the West Bank to engage in trade independently of Amman and left the way clear for those larger landowners and importers – Palestinians and East Jordanians – who were favoured by the Hashimite regime. Throughout the 1950s the newspapers were filled with protests and complaints issued by chambers of commerce in the West Bank decrying the economic stagnation that resulted from Amman's neglect. Chamber members were also unhappy about their inability to obtain import and export licences and the capital needed for the development of both industry and agriculture. The chambers of both Jerusalem and Nablus, for example, protested that

> trade had begun to be concentrated in designated places and in the hands of those designated . . . The tragedy which has affected our country has resulted directly and indirectly in an economic revival which is concentrated in the city of Amman and which has brought it profits on account of the decline in exports [of traditional crops] to it compared with earlier times.[71]

The fact that the post of Minister of Agriculture was reserved for those large landowners and members of the sharifian families like the Nashashibis, Jaiyussis and Tuqans who supported Jordanian rule in the West Bank made it even more difficult for the smaller landholders to be heard in Amman.[72] Since these same landowners and families, as we shall see, dominated other important posts in the ministries and in the civil service, the remnants of the ruling class who remained opposed to the annexation as well as the nascent industrial bourgeoisie and smaller peasants suffered as well. By 1956 these groups, supported by the urban workers and the unemployed agricultural labourers housed in the refugee camps, together with the independent intellectuals, were ready to challenge both the Hashimite hegemony and the domination of those Palestinian notables sympathetic to the monarchy. However, before discussing this in detail, we need to look further at the other benefits enjoyed by the pro-Abdullah faction under Jordanian rule, namely their privileged access to state positions in government, the civil service and the army.

Participation in Government

The restoration of Arab rule in the West Bank was greeted with great enthusiasm by large segments of the *ashraf*, who hoped to regain the influence they had enjoyed under the Ottomans but which had been destroyed under the British. However it soon became clear that while Abdullah intended to draw on the skills and talent of Palestinians to administer both his own desert kingdom and the newly annexed West Bank, he had no intention of restoring the collective power which the *ashraf* had enjoyed under the Sultans.[73] Instead the criteria for selection was determined above all by the support shown by certain families — and individuals — for the Hashimites (including King Abdullah's grand-nephew, King Faisal II of Iraq) and for the British who supported both his throne and his claims to the West Bank. This excluded those families who remained loyal to the Hussainis and those who favoured the continuation of the conflict with Israel in an effort to liberate their country.

As a result the *ashraf* were divided in their loyalty to Abdullah and his successors. Individuals within a given leading family often took opposing stands on their view of the Jordanian monarchy and the role that the sharifian families should play in either supporting or participating in it. While some, like Sulaiman Tuqan, gave total allegiance to the throne to the extent of serving on the Regency Council, others accepted high government positions primarily with the hope that the King could be persuaded to renew the battle to achieve Palestinian statehood, or, at minimum, to provide the political and economic framework in which the national struggle could continue.[74] Although, as we shall see, this latter position became increasingly untenable from the late 1950s onwards, many of the leading members of the *ashraf* and their sons nevertheless continued to serve the King loyally in return for obtaining the economic and social benefits that were denied their more militant kin.

The provision of posts to leading Palestinian supporters of the Hashimites began with the Arab Legion's occupation of the West Bank in the second half of 1948. Two Palestinians, 'Arif al-'Arif – who had served in Trans-Jordan under the British – and Ahmad Hilmi Pasha, were appointed to serve as district military governors under Ibrahim Hashim (who was succeeded in October 1948 by 'Umar Matar, another East Jordanian). After the Jericho Congress another Palestinian, 'Azmi al-Nashashibi, was appointed Deputy Military Governor, based at Ramallah. Following the replacement of military rule by a civilian administration, central Palestine was divided into three provinces and in March 1949 two Palestinians – Ahmad Khalil, the former Mayor of Haifa who had helped to organise the Jericho Congress, and Naim Tuqan – were appointed to head the Ramallah and Hebron districts respectively.[75] In September 1949 another Nashashibi, Raghib Bey – the former Mayor of Jerusalem – was appointed Governor-General for Arab Palestine.[76]

A few months earlier, in May 1949, the King had reshuffled his Cabinet to include three of his other close Palestinian supporters: Musa Nasr, a landowner and former District Officer for Ramallah under the British; Ruhi Abdul Hadi (who in addition to being from one of the leading landowning families had also served as Principal Assistant to the Chief Secretary of Palestine during the Mandate) and Khulusi al-Khairi, the former Director of the Arab Office in Washington under Musa Alami.[77] In August Raghib Bey al-Nashashibi was appointed to head a new ministry for refugees and rehabilitation. The post gave him almost exclusive control over the distribution of the huge aid funds and food stocks sent by the United Nations and other charitable organisations to help alleviate the plight of the displaced Palestinians.

Other royal appointments to the legal administration of both Jordan and the West Bank followed, dashing in the process any hope still held by the *ashraf* that they would regain their former powers as a whole. Two of the men most bitterly opposed to the Supreme Muslim Council and to the Mufti during the Mandate were among the King's first appointees: Sheikh Hussain al-Din al-Jarallah, who was appointed Mufti of Jerusalem (replacing Hajj Amin al-Hussaini) and Chief Qadi on 20 December 1948 and, again, Raghib Bey al-Nashashibi, who became the Custodian of the Holy Places and the Supervisor of the Haram al-Sharif (the Noble Sanctuary) – one of Islam's most sacred shrines – in Jerusalem. Finally the King ordered the establishment of a new Supreme Muslim Council which was to be headed by 'Awni Abdul Hadi.[78]

The fact that these men were appointed by royal decree dealt a final blow to the collective powers of the *ashraf* who had hoped the King would restore the rights to choose leaders and to interpret and administer the law free from secular interference which they had enjoyed under the Ottomans. The enactment in 1951 of a new Criminal Code, the establishment of formal Criminal Procedure Rules and the subsequent passage of a Court Establishment Law (which set up a series of civil courts based on British models) in effect confirmed that those *ashraf* who had been trained in Islamic and Ottoman schools would be unable to practise law (although they did retain some rights to adjudicate matters of personal status). Because all three of the enactments followed the British pattern established in Palestine, lawyers like Rashad al-Khatib and Fuad Abdul Hadi who had been trained in the British system and who had loyally served in the government of Palestine during the Mandate found themselves in an extremely advantageous position *vis-à-vis* their erstwhile colleagues.[79] The decision of the King's advisers and of the Cabinet to retain tribal, or customary, law and to give the Tribal Courts jurisdiction in all matters affecting the Bedouin (except for disputes involving land ownership and those in which the Commander of the Arab Legion chose to intervene) further circumscribed the collective power of the *ashraf* and to a certain extent those of Palestinians trained in Western law as well.[80]

The passage of new electoral laws in 1949, giving Palestinians the vote and allowing them to be represented in the lower house of Parliament, the Chamber of Deputies, also increased the divide separating those sharifian and landowning families which supported independence from those which supported the Hashimites.[81] In elections held in April 1950, 65 candidates from the West Bank stood for 20 seats in the Chamber, 3 of which were reserved specifically for Christian Palestinians. Members of the sharifian and large landowning families who supported the monarchy dominated the list of the victorious candidates. They included Tahsin Abdul Hadi, Rashad al-Khatib, Abdul Rahim Jarrar, Anwar Nusaibah and Qadri Tuqan.[82] These men, or other representatives of their families, together with the representatives from a handful of other landowning families subsequently elected to the Chamber (such as Abdul Qadir al-Salih, Hashim al-Jaiyussi and 'Umar Salah al-Barghouthi) dominated the lower house until it was prorogued by royal decree in April 1957. Many later assumed top positions in the Cabinet or served as mayors of their home towns.

The families were even more prominent in the Chamber of Notables, where the members were appointed directly by the King. Under the new legislation Palestinians were guaranteed equal representation for the lower house only, but the King rewarded his most faithful Palestinian followers with seats in the upper Chamber. They were invariably chosen from the most powerful families in the West Bank: the Nashashibis, the Tuqans, the Salahs, Dajanis, Abdul Hadis and Khalidis. Sheikh Muhammad 'Ali al-Ja'abari and Sheikh Sulaiman al-Taji al-Faruqi, both of whom had been so influential in obtaining Palestinian support for the annexation of the West Bank, were given seats in the Chamber in April 1950.[83]

The same families also dominated Palestinian representation in the Cabinet. Hashim al-Jaiyussi, for example, served in six Cabinets between 1950 and 1957, as Minister of Communications, Interior, Commerce, Finance, Agriculture, Posts and Civil Aviation. Anwar Nusaibah, a member of a leading sharifian family from Jerusalem who was first appointed to the Cabinet in September 1952, served as Minister of Development and Reconstruction, and subsequently as Minister of Defence and Education. Ahmad Tuqan, a graduate of Oxford University who had worked under the British in the Department of Education in Palestine, served as Minister of Education, Foreign Affairs, Defence and Prime Minister; at one stage in the 1950s he headed four ministries simultaneously.[84]

Aside from the influence which the holding of a Cabinet post entailed, it also gave the large landowning and sharifian families the ability to obtain posts for their relatives and friends in the civil services. Although Trans-Jordanians usually staffed the upper echelons of the more sensitive ministries, such as Defence and Interior, Palestinians were predominant in several others, notably Education, Social Welfare and Foreign Affairs, where the number of employees was particularly high. In the case of Foreign Affairs, for example, the Palestinian control of this ministry during most of the 1950s and 1960s helped to ensure that Jordan's corps of ambassadors was largely staffed by Palestinians, and especially by members of the favoured families. At various times in the 1950s and 1960s their ranks included Yusif Haikal, the former Mayor of Jaffa (Washington, London and Taipei); Hazim Zaki Nusaibah (United Nations); 'Awni Abdul Hadi (Cairo); 'Isa Bandak, the former mayor of Bethlehem (Madrid); Jamal Tuqan (Beirut); Abdullah Salah (Kuwait, New Delhi, Paris); 'Adil al-Khalidi (Madrid); and Anwar al-Khatib (Cairo).[85]

This domination of the pro-Abdullah faction also extended to the municipal and provincial administrations in the West Bank. Jerusalem, the seat of the Hussainis and of other sharifian families opposed to the Hashimites, was subordinated to Amman and its leading families lost the dominant influence they enjoyed. Political power and the ability to exploit the area's economic resources passed to Nablus, Hebron and Ramallah, where the leading families supported the King. The electoral laws, and the way in which the electoral districts were drawn up, encouraged this diffusion of power: while the Jerusalem district, for example, had a population of more than 150,000 in the 1950s, it was represented by only three members in Parliament; Hebron, with a population of only 135,000, was allocated four members.[86]

The 1955 Municipal Law also gave the Minister of the Interior the right to subdivide municipal districts arbitrarily, thereby enabling him to increase the size of the urban council and to determine which of the districts within the municipality would have the most seats. In addition he was empowered to appoint two council members directly in each municipality and to appoint the mayor as well. This meant, for instance, that Sheikh Ja'abari could be appointed to the Hebron City Council and to the office of mayor irrespective of his actual electoral support, and that any opposition, either within the city or in the West Bank as a whole, could be neutralised.

Further restrictions in the Municipal Law, limiting suffrage to those persons who paid property taxes or a certain amount of municipal taxes each year, also favoured the large landowning and merchant families, to the extent that these families tended to dominate the municipal councils in their area throughout the period of Jordanian rule. Hajj Mazuz al-Masri, for example, was elected to the Nablus municipal council in three of the four elections held between 1951 and 1967; 'Adil al-Shaka served on the same council for the entire period of Jordanian rule. While members of the Khatib family served in high-level positions in Amman — in the Cabinet and the Chamber of Deputies — their rivals, the Ja'abaris, dominated both local government and the higher religious posts in Hebron. Other Khatibs were appointed to serve in Jerusalem, as Governor in the mid-1950s and as mayor in 1967.[87] In this way the pro-Abdullah faction not only gained access to high-level posts in the Jordanian government and civil administration but also obtained a pre-eminent role in the West Bank throughout the period of Jordanian rule.

Finally, although Palestinians in general could not hope to aspire to high positions in the Arab Legion, the leading families nevertheless managed to obtain certain influential posts in the military during the period of Jordanian rule. This effectively allowed them to participate in the efforts of the Arab Legion to pacify the indigenous resistance to the annexation and to ensure that the border with Israeli-occupied

Palestine was sealed. As early as August 1949 Ahmad Tuqan, then Director of Education in the West Bank, announced that all secondary school pupils in the West Bank would receive military training. The following month a National Guard, consisting mainly of Palestinian villagers drawn from the border areas, was set up. It was supplied and trained by the Arab Legion and acted as an auxiliary force under the Legion's command. Five months later compulsory military service for all men over twenty was introduced.[88]

Although many of the leading landowning families in the West Bank at first opposed the creation of the Guard, arguing that it was dangerous to arm the peasants, the need to pacify the continuing resistance of elements which had continued the struggle with Israel and to patrol the border areas was regarded as more important. Furthermore, by recruiting villagers into a Legion-controlled force, the attraction of the other armed units loyal to the Hussainis was minimised and, more importantly, these other units — particularly those of the Jaish al-Inqadh still in the West Bank — were forced underground. By 1956 the National Guard had succeeded in becoming the only legal armed force in the West Bank, aside from the Legion itself, and its forces numbered some 30,000 men.[89]

Meanwhile Palestinians from the leading families were recruited directly into the Legion as officers within the army and air force. While subsequent events were, as we shall see, to demonstrate that not all these officers were loyal to the throne, their presence effectively prevented a unified armed opposition to the King, and to the domination of the leading families in the West Bank, from developing in Jordan until 1967, after Israel occupied the West Bank and forced the Legion back to the East Bank.[90]

The New Nationalist Challenge

The ascendancy of the pro-Hashimite faction within the former Palestinian ruling class was not achieved without difficulty. In the West Bank the armed resistance, supported by the Mufti from his base in Egypt, continued to carry out raids against Israeli-occupied territory even after the formal annexation of the area by Jordan. In July 1951 King Abdullah himself fell victim to the discontent: he was assassinated by a Palestinian tailor on the steps of Al-Aqsa Mosque in Jerusalem. Colonel Abdullah al-Tal, a Jordanian officer who had commanded the Arab Legion forces in East Jerusalem in 1948 and who had served as a messenger for Abdullah's secret talks with the Israelis, and two of Hajj Amin's closest associates were implicated in the assassination.[91]

One year later the monarchy of King Farouk was overturned, and while this removed the Mufti's base of support, the ardent nationalist rhetoric of Nasser and the Free Officers who came to power raised the hopes of Palestinians everywhere. The effects were soon felt in the West Bank, where the discontent with the repressive measures adopted by the Arab Legion and the lack of action to alleviate the plight of the refugees further fuelled opposition to the annexation. In November severe rioting broke out in Jerusalem, Nablus and Ramallah as well as in Amman. Aside from protesting against the wide-scale imprisonment of 'infiltrators' who had crossed the border into Israeli-occupied Palestine, the crowds shouted slogans denouncing British imperialism and calling for the right of all Palestinians to return to their homeland.[92]

King Hussein's accession to the throne in May 1953 brought a short period of relative calm. But by the autumn of that year the Palestinians were in the streets once again. Rioting followed in December, and there were massive demonstrations against the monarchy in the spring and summer of 1954.[93] Much of the protest centred on the failure of the Arab Legion to respond to pleas by the Palestinian-manned National Guard for reinforcements after the Israelis had staged particularly brutal raids on border villages in October 1953 and again in March 1954.[94] Matters came to a head on election day, 16 October 1954, when the Arab Legion opened fire on civilian demonstrators in Jerusalem, Ramallah and Amman, leaving at least nine dead and several dozen wounded.[95]

For the Palestinian families which supported the throne, the King's evident determination to save the monarchy even at the cost of Palestinian lives raised a cruel dilemma. They could follow the lead of nationalist politicans like Sulaiman al-Nabulsi, a young banker from an influential family of Palestinian origin, and withdraw from the elections in protest, or they could ignore the Legion's actions and support the repression. The first course of action promised to save their credibility among their own countrymen but at the cost of losing the privileges allegiance to the Hashimites had provided; the second would preserve their powers, but also entailed the risk that Palestinians who did not share these privileges would stage an uprising against their own leaders in the kingdom. Either way the loyalists among the Palestinian ruling class stood to lose.

The nature of the dilemma was not fully apparent, however, during the first years of annexation. While the displaced, dispossessed and destitute marched in the streets, the monarchist supporters of the King

within the Palestinian nobility concentrated their attention on expanding their power within what was then primarily still a tribal state
unaccustomed to Western-style democracy and modern administration.
For the most powerful families in the West Bank this was largely a
matter of expanding Palestinian representation in the government of
Jordan and ensuring that the parcelling out of appointments reflected
the weight and prestige of their own clans.

One of the first major disagreements within the loyalist faction
occurred in the spring of 1951, when Parliament was debating the
budget. After several deputies — Palestinian and Trans-Jordanian —
protested against the fact that 65 per cent of the funds were allocated
to the army and the police and another 25 per cent to the royal household, the Chamber issued a vote of no confidence in the government.[96]
Aside from provoking the King's wrath, the action led to a split between those Palestinians like Ahmad Tuqan, Raghib al-Nashashibi and
Anwar al-Khatib, who served in the Cabinet and who feared the loss
of their positions should the government fall, and those in the Chamber
of Deputies such as Tawfiq and Qadri Tuqan, Tahsin Abdul Hadi,
Anwar Nusaibah and Hikmat al-Masri, who wanted to use the newly-
introduced constitutional rights to increase the power of themselves
and their families in the administration of the enlarged state.[97] The
matter was solved, in the Cabinet's favour, when the King responded
to the vote of no confidence by summarily dismissing the Chamber
and dissolving Parliament while retaining the Cabinet.[98] The decision
of two of the West Bank deputies, Abdul Qadir al-Salih and Qadri
Tuqan, to stand as Communist-sponsored candidates when elections
were held again the following September, demonstrated the degree to
which some of the younger sons of the nobility disagreed with their
elders, and with the more conservative elements in their class.[99]

The next year another major disagreement arose over the country's
foreign policy and specifically over Jordan's close ties with Britain.
While the monarchy and the Cabinet firmly supported the treaty with
Britain (which provided the bulk of the country's financial support and
most of its military weaponry), some of the Palestinian deputies in the
Chamber wanted to amend the pact to remove Britain's right to inter-
fere in the country's internal affairs. This time the Cabinet, led by
the King's loyal Prime Minister, Tawfiq Abul Huda, resorted to the
unusual tactic of taking a vote on the issue while the opposition was
absent.[100] Once again the Cabinet and the throne had won, but at the
cost of further increasing discontent within the ranks of the Palestinians
represented in the government.

By 1954 the combination of protest in the streets and growing opposition in Parliament threatened to provoke still more demands for democratic reform and for an end to the British presence in Jordan. In October Prime Minister Abul Huda, at the King's insistence, ordered the arrest of several opposition candidates, including Nabulsi, and attempted to rig new elections in the government's favour. Party publications were banned and known militants turned away from the polls. But the fury of the crowds, who resorted to the burning and pillaging of private villas and government installations in Amman, dissuaded the Cabinet and the Palestinians in it from making further protests against the electoral manipulation, lest their own properties be harmed. As a result the Prime Minister was able to obtain a Chamber that included 35 government-sponsored deputies and only 5 opposition candidates. Within the Palestinian camp, pro-government deputies like Abdul Rahim Jarrar, 'Umar Salih al-Barghouthi, Antun Atallah and Sheikh Ahmad al-Dawar replaced men like Qadri Tuqan, Rashad al-Khatib and Abdullah al-Rimawi, all of whom supported the nationalist cause and, in the case of Rimawi, pan-Arabism as well.

Despite this, the government's victory was far from decisive. The new Chamber, recognising the threat that such electoral manipulation posed to its own freedom of action, insisted on revising the constitution to prevent its summary dismissal by royal decree. Under the amended version, a Cabinet which sanctioned the dissolution of Parliament would itself be obliged to resign within a week to make way for new elections. In addition, the revised constitution stipulated that a vote of no confidence in the government could be carried by a simple majority, rather than by the two-thirds vote previously required. Although the government had managed once again to preserve its authority against the wishes of the electorate, the powers of the Cabinet and of the King were severely reduced.[101]

Armed with the new amendments, the dissidents within the ruling families who had been excluded from power waged an intense campaign over the next two years to force new elections to the Chamber.[102] Led by Nabulsi, they helped to form a new party, the National Socialists, which brought together both Palestinians and Trans-Jordanian sheikhs and landowners as well as representatives of the emergent bourgeoisie who wanted economic, as well as political, reforms. The new party sought to make a wider appeal to the public rather than relying on the exclusive support of the King and Court. In addition to recruiting leading Palestinians like Anwar al-Khatib, Fuad Abdul Hadi and Abdul Qadir al-Salih to stand for election to Parliament,

the party formed a united front with the more militant parties –
notably the Ba'ath (Arab Renaissance) Party and the Communists –
which had been banned and which drew their support from the lower
ranks of the civil service as well as from the intellectuals.

Meanwhile the Cabinet, sensing the winds of change in the country,
had opened secret negotiations with Britain to amend the Anglo-
Jordanian Defence Treaty in an effort to avoid its abrogation altogether. However when news leaked of the talks – and of further discussions on forming a wider pro-Western Baghdad Pact – the four
Palestinians in the Cabinet – 'Azmi al-Nashashibi, Naim Abdul Hadi,
'Ali Hasanah and Sama'an Daud – were forced to resign. In December
1955 an attempt by Hazza al-Majali, a close ally of the King, to
replace them with, among others, the mayors of Jerusalem and
Ramallah, only provoked further discontent within the Palestinian
nobility, since both the mayors were opposed by strong rivals in their
local areas who promptly joined the opposition in calling for new
elections.[103] Order was preserved only after the Chamber of Deputies
– despite severe rioting in the streets – overturned the Prime Minister's
decree dissolving Parliament on a technicality and itself remained in
power despite the lack of a Cabinet.[104]

Aside from the political and economic chaos that resulted from such
a situation, the constant reshuffles in the government and the resigna-
tions and re-nominations by the Prime Minister demonstrated the
extent to which the pro-Hashimite faction within the Palestinian
nobility had become fragmented and divided. Personal rivalries, rather
than policy, dictated the stance taken by the King's supporters in both
the Cabinet and the Chamber. Outside Parliament the Palestinians in
the opposition, who had reached agreement on a new set of both domestic and foreign policy reforms, found themselves helpless to install a
new government since there were always rival candidates from one or
other of the West Bank families ready to take up a position left vacant
by the resignation or dismissal of a Palestinian representative. Only
in June 1956, after the King himself had approached the neighbouring
Arab states for additional financial aid and after the Chamber had voted
for the abrogation of the Anglo-Jordanian Defence Treaty – a fruitless
attempt to stave off the call for new elections – did the Prime Minister
finally dissolve the House and pave the way for the election of a new
government under the revised constitution. Three months earlier King
Hussein himself had been forced to dismiss the British Commander of
the Arab Legion, John Glubb, and to order the withdrawal of British
officers serving with the Legion.[105]

The victory of the opposition in the elections held in October ushered in a nationalist majority in the Chamber of Deputies and in the Cabinet. Nabulsi's party, which secured 18 per cent of the 405,000 votes cast, was the clear winner and obtained 12 of the 40 seats in the Chamber. Together with the Ba'ath, which secured 2 seats, the Communist-led National Front, which obtained 3 seats, and the votes of 3 independent deputies, he was able to form a coalition which, with a total of 20 seats, commanded half the votes in the Chamber. The pro-government deputies, who had numbered 35 in the previous Chamber, were reduced to 8.[106]

Within the Chamber the Palestinian representatives included several who had not served before and did not come from the sharifian or land-owning families. In the Cabinet National Socialists and Ba'athists replaced the King's allies drawn from the Nashashibis, Nusaibahs and Tuqans. Dr Hussain Fakhri al-Khalidi's post, Minister of Foreign Affairs, was given to the young editor from Ramallah, Abdullah Rimawi, who had helped to found the Ba'ath Party and who had been imprisoned on several occasions for his opposition to the monarchy and to Britain.[107]

The new regime, despite its radicalism, was not opposed to the throne entirely nor committed to republicanism. It called for the establishment of basic public feedoms, democratic rights and economic and social reform at home, measures which would have converted the system of government from one in which the King enjoyed almost absolute authority to something resembling a European constitutional monarchy.[108] As Nabulsi himself said later, 'What I and my friends . . . demanded was the establishment of genuine democratic rights. We were not against the regime or against King Hussein.'[109]

To this extent the Nabulsi government did not pose a direct threat either to the King or to the monarchist faction within the Palestinian nobility. What it did threaten was the pro-British policies favoured by the King and by the loyalists among his Palestinian supporters who feared that the abrogation of the defence treaty with Britain would leave them vulnerable not only to Israeli attack but also to the masses of Palestinians who demanded an end to Jordanian rule in the West Bank and the liberation of their homeland.

Much as these elements feared, the new government lost little time in reversing Jordan's foreign alliances. It declared that Jordan and the people of Jordan were a part of the wider Arab nation and called for the emancipation of Arab lands from both British and French domination. When, a week after the installation of the Nabulsi cabinet, Israeli troops crossed into the Sinai Peninsula, ostensibly to destroy 'commando bases', the country went wild. As the French joined the Israelis and as British bombers strafed Cairo and the Suez Canal, huge crowds attacked British installations in the East Bank and sacked the French embassy in Amman. More rioting followed the landing of British paratroopers in the Nile Delta a few days later. The King, who before the Suez war had opposed the government's change of direction, reversed his own stand in an effort to save his throne, telephoned his support to Nasser and promised 'all my forces and resources' in the fight against the Israelis, the British and the French.[110]

By the end of November 1956 Nabulsi had the support of the entire Cabinet, the Parliament and the country when he denounced 'imperialism and all its facets' and announced his government's intention to end the Anglo-Jordanian Treaty and 'to ask for the withdrawal of British forces from ... the Jordanian lands'.[111] This was formally achieved three months later when he announced the termination of the Treaty, the withdrawal of British troops and the liquidation of British bases in the country. An annual grant of £12.5 million sterling in aid was to be provided by Egypt, Syria and Saudi Arabia to replace the £10 million sterling subsidy paid by Britain to Jordan each year. The new funds, unlike the British payments which were made directly to the Arab Legion and to the Court, were to be used to finance both the National Guard on the West Bank and the newly formed Jordanian army (which replaced the Legion) as well as to provide finance for much-needed economic and social development projects.[112] Finally, as part of the new re-alignment, diplomatic relations were established with the Soviet Union and with the People's Republic of China.[113]

However the unity of the Court, the Cabinet, Parliament and the country lasted only a short time. As the threat of invasion — and of an internal uprising — receded, the King, backed by the Court and those Palestinians loyal to him and to Britain, moved to reverse Nabulsi's policies. In this he had the strong support of the United States, where President Eisenhower had recently announced his new 'Eisenhower Doctrine' aimed at combating communism (and neutralism) in the Middle East. In January 1947 the King informed the United States, through its ambassador in Amman, of his support for the doctrine; however because of the uproar this would have caused in Parliament and in the country he decided to keep his views secret, at least for the time being.[114]

As a next step, the King initiated plans to direct foreign policy himself, thereby circumventing the Cabinet and Parliament. Meetings aimed at forming an Islamic alliance and at countering what was seen as Soviet-inspired leftism were arranged with other Arab heads of state, but the news of these secret contacts by the King soon leaked to the press.[115] A constitutional crisis, centring on the respective powers of the Court and of the elected government, was not long in coming. When the Cabinet ordered the retirement of several leading advisers to the Court and sacked a number of ambassadors appointed by the King, he retaliated by demanding the immediate resignation of Nabulsi.[116] On 10 April 1957, in accordance with the constitution, the Prime Minister complied.

Severe rioting broke out almost immediately and continued during the next fortnight. An attempted *coup*, aimed at toppling the King, was averted only at the last moment by the King's decision to proceed to the site of the rebellion himself.[117] On 25 April, after he had found it impossible to install a government more to his liking and after even more widespread rioting in Amman, Jerusalem and Nablus, the King suspended the constitution, dismissed Parliament, declared martial law, banned political parties and ordered the army into the streets. A total 24-hour curfew was imposed on Jerusalem, Nablus, Ramallah and Irbid (where some army units had also revolted).[118]

The next day several hundred of his leading opponents, including Nabulsi, Naim Abdul Hadi and Abdul Halim al-Nimr, were arrested and ordered to stand trial in military courts. A Cabinet, which included several Palestinians loyal to the King, was appointed by him directly. Sulaiman Tuqan, who had served on the Regency Council, was named Defence Minister and Military Governor for the entire country.[119] On the 29th, faced with the end of the British subsidy and the refusal of the Arab states to provide the aid they had promised to Nabulsi's government, the King obtained a $10 million emergency grant from the United States which he used, in part, to increase the salaries paid to the army.[120] Another $20 million was received from Washington at the end of June, and a further $10 million in November.[121] Armed with this financial aid the King rapidly severed his few remaining ties with the republican regimes of Egypt and Syria and withdrew diplomatic recognition of the Soviet Union and China.

The sentencing in September of twenty men to long prison terms for their part in the riots and the trial, *in absentia*, of Major-General 'Ali Abu Nuwar and others implicated in the April *coup*, was followed by further wide-scale arrests and arms searches. The civil service, which had already been purged, lost still more Palestinians from the West Bank who were suspected of belonging to parties, like the Ba'ath, the Arab Nationalists and the Communist Party, which were banned and forced underground.[122] But although the home front may have seemed more secure as a result of the repression, the King's problems were not over yet.

Abroad a war of words broke out between Jordan on the one hand and Egypt and Syria on the other. When Syria moved troops to the border, war seemed imminent. Then in February Egypt and Syria announced their intention to merge into a United Arab Republic. The King's enemies within the Arab world seemed stronger than ever and the King countered by forming a union with Iraq, where the Hashimite dynasty also ruled. However any hope he had of receiving military aid from Iraq in case of an attack by Egypt and/or Syria was dashed only a few months later in July when his cousin, Faisal II, was overthrown in Baghdad by a military *coup*. Fearing he might be next, Hussein asked for emergency military assistance from Britain and the United States. While American troops landed in the Lebanon to buttress the authority of the pro-Western government of President Camille Chamoun (who also faced a challenge from the Nasserists and other nationalists), two battalions of British paratroopers landed in Amman.[123] With the aid of the British the King was able to effect a complete re-organisation of the army, remove many of its Palestinian officers and further expand his internal security forces at home.

The break-up of the United Arab Republic three years later eased the pressure somewhat, and in 1962 he released many of those imprisoned. But by then the question of Palestinian rights, and of the pursuit of Arab unity in general, had been taken out of his hands. In the meantime the mass of the Palestinians in Jordan had come to regard the King's action and the British intervention as the final betrayal of their attempt to recover their land by peaceful means. After 1958 many of them were to join other Palestinians exiled elsewhere in the Arab world to begin preparations for the renewal of armed struggle against Israel.

For those within the Palestinian nobility still loyal to the throne in Jordan, the defeat of Nabulsi and of his sympathisers amongst their own ranks brought a sigh of relief. They had been spared the wrath of their compatriots − unlike the fate that had befallen them in the 1936-9 revolt − and were rewarded for their loyalty with high positions in the government and substantial economic benefits as well. But the cost was high: as a result of their allegiance to the House of Hashim and to Britain, they lost any credibility they still enjoyed among their own countrymen and became totally dependent on the King and Court, incapable of ruling in their own right.

Those amongst their number who had joined the opposition and who had sought to preserve the allegiance of their compatriots by forging links with the emergent bourgeoisie in Jordan and, to a lesser extent, with the intellectuals and displaced peasantry, were faced with a sombre choice: either to join other Palestinians in exile and to accept their exclusion from power or to forsake their ties with the Palestinian masses in return for the patronage the King could offer. While some of the younger generation, like Kamal Nasser, the poet and editor of the militant newspaper *Al-Jil al-Jadid* (*The New Era*), and the Ba'athist, Dr Hamdi al-Taji al-Faruqi (a relative of the man who had helped to set up the 1948 'National Congress' in Amman), fled abroad to continue the struggle, many others chose to remain loyal to the King. By 1967 people like Anwar al-Khatib, Anwar Nusaibah, Sheikh Muhammad 'Ali al-Ja'abari and some of the former dissidents within the Tuqan family were counted among the King's most loyal supporters in the West Bank.[124] Dependent on the salaries they drew as ministers, deputies, ambassadors, mayors and judges, they pursued this course even after the Israeli occupation of the West Bank in 1967 and the civil war in Jordan in 1970 and 1971. Together with the loyalist elements in the ruling families and the tribal leaders faithful to Hussein, they helped to prevent the development of a specifically Palestinian national consciousness in the West Bank and in Jordan until the late 1960s.

5 NATIONALISM AND THE BOURGEOISIE

Jordan was not the only country in the Arab world to suffer the ill effects of the loss of Palestine. In Egypt the monarchy of King Farouk fell in July 1952 partly because of the dissatisfaction and disillusionment experienced by a new generation of army officers during service in Palestine in 1948.[1] In Syria the first of a succession of military *coups* occurred in March 1949. Popular discontent with the National Bloc of Shukri al-Quwatli was intensified by reports of corruption and incompetence during the abortive Syrian intervention in Palestine. In 1955 Nasser himself was subjected to bitter denunciation by thousands of angry Palestinians demanding arms after the Israeli army attacked Egyptian outposts and civilian targets in Gaza in February, leaving 39 dead. The Suez invasion eighteen months later produced massive rioting in a score of Arab cities, from Dhahran on the Gulf coast to Beirut, Cairo and Algiers. Then, shortly after the landing of American troops in Lebanon in 1958, the Hashimite monarchy in Iraq was overthrown in a bloody *coup d'état* led by Major General Abdul Karim Qasim.[2] Radical Arab nationalism seemed the order of the day as everywhere the existing regimes were challenged by the military and the masses alike.

With hindsight, however, it is clear that while many in the Arab world thought that the day of liberation from the remnants of the inter-war colonial period was at hand, the region was in fact undergoing a new stage of Western encroachment, this time in a more indirect, 'neo-colonial' form. By far the most significant development occurred with the rapid expansion of oil production in the Gulf states. Oil exports from Iraq had begun as early as 1934; however the outbreak of the Second World War and the threat of sabotage by Arab nationalist elements opposed to the British presence in the country prevented a substantial increase in production. After the war the international oil companies which had obtained concessions in Iraq, Saudi Arabia and the Gulf sheikhdoms prior to the outbreak of hostilities lost no time in exploiting their new finds. Encouraged by the huge rise in oil demand in war-torn Europe and by the incredibly low cost of producing oil in the Middle East, they set out to develop their concessions as quickly as possible.

Map 4. Palestine and the Palestinians, 1983*

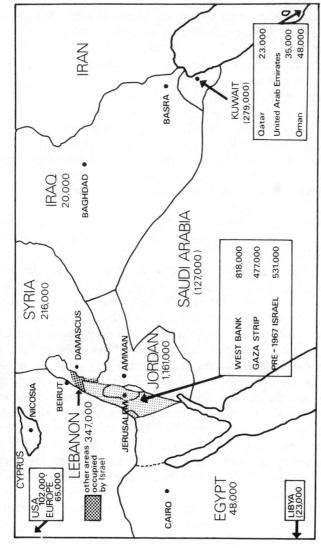

KUWAIT (279,000)	
Qatar	23,000
United Arab Emirates	35,000
Oman	48,000

WEST BANK	818,000
GAZA STRIP	477,000
PRE-1967 ISRAEL	531,000

USA	102,000
EUROPE	65,000

LEBANON
other areas 347,000
occupied by Israel

LIBYA (23,000)

EGYPT 48,000

IRAN

IRAQ 20,000
BAGHDAD

SYRIA 216,000
DAMASCUS

SAUDI ARABIA (127,000)

JORDAN 1,161,000
AMMAN

JERUSALEM

BASRA

CYPRUS
NICOSIA

BEIRUT

CAIRO

* The population figures are based on the 1980 Statistical Abstract published by the PLO (see text). It is estimated that since then the numbers in Syria, Jordan, Cyprus, Saudi Arabia, Kuwait, the UAE and Europe have risen substantially, while those in Lebanon and Egypt have declined.

In Iraq, after a hiatus caused by the loss of the export terminal and refinery at Haifa, production rose nine-fold from a pre-war level of 4 million tons in 1939 to 35.8 million tons in 1958. Saudi output, which had amounted to less than 500,000 barrels in 1938, the first year of production, rose to 546,703 barrels *a day* by the end of 1950. Ten years later it reached 1.2 million barrels a day (456 million barrels a year), almost 1,000 times as much as before the war. Production in Kuwait began in 1946, but output remained relatively low until the nationalisation of the Iranian oilfields by Prime Minister Muhammad Mussadeq. The ensuing 'Abadan crisis' and the virtual halt in Iranian exports led to a huge increase in Kuwaiti output, which by 1956 reached 54.1 million tons, a figure which made it the largest producer in the Gulf at the time. The opening of new fields in Qatar in 1949, in Libya in the early 1960s and in Abu Dhabi in 1963 added still more to the oil wealth of the region and to the surge of development that accompanied it.[3]

The oil boom also led to the expansion of other cities in the area as a result of the influx of imports, the opening up of new companies to service the oilfields, the construction of oil refineries and export terminals on the Mediterranean coast and the rapid growth in consumer demand. Beirut, which had already experienced a remarkable growth in the immediate aftermath of the 1948 defeat in Palestine, became a major transhipment centre for trade to and from the Gulf and, from the mid-1950s onward, a focal point for the re-cycling of Arab oil wealth.[4] Amman, which as we have seen grew from a small town to a major city almost overnight in the wake of the Palestine defeat, also provided new opportunities for Palestinians with capital to invest, particularly in the early 1950s and, later, in the 1960s and 1970s when demand was fuelled by the remittances which Palestinians working in the Gulf sent back to their families in the West Bank and in East Jordan.

For the hundreds of thousands of Palestinians who had lost their homes and livelihoods in 1948, these countries represented one of the few avenues of hope. However the new opportunities which the exploitation of Arab oil and the influx of Western capital created were not equally available to all Palestinians. For many, especially those living in the camps or in the mushrooming shanty towns and bidonvilles which surrounded the major cities of the countries bordering Israel, the greater oil wealth and the capitalist penetration which accompanied it simply brought higher rents and prices, as well as the separation of families as sons and brothers left the refugee camps to take low-paid manual jobs in the Gulf states and in the larger cities and towns of Lebanon, Syria and Jordan. On the other hand, Palestinians with capital to invest or with the educational qualifications needed to obtain highly paid jobs in Western companies, government ministries and private industry in the Gulf states found themselves at a distinct advantage. Unlike the manual labourers, Palestinians with these assets could afford to take their families with them to the Gulf, or to settle permanently outside the camps in Beirut, Amman, Cairo, the United States and Europe, often with the added advantage of being able to obtain local citizenship and a passport as well.

Thirty years after the defeat those Palestinians who had managed to transfer sufficient capital from Palestine to start new businesses, who had managed to settle in the Gulf states or to take part in the rapid economic development of the other major cities of the Arab world formed a new class within Palestinian society. Population figures for Palestinians resident in the Gulf in 1970 (the first year for which they are available) give us a rough idea of the size of this new class. They show that a total of 189,000 Palestinians were living in the Arab oil states of Iraq, Saudi Arabia, Kuwait, Qatar and the emirates of the lower Gulf. Another 5,000 were settled in Libya, bringing the total up to 194,000 or about 6.6 per cent of the total Palestinian population. Kuwait, which had experienced the most rapid development of its oil-fields in the 1950s, and which initially encouraged Palestinian immigration, had by far the largest number: 140,000, or about three-quarters of all those in the oil states of the Gulf and Libya. By 1980 the number of Palestinians in the Gulf states and Libya comprised an even larger percentage of the total Palestinian population: 12.6 per cent, almost double the 1970 figure. Of the 554,000 total, half (278,800) lived in Kuwait alone; another 127,000 lived in Saudi Arabia, five times as many as in 1970.[5]

Although it shared some similarities with its counterparts in nineteenth-century Europe, this new bourgeoisie was different in important respects, primarily because it lacked access to the ownership of property in the form of either landed estates or industry and because it did not have a territorial base, i.e. a state, of its own in which to operate. As a result, its open espousal of Western-style capitalist development and of free enterprise was accompanied by political action of a more radical kind than was the case in Europe, namely support for armed struggle and guerrilla war. Although some members of this class, particularly those who formed the new intelligentsia of the 1960s, advocated radical social change within Palestinian society and in the

Table 5.1: The Palestinian Population, 1970

		Number	Per Cent of Total
Arab Oil States:		194,000	6.6
Kuwait	140,000		
Saudi Arabia	20,000		
Iraq	14,000		
The Gulf	15,000		
Libya	5,000		
Other Arab States:		1,328,000	45.4
Jordan (East Bank)	900,000		
Lebanon	240,000		
Syria	155,000		
Egypt	33,000		
Europe and the Americas:		27,000	1.0
West Germany	15,000		
United States	7,000		
Latin America	5,000		
Occupied Palestine:		1,374,000	47.0
West Bank	670,000		
Gaza Strip	364,000		
Israel	340,000		
Total		2,923,000	100.0

Source: Nabil Shaath, 'High-Level Palestinian Manpower', *Journal of Palestine Studies*, vol. 1, no. 2 (Winter 1972), p. 81.

Arab world as well, the majority confined their support to those organisations within the Palestine Liberation Organisation (mainly Fatah) which eschewed involvement in the internal affairs of the other Arab states and concentrated solely on the liberation of Palestine and the replacement of the Zionist state with a democratic, secular state open to Jews, Muslims and Christians alike. A commitment to social change, or to a particular economic system, was carefully avoided, lest it result in conflicts within the nationalist movement.

This chapter looks at the origins of the bourgeoisie, its growth in the 1950s and 1960s, its alliances with other classes in Palestinian society and its relations with its counterparts in the Arab world from 1948 until the early 1970s when the civil war in Jordan and the growing challenge posed by the rise of local bourgeoisies in the Gulf states led to new strains between this class and their host countries and to the decision to pursue a negotiated settlement with Israel, a policy formerly advocated only by the remnants of the aristocracy who survived in the West Bank and in Jordan.

The Transfer of Capital

Palestine, as we have seen, was not the backward, undeveloped country in 1948 that Zionist propaganda often portrays. The construction boom, the rapid development of industry and the influx of capital precipitated by the British military presence during the Second World War had led to a phenomenal growth of the economy and to unprecedented levels of income for almost all classes of Arab society, including those peasants who owned land and who benefited from the record high prices they obtained for their agricultural produce. While much of the wealth which flooded into the rural areas was spent on providing the schools, hospitals and clinics which the government failed to build in these areas, the villagers used part of their income to pay off debts to money-lenders, to purchase new agricultural tools and equipment, to invest in land or to buy the gold and jewellery they needed for dowry payments.

In contrast, the merchants, traders and entrepreneurs in the urban areas, particularly along the coast, who benefited from the wartime prosperity tended increasingly to invest a larger share of their profits in interest-bearing bank deposits (both at home and abroad, primarily in Britain), in shares, government bonds, commodity stocks and the other forms of financial paper that had become available with the integration of the economy into the world market. While a full breakdown of the total capital assets held by Palestinian Arabs both at home and abroad at the time of the creation of Israel is still unavailable (and may never be known because of the destruction of documents during the British withdrawal and the intense controversy which surrounds the issue of 'compensation' for those who were forced to flee), some estimates of Palestinian wealth and capital assets can be made from the data provided by the government of Palestine to the Anglo-American Committee of Inquiry in 1945 and 1946.[6]

The figures are approximate estimates only, and do not include Arab holdings in urban buildings nor investment in improvements on these buildings. Nevertheless they indicate that at least one-third of the Arab

Table 5.2: Ownership of Capital in Palestine, 1945ᵃ (£P millionsᵇ)

	Total	Arab-owned
Foreign liquid assets	114.7	39.3
Rural land	99.1	74.8
Industrial capital	20.5	2.1
Insured commercial stocks and commodities	13.5	2.0
Motor vehicles	3.2	1.3
Agricultural buildings, tools and livestock	29.6	13.1
Total	280.6	132.6

Notes: a. The figures for rural land, motor vehicles and agricultural investment are for all non-Jewish holdings, including those owned by the government, non-Arab Christians and foreign residents. b. £P1 = £1 sterling, or $4.00 at 1945 exchange rates.
Source: Government of Palestine, *A Survey of Palestine* (2 vols., Jerusalem, 1946), vol. 2, p. 569.

community's total capital assets consisted of movable assets; that is, of sterling deposits held abroad, government bonds, commercial stocks, insured commodities and motor vehicles.[7] The actual figure would have been somewhat higher, since part of the capital held in industry and in agriculture included shares, tools and livestock which, in theory, could also be transferred either to the Arab-held sectors of central Palestine, Gaza or Himmah (the area north of Tiberias occupied by Syrian forces in 1948) or abroad. Similarly, since the custom of insuring commercial stocks with Britain's War Risks Department was only of recent origin, a substantial share of such stocks which were not insured was excluded from the government estimates, and the figure given is therefore less than the actual total held by Palestinians in this category.

In addition to foreign liquid assets and local shares and stocks, Palestinians had also amassed considerable cash holdings in the two local Arab banks which existed in Palestine in 1945. Figures on Arab bank deposits in October 1945 show that they rose from a total of £P532,515 at the end of 1941 to just under £P7 million by the end of October 1945. (The magnitude of such a sum can be gauged by the fact that this £P7 million amounted to almost £P1 million more than the entire civilian budget of the government of Palestine in the fiscal year 1944/5.[8]) Such phenomenal growth also enabled the banks, by the end of the war, to increase their dividends to shareholders and to place new shares on the market, most of which were purchased by

Arabs in Palestine.[9] Additional sums were held in the Ottoman Bank in Jerusalem and in the local branch of the British-based Barclays Bank in the form of bank deposits, gold, bonds and other valuables placed in safe deposit boxes. Arab bank deposits in those two institutions amounted to approximately £P3 million by the middle of 1948. Another £P300,000 was held in Israeli banks.[10]

Table 5.3: Deposits, Capital and Reserves of Arab Banks in Palestine, 31 October 1945 (£P)

	Deposits	Reserves	Paid-up Capital
Arab Bank Ltd	3,777,821	844,154	815,296
Arab National Bank	3,192,907	133,723	600,456
Total	6,970,728	977,877	1,415,752

Source: *Survey*, vol. 2, p. 562.

Of the total capital assets held in Palestine at the time of the 1948 defeat, only a small portion was transferred to the host countries or to other places of exile by the Palestinians who left. In particular, the capital held in land — mainly by the aristocracy and by the peasantry — outside the West Bank and Gaza, and the rents and income which had been derived from it, were lost totally, Israel having failed to provide compensation to its owners despite continuous United Nations resolutions urging it to do so. Other capital held in private homes or invested in buildings and immovable commercial property located in those areas which came under Israeli control was also lost completely.[11] Nevertheless the wealth of the country was such — and the exodus of sufficient duration — to allow for the transfer of substantial sums abroad, some of which were used to form a new base for the trading and industrial bourgeoisie that had begun to emerge in force during the Second World War in Palestine.

Of the movable assets, certain kinds were relatively easy to obtain in exile. The balances held in sterling accounts in London, which made up the bulk of the total liquid assets held abroad, are one example.[12] Another consisted of the sums held in bearer bonds issued by the government of Palestine before the end of the Mandate. The value of these held by Palestinian exiles outside Israel in 1949 was estimated by the United Nations to total £P1.7 million.[13] The transfer of banknotes was also substantial: of the £P60 million in circulation at the time of the defeat, only about £P27 million was turned into the government of Israel for conversion into Israeli currency. Another £P12.5 million was held in the remaining areas of Arab Palestine. Of the rest, an estimated £P10 million was brought into Jordan (where the Palestinian pound remained legal currency until 1950), £P3 million to Lebanon, £P1.5 million to Syria and £P100,000 to £P200,000 each to Egypt and Iraq.[14]

While complete figures on the transfer of bank deposits are unavailable, some indication of the amount of transfers can be ascertained from a study conducted by the bankers concerned in the early 1950s. They estimated that transfers made by depositors who sought refuge in Jordan amounted to about JD10 million (£P10 million).[15] The Arab Bank in particular went to great lengths to ensure that all the exiles with deposits in their branches were able to recover their sums despite the loss of their headquarters in Jerusalem (see Chapter 6). Other deposits, held in the Ottoman Bank or in Barclays, were recovered later following negotiations between Barclays and the government of Israel. By the end of August 1956 a total of £2,633,175 had been released to Palestinians whose accounts had been blocked. (The sums released were designated in pounds sterling, since the Palestinian pound, equivalent to £1 sterling in 1948, had ceased to exist.) The majority, about £1.6 million, went to Palestinians in Jordan. Those in Lebanon obtained a total of just under £700,000. Smaller sums were released to account holders in Syria, Egypt and other Arab countries as well. Another £25,516 was released in the period from August 1956 to 1958, bringing the total up to just under £2,660,000.[16]

At the same time 154 safe deposit lockers containing personal valuables and others holding both government and private bonds were also released. (However negotiations for the transfer of the personal valuables held in the safe deposit boxes were only concluded with the governments of Jordan and Lebanon, and only Palestinians living in those countries could actually obtain their contents.[17]) Of the £P300,000 held in deposits in other Israeli banks, about £P160,000 had been released by the end of 1958.[18]

While considerable amounts of the total holdings in sterling, bonds and deposits transferred abroad were, as we have seen, invested in land and urban real estate or in building private homes in East Jordan, the lack of citizenship and the legal restrictions which limited property ownership in the other host countries almost invariably meant that the larger sums brought to countries like Lebanon, Syria, Egypt and the Gulf states were invested in local enterprises or in starting new Palestinian companies. Yusif Baidas, a former bank clerk and foreign exchange dealer in Mandatory Palestine, used funds obtained by colleagues from the release of accounts in Barclays, and other earnings he made after the devaluation of the Palestinian pound, to start a new money exchange business in Beirut. It later became a multi-million dollar bank and holding company with operations throughout the Arab world and in many parts of Europe (see below).[19]

The Tuqan family of Nablus used its funds to expand operations in East Jordan and to start related industrial enterprises such as the Vegetable Oil Company of Jordan whose Board of Directors by 1964 included four of the wealthiest merchants in Nablus as well as merchants and industrialists from Amman.[20] Palestinians employed by the Mandatory government who received pensions or special war compensatory allowances paid in sterling set up small travel and trading companies both in the Arab world and in Europe, opened offices in their particular professions (such as law or accountancy) or used their funds to provide university educations for their sons and daughters in Europe and America.[21]

While most firms which existed in Palestine before 1948 were owned by individuals, families or partnerships of one kind or another, the rapid growth of corporate forms of organisation and of limited companies in the period following the Second World War meant that some Palestinians were also able to transfer their wealth abroad in the form of shares and securities. This enabled many of the larger firms to re-start their businesses abroad. Middle East Airlines, which was founded in 1943, and the Arabia Insurance Company both re-opened in Lebanon after 1948.[22] By the end of the 1950s, when both companies had experienced an impressive growth in their profits, their shareholders included some of the wealthiest Palestinians in the Arab world.

Other Palestinians, like Fuad Saba, whose accountancy firm included offices in Syria, Trans-Jordan and Lebanon as well as in Palestine, were able to transfer funds to their branches abroad prior to the final defeat and to avoid the crushing finanical losses which befell their colleagues.[23] Members of the Shoman family, which had founded the Arab Bank in Palestine in 1930, managed to transfer the bank's Jerusalem headquarters to Amman in the late 1940s after a daring series of exploits which involved smuggling out documents, safe deposit boxes, cash and the bank's accounts.[24] The bank was able to pay its shareholders and depositors and to establish a firm base for further expansion in the Arab world and in Europe in the 1950s and 1960s.

In addition to transferring sterling, bonds, bank deposits, stocks, shares and securities abroad, many Palestinians were also able to bring with them small amounts of gold, jewellery and other valuables as well as some agricultural tools, livestock and household goods. The gold and jewellery were usually owned by the married women, who had obtained it along with the household goods as part of their dowries. As far as one can ascertain, wealth held in this form was not generally used to invest in property or in industry. Instead mothers sold their possessions in small amounts to provide for their families during the first barren years of exile.[25] Most of the livestock that was brought out, mainly by farmers living near the borders of Lebanon, Jordan or Syria, either died in the harsh conditions or had to be slaughtered or sold because of the lack of fodder. A few re-established their herds on the West Bank or in the Sinai, usually with the help of relatives and kin living in the area. Agricultural tools were of little use if there was no land to till; their main value lay in enabling some refugees to work as hired hands for local landlords and to avoid the harsh restrictions and dire poverty of life in the refugee camps.[26]

Trade and Investment in the Diaspora, 1948-74

Once in the neighbouring Arab states the Palestinian refugees had to face severe restrictions on their freedom as well as the dislocation and disruption which sudden exile entailed. Conditions varied from country to country and from city to city. In the Lebanon the restrictions were particularly harsh, partly because the influx of refugees threatened to upset the delicate confessional balance between the various Christian and Muslim communities and to undermine the extensive privileges which the Maronite Christians enjoyed in the state bureaucracy and in commerce. Passports and residence visas could be obtained only with the help of a powerful local leader who often charged an exorbitant fee for exercising his *wastah* (influence). Property ownership and short-term leases on buildings were allowed only with the consent of the President. Palestinians, like foreigners resident in the country, were required to obtain work permits before taking up employment, practising a profession or engaging in trade, commerce or agriculture. Refugees drawing food rations were forbidden to change their residence without official permission and those who did not have passports from another country and who wished to travel abroad were only rarely granted a return visa or re-entry permit.[27]

Palestinians who fled to Egypt and who were not members of the upper class or related by marriage to an Egyptian were returned to the

Gaza Strip *en masse* in October 1949. Some 6,000 to 8,000 were affected, although a few hundred were later allowed to return to study at Egyptian universities. Once in the Strip they were subject to the military rule imposed on the area in the aftermath of the 1948 defeat. Freedom of movement and of association were almost totally restricted and the exceptionally high degree of poverty and unemployment entailed by the huge concentration of refugees in so small an area meant that many, despite their wealth or skills, were forced to emigrate to survive or to take up residence in the camps supervised by the United Nations when they had exhausted their savings.[28]

Conditions were better in both Syria and Jordan, where the Palestinians were generally allowed to work and to engage in trade without work permits. However Palestinians in Syria, unlike those in Jordan, were not granted citizenship automatically and were forbidden to buy or acquire land or property in the country without the permission of the government. Self-employed professionals — writers, lawyers and doctors — were allowed to practise freely by law in Syria but like all the refugees found it difficult to return to the country once they had left for travel or work abroad.[29] In Iraq Palestinians were allowed to work in both the public and private sector and to open shops and small businesses on an equal footing with Iraqi citizens but were not granted the right to vote.[30]

In the Gulf states the Palestinians encountered a style of life far different from their own. The lack of the most basic social services and physical facilities automatically hindered geographical and social mobility and made travel abroad difficult even though there were no laws as such forbidding Palestinians from leaving and returning once they had obtained a sponsor in the country. Some one thousand Palestinians employed at the Dhahran air base in Saudi Arabia were granted Saudi citizenship in August 1951 and others were allowed to remain in the country after arriving on pilgrimage to the Holy Cities of Mecca and Medina.[31]

Those who sought refuge in the smaller sheikhdoms along the coast were almost totally prevented from obtaining citizenship and relegated to second-class status along with the indigenous merchant communities which had originally immigrated from Persia. While Palestinians in Kuwait could own their own homes and a small surrounding plot of land, they were forbidden to sub-lease them to others or to sell them. Ownership of other land and of company shares was forbidden, and the spectacular rise in land prices in the 1960s and 1970s prevented many Palestinians who arrived in the country during this period from purchasing their own homes. Gradually as more and more Palestinians sought to enter the country the restrictions were tightened and only those with relatives or a work permit obtained from a local sponsor were allowed in. Re-entry after leaving for study or business abroad was not guaranteed and any form of political activity could be used as grounds for deportation. However once in the country Palestinians were not required to pay income tax — as they were in Lebanon, Syria, Jordan and Iraq — and were free to engage in trade and to set up businesses of their own under certain conditions.[32] In addition profits from their businesses could be transferred abroad — for investment in property or in securities and deposits which earned high interest rates — since the Gulf states, like Lebanon, allowed their inhabitants to engage in foreign exchange dealing freely and to repatriate their funds abroad without any restrictions.

While all the Palestinians in exile found their basic freedoms curtailed, those with wealth, influence or professional skills were often able to circumvent the regulations or to obtain special consideration. In Lebanon the law regulating work permits gave priority to those with an advanced education or specialised training, those who were originally from Lebanon and those who were married to Lebanese women. The first category allowed those Palestinians who had operated businesses or practised in the professions — accountants, lawyers, doctors, engineers — to set up their own firms or to open offices in Beirut and other parts of Lebanon and to avoid some of the restrictions on foreign travel. Some Palestinians like Emile Bustani, the founder of the Contracting and Trading Company (CAT), who had originally been born in Lebanon but who had emigrated to Palestine during the Mandate, were able to transfer their company operations to Beirut after the 1948 defeat. Those married to Lebanese women could obtain residence visas and invest in property in addition to obtaining work permits.

However the most important exception applied to those Palestinians who found work with the many foreign companies which set up operations in Lebanon in the late 1940s and 1950s. Since foreign companies were allowed to employ a certain number of non-Lebanese under a quota system without recourse to the authorities, those Palestinians who had the qualfications these firms required quickly found themselves in a far better position than their compatriots.[33] Again, the urban middle-class Palestinians benefited in particular since many had received not only an education in Palestine but one in which English had been the mode of instruction. This enabled them to take up posts at the American University of Beirut, National Cash Register, IBM, Time-Life, Shell, the Trans-Arabian Pipeline Company (Tapline) in Sidon, the Iraq Petroleum Company offices in Beirut and Tripoli and in other firms owned or operated by American or British interests. Still others who had acted as commission agents, freight forwarders, importers, wholesalers and retailers or who had obtained franchises from American and British firms in Palestine during the Mandate used their contacts abroad to re-open similar businesses in Beirut.

As a result small communities of relatively prosperous Palestinians grew up in Ras Beirut and Sidon where their style of life stood in marked contrast to the tens of thousands of others housed in the camps or in the sprawling shanty towns located outside the major cities. By the early 1970s many of these more prosperous Palestinians had also been able to obtain Lebanese citizenship and to escape the restrictions on investment in property and industry as well as on foreign travel. In the Hamra area of West Beirut, then one of the most modern areas in the entire country, 86 per cent of the Palestinians residing in the district had obtained Lebanese citizenship by 1973.[34] In addition to providing Palestinian society with many of its leading academics, journalists, entrepreneurs, physicians and engineers, the community provided a haven for Palestinian activists deported or banned from other Arab countries and became a base for the Palestinian resistance movements which flourished in the area from the late 1960s until 1982.

In Syria the more relaxed laws governing Palestinian activity enabled those with capital to open shops, establish businesses and form companies or partnerships on equal terms with Syrians. In contrast Palestinian workers, who had to compete with their Syrian counterparts for scarce jobs, found the process of obtaining employment more difficult. Refugee peasants drawing rations from the United Nations Relief and Works Agency (UNRWA) were even less privileged; they were forbidden to change their residence without the approval of the Department of Public Security.[35]

Palestinian traders who had enjoyed close relations with their counterparts in Damascus and Aleppo or who had been accustomed to taking their summer holidays at Syrian resorts were also in a position, unlike the workers and peasants, to find suitable accommodation outside the camps on their arrival in the country in the months following their departure from Palestine. This crucial difference was to give them a distinct advantage in future years when their relative freedom of movement and greater ability to obtain Syrian passports allowed them to expand their contacts abroad and to take part in the rapid growth of the Gulf economies. By the late 1970s it was estimated that ten Palestinians had become millionaires in Syria. However, unlike their counterparts in Beirut, they preferred to remain with their compatriots in the camps, where the Syrians provided more amenities than elsewhere in the Arab world, rather than move to the more fashionable districts of Damascus. Nevertheless they tended to invest their wealth in property and businesses located outside Syria where the taxes were lower and where there were fewer restrictions on the transfer of funds. Their assets outside Syria were also less likely to be confiscated in times of political upheaval.[36]

Palestinians who settled in Saudi Arabia in the late 1940s found themselves particularly well placed to take advantage of the huge growth of the economy that began with the rapid expansion of oil production. Many obtained Saudi nationality and had brought some capital with them. The lack of regulations governing commerce and trade in the early days of the boom years and the huge amounts of investment and aid provided by the Arabian American Oil Company (Aramco), the United States Agency for International Development (AID), Washington's Point IV Programme and other American funding programmes gave ample scope to those who had the training and initiative to take advantage of the increased demand generated by Aramco's needs and by the rapid development which followed in other areas. Those with professional qualifications could find employment as physicians, teachers, accountants, engineers, managers and consultants. Others found work as sub-contractors, commission agents and business representatives and either sent their earnings back to their families living outside the country or used them to start businesses of their own. The kingdom's heavy reliance on Palestinians to man its overseas consulates and embassies also enabled the Palestinian community in the country to obtain contacts with exporters of arms, industrial equipment and consumer goods in the United States and Western Europe outside the Aramco framework and to enter close business relationships with the indigenous mercantile families who expanded their operations in the 1960s and 1970s.[37]

In Kuwait and the other Gulf states the presence of British firms and advisers in the early 1950s provided opportunities for Palestinians who had either worked for the British government in Palestine or who had received an education in British schools in Mandatory Palestine. One of the earliest arrivals was Muhsin al-Qattan, who played a key role in the development of the educational system in Kuwait and who enjoyed close connections with the ruling family and with the sons and daughters of the most prominent merchant families as a result. His son, Abdul Muhsin al-Qattan, became Deputy Undersecretary at the Ministry of Public Works and, in 1959, founded the Al-Hani Contracting Company of Kuwait which built the Sheraton Hotel and Kuwait Airways office complex as well as huge water reservoirs, residential buildings and drainage systems in Kuwait. By the late 1960s the firm was also reaping big contracts in Saudi Arabia and Jordan, as well as in Kuwait, importing building materials, machinery and equipment. In 1968 Abdul Muhsin, who by this time had amassed considerable personal wealth, was elected President of the Palestinian National Council, partly as a result of his substantial support for Fatah since the late 1950s.[38]

Other Palestinians found work with one of Kuwait's largest merchant families, the al-Ghanims, and then went into business on their own providing contracting, construction, transport, engineering, public relations and consultancy services to government and private industry. By the late 1950s, when a young engineering student from Cairo named Yasser Arafat arrived in Kuwait to work for the Ministry of Public Works, the Palestinian community in Kuwait numbered several thousand and was the wealthiest in the diaspora. Twenty years later it had grown to more than 400,000; its financial contributions to Fatah and to the Palestine Liberation Organisation, which were paid in the form of a tithe on Palestinian incomes and deducted directly by the government, played a vital role in enabling Fatah and the PLO to survive and grow in the 1970s despite the losses which the resistance suffered in Jordan and Lebanon.

Elsewhere in the Gulf Palestinians were also attracted to the small sheikhdom of Qatar. They were helped by Abdullah Darwish, a prominent merchant who together with his father and other brothers enjoyed a close relationship with the ruling family and with the British resident in Doha. Named as the chief purchasing agent for the Qatar Petroleum Company (in which both British Petroleum and Shell had substantial holdings) and later as the government's chief labour contractor, Darwish formed a partnership with the Contracting and Trading Company (CAT), a firm which had won sizeable military contracts in Palestine during the Second World War before moving its headquarters to Beirut after 1948 (see below). CAT won several multi-million dollar contracts from both QPC and the government and by the mid-1950s had imported some six hundred personnel, mostly Palestinian engineers. administrators and skilled craftsmen, into Qatar. Darwish in turn amassed a small fortune from the partnership in the form of commission fees and profits made on his trading and importing side of the business.[39] By the mid-1970s the Palestinian community in Qatar had risen tenfold. As in Kuwait it provided a fertile recruiting ground for the emissaries from Fatah in the late 1950s and early 1960s. Through its contributions to the PLO after the 1967 war it too became a mainstay of the resistance movement in the 1970s.

In the United Arab Emirates Palestinian emigration was delayed until the discovery of oil in 1963. The community, which numbered only about 450 at the time, grew considerably after the 1967 war when the demand for engineers, civil servants and others increased along with the flow of oil revenues. Further immigration occurred after the outbreak of the civil war in Lebanon; the Emirates, whose income had risen rapidly after the fourfold rise in oil prices in 1973 and 1974, welcomed Palestinians whose training in higher education made them particularly useful. Palestinian-owned firms located elsewhere in the Gulf also opened branch offices in Abu Dhabi, Dubai and the other emirates and began hiring their compatriots from Lebanon and Jordan. State ministries and overseas embassies were also staffed extensively by Palestinians. By 1975 the comunity numbered almost 27,000 and, like its counterparts in Kuwait and Qatar, provided considerable support for the resistance movement.[40]

Further afield the United States and the South American countries of Chile, Brazil and Argentina attracted members of several Christian villages whose relatives had emigrated earlier in the century to set up small trading concerns or to promote the export of artefacts and goods 'made in the Holy Land' (see Chapter 3). By the mid-1960s sizeable communities of Palestinians from Ramallah, Bir Zeit and Bethlehem existed in Connecticut, Detroit and San Francisco; a lawyer from the West Bank town of Ramallah, Aziz Shihadah, estimated in 1978 that 'some 80 per cent of the landowners in this town live in the US'.[41] While emigrants from these communities specialised in small trade (wholesale and retail), some obtained advanced educations in the United States and went on to play a significant role in the professions, the universities and the church.

By the early 1970s the Palestinian community in Chile numbered some 80,000, 30,000 of whom were from Bethlehem. In addition to the immigrants who had come after 1948 the community included several thousand who were descended from the original settlers who had left Palestine before the First World War to escape conscription by the Ottomans. A handful of these had become extremely wealthy, mainly through their activity in the textile industry. Unlike their counterparts in the Gulf, however, the older Palestinians in Chile tended to be conservative in matters affecting local politics. Some were vehemently opposed to the election of President Salvador Allende and later sympathised with the military government of President Pinochet.[42]

Elsewhere in South America sizeable communities of Palestinians are to be found in the cities of Sao Paulo and Buenos Aires as well as in Uruguay and parts of Central America. In Brazil and Argentina they often joined forces with the large communities of Lebanese and Syrians who had opened up importing and exporting businesses, shipping and transport companies and textile firms after emigrating at the time of the First World War.[43]

In Europe, a small community of Palestinians composed primarily of former civil servants and advisers to the Mandatory government, as well as others engaged in the professions and in the communications sector (journalists, public relations advisers and advertising agents), existed in London throughout the 1950s and 1960s and played a major role in espousing the Palestinian cause in Britain at a time when it was still unpopular in the West. Their numbers increased considerably after the Lebanese civil war in the mid-1970s when Palestinians from Beirut and other Lebanese cities took refuge in London. While many came to study or to work for Arab-owned firms, their numbers also included several enterprising businessmen and women who, because of their access to capital and/or professional skills, were exempted from the restrictions on immigration and work permits and allowed to set up commercial companies which specialised in trade, travel, publishing and consultancy.

Palestinian Corporations and the New Entrepreneurs

Unquestionably the majority of those Palestinians living in the diaspora who could be distinguished from the aristocracy on the one hand and from the working poor and displaced peasantry on the other consisted of what might, for lack of a better term, be called the 'petite bourgeoisie'; that is, shopkeepers, owners of workshops, small travel or vehicle-hire firms, printing and distribution companies, laundries and mechanical repair firms as well as others, such as teachers and clerks, employed in the service sector. Further up the scale were those who had managed to set up businesses based on their technical or professional skills: teams of consulting engineers, architects, doctors, urban planners and financial advisers.

At the top of the scale, however, there existed a handful of Palestinian entrepreneurs who, although small in number, had a profound impact not only on Palestinian society but also on the development of the entire Middle East. Because of their extensive business contacts in the neighbouring Arab countries, they were able to re-build their companies abroad, usually with capital transferred from Palestine before the defeat or with assets recovered soon afterward. They were therefore in a position to take advantage of the rapid growth in demand in the Gulf on the one hand and, on the other, of the huge reservoir of highly skilled but unemployed Palestinian labour which existed in the area in the late 1940s and early 1950s. By the mid-1960s their interlocking network of companies and corporations constituted a formidable financial and trading empire which specialised in construction, contracting, transport, banking and real estate management throughout the Middle East and, to a certain extent, in Europe, the United States, Africa and South America as well.

While lack of space precludes a more detailed and comprehensive study of these larger firms, a few illustrations may help to demonstrate the extent to which these companies and their owners were able to amass considerable wealth and the way in which they were able to exert a profound influence on the economic and social development of the Arab world in the first two decades following the defeat in Palestine.

One of the oldest Palestinian-owned corporations is the Arab Bank, which was founded in Jerusalem in 1930 by a Palestinian peasant from the village of Beit Hanina, Abdul Hamid Shoman. Shoman left school at the age of seven and started his working life as a labourer in a quarry near the village before emigrating to the United States at the age of twenty in 1911. There he worked as a travelling salesman selling textiles and small goods throughout the American South, saving his earnings to open a shop in Baltimore and then a huge department store in New York. By 1929, when he returned to Palestine, he was already a rich man.[44]

Convinced that the indigenous economy in Palestine had suffered because of the lack of Palestinian-owned financial institutions, Abdul Hamid first sought to open a bank in Palestine with capital raised among Arab emigrants in the United States. When that attempt failed, he approached Egyptian investors, but they were fearful that the riots which broke out in Palestine in 1929 would affect profits. Finally he decided to act on his own and opened the Arab Bank in Jerusalem in July 1930 with his private savings, amounting to £P15,000. Under the laws existing at the time, he needed seven shareholders in order to register it as a private limited company. His son, Abdul Majid Shoman, describes the way he went about finding the seven: 'My father picked six of his relatives and friends as shareholders. He gave them a few shares. There was one man he gave a loan to so he could buy four shares in order to complete the seven.'[45]

Among the bank's first big borrowers was none other than the Supreme Muslim Council which, in 1931, was facing bankruptcy as a result of a change in the way the Mandatory government assessed and paid the tithe on agricultural lands and *awqaf* (see Chapter 3).[46] Later when the Council and its President, Amin al-Hussaini, regained their wealth and embarked on a huge campaign throughout the country to raise funds to buy Arab land, the bank benefited by acting as depositor for the funds. Abdul Hamid himself enjoyed a close relationship with the Mufti, as well as with Ahmad Hilmi Pasha before he left the Arab Bank to set up a rival institution, the Arab National Bank, in the mid-1930s (see Chapter 4).[47] When the general strike broke out in 1936, Abdul Hamid was twice detained by the British for his support of the nationalist cause, but the bank nevertheless honoured all claims made by its depositors while at the same time postponing the debts owed by borrowers who had been adversely affected by the stoppages and the subsequent revolt.

This well-earned reputation for paying out despite political circumstances stood it in good stead when the economy grew dramatically during the Second World War and enabled the bank to compete on equal terms for Arab deposits with the British-owned banks in Palestine. When in 1948 the bank again paid out all claims immediately — unlike Barclays and the Ottoman Bank — despite the loss of its branches in Haifa, Jaffa and Jerusalem, its reputation for financial soundness and above all for security was well established. This helped the bank to transfer its headquarters to Amman in 1948 and to attract new deposits in Jordan and the other Arab countries. It brought an interest in the newly established Development Bank of Jordan, which channelled British and American aid funds to local businesses and provided funds to set up the Jordan Petroleum Refinery Company in 1956.[48]

By 1967, when the bank again lost branches in Palestine and had to weather a run on deposits by refugee claimants fleeing Israeli troops, the bank had more than a dozen branches in the Arab world as well as affiliates in Switzerland, West Germany and Nigeria. The existence of these offices enabled the bank to spread its losses while still attracting new business. A year later its reserves had risen to more than JD8.5 million ($24 million) and its capital amounted to JD5.5 million ($15 million). However these figures represented only a small portion of its annual turnover: the Lebanese branch in Beirut alone handled business worth more than $130 million in 1968.[49]

Shoman, his son, Abdul Majid and another relative, Khalid Shoman, also helped to encourage the growth of a number of related companies that supplemented the bank's widespread activities in the Arab world. One of these, the Commercial Buildings Company, was set up in Beirut in August 1966 with almost 14 million Lebanese pounds (LL), the equivalent of $4.5 million, in capital to finance and manage property investments. Other founders included Amin Shahin, a Palestinian from the West Bank whose family operated a large construction firm in Jordan; Sulaiman Tannous, a member of the Arab Bank's board of directors; and Sami Alami, the bank's regional manager in Beirut.[50]

Tannous, together with other Palestinians, including Basim Faris, Farid 'Ali al-Sa'd — who had served as a district officer in the Mandatory government and then as manager of the Arab Bank branch at Haifa until 1948 — and Abul Wafa al-Dajani — a businessman from Jerusalem — also helped to set up the Arabia Insurance Company in Beirut which, by 1967, had branches in Jordan, Kuwait, Bahrain, Qatar, Dubai, Abu Dhabi, Sudan, Libya, Tunisia, Morocco and Britain as well as Beirut. Although the company, which was originally founded in Palestine in 1944, specialised mainly in insurance for the construction, shipping and property markets of the Arab world, it also invested in a number of other manufacturing and investment firms, including the Cortas Canning and Refrigeration Company of Lebanon and the Al-Mashriq Financial Investment Company of Beirut, whose board of directors included Faris, Tannous and a number of other prosperous Palestinian businessmen.[51]

The prime mover behind the formation of Al-Mashriq in 1963 was a well-known Palestinian accountant, Fuad Saba, who had served as the managing director of a limited company by the same name in Mandatory Palestine as well as running his own highly successful team of accountants, Saba and Company. First founded in Haifa in the 1920s, Saba and Company have served as auditors for the Arab Bank since the bank's formation in 1930. The firm has also handled the accounts of Intra Bank (see below), CAT, Arabia Insurance and scores of other Palestinian-owned firms. Saba himself helped to set up the Palestinian National Fund in 1930 and was appointed secretary of the

Arab Higher Committee in June 1936 before being deported by the British for his political activities in 1937. After the defeat of 1948 the company moved its offices to Beirut and Amman and from there expanded its operations throughout the Middle East. In 1955 it obtained a contract from John Paul Getty to work for the Getty Oil Company in the neutral zone between Saudi Arabia and Kuwait. Through Getty's help the company entered into a partnership with the huge US accountancy firm of Arthur Andersen and Company, a move which opened the door to extensive business from US firms doing business in the United States.

Former employees of Saba and Company, such as Talah Abu Ghazalah, have since branched off into their own companies. Abu Ghazalah's firm, based in Kuwait, prospered after the 1973/4 rise in oil prices and in 1978 donated a huge sum, reportedly totalling $10 million, to help set up a graduate school of business administration and management at the American University of Beirut. Another member of the Saba family, Fawzi, opened his own accountancy firm in Saudi Arabia which by the mid-1970s was doing substantial business for both Saudi and Western firms, including several international oil companies which sought the firm's advice on financial and tax problems.[52]

Although the interlocking network which surrounded the Arab Bank and its associated companies registered phenomenal growth in the 1950s and the 1960s, its investment policies remained conservative. Its reserves were kept high, its profits were re-invested in the company and, unlike other banks, it maintained a high level of liquidity.[53] In contrast the Beirut-based Intra Bank prided itself on taking risks that other entrepreneurs avoided and expanded its holdings to include property, real estate, construction, trade, transport and manufacturing companies in addition to engaging in the more traditional commercial banking and investment management services which characterised the Arab Bank. Founded in 1951 by Yusif Baidas, a former foreign exchange dealer in Jerusalem (see above), Intra by 1965 had become the largest single financial institution in Lebanon, with assets amounting to just under LL1,000 million ($325 million).[54]

By skilfully deploying the wealth of Palestinian talent at his disposal and by practising an aggressive and competitive policy of acquiring prime properties and industrial equities at a time when their future prospects were only faintly visible, Baidas almost single-handedly led the bank from one success to another. In Lebanon its holdings included controlling interests in Middle East Airlines, the Beirut Port, the

Phoenicia Hotel, the Beirut Hilton, Lebanese television and two major insurance companies. In addition it also owned sizeable interests in other manufacturing, telecommunications, publishing, property, shipping and investment companies. By 1966 it had expanded into Europe, the United States, Africa and South America as well, picking up important shareholdings in France's second-largest shipyard (Chantiers Navals de la Ciotat), mining companies registered in England, lucrative real estate along the Champs Elyseés in Paris, Manhattan's Fifth Avenue and London's Park Lane as well as banks, brokerage houses and trading companies in Geneva, Rome, Frankfurt, New York, Sao Paulo, Dubai, Liberia, Sierra Leone and Nigeria.[55]

In addition to helping many other Palestinian-owned companies to build up their businesses in the Middle East and in the oil states of the Gulf, Intra and its affiliates imported many of the basic materials needed in the area – wheat, building supplies, manufactured goods and transport equipment – while at the same time advising the royal families of the Gulf and their governments on how to invest their funds abroad. Long before the oil 'boom' of the 1970s, Intra under Baidas had recognised the vast development potential of the Gulf states and the huge opportunities that arose from the 'recycling' of petrodollars. At its height Intra was able to compete on equal terms with the huge multinationals of Europe and the United States and, in some cases, to undercut their business in the Arab world through its unrivalled knowledge of the local market and its ability to marshal an impressive array of managerial talent skilled in both the ways of the West and the East.

Palestinian expertise also contributed to the growth of another huge firm which had a major impact on the construction industry in the Middle East in the 1950s and 1960s: the Contracting and Trading Company (CAT). CAT was started in 1941 by a Lebanese entrepreneur, Emile Bustani, who had studied engineering in Britain before emigrating to Palestine after the outbreak of the Second World War. In Palestine the company quickly became a major contractor for the Mandatory government, building housing and other military projects for the British Army. In 1943 it also obtained contracts from the British for the construction of military facilities in Beirut and expanded its operations to include two other partners: Abdullah al-Khoury, a Lebanese businessman, and Shukri Shammas, a Syrian merchant from Homs.[56]

After the war CAT, through Shammas, extended its operations to Syria where it became involved in the expansion of the huge Iraq Petroleum Company (IPC) pipeline from Iraq to the Mediterranean coast. In 1951 it formed a partnership with a British-registered company, Motherwell Bridge and Engineering, and set up a second company, Mothercat, which specialised in the building of refineries, pipelines and oil tank farms. At the time it was reported to be the only company in the world which was capable of providing the kind and size of pipe needed to develop the oilfields of the Middle East.[57]

Through its work for IPC, then owned by British Petroleum and Shell as well as other oil companies from France and the United States, CAT and Mothercat were able to expand into the other British-ruled territories of the Gulf coast, winning major contracts for the construction of oil pipelines, oil terminals and storage depots, roads, power plants, water-supply installations, port and harbour works, pumping stations and commercial buildings in Kuwait, Qatar, the Emirates and, later, in Saudi Arabia and Oman as well. In Qatar, as mentioned earlier, CAT obtained a virtual monopoly on foreign trade and construction for the oil industry in the early 1950s through its partnership with Abdullah Darwish. All of Qatar Petroleum Company's installations were built by CAT or Mothercat, which were then the only foreign firms allowed in the sheikhdom. Under its arrangement with QPC, the oil company normally furnished the necessary heavy machinery, as well as cement, steel, timber and other imported materials, while CAT provided the technical staff, skilled craftsmen, some vehicles and light machinery and locally available building materials such as sand and stone. CAT also operated a gypsum plant and tile factory in Qatar.[58]

In South Yemen, then also under British rule, CAT obtained an important contract for the expansion of the port and oil terminal facilities at Aden. After the opening of the British Petroleum refinery in 1954, the colony of Aden experienced a huge economic boom that generated still more contracts for both CAT and the colony's local merchants.[59] Then, in the early 1960s, the company moved into Nigeria where it again obtained work from British Petroleum, Shell and the government as the economy expanded rapidly following the development of the country's oil reserves and the start of oil production in 1958.[60]

At home CAT's influence in the Lebanon was also increasing, largely through the efforts of Bustani, who had been elected a member of the Chamber of Deputies in 1951. When in 1956 he became Minister of Public Works and Planning, he was able to obtain access to the offices of Gamal Abdul Nasser and other Arab leaders who, in the aftermath of the Suez invasion and the subsequent rising tide of Arab nationalism, were eager to promote the use of Arab-owned companies on development projects.[61] While Bustani's professional expertise and his reputation for honesty and good work were undoubtedly important factors in the company's success, an even more important element may have been the desire of Nasser and the conservative regimes in the Gulf to avoid the kind of political and social instability that had occurred in Jordan in the 1950s as a result of the high unemployment that existed among the Palestinian refugees. Bustani argued convincingly that his company, by tapping the wealth of Palestinian talent at its disposal, could help to make Palestinians self-sufficient and promote their integration into the economy of the Arab states while at the same time contributing to the development of the region's infrastructure and to the profitable deployment of its oil revenues.[62] Unfortunately there were those in the area, as we shall see, who were bitterly opposed to the integration of the Palestinian businesses which could successfully compete with local firms and local merchants. Bustani's own untimely death, in an air crash in 1962, shortly before he was expected to campaign for the presidency of Lebanon, has never been fully explained.[63] There are many Palestinians who still feel that his death was not accidental and that he and CAT had become too successful, through the employment of Palestinians and the marshalling of their skills to the benefit of the region as a whole, to suit his potential Arab rivals.

In 1963 three other Palestinians started another construction company that was destined to overtake CAT by the late 1960s. The three, Hassib Sabbagh, Muhammad Kamal Abdul Rahman and Sa'id Tawfiq Khouri, started with only LL10 million ($3 million) but by 1967 the firm, Consolidated Contractors Company, was doing business worth LL55 million ($18 million) a year. Abdul Rahman, Sabbagh and Khouri soon became wealthy men in their own right and invested in still other companies and firms doing business throughout the Middle East. Abdul Rahman, who was born in Jerusalem, became a director of a dozen Arab companies operating in the area, including Middle East Airlines, the Beirut-based Banque Foncière Arabe, the Société Nationale pour l'Industrie de la Chaux Hydraulique and the United Investment Corporation.[64] Sabbagh, whose family had originally owned an extensive textile and dyeing business in Safad, bought properties in Beirut and London in addition to his other investments which included an apartment in Beirut furnished with fifteenth-century oak panelling shipped from Syria, Gothic tapestries and Italian works of art.[65] Khouri set up a property company in Beirut that invested in commercial real estate and later became chairman of the Sharjah-based Investment Bank for Trade and Finance and a director of the Banque d'Investissement et de Financement of Beirut whose shareholders included members of the royal families of Sharjah, Ras al-Khaimah and Kuwait.[66] By the early 1970s CCC and its related companies were doing business worth an estimated $60 million a year in the Gulf states, Libya and Nigeria.

Challenge and Retreat, 1964-74

While the Palestinian entrepreneurs were expanding their economic base in the Arab world, new forces were arising within the Arab states that eventually were to bring about conflict and dissension between the Palestinian bourgeoisie and their counterparts in Saudi Arabia, Kuwait, Lebanon, Jordan and elsewhere in the Arab world. The Palestinian economic expansion had been made possible to a large extent by the existing state of underdevelopment in the Gulf states and by the early experience of capitalism which the Palestinians had obtained under the British Mandate in Palestine, particularly during the Second World War.

By the late 1950s, however, local bourgeoisies were beginning to expand and to challenge their Palestinian rivals. A series of strikes in the mid-1950s led by Palestinian workers angered at the appalling conditions which prevailed in the oil industry (and which were also supported by local nationalist elements opposed to the British role in Suez and to the continuation of Western economic domination) led to the deportation of hundreds of Palestinians from Saudi Arabia, Kuwait, Iraq and Libya (see Chapter 6).[67] Local merchants, anxious to obtain a greater share of the oil revenues, argued that the use of Palestinian labour, rather than ensuring stability, actually undermined it. They pressed their governments to enact tighter controls on the awarding of contracts to Palestinian firms. Others argued that the foreign oil companies, by favouring outsiders (Westerners as well as Palestinians) were preventing the development of local capital and insisted that the local citizens be given more opportunity to set up their own enterprises.

In Saudi Arabia a new agreement concluded in 1957 between the government and the American oil companies which ran the oilfields included a provision that not less than 70 per cent of those employed in the industry's operations in the kingdom should be Saudis. Although the companies initially had difficulty finding suitably qualified candidates, by 1964 the percentage of Saudis employed in supervisory and management posts in the industry had risen to 52 per cent.[68] Furthermore, since the 1957 agreement gave preference to citizens from other Arab League countries in cases where Saudis were not qualified, Arabs from countries like Lebanon, Egypt and Syria received priority over Palestinians for the remaining jobs; Palestine, having ceased to be an independent state in 1948, was not recognised as an Arab country even though it did have an *ex officio* representative attached to the League. The result was that the influence of Palestinians in the middle ranks of the oil companies was reduced, and the opportunities to provide compatriots with contracts, export-import licences, work permits and employment diminished.

In Kuwait a similar agreement was signed between the oil companies and the government in 1958. In 1961 an agreement between the government and Shell Oil was amended to provide for the training of Kuwaitis and their preparation for taking over supervisory positions. However, unlike the situation in Saudi Arabia, the Amir of Kuwait was personally empowered to choose other Arabs for employment by the government, by Shell or at local schools and institutes without regard to whether or not they were actually citizens of an Arab League country.[69] This stipulation helped to minimise the impact which the legislation had on Palestinians, and a sizeable number were able to retain their positions in the oil sector and in related industries even though the overall influence of Palestinians in the operation of the oil-fields was reduced.

In addition to tightening restrictions on the employment of Palestinians in the oil companies, the governments of Saudi Arabia, Kuwait and other Gulf states began to insist that outside contracts placed by the oil companies be given to local citizens wherever possible. While pressure of this kind had been felt by the companies as early as 1951 when the nationalist regime of Iranian Prime Minister Muhammad Mussadeq attempted to take over control of the refinery at Abadan and to nationalise the western oil companies in Iran, it was only in the mid-1950s that its effects began to be felt within the Palestinian communities in the Arab oil states. Aramco, which had set up a special department on Arab Industrial Development (AID), began to farm out construction and maintenance jobs to Saudi contractors and to provide them with the capital, tools, equipment and raw materials needed to complete the job. At the same time the company began moving into areas not directly related to the production and export of oil, such as the construction of roads, schools, housing, hospitals, power plants and water supply facilities. In 1955 alone it paid out some $9 million to 126 Saudi contractors.[70] (The magnitude of this sum at the time can be gauged from the fact that it represented almost three-quarters of the country's entire educational budget for the year.)

By the end of the decade Saudi entrepreneurs, who had used the profits from these contracts to buy their own equipment, spare parts and imported goods, were in a position to compete with their rivals from amongst the Palestinian, Lebanese and Egyptian communities and to bid directly for more substantial contracts covering the supply of transport goods, agricultural produce and building materials as well as the construction of the bigger projects such as electricity stations, factories and schools formerly done by outside firms. Palestinians who lacked easy access to Aramco's capital subsidies and technical advice and to government ministries responsible for supplying import licences and work permits often found it difficult to compete.

In Kuwait this process of giving priority to the local citizens was taken another step further in the early 1960s when a series of measures were passed restricting the activities of non-Kuwaiti firms and giving preference to local companies in certain economic sectors. This culminated in a new Industrial Law in 1965 which gave the government extensive control over all sectors of the economy, including imports and trade, manufacturing, construction and banking. All industrial firms were nationalised under regulations which stipulated that they must be controlled by Kuwaiti shareholders; that is, a 51 per cent share or more. An Industrial Development Committee was set up and empowered to grant or withhold import licences, planning permission and building permits as the government deemed necessary to promote the establishment of Kuwaiti-owned enterprises. Non-Kuwaiti firms were banned from setting up banking and financial institutions altogether.[71]

Such measures not only prevented Palestinians from competing on equal terms with Kuwaitis but also made it increasingly difficult for Palestinians to own and operate their own firms without paying large fees to Kuwaiti partners. As one observer, describing the 51 per cent rule, remarked: 'At times this means the foreigner [i.e. Palestinian] does all the work but the Kuwaiti collects most of the money.'[72]

Elsewhere in the Arab world the advent of radical regimes in the late 1950s and early 1960s further limited the opportunities open to Palestinian entrepreneurs. The fall of the pro-British monarchy in Iraq in 1958 and the installation of a military government led by Major-General Abdul Karim Qasim led to sweeping changes in the economy that removed the right of foreigners to repatriate profits and to engage in banking and foreign exchange transactions. In 1964, under a new

Ba'athist regime headed by 'Abd al-Salam al-'Arif, all industrial sectors in the country came under direct government control. Public owned companies were established to run major areas of the economy and given an exclusive right to engage in foreign trade. In 1972 the Iraq Petroleum Company, owned by a consortium of Western interests, was completely nationalised and the oilfields taken under state control.[73] Companies like CAT, whose clients were allied to the pro-British factions in pre-revolutionary Iraq, found themselves excluded in favour of local firms and state-owned enterprises.

In Syria the restrictions on private economic activity introduced during the period of union with Egypt (1958-61) left some scope for activity in retail trade as well as in construction and transport. However the continued threat of Israeli aggression, which culminated in a series of attacks and reprisals in the mid-1960s and finally in the 1967 war, left the economy paralysed and dependent on outside aid. Palestinians who were educated or skilled in commerce left for the more promising countries of the Gulf states or renounced the opportunities for advancement available to their compatriots in Saudi Arabia, Kuwait and the Emirates altogether in favour of direct military and political action against Israel.[74]

In Libya the overthrow of King Idris and the installation of a republic headed by Muammar Qaddafi in September 1969 led to the arrest of many of the Palestinians who had served as advisers to the King or as civil servants in the administration. Individuals and companies suspected of doing business with the former regime had their bank accounts frozen.[75] Banks, insurance companies and manufacturing industries were nationalised a year later and the local offices of Palestinian-owned firms like the Arab Bank and the Arabia Insurance Company were forced to leave or to submit to a Libyan takeover of their assets.[76] At the same time Libyans were encouraged to take a greater role in those areas reserved for the private sector — retail and wholesale trade, foreign commerce, construction and agriculture — through a system of subsidies and exemptions from tax and import duties. Once again Palestinian firms found it difficult to compete and even when they could, the uncertainty of the political climate and of their own status within the country led them either to emigrate to more receptive shores or to invest their funds elsewhere.

Aside from the growing competition posed by the emergence of local bourgeoisies and the adverse impact of restrictions on private enterprise, Palestinian entrepreneurs faced other more intractable problems that stemmed from their inability to translate their growing economic influence into political power. In Lebanon the death of Emile Bustani and the decline of CAT was followed by the dramatic collapse of Intra Bank in October 1966 after a series of sudden withdrawals by members of the ruling families in Kuwait and Saudi Arabia.[77] The refusal of the Central Bank of Lebanon to provide a loan to Intra, even though its assets outweighed its liabilities by $50 million, and its premature action in declaring Intra bankrupt in January 1967 provoked an outcry both among the bank's 16,000 unsecured depositors – many of whom were Palestinians – and the Lebanese left. They claimed that such precipitate action by the Central Bank reflected the desire of the Lebanese Maronite community to reduce Baidas's influence in Lebanon and to remove the challenge he posed to their own attempts to participate in the country's banking sector.[78]

Efforts by Baidas to raise additional funds and to transfer assets from Intra's branch in New York were blocked by three US banks, and Intra Bank, together with all of its affiliated companies and real estate holdings, was turned over to a management committee representing Intra's four main creditors: the governments of the United States (which had lent Baidas $22 million to finance a wheat purchase agreement), Kuwait, Qatar and Lebanon.[79] A US investment firm, Kidder Peabody and Company, was called in and subsequently set up a new holding company, Intra Investment Company, which proceeded to sell Intra's prized real estate in Paris and other European capitals to the governments of Kuwait, Qatar and Lebanon. Its overseas banking interests were subsequently turned over to a number of US, British and German banks.[80]

Kuwait, Qatar, Lebanon and the United States, together with a number of private Gulf investors, also acquired a controlling interest in all of Intra's affiliates, including its huge shipyard in France, Middle East Airlines, the Port of Beirut, the Casino du Liban and its publishing, radio and television interests. Baidas, who was left bankrupt, was excluded from the new company and died of a heart attack in Switzerland three years later. For the scores of Palestinian companies which he had assisted the collapse of Intra was a bitter blow from which many never recovered. For hundreds of others who had been unable to obtain an education in the Arab world it meant the loss of a unique opportunity to obtain training and professional experience in modern finance and industry.

Whatever the merits or faults of Intra – and the controversy about it and Baidas still continues – Palestinians of all walks of life drew the conclusion that the bank had failed, or been allowed to fail, solely because it was Palestinian.[81] Henceforth, they argued, Palestinians would either have to share their profits with their Arab rivals – and so defuse potential jealousy – or invest their funds in an area where Palestinians had a say in the government and in the way affairs of the economy were handled. Since no Arab state except Jordan gave the Palestinians a right to participate in governmental affairs – and there they had little power to decide policy – the only answer to many Palestinian businessmen in the diaspora after the collapse of Intra seemed to be the creation of a place where economic influence could be secured and maintained by political power, namely through the establishment of a state of their own.[82]

Less than a year after the collapse of Intra the loss of the entire West Bank and of Gaza to the Israelis during the June war led to even greater support for Palestinian nationalism among those elements in Jordan who, unlike their colleagues in the Gulf states, had up to then eschewed active involvement in Palestinian politics. However the greater freedom enjoyed by Palestinian entrepreneurs in Jordan and the fact that it remained one of the few countries in which Palestinians could own property delayed the development of national sentiments among some sections of the bourgeoisie until after the civil war of 1970-1.

Later, when King Hussein abandoned his claims to the West Bank at the 1974 Arab Summit Conference in Rabat and endorsed the Palestine Liberation Organisation as the sole legitimate representative of the Palestinians, Palestinian businessmen in Jordan suffered a fate similar to that experienced by their colleagues in the Gulf a few years earlier. The King's recognition of the PLO was followed by the 'Jordanisation' of the kingdom and the removal of Palestinians from influential posts in the Cabinet and civilian administration. As a result Palestinian merchants, financiers and industrialists who in the past had depended on the government for contracts and funds found themselves at a disadvantage *vis-à-vis* their Jordanian rivals, who increasingly obtained a privileged position in the economy even though they were usually less experienced than the Palestinians.[83]

By the end of the year even those elements of the landed aristocracy in the West Bank which had supported the monarchy against the nationalist demands of the Palestinian bourgeoisie in the other Arab states had begun openly to declare their support for the PLO and to demand the creation of a separate Palestinian state in the West Bank and Gaza. While they, like the bourgeoisie, had come to believe that their interests could only be protected in a state of their own, their action was also prompted by the growing radicalism which had spread among the dispossessed peasantry and proletariat of the West Bank, Gaza and the refugee camps of Jordan and the other Arab states. This radicalism, as we shall see, provided the Palestinian resistance move- ment with its fighters and theoreticians and enabled the leaders of Fatah in particular to transform the political and financial support they received from the bourgeoisie into a fighting force that rapidly caught the world's attention and, after years of neglect, made the word 'Palestine' a household name in the West as well as in the Arab East.

6 THE FRAGMENTATION OF THE PEASANTRY

The defeat of the Arab resistance and the creation of the state of Israel led to a massive exodus of refugees from the area occupied by Jewish forces.[1] Although some, as we have seen, managed to leave early and become self-supporting in the cities of the neighbouring countries, the vast majority of the peasants found themselves without food, shelter and the basic necessities of life. Many initially sought safety in Lebanon or in other parts of Palestine, particularly during the heavy fighting in the Galilee in the spring of 1948 and after the massacre of 254 villagers in Dair Yassin in April. Others fled to the West Bank and to Trans-Jordan after the entry of the Arab Legion in May. Still others, including many from Jaffa, sought the protection of the Egyptian army and fled to southern Palestine and later to Egypt and the Gaza Strip.

At first most lived in the open — in orchards, barns and caves; others found temporary accommodation in army barracks, convents, schools and charitable institutions. As the exodus continued through the autumn and winter of 1948 efforts were made to register the refugees as they accumulated in various centres of assembly. By January 1949, when a programme of food rations was organised, the number of refugees registered for relief was estimated to total almost 1 million.[2] Compared to the pre-1948 population of Palestine, this figure meant that nearly three out of every four Palestinians had either fled their homes or been reduced to destitution.[3] As the international relief organisations, which included the International Red Cross, the League of Red Cross and Red Crescent Societies and the United Nations, began to open up routes for the supply of tents, medical supplies and clothing, as well as food, makeshift camps were established in the West Bank and Gaza as well as in the surrounding Arab countries where Palestinians had sought refuge. Designed to be temporary pending a full repatriation of the Arab population of Palestine, they rapidly became permanent as the prospects of return dwindled. By the end of 1949 an estimated 430,000 Palestinians were living in them. Another 250,000 had managed to find accommodation outside the camps but were registered for free food rations.[4]

The overwhelming majority of those who were forced to seek relief were peasants who had owned their own homes and land in Palestine or tenant farmers and sharecroppers who had tilled plots in or near their native villages. Unlike those who had experienced urban life, who had received an education or who had business contacts abroad, they had been unable to transfer their possessions or to find new jobs in their places of refuge. Deprived of the land and consequently of their sources of livelihood, they were reduced to almost total dependency. Their skills were of little or no use in societies where arable land was scarce and manual labour in abundant supply. Moreover, their social ties consisted almost entirely of links with their fellow villagers who had suffered a similar fate. While a few managed to enlist the aid of an Arab relative abroad or to find temporary day labour, the majority became dependent on relief for their physical survival.

Over the years the natural increase of the refugee population also affected the numbers registered for relief. By the end of March 1966 the figure stood at just over 1.3 million.[5] The occupation of the remainder of Palestine in June 1967 increased the list of those needing aid still more: in addition to those who were forced to flee for the second time in their lives, tens of thousands of others found themselves cut off from their lands and livelihoods and sought refuge in the neighbouring countries.[6] By 1972 the number of Palestinians registered for relief had risen to 1.5 million, or about half the total Palestinian population. Forty-two per cent of these, 640,000, were housed in refugee camps of one kind or another.[7] Three years later the outbreak of civil war in Lebanon added still more to the list. The fighting, which resulted in the wholesale destruction of the refugee camps of Tel Zaatar and the shanty town of Qarantina, combined with the continuous Israeli attacks on Palestinian camps in southern Lebanon, sent the numbers up to 1.8 million by 1979.[8] By the autumn of 1982 the figure was thought to be well over 2 million, as hundreds of thousands of Palestinians in Beirut and southern Lebanon lost their homes and livelihoods yet again as a result of the massive Israeli onslaught in June.[9] The dispersal of the peasantry and the sudden separation of a whole class of people from their source of livelihood created a new landless proletariat within Palestinian society. Penned up in camps and at the mercy of the local police and the relief organisations, their daily life became consumed by the sheer struggle to survive in the face of overwhelming odds. For many this meant finding employment wherever possible: in the fields of a local landlord during the harvest, in the streets selling food and other small wares or in the workshops and offices of the relief organisations set up in the camps. However the majority who did manage to find work remained outside the local economies of the host countries and subject to the vagaries of a labour market that was usually too small to provide anything but a temporary wage well below that needed to provide for a family.

While a new generation of Palestinians born in the camps was able eventually to obtain an education and to seek more permanent work in the oil states of the Gulf, most of the generation of peasants and sharecroppers that grew up in Palestine (Jeel Filistin) found little or no outlet for their skills and remained unemployed for most, or all, of their lives after leaving Palestine. As their sons left the camps in the 1960s and 1970s, the camps became simultaneously the focal point for armed resistance as well as the abiding refuge of the elderly, the women and the children.

This chapter looks at the fragmentation of the Palestinian peasantry as a class and at their subsequent tranformation in the diaspora. While some mention is made of those who remained in that portion of Palestine that became Israel in 1948, and of those living in the West Bank and Gaza who were not displaced, the chapter focuses primarily on those who sought refuge in the Arab portion of Palestine (the West Bank and Gaza) and in the neighbouring Arab countries.

The Subjugation of the Refugees, 1948-64

The Role of the United Nations

Although the United Nations in December 1948 had urged that 'refugees wishing to return to their homes and live at peace with their neighbours should be permitted to do so at the earliest practicable date, and that compensation should be paid for the property of those choosing not to return', the refusal of Israel to implement the resolution and the inability of the United Nations to enforce compliance with it left the refugees in a state of total upheaval and uncertainty.[10] A year later the United Nations Economic Survey Mission, which had been despatched to the area by the General Assembly to assess the situation, recommended that in view of the continuing political stalemate and the lack of repatriation member states of the United Nations should continue their voluntary contributions to provide emergency relief until 1 April 1950. It recommended further that after that date a special agency should be set up to begin a public works programme and to direct the relief.[11] The Mission felt, as the UN Secretary-General later explained, that such a proposed public works programme in Jordan, Arab Palestine, Lebanon and Syria, providing temporary employment for the refugees by mobilising a great body of manpower, at that time idle, would halt the demoralising effect of a dole, increase the practical alternatives available to the refugees and would also improve the productivity of the countries where the refugees were residing.[12]

The General Assembly accepted the recommendations in December 1949 and ordered the United Nations Relief and Works Agency (UNRWA) to be set up as of 1 May 1950.[13]

Funding was to be provided through voluntary contributions from governments, and the relief was to be channelled into projects approved by the host governments. The Agency's long-term aim, as the Secretary-General later commented, was 'to transfer refugees from relief to wage-paying work that will contribute to the economy of the countries which participate in the programme'.[14] Political questions, whether concerning a solution to the conflict or matters of repatriation, resettlement and compensation, were specifically left outside the scope of UNRWA's tasks and delegated to the United Nations Conciliation Commission for Palestine (UNCCP), a body which had been set up in December 1948 to enforce compliance with UN resolutions.[15]

The recommendations of the Mission and the way in which UNRWA was set up marked a crucial turning point in the future of the refugees. In effect they were to become the wards of international charity and a pool of cheap labour for the Arab countries. Despite the General Assembly's specific call for repatriation and resettlement of the refugees in their own country, UNRWA became an agency whose primary aim was to ensure that they were assimilated in the neighbouring Arab countries rather than returned to their homes in Israeli-occupied territory. Although the Arab League states, except for Jordan, protested at the manner in which UNRWA's tasks had been defined and insisted instead that the need for 'repatriation, resettlement and compensation', rather than 're-integration' – as UNRWA defined its role – should be given priority, their pleas were to no avail.[16] The Conciliation Commission, unable to reach agreement with Israel on repatriation, was reduced to a talking shop and from 1950 onwards contented itself with drawing up lists of Arab property in Israel calling, in vain, for the Israelis to accept resettlement and/or compensation of the refugees.[17]

In the eyes of the refugees, the Mission's recommendations and the establishment of UNRWA amounted to a total betrayal of their rights and of their identity as a separate people. The injury was felt all the more acutely since it was the United Nations – then dominated by the wartime allies of the United States, Britain, France and the Soviet Union – which had ordered the partition of Palestine in the first place and which had sat idly by while the Israelis proceeded to conquer lands allocated by the UN to a future Arab state.

Throughout the area the refugees took to the streets to protest against the plan to assimilate them into the neighbouring countries and to demand the right to continue the fight against partition and against the creation of a Zionist state in Palestine.[18] By 1952 several clandestine groups had formed which sought to channel refugee discontent into concrete political and military action aimed at regaining their homeland. One of these, the Organisation to Oppose the Peace with Israel, began distributing its own newspaper, *Al-Thar* (*Vengeance*), in the camps while at the same time providing basic medical, educational and welfare services. Sponsored by the Beirut-based Arab Nationalist Movement, its leaders included a number of refugee doctors and medical students, notably George Habash, Wadih Haddad and Ahmad Yamani, all of whom later helped to set up the Popular Front for the Liberation of Palestine.[19]

In Cairo groups of refugee students from Gaza formed the General Union of Palestinian Students in Egypt – the first Palestinian institution to be established since the 1948 defeat. Some of its members, like Yasser Arafat, had fought alongside the Mufti's forces in the defence of Palestine in 1948. Others, like Salah Khalaf (Abou Iyad) and Muhammad Najjar (Abu Youssef) who were to help Arafat set up Fatah in the late 1950s, joined the organisation in Cairo. Throughout the early and mid-1950s, especially in the aftermath of the Israeli raid on Gaza in February 1955 and the Suez invasion in 1956, it played a major role in recruiting displaced peasants, workers and intellectuals to the Palestinian cause and in providing military training for its recruits.[20]

Still other groups, like those centred around the National Front (al-Jabhah al-Wataniyyah) and the Communist Party of Jordan, concentrated on organising Palestinian workers and on providing political education amongst the refugee population.[21] Both the Muslim Brethren and the Islamic Liberation Party (Hizb al-Tahrir al-Islami) were also active in the refugee camps, where they helped to organise mass demonstrations against the re-settlement projects and against Israel.[22]

Although these initial attempts at resistance failed to achieve the repatriation of the refugees, they did succeed in preventing UNRWA from carrying out several important development projects which the refugees feared would have led to the permanent absorption of the Palestinians in the neighbouring countries.[23] Israel's reluctance to allow the utilisation of the Yarmouk and Jordan river basins for the development of large-scale irrigation projects in Jordan and Syria and the failure of UNRWA's sponsors to honour all their financial pledges also helped to reduce UNRWA's scope of operations severely.[24] By the late 1950s, UNRWA was forced to give up its longer-term plans and to limit its activities primarily to the provision of food rations and basic health and educational services. Its ability to carry out these tasks depended upon two main factors: (1) the receipt of adequate funds from the donor governments and (2) the co-operation of the host Arab governments.

Although UNRWA's budget allowed for considerable expenditure on works projects during its early years of existence, donor governments proved reluctant to provide more funds once the Palestinians' resistance to any long-term programme of re-integration in the neighbouring countries became evident. By 1966 UNRWA's expenditure on basic rations (including supplementary feeding, hardship assistance and other related costs) amounted to only $13.24 a year for each refugee registered with the organisation. This made it impossible to add meat, fruits or vegetables to the basic rations, which consisted of flour, sugar, rice, pulses and oil amounting to only about 1,500 calories a day. Expenditure on medical and health services amounted to only $3.79 a year for each refugee, while education received only $11.87 a year. In other words, UNRWA's total expenditure on relief for each refugee amounted on average to less than $30 a year.[25] After 1967 even these small amounts were reduced as the Agency's budget failed to keep pace with the enlarged list of Palestinian refugees needing aid.

It is not surprising then that UNRWA's Commissioner-General in 1966 was moved to express his sympathy for the refugees. He said in his annual report for the year:

> During the long period of their dependence on international charity their life has been one of hardship and privation. The relief accorded by UNRWA, though indispensible, has been no more than a bare minimum ... The rations are meagre and unvarying and would hardly sustain a person who depended solely on them for any long period.[26]

Aside from the lack of all but the most basic services, the Palestinian peasantry which had been forced to flee also encountered living conditions in the neighbouring countries and in the camps which were deplorable and long lasting. By 1966 the Secretary-General was moved to comment that 'It is clear that a large part of the refugee community is still living today in dire poverty, often under pathetic and in some cases appalling conditions.' Some families, he pointed out,

> still live in dwellings which are unfit for human habitation: some in dark cellars, others in crumbling tenements, others in grossly over-crowded barracks and shacks ... Nearly all the UNRWA camps are extremely overcrowded with five or more persons living in one small room. They lack adequate roads and pathways and many camps are deep in mud in winter and dust in summer.

Water supplies, he added, were inadequate, especially in the summer months, and there were rarely any sewers or stormwater drainage systems.[27] Yet no matter how difficult their living conditions and physical surroundings were, the refugees' bitterest complaints were reserved for the Arab governments in whose countries they lived and whom they held responsible for their plight and for their inability to take their fate in their own hands. This was particularly true in Lebanon and Jordan, but neither Egypt, which administered the Gaza Strip, nor Syria escaped criticism even after more progressive regimes came to power in the 1950s.

The Attitude of the Arab Host Governments

The Palestinian refugee's attitude towards his hosts has been eloquently summed up by Fawaz Turki, a Palestinian writer who was forced to flee from his home in Haifa in 1948 when he was only a small child:

> As I grew up my bogeyman was not the Jew, nor was he the Zionist, nor was he ... the imperialist or the Western supporters and protectors of the state of Israel, but he was the Arab. The Arab in the street who asked if you'd ever heard the one about the Palestinian who ... The Arab at the Aliens Section who wanted you to wait obsequiously for your work permit, the Arab at the police station who felt he possessed a *carte blanche* to mistreat you, the Arab who rejected you and, most crucially, took away from you your sense of hope and sense of direction. He was the bogeyman you saw every morning and every night and every new year of every decade tormenting you, reducing you, dehumanising you, and confirming your servitude.

While the older generation of exiles vividly remembered what they had lost and tended to blame both Israel and Britain for the loss of their homeland, those who grew to maturity in the camps and who were unable to find new homes and jobs in the diaspora took little comfort in the fact that they had escaped Israeli occupation. As Turki concludes:

> To the Palestinian, the young Palestinian, living and growing up in Arab society, the Israeli was the enemy in the mathematical matrix; we never saw him, lived under his yoke, or, for many of us, remembered him. Living in a refugee camp and growing hungry, we felt that [while] the causes of our problem were abstract, the causes of its perpetuation were real.[28]

The attitude of the Arab host governments was conditioned by their fear that the Palestinians would drag their countries into another war with Israel and by their concern that the embittered refugees could threaten their own legitimacy at home. Nowhere was this more consistently true than in Jordan, which, unlike the other Arab countries, had welcomed the partition plan and successfully waged a military and diplomatic campaign against the creation of a separate Palestinian state in those parts of the country not occupied by Israel. Under the terms of the armistice agreement signed with Israel at Rhodes in April 1949, the government of Jordan agreed that 'no element of [its] land, sea or air, military or para-military forces . . . including non-regular forces, shall commit any warlike or hostile act against the military or para-military forces of the other Party or against civilians in territory under the control of that Party'.[29] This clause committed the Jordanian government to ensuring that all those who lived within its borders — Palestinians as well as Jordanians — observed the ceasefire and respected the new international boundary. Yet, as we have seen, the refugees, particularly in the first years following the defeat, were the ones most desperate to return. One knowledgeable observer has written that the refugees, particularly from the border villages,

> either . . . slipped across the border to snatch, say, a sack of oranges or some small piece of movable property from the fields they had formerly owned; or else they risked their lives ploughing and sowing overnight the lands the Israelis were using as buffer territory. The first of these hazards became known as 'infiltration', the second as 'illegal cultivation', and together with the innocent strayings of

divided families trying to find each other and the criminal activities of smugglers of both countries who were profiting from Israel's readiness to pay almost any price for meat and rice from Jordan, they created an acute frontier problem . . . Scavenging [was] carried out, often as not, by mothers of starving families.[30]

The response of the Israeli troops, who had orders to 'shoot on sight' any such infiltrators soon led to the loss of many fathers, sons, mothers and daughters who were killed, often as not, in their own olive groves or villages.[31] Soon the refugees crossed the border armed. There they joined those fighters who had remained behind the lines and who continued to engage in sporadic resistance against the Israeli occupying forces.[32] When Palestinians loyal to the Mufti and others, angered by the massive Israeli attack on the border village of Qibya in October 1953, began to engage in organised resistance, the Arab Legion, under orders from its British commander John Glubb, also began to fire on Palestinians who crossed the border. Legislation was introduced which made a mere crossing of the line punishable by six months' imprisonment. According to David Hirst, 'At one time at least half the prisoners in the West Bank were serving terms for this offence.'[33]

For the refugees, the inability to regain any of their household possessions and agricultural produce was bad enough; even worse was the clear determination of the government to prevent them, at all costs, from making any serious attempt to oppose the occupation of their homeland. What was intolerable above all was to be unable to defend oneself and one's family from Israeli reprisal raids across the border into Arab territory.

Gradually, as the resistance within Jordan was disarmed and as the refugees, together with Jordanian villagers affected by the reprisal raids, began to vent their outrage on the streets of the major cities, the regime began to clamp down totally on all forms of political opposition as well. For King Hussein, such repression apparently seemed vital to his own personal survival as well as to that of his kingdom. It could not have been far from his mind throughout the decades after his accession to the throne that his own grandfather had been shot down in front of his eyes by an embittered Palestinian refugee. Palestinians who sought a way out of the camps, into more amenable jobs in the cities or into educational institutions where they might hope to improve their own lot, found themselves forced to give up all political activity and to acquiesce in the innumerable restrictions which the regime imposed on them.[34]

In the Lebanon the restrictions were also harsh. Again it was the dispersed peasantry that was the most affected. All were disarmed and prevented from crossing the border to regain their household goods and tools or to harvest their grain.[35] At one point a tax of LL25 was imposed on each adult who sought to enter the country.[36] Such a measure not only discriminated against the poorer Palestinians who sought refuge in Lebanon but also made it difficult for broken families to be reunited with their kin. Palestinian Christians were also separated from their Muslim compatriots, a move that most Palestinians found incomprehensible.[37] Later, Palestinians who had settled in the southern part of the country to be near their villages across the border in Galilee were moved into camps further north, near Tripoli and Beirut, as well as in the Beqaa Valley of east central Lebanon.[38] Movement from one camp to another, or from the camp to the city, was forbidden without express permission from the government authorities; curfews and police searches became commonplace.[39]

Aside from their fear that Palestinian anger might force Lebanon into another war with Israel, the Lebanese government was also concerned that the Palestinians, who were largely Sunni Muslims, would upset the delicate internal balance between the various religious sects in the country which guaranteed the Maronite Christians dominance of the country's ruling institutions and of its economy. Contact between the refugees and the impoverished Shiʻa Muslims of southern Lebanon was also seen as dangerous: the Lebanese authorities feared that they might join the uprooted Palestinians in pressing for fundamental political change in Lebanon itself.[40]

In the Gaza Strip the refusal of the Egyptian government, both under King Farouk and in the early days of Nasser's regime, to allow the refugees to travel outside the Gaza Strip into Egypt was compounded by the government's refusal to allow them to take up arms to counter Israeli raids into the Strip. By the middle of 1956 these attacks had left more than 134 people dead and 81 wounded. Some 40 people, most of them Palestinian refugees or Bedouin from Gaza and Sinai, had been taken prisoner by the Israelis during the period up to mid-1956.[41] Despite riots, demonstrations and protests by the refugees, the Strip was treated as occupied territory under military rule and the Military Governor had extensive powers to detain persons suspected of crossing the border, of carrying arms or of engaging in proscribed political activities.[42] Freedom of association and movement within the area was severely curtailed for security reasons and travel outside the area was restricted to those few who carried passports issued by other Arab governments.[43]

Only after a particularly brutal Israeli attack on Gaza in February 1955, which was followed by three days of rioting throughout the Strip and attacks by stone-throwing youths on Egyptian army posts, did Nasser allow some hand-picked Palestinians to bear arms and to begin a series of counter-raids on Israeli territory.[44] However the armed units remained totally under Egypt's control and under the command of the Egyptian army. While they were allowed to do the work of the Egyptian army in opposing Israel's incursions and to participate in the defence of Cairo and the Suez Canal during the combined Israeli-French and British invasion in October 1956, they were not allowed to organise their compatriots in the camps or to provide them with military training. For Yasser Arafat and other future leaders of Fatah, Nasser's reluctance to allow such moves was a major factor in leading them to conclude that only by setting up their own military and political organisation could Palestinians hope to achieve their liberation.

Conditions were better in Syria, where the government set up its own organisation, the Palestine Arab Refugee Institution (PARI), to provide food, clothing and housing to the refugees. Camps run by PARI were fitted with better educational, social and health services than those available in the UNRWA camps and special cash subsidies were granted to those refugees most in need. Housing grants for each family were also provided, with the result that the camps in Syria, especially those in Yarmouk, near Damascus, and in Latakia, more closely resembled suburban neighbourhoods than impoverished shanty towns, as is still the case in parts of Lebanon and Jordan.[45] However the Palestinians, as in other Arab countries, were forbidden to carry arms until the mid-1960s and, for most of the period since 1948, have been forbidden to form political parties or associations without the permission of the government.[46]

The experiences of the Palestinian peasantry in the diaspora were also conditioned by the attitude of the general public towards the refugees. Unlike the governments, whose aid was often more rhetorical than substantive, the citizens of the surrounding Arab countries were often the first to come to the rescue of the refugees by providing food and shelter in the first critical weeks of the dispersion.[47] However as the exodus increased and the trickle became a flood, opinion rapidly changed. In part this reflected the sheer magnitude of the dispersal, which amounted to a massive transfer of population to countries already affected by years of economic stagnation and neglect under foreign rule. The indigenous residents of a country like Syria, which took in relatively small numbers of refugees compared to Palestine's other neighbours, and which had large amounts of uncultivated land available, were less likely to feel that their own livelihoods were threatened than was the case in Jordan, where the refugees on relief (including those in the West Bank) constituted almost half the total population, and in Lebanon where, even though the refugees made up only 10 to 12 per cent of the total inhabitants, they were regarded with suspicion by a large segment of the Christian population.

The attitudes of the Arab host population to the refugees were also conditioned both by the disparity between their own societies and customs and those which prevailed in Palestine during the Mandate and by the heightened political consciousness which the refugees brought to bear on developments in the neighbouring countries. In Syria, where the customs were similar and where historical and economic ties with Palestine had existed over a long period, the Palestinians did not find it difficult to adapt to the prevailing cultural patterns, although their own sense of defeat and of alienation from their homeland made adjustment more difficult than it might otherwise have been. In Jordan the problems were immense. Unlike the Palestinians, the indigenous citizens of the country were mainly Bedouin, organised along tribal lines, whose customs and economic way of life still reflected their nomadic, or semi-nomadic, origins. Centuries of hostility between the Bedouin and the settled peasantry on both sides of the Jordan Valley were not easily overcome, and the latent hostility between the two groups became more overt as the Palestinian refugees began to oppose the monarchy and its close alliance with British interests.[48]

In all the neighbouring countries, and to a lesser extent in the West Bank as well, the traditional antipathy between the urban residents (*madaniyyin*) and the peasantry (*fellahin*) was exacerbated by the conditions of flight and the segregation of the peasantry from both their compatriots who had managed to find jobs and homes in the cities of Beirut, Damascus and Amman and from their Arab kin who had little regard for those who tilled the soil.[49] The conditions which the peasantry experienced in the refugee camps in turn reinforced their sense of class solidarity and the traditional familial and village ties which were seen as one of the few elements of continuity and identity in a time of almost total social disintegration and massive insecurity.[50]

During the long years of exile the peasant refugees of Palestine were to undergo changes in their way of life that few could have envisaged. Many were to find themselves on the move again as the Israelis advanced

Table 6.1: Palestinian Refugees Registered for Relief: Geographical Distribution, 1950-79 (thousands)

	1950[a]	1966[b]	1972[c]	1979[d]
Palestine:				
Israel (pre-1967 borders)[e]	50	–	–	–
Gaza	201	304	325	363
West Bank	362 ⎫		278	318
	⎬ 702			
Jordan (East Bank)	138 ⎭		552	700
Lebanon	129	164	184	219
Syria	82	139	168	204
Total	962	1,309	1,507	1,804

Notes: a. Figures drawn from United Nations Department of Economic Affairs, *Review of Economic Conditions in the Middle East, 1951-2*, UN Document E/2343/Add. 1, ST/ECA/19/Add.1 (New York, March 1953), except for those given for the East and West banks, which are taken from Jamil Hilal, *The West Bank: Economic and Social Structure 1948 to 1974* (Beirut, 1975) (in Arabic), p. 79, and which are for 1951.

     b. UNRWA, *Registration Statistical Bulletin for the First Quarter 1966*, no. 1/66, cited in Harry N. Howard, 'UNRWA, the Arab Host Countries and the Arab Refugees', *Middle East Forum*, vol. 42, no. 3 (1966), p. 34.

     c. *Report of the Commissioner-General of UNRWA*, 1 July 1971 to 30 June 1972, p. 76, cited in E. Hagopian and A.B. Zahlan, 'Palestine's Arab Population: The Demography of the Palestinians', *Journal of Palestine Studies*, vol. 3, no. 4 (Summer 1974), pp. 32-73.

     d. Central Bureau of Statistics, Palestine National Fund, *Palestinian Statistical Abstract* (Damascus, 1980), p. 361.

     e. After 1950 no figures on the number of Palestinian refugees – as opposed to those who remained in their homes – in Israel are available.

still further into Arab territory and as their presence became an anathema to one or other of the local Arab regimes. Throughout it all the peasantry held steadfastly to their goal of return and to their collective identity as a people and as a nation. While the older generation instilled in their children the same love of the land they themselves had absorbed in their homeland and sacrificed their own hopes of a better future to ensure that their families survived the physical oppression of exile, the younger generation turned its attention to acquiring the skills and material resources they needed to escape their surroundings and to build a movement capable of liberating their homeland.

Class Transformation of the Peasantry

The history of the displaced peasantry in the diaspora since 1948 is largely unknown and may remain so for a long time to come. The conditions of exile and the need to concentrate resources on basic needs have prevented many Palestinians from undertaking study in this area. Outsiders have shown little interest and those few statistics which are available, usually from UNRWA or the Israelis (after 1967), tend to be either incomplete or highly selective. The looting and destruction of Palestinian archives during the Israeli occupation of Beirut in 1982 has also made research extremely difficult. However a crude calculation, based on the little demographic information that is available, indicates that the percentage of those registered for relief had fallen from about three-quarters of the total population in 1949 to less than half thirty years later.

Table 6.2: Palestinians Registered for Relief as a Percentage of the Total Palestinian Population, 1949-79[a]

Year	Number Registered for Relief	Total Population	Per Cent
1949	1,000,000	1,304,000	76.7
1979	1,804,000	4,390,000	41.1

Note: a. The percentages are rough estimates only. The percentage for 1949 is actually based on a total population figure drawn from the 1947 figure as given in Janet Abu Lughod, 'The Demographic Transformation of Palestine' in Ibrahim Abu Lughod (ed.), *The Transformation of Palestine* (Evanston, 1971), p. 155. (No population figure for 1949 is available.) The percentage for 1979 is based on a total population figure provided by the Palestine Liberation Organisation in the *Palestinian Statistical Abstract* for 1980, p. 28. Figures on the numbers of refugees registered for relief are taken from the relevant UNRWA annual reports.

The figures suggest that despite the huge increase in the total population between 1949 and 1979 and in the number needing relief, a substantial share of the displaced peasantry managed to become self-supporting within the thirty-year period. The evidence available suggests that they accomplished this by finding work in one of three main areas: (1) in agriculture, primarily as sharecroppers, tenants and labourers; (2) in the services sector, mainly the building trades; and (3) in industry, workshops and other skilled crafts. Smaller numbers of refugees on relief managed to set up small shops and businesses of their own either in the camps or in the shanty towns and urban quarters of the larger cities where Palestinians lived, while others found work as salaried employees of the United Nations and other aid agencies as well as with the host governments.

The ability to find work sufficiently well paid to leave the camps or to forgo rations was primarily limited to able-bodied young men, especially those who had obtained either vocational or professional training during their years in the diaspora. However the willingness of the younger men to provide an education for their sisters and brothers and to take on the responsibility of providing not only for their own immediate families but also for a host of in-laws, brothers, sisters and cousins enabled many more to leave the camps over the years and to escape the humiliation of total dependence on UNRWA. The eagerness of the women to sell their dowries and to take in home work such as sewing and laundry added still further to family resources and often supplied the vital extra funds needed to find accommodation in the city or to provide an education for one or more of the children.

Agricultural Labour

Although the peasantry made up the overwhelming share of those who were forced to seek relief after 1948, the percentage of the population that still worked in agriculture thirty years later had fallen considerably. Only a few rough estimates and sample surveys are available, but the figures from these show that the percentage working in this sector ranges from a low 7.9 per cent of the active Palestinian labour force in Syria to about 28 per cent in the West Bank.[51] However since the figures for both the Gaza Strip and the West Bank include those Palestinians who retained their lands and tenancies and who were not forced to flee in 1948, the actual percentage of Palestinian refugees working in agriculture is probably even lower than these figures indicate.

Furthermore, while the majority of the peasants owned or had access to some land prior to 1948, very few of those who were forced to flee have been able to acquire permanent holdings of any kind since then. The ban on the purchase of arable land which affected Palestinian refugees in Syria, Lebanon, Egypt and other parts of the Arab world meant that only those who remained in the West Bank and Gaza Strip or those who obtained citizenship in Jordan could legally purchase plots of their own. However the huge rise in land prices in the West Bank, the scarcity of land in the Gaza Strip and the closure of Palestinian banks and credit institutions after 1948 placed this option beyond the reach of almost all but the wealthier landowners and

Table 6.3: Palestinian Labour Force, Percentage of Workers in Agriculture

Country or Area	Economically Active Population	Agricultural Sector[a]	Per Cent in Agriculture
Syria[b]	43,593	3,462	7.9
Jordan	n.a.	n.a.	n.a.
Lebanon[c]	19,020	4,020	21.1
Gaza Strip[d]	80,800	17,500	21.7
West Bank[e]	132,800	36,700	27.6

n.a. − not available.

Notes: a. Including forestry, hunting and fishing; b. 1979 estimate; c. based on survey of five camps only, 1971; d. 1978; e. 1978. Not all the data are comparable between countries; for example, the Syrian figures on the economically active portion of the Palestinian population in the country include all those over 10 years of age while those for the West Bank begin at the age of 14.

Source: *Palestinian Statistical Abstract 1980*, pp. 58, 63, 100, 105, 177 and 222.

merchants. Only in the East Bank of Jordan were some refugee families able to acquire plots of their own, usually through government aid funds or with the help of a wealthier relative. Two tribes of Palestinian Bedouin, the Al-Magharbah and the Bashatwah, who had fled their lands on the West Bank south of the Sea of Galilee, were given land in 1956 and sufficient sheep, camels and fodder to provide a living for 289 families. Cash grants from UNRWA enabled them to purchase farming implements and the government of Jordan provided irrigation canals using water from the Yarmouk river. By the end of the first year of operation the families were self-sufficient in food and able to produce a small surplus of wheat for sale on local markets. However the outbreak of hostilities in 1967 devastated their crops, canals and orchards. Since then the diversion of the waters of the Yarmouk by Israel has reduced the amount of crops that can be cultivated and the land now produces only about a quarter of what it did before 1967. Most of the families have now taken up residence in nearby towns; some have found work outside the agricultural sector, but a few have had to apply for relief once again.[52]

Elsewhere in Jordan Palestinian peasants from the Hebron area who had traditionally traded with the tribes of Al-Karak in the East Bank managed to obtain some land near the town after 1948, usually by signing *murabi'* contracts which guaranteed them food for subsistence and the protection of the Bedouin in return for their labour. Gradually they were able to improve these contracts and to increase their share of the harvest. Some eventually were able to purchase plots of their own, partly with the help of other Palestinians from Gaza who had built up the town's market district after 1948.[53] In the same area Bedouin from the Negev tribe of the Azazmah have been able to maintain their traditional summer pasture lands on the East Bank and raise sheep and goats. They obtain additional income by selling produce from their herds in local markets and by continuing to engage in trade with their Bedouin kin on both sides of the border, thereby overcoming some of the obstacles that the loss of their land in the West Bank entailed.[54]

Grants from UNRWA and other funds made available by the government of Jordan in the 1950s enabled some refugees to set up small farming projects on re-claimed land elsewhere in the Jordan Valley.[55] One of the most successful series of projects took place at Karamah, a settlement located only four miles east of the ceasefire lines. Originally nothing more than a tent encampment of refugees, by 1967 it had become a major centre for the production of early vegetables which were exported to Jerusalem, Amman, Lebanon, Syria and the Gulf states. More than one-third of the chickens consumed in Jordan each year came from Palestinian farms at Karamah. Water and electricity services were organised by the refugees themselves and the tents soon gave way to houses built of dried mud. At the time of the 1967 war it housed some 25,000 inhabitants and two UNRWA training centres. However once again Israeli reprisals, combined with the influx of another 25,000 refugees during and immediately after the war, strained resources. Cultivation under almost constant shelling was difficult and in March 1968, when the Israelis launched a massive reprisal raid — which for the first time led to their retreat in the face of heavy guerrilla resistance — the town and its farms were left devastated and vacated. Many of its former inhabitants were forced to migrate to find work in Amman or in other Jordanian cities and towns.[56]

Throughout the East Bank the lack of legalised shareholding arrangements and the absence of a pattern of communal distribution of land along the lines of the *musha'* system which operated in Mandate Palestine served to reduce the economic power of those refugees who did obtain access to land. Unable to ensure that land rights were granted in accordance with those they had formerly enjoyed, they were open to extreme exploitation at the hands of the more unscrupulous landowners. Only in the 1970s, when the government passed a series of measures giving small farmers and tenants greater security of tenure, did the position of the Palestinian peasants improve significantly. The huge emigration of skilled workers to the Gulf in the mid-1970s, which led to a severe shortage of labour in the agricultural sector of the East Bank, also helped to raise wages and to improve conditions for those tenants and sharecroppers who remained.[57]

As in the East Bank, the displaced peasantry in the West Bank also faced considerable obstacles in obtaining access to land and the situation was aggravated by Israel's invasion in 1967. Five years later Israel had taken over 1.5 million *dunums* of land in the territory, or about 27.3 per cent of the total land area. Of the 850 million cubic metres of water available each year, only about 100 to 120 million cubic metres were available to the Palestinian population. The remainder was piped to Israel, used by the Jewish settlements or kept as a reserve. Palestinian farmers, both the indigenous holders and the refugee tenants and sharecroppers, were prevented from drilling wells; many of those which already existed dried up while in others the water levels fell too low to provide enough for cultivation.[58]

Nevertheless the huge emigration of workers from the West Bank to Europe and the Gulf states after 1967, as in the East Bank, led to a greater demand for agricultural labour, particularly at harvest time. Women and children were employed by the wealthier Palestinian landlords to work on a seasonal basis in the citrus, almond and olive groves as well as in the harvesting of vegetables and fruits.[59] Others found similar work in the Jewish settlements and, to a certain extent, in Israel as well.

At the same time the spread of irrigation and of new agricultural technology, the development of greenhouse farming and the use of more advanced marketing systems, particularly for export to the Gulf states, created a new demand for sharecroppers willing to work land that had formerly been un- or undercultivated. Refugee peasants who had obtained sharecropping contracts and who had funds either from a member of the family working abroad or from wealthier relatives could benefit from the introduction of commercial methods to the extent that they were able to finance their share of the capital inputs. However this was the exception rather than the rule. Most of the refugee peasants who had obtained access to the land as sharecroppers in the 1950s and 1960s were unable to meet the new financial requirements and found themselves reduced to simple croppers, tenants or wage labourers.[60] While their access to land, however small, enabled them to reduce their dependence on UN food rations, the inability to obtain all their basic needs from the land often meant that they were able to leave the camps permanently only if they could find additional work as labourers, porters, nightwatchmen and the like in the cities, or if their income could be supplemented by remittances sent by another member of the family working abroad.[61]

Elsewhere in the West Bank the spread of the towns and increased urbanisation in the 1970s fuelled speculation in real estate on the outskirts of the populated areas and led to the emergence of a new stratum of land speculators and rentiers among the indigenous peasantry. These in turn leased land to refugees from the camps on short-term contracts. One study, conducted by the Palestinian sociologist Salim Tamari, showed that this pattern was particularly pronounced in the village of Ballata, which is located just outside Nablus near a large refugee camp. However Tamari found that 'such a situation [is] relevant to a substantial area in the region', i.e. to the rural periphery of the big towns which had access to the labour of the refugee peasantry.[62]

In Gaza the lack of available land and the high proportion of refugees compared to the indigenous population made it virtually impossible for the refugees to obtain landholdings of their own. However the local citrus industry provided employment for some in the 1950s and 1960s, primarily in packaging and sorting. After 1967 others, primarily women and children, were employed as agricultural labourers in the Jewish settlements which were established in the area and in Sinai as well as in Israel itself. Most worked in the almond and citrus groves, in the vegetable and flower fields or in the greenhouse complexes established in the 1970s. While the wages were extremely low and often entailed travelling long distances, the extra cash income helped to supplement the meagre UN rations and to provide funds for education and training. Some workers in Gaza, who were forced by the Israelis to move into new housing projects set up in the late 1960s and early 1970s had to work even longer hours to pay the electricity and water rates charged by the municipality of Gaza.[63]

In Lebanon the refugees in the camps were forbidden to own land and the nature of the existing land tenure system, which differed considerably from that of Mandate Palestine, made it almost impossible to obtain a tenancy or shareholding. However some refugees could obtain seasonal work in the citrus and banana groves along the coast, in the vegetable and wheat fields of the eastern Beqaa Valley and in the orchards and tobacco-growing areas of southern Lebanon. Families often saved their meagre earnings for years and were eventually able to open workshops, small grocery stores and/or garages in or near the camps.[64] Others managed to send a child to school or to profit from a younger son's success.

One camp dweller from Nahr al-Barid, north of Tripoli, told Rosemary Sayigh about the conditions which the workers faced in the early years of their exile:

> First I worked moving sacks of onions for £ Lebanese 0.25 [7 US cents] a day, though because I was a kid I didn't even get paid my salary. Then I worked in a sugar factory, walking seven or eight kilometres to work ... At first [my earnings] were just enough because people didn't want more than a mouthful of bread. If we ate meat once a year we thought it was great.[65]

Because of his age, this refugee, like so many others, had been unable to attain any education: he was too young in Palestine and too poor to pay the fees demanded once he had arrived in Lebanon. The lack of industrial work near his camp, together with his lack of skills, left him no alternative but to accept the appalling conditions, from which there was no escape:

> Agricultural work is seasonal, one month you work, the next you don't. There's more than one harvest, but there are also periods without any harvest. One day you work with the shovel, the next with the pruning knife. Changing jobs all the time, we had to work like donkeys to prove our worth to each new employer.[66]

For those in camps closer to the major cities the opportunities were greater. Sayigh describes the history of one man who managed to better his conditions after working as a child labourer in the citrus groves of southern Lebanon.

> Married at sixteen to a girl from his village he went, as custom prescribed, to pay his respects to her family in Bourj al-Barajnah (a camp located on the outskirts of Beirut which was virtually destroyed in the Israeli invasion of 1982). There his wife's relatives told him he could earn more in Beirut than in the south, even in agricultural labour. So he moved to Beirut, where he bought a hut of flattened petrol cans ...

> Conditions in the Beirut camps were no easier at the beginning than anywhere else, but they did have the great advantage of being nearer to the centre of things. Beirut was the location of UNRWA's headquarters, employing some 2,000 Palestinians. It had large offices

and banks, three universities, and numerous small private training establishments. Above all it was a place for personal contacts, all important in the struggle to survive.

This refugee, Sayigh continues, found work in agriculture,

> then got a job in UNRWA at £ Lebanese 50 [$17] a month, serving coffee in the canteen ... He started attending English classes. He was promoted to clerk at £ Lebanese 150 a month, then to the switchboard at £ Lebanese 350 a month.[67]

In addition to providing for himself and his young wife, he was able, after his promotion, to bring his parents, brothers and sisters from the south to join him in Beirut.

Another example is provided by Sayigh from Bourj al-Barajnah camp, this time concerning a young woman who married an educated man at the age of fifteen in 1953. Although her husband, like everyone else at the time 'worked with the hoe', he eventually managed to obtain a job as a nightwatchman in a bank, earning LL50 ($17) a month. She describes what happened next:

> As soon as he got employed with the bank we bought a cow. It gave 30 kilos of milk a day. It ate for £ Lebanese 3, so we made £ Lebanese 7. We sold a lot of milk and we bought another cow ... I used to have to bring them water from the tank, I'd carry one jar on my head, one under my arm. I was six months pregnant.

After one of the cows died, they sold the other. Then her husband bought her a sewing machine.

> I learnt to embroider and take the work to a shop. I'd make £ Lebanese 20 to 25 a day ... My younger brother and sister used to work there. They'd bring me the pieces, about one dozen a day, and I'd do the machine work on them. I'd work from 8 a.m. until midnight.[68]

By 1971 the number of Palestinians working in agriculture had declined, as we have seen, to an estimated 21 per cent of the Palestinian labour force in Lebanon. A sample of the population conducted by Samir Ayoub that year also showed that some 74 per cent were employed in services, and 9 per cent in industry.[69] In other words, while many Palestinians from the camps in Lebanon had become self-supporting and had escaped the poverty of agricultural labour, they had achieved this only by becoming wage labourers in other sectors of the economy. Whereas almost three-quarters of the grandfathers of the Palestinians surveyed in the sample had been self-employed – mainly as peasants, small traders and craftsmen – 79 per cent of their grandchildren in exile in Lebanon were employed by others.[70]

By the mid-1970s even these gains were being eroded. The civil war in the Lebanon, which particularly affected the camps around Beirut, and the invasion of Israeli forces in 1978 disrupted the economic and social life the population had built for themselves either in the camps or in the shanty towns and urban quarters of the larger cities. In 1982, when the Israelis occupied almost all of Lebanon south of Beirut, the camps of 'Ain al-Hilwah, Rashidiyyah and Bourj al-Shemali were almost totally destroyed. Others in Beirut, such as Bourj al-Barajnah, Sabra and Chatilla, were heavily shelled and their populations either killed brutally or forced to evacuate. Damour, south of Beirut, was razed to the ground; its inhabitants, many of whom had fled to the town after the massacre of Tel Zaatar camp in 1976, were forced to move yet again. With some 300,000 homeless and more than 1,500 dead and injured, the Palestinians – who made up half the population of southern Lebanon – found themselves in a situation very similar to the one they had experienced in 1948.[71] Despite three decades of struggle their physical survival, jobs and homes remained precarious indeed.

Compared to their compatriots in Lebanon, the West Bank, Gaza and Jordan, the peasants from Palestine who settled in Syria have experienced much less hardship. Here again, however, they have been prevented from re-establishing their economic way of life by the government's refusal to allow them to buy land or to set up small farms on land leased from others. By 1979 less than 8 per cent were working in the agricultural sector even though the majority of the refugees in the country had worked on the land before their exile. Jobs in the sector were reserved for the indigenous population, almost half of whom were working on the land in one form or another.[72] The majority of the Palestinian refugees who eventually became self-supporting found work in construction and in the building trades, in the services sector or by emigrating to other parts of the Arab world (see below).[73]

The Building Trades and Industry

For the refugees on relief the only other major source of work in the early years of their exile aside from labour in the agricultural sector was that which was provided in the workshops of UNRWA itself. The Agency's huge need for household goods and basic tools of all kinds, coupled with the revenue it received from the United States, Britain and other Western governments made it possible to provide some form of paid employment for hundreds of refugees living in the camps. UNRWA opened workshops for craftsmen in the host countries and supplied the raw materials as well as power, water and fuel. The products produced in the shops were used almost exclusively by the Agency to assist relief work. Carpenters were employed to produce furniture for UNRWA offices and schools. Shoemakers, tailors and dressmakers produced clothing for distribution to the refugees. Tinsmiths supplied utensils and cooking pots; other workers made wheelbarrows, rubber baskets (from old tyres), rush matting, soap and bricks. Still other workmen were employed on new road-building projects to enable relief supplies to reach the more remote camps, to lay new water pipes and drains and to help in the construction of a number of schools, medical clinics and office buildings.[74] While such work often enabled a refugee family to supplement its meagre rations, employment with UNRWA also tied the refugee to the camps and made it difficult for him to leave without sacrificing his employment. Furthermore such projects, however useful in the beginning, were never sufficient to provide work for more than a few thousand camp inhabitants at most. Compared to the huge numbers needing work, UNRWA's efforts represented little more than a good intention that had almost no practical impact on the standard of living of the mass of displaced peasants.

The same holds true for UNRWA's individual grants programme established in 1954. Of the 714 projects approved by UNRWA before the funds for the scheme were stopped in 1957, only 176 were concerned with the establishment of new workshops and small industries. Although a handful of craftsmen benefited, most of the funds for these projects went to the wealthier refugees from the cities and towns of Palestine who had had prior experience in industry and trade and who also had some capital of their own.[75]

More useful were the vocational schools and training centres set up by UNRWA in the mid-1950s and later. The first was established at Kalandia camp near Jerusalem and provided facilities for the training of 600 boys and young men.[76] By the end of 1977 there were seven such centres in Jordan, the West Bank, Gaza, Syria and Lebanon with an annual attendance of more than 2,000.[77] Specialising in the building trades, textiles, electronics and light manufacturing, these schools enabled many young Palestinian workers, both men and women, to find work in the host countries or the Gulf states and to provide a better standard of living for their families.

Aside from UNRWA, the Palestinian's own aid organisation, SAMED, was also able to provide both jobs and training facilities for Palestinian workers after its formation in 1970 by the Palestine Liberation Organisation. Although it was originally established to provide work for the sons and daughters of Palestinian fighters killed in action and for disabled Palestinians, SAMED gradually began to expand its activities to help relieve the huge problem of unemployment among the refugees, particularly those living in the camps and shanty towns of the West Bank, Lebanon and Syria. By the mid-1970s the organisation had set up knitting mills and embroidery shops in six Lebanese camps and in another in Syria; woodworking and craft centres in the occupied territories; and several other workshops in Lebanon to produce furniture, clothing and artefacts.[78] Plans were also under way in the early 1980s to set up new light industries and agricultural projects in the occupied territories and to employ Palestinian workers to build new housing and schools in the West Bank and Gaza with aid provided through the Palestine National Fund, the PLO's 'Treasury'.[79]

Still other work was available in the workshops and clinics set up by the Palestinian Red Crescent Society, the PLO's equivalent of the Red Cross, in the 1970s. The workshops produced chairs, couches, blankets, furniture, linens, uniforms and medical equipment for use by the Society and for sale to the refugees in the camps. Other facilities provided work for Palestinian men and women skilled in the traditional crafts of weaving, carving and embroidery as well as training for young men and women from the camps in radio and television repair, sewing, languages and visual arts. Altogether the Society provided work for more than 8,000 Palestinians in 1980. Nearly 3,000 of these were refugees living in the occupied territories of the West Bank and the Gaza Strip.[80] Although the Israeli occupation of the Lebanon in 1982 destroyed many of the facilities set up by SAMED and the Red Crescent Society, both organisations continued to help provide employment for Palestinian refugees in other parts of Lebanon and Syria as well as in the occupied territories.

Within the host countries the gradual expansion of the local economies after 1948 and the development of their infrastructure and industrial base provided other opportunities for Palestinians seeking work in the 1960s and 1970s. In Syria the rapid growth of the residential areas in and around Damascus and the other major cities, together with the demand for new factory and office accommodation, led to a rapid increase in the number of Palestinians employed in the building trades. By 1981 some 7,800 Palestinian refugees — about 18 per cent of the Palestinian labour force in the country — were employed in construction and related fields. (This represented about 7.3 per cent of the total Syrian work-force employed in the same sector.[81]) Many of the skilled workers were trained at UNRWA's vocational centre in Damascus which opened in 1961. By 1981 4,000 Palestinians had graduated from the centre. While most had trained as bricklayers, plumbers, carpenters, building technicians and draughtsmen, others had finished courses in auto mechanics, radio and television repair and pharmacy.[82]

The high number of Palestinian refugees who found work in the building trades was a direct result of official government policy, which aimed to channel Palestinian labour into those sectors of the Syrian economy most in need of labour. While some refugees still complain that they are discouraged from taking more advanced courses or from finding more amenable jobs in the services sector or as self-employed workers, others have accepted the opportunities provided because of the need to support large families and/or to finance the high cost of education. One student at the UNRWA centre in 1981, Fawaz Sharani, summed up the feeling of his fellow trainees: 'After two years of study at the centre I will earn as much as I would after studying for six years to become an architect.'[83]

In Lebanon a total of 4,845 Palestinians from the refugee camps were employed in industry, construction, power and water in 1971. Together they accounted for just under a quarter of the total number of economically active Palestinians in the camps or about 4 per cent more than the share employed in agriculture.[84] Most were unskilled labourers and four-fifths were employed on a daily or casual basis. Only 390 had permanent jobs, primarily in industry or as employees of the state-owned electricity and water departments.[85]

Unlike Syria, where the refugees had greater access to training, those in Lebanon were often forced to take the lowest-paid jobs because of the difficulty of competing with skilled Lebanese workers and inability to obtain working permits for more permanent positions. Those in employment were often required to pay an initial sum, or part of their wages, to middlemen of one kind or another — a government official, labour contractor or a member of one of the local families. The destruction of much of Lebanon's industrial base during the civil war of 1975-6 and later as a result of Israel's invasion in 1982 made the workers' lot even more precarious. Many now must work at two, or even three, jobs just to provide a minimal standard of living for their families. As a result attempts to organise Palestinian workers in Lebanon into trade unions have failed, particularly since most feel they are the victims of national as well as class oppression.[86] Only in a few limited areas, mainly among the dock workers of Beirut and those who work in the oil refineries and distribution centres, have efforts to obtain higher wages, better working conditions or compensation for unemployment been successful.[87]

Figures on the numbers of Palestinian workers employed in construction and in industry in Jordan are almost totally lacking, primarily because government records do not distinguish between Palestinians and Jordanians. However it is clear that in the early years of exile the influx of capital brought by the wealthier Palestinian refugees provided considerable numbers of jobs for the camp population in construction and transport. Later the lack of a more permanent base for industrial growth impeded economic development although some jobs were available in public sector companies providing power, water and (after 1960) refined petroleum products, as well as in smaller, family-owned workshops.[88]

Most of the jobs — in construction as well as in industry — were only available in the larger cities and towns, particularly in Amman, Irbid and Zarqa. As refugees from the more remote camps flooded into the capital and larger towns looking for work and for better medical and educational services, wage levels fell and huge shanty towns grew up around the more populated areas. In 1960 the unemployment rate in Amman was 50 per cent, and most of the employed made barely enough to pay their rent and buy their food.[89] However in the 1970s the influx of 'petrodollars' and increased foreign aid made it possible to improve health services, housing, schools, roads and communications, thereby adding to the opportunities to find employment in the building trades. New industries, to produce dairy foods, beverages, plastic products, animal feed, cigarettes, textiles and clothing were established in Amman and in Zarqa. Smaller workshops, to fabricate metal products, automobile batteries and steel tubing, were also set up. Many of them employed Palestinian workers, both men and women.[90] Combined with the possibility of finding work in agriculture, or by emigration to the Gulf states, these new opportunities in construction and industry led to higher wages and to a demand for labour of all kinds. By 1982 only an estimated 15 per cent of the population in the East Bank remained in the camps, and these consisted for the most part of the very old, the very young and the mothers and wives of

Palestinian men who had emigrated either to the main cities or to the Gulf states.[91]

For the West Bank almost no figures on the size of the working class are available for the period 1948 to 1967, when the area was under Jordanian occupation, since the authorities in Amman tended to lump all workers — Palestinians and Jordanians — together. However it is known that the policies of the government discouraged the growth of industry in the West Bank and led to stagnation in this sector until 1967. Employment on private construction projects provided work for some refugees, particularly in the 1960s as remittances from Palestinians working abroad began to flow into the West Bank. However, since much of this work was residential — consisting of buildings or expanding houses and apartments — a large portion was carried out by family members who exchanged their labour with one another for other services. Smaller numbers of workers were employed by the municipal services, to build roads and to provide power and water, but the lack of sufficient public investment for these purposes made it difficult to increase significantly the number of refugees which could be gainfully employed.[92]

In the Gaza Strip employment in construction and industry was also extremely limited during the period from 1948 to 1967 when the area was controlled by Egypt. UNRWA undertook a number of improvement projects in the mid-1950s such as the building of roads, a drainage system for the town of Gaza and the construction of a small port.[93] However most of the work on these projects was temporary; they did not materially affect the size of the working class or lead to permanent employment in construction and/or industry. On the other hand, Gaza's important textile, rug-weaving and soap industries did manage to survive the 1948 defeat, partly with UNRWA's help. In 1980 these occupations provided employment for about 2,500 persons, some of whom were drawn from the refugee population.[94]

After the Israeli occupation of the West Bank and the Gaza Strip in 1967 thousands of new jobs in construction and industry became available in Israel and in the Jewish settlements established in the occupied territories. The establishment of food-processing and fruit- and vegetable-packing plants, dairies, poultry farms, metal-fabrication workshops and other small-scale industries also required Palestinian labour, mainly unskilled male and female workers who were employed at harvest time or as casual labour.[95] By the end of 1977 the number of Palestinians working in industry within the occupied territories totalled 32,000, or about 16 per cent of the total Palestinian labour force.

Nearly two-thirds of those employed in this sector worked in Israeli factories, commuting daily to their jobs.[96]

Although it is impossible to tell from the figures how many of these were refugees from the 1948 and 1967 dispersions, the figure working in Israeli factories is thought to amount to at least half the total. Unlike the indigenous residents who had been able to remain in their homes, the refugees found it necessary to accept work in Israel and in the settlements because of the huge unemployment levels which existed in the camps. Although most received lower wages and fewer benefits than their Israeli counterparts and had to pay a larger portion of their wages on travel and food, the demand for Arab labour during this period enabled many refugee families to improve their standard of living and to escape life in the camps.[97] However by the end of the 1970s the deep recession in the Israeli economy, together with the increased scale of military repression ordered by the Begin government, closed this avenue to many and the younger workers in the camps often found it necessary to emigrate to find work (see below).

Aside from work in Israel and in the Jewish settlements, there were also some jobs available in construction and in local industry in the West Bank and Gaza. Although the economic integration of the occupied territories with Israel in the early 1970s imposed new stresses on the indigenous Arab economies, the economic expansion which Israel experienced during the period following the 1967 war led to an increased demand for products made in the West Bank and in Gaza and to an increase in investment in the territories. Small-scale industries producing wood and paper products, building materials, chemicals, electrical goods, textiles and clothing were able to expand their labour force even though others, such as the food-processing industries, were adversely affected by integration. Still other industries, producing building materials, soap and plastic products, found it possible to increase their exports to Jordan and other Arab states as a result of the economic expansion of the region in the mid-1970s. By the end of 1977 the number of workers employed in the indigenous industries of the occupied territories totalled some 12,000.[98] The subsequent economic recession in Israel led to a decline in the number of jobs available in Arab-owned factories as demand for products made in the West Bank and Gaza fell sharply. The local industries were also adversely affected by a lack of investment, rising costs for raw materials and the imposition of new sales taxes. As a result many workers who had been hired during the period of economic expansion were laid off in the late 1970s, while others found it impossible to demand the higher wages they needed to cushion themselves against inflation. Since the refugee workers were often the least skilled among those employed and the last hired, they were usually the first ones to lose their jobs.

Emigration and Migrant Labour in the Gulf States

Aside from employment in agriculture, construction and industry, the other main avenue of escape from the refugee camps involved emigration to areas which were short of labour. The rapid development of oil production in Saudi Arabia and the Gulf states in the 1960s and 1970s, combined with the import of labour by some industrial countries such as West Germany and Canada during the same period, helped to open up opportunities for those sections of the Palestinian peasantry which had obtained vocational training of one kind or another. The earnings which these workers sent back to their families in the camps helped to improve their material conditions and allowed some to send another son, or daughter, abroad for further education.

The first major wave of emigration by Palestinians occurred in the early 1950s when hundreds found their way to the expanding oilfields and construction centres of Saudi Arabia and the Gulf states. Many of the emigrants were young artisans, craftsmen or skilled workers who had obtained their training in Palestine on government-funded construction projects subcontracted to Palestinian employers or in government-run industries and services such as the public utilities and police. Palestinian labourers were preferred by the Arab American Oil Company (Aramco) in Saudi Arabia and by the Kuwait Oil Company (then a joint venture of Anglo-Persian and Gulf Oil) because of their knowledge of English, their experience with modern tools and equipment and their ability to work in supervisory positions where their knowledge of Arabic and Arab customs was seen to make them ideal foremen.[99] By the end of 1953 some 3,000 Palestinians were employed by Aramco in Saudi Arabia alone.[100] Other Palestinian workers were imported to build commercial port facilities in Dammam, the Dammam-Riyadh railway (which at one time provided work for an estimated 15,000 workers, mostly immigrants) and the new towns, schools, hospitals and housing estates which sprang up throughout the Gulf.[101]

However the Palestinians, in addition to bringing both skill and energy to their jobs, also brought with them their experience of labour organisation and a more progressive political consciousness than the host governments were willing to tolerate. A three-week strike against Aramco in 1953 and another in 1954 in which the workers demanded the right to form trade unions, an improvement in their housing conditions and a more equitable distribution of the oil revenues led to the arrest of more than 160 Palestinian workers and their subsequent deportation. Another 100 Palestinians were arrested in 1955 for engaging in unauthorised political activity. Although Aramco initially opposed the arrests, fearing that such precipitate action by the government might deter other trained Palestinians from seeking work with the company, it was later forced to accept the action under pressure from the Saudi government.[102] Similar unrest in Kuwait, Bahrain and Qatar in the early 1950s led to fears that the discontent might spread to other immigrant workers or to sections of the indigenous population and provoked repression like that which the Palestinians had encountered in Saudi Arabia. During the following years the number of Palestinians allowed to work in sensitive installations and in the oilfields was reduced considerably.[103]

The outbreak of demonstrations and strikes in 1956 during the Suez war, in which Palestinians played a leading role, added still more to the concern felt by the ruling families in the Gulf and by their British advisers. This, combined with the increasing tendency of Aramco and the other Western oil companies operating in the area to turn construction projects and supply contracts over to local entrepreneurs (see above), led to a marked reduction in the import of foreign labour as a whole. By 1958 only those Palestinians with professional qualifications in fields such as engineering, urban planning, medicine, English and education were being allowed into the region in large numbers. Palestinian workers left idle in the camps of Lebanon, Syria, Jordan, the West Bank and Gaza found the door to emigration tightly closed and only those who managed to find work locally — for UNRWA, other Palestinian employers or in the larger cities and towns of Jordan, Lebanon and Syria — managed to escape years of unemployment and the loss of their skills which such prolonged idleness entailed.

Ten years later the rapid influx of oil revenues led to an easing of the restrictions on immigration in the Gulf. Palestinian workers who had Jordanian passports and others with valid travel documents provided by the Lebanese and Syrian authorities were recruited to work in private construction, hospitals, print shops, laundries, garages and workshops, as well as on projects established by the government. Unlike the earlier generation which had been trained in Palestine, these new *émigrés* were for the most part young single men who had manged to obtain vocational training in the camps or in the larger cities and towns of the non-oil states. Some had benefited from the intervention of relatives and neighbours already working in the Gulf states; others had waited for years to earn the money and influence needed to obtain an exit visa, working permit, identity card or training certificate.

Once in Saudi Arabia, Kuwait, Qatar or the United Arab Emirates they faced difficult living conditions and severe restrictions on their social and geographical mobility.[104] Most of the work was of a temporary nature and there were few guarantees that an immigrant could find additional work once the project on which he was employed had ended or a local citizen had been trained to take his place. Unlike their compatriots who had managed to obtain a university education or to establish a local business, they were often deported after only a year or two of work. Nevertheless their remittances sent back home helped to provide a ray of hope for their families and contributed greatly to the economies of the labour-exporting countries, such as Jordan and Lebanon, which benefited from an influx of *riyals*, *dinars* and *dirhams*. This was especially true in the West Bank, where the savings accrued during a spell in the Gulf often made it possible for a refugee family to build a home or start a small business outside the camps.

By the end of the 1970s a new stratum of Palestinian workers had come into being which was distinguished on the one hand from those still in the camps or employed as agricultural labour and on the other from those who, because of their advanced education, had obtained the benefit of a residency permit. These workers eschewed political activity in the countries where they worked in favour of earning money for their families. The difficulty of organising themselves locally given their temporary status, the multitude of work sites often located in remote areas and the cultural differences that separated them both from the Arabs of the Gulf and from other foreign workers, in addition to the ever present fear of deportation, led them to concentrate their attention on the material and social advancement of their families. While many sympathised with the views of the more leftist organisations in the PLO and with the Communist and socialist parties of Jordan, Syria and Lebanon (most of which had been banned by the late 1970s), as well as with Fatah, they tended either to eschew political work altogether or to return to the camps where they enrolled in the Palestinian movements as full-time workers or fighters. Their sense of a common identity as workers was subordinated to the nationalist struggle which was regarded as the main priority.

Only in the 1980s, as the opportunities to emigrate declined sharply due to the fall in oil revenues in the Gulf and economic recession in Europe, did a concerted sense of class consciousness begin to emerge once again. By then, however, the appalling physical destruction of the camps in Lebanon, the imprisonment of thousands of fighters in Israel, the increased repression in the West Bank and Gaza and the growing insecurity felt by the Palestinian communities in Kuwait and the Gulf states brought new, more immediate, concerns to the fore. The effort to reunite families, to obtain the release of family members held in Israeli jails, to provide for needy relatives and to make plans for the days when even wealthier kin might no longer be welcome in the Gulf absorbed what little energy was left after the daily struggle to survive. Divisions within the Palestine Liberation Organisation and the loss or closure of many of the welfare organisations which had been built up by the PLO in Lebanon, Syria and other parts of the Arab world added to the sense of insecurity which the workers felt both individually and collectively. Under such conditions political activity, whether as a nationalist or as a worker, was often regarded as a luxury that few could afford even though their sympathies and support for the cause remained undiminished.

7 NATIONALISM AND CLASS STRUGGLE, 1948-1983

The formation of the Palestine Liberation Organisation in 1964 and its subsequent takeover by Fatah and other guerrilla organisations in the aftermath of the 1967 Arab-Israeli war opened a new chapter in the history of the Palestinian people. Palestinian nationalism and the demand for the creation of an independent secular state were back on the agenda. Nineteen years later, in the wake of the Israeli invasion of Lebanon, Western journalists were busy writing the PLO's obituary. The physical removal of the PLO leaders and several thousand fighters from Lebanon, the incarceration of at least 4,000 others by the Israelis, and the outbreak of civil war within Fatah appeared to underline the fact that the movement had suffered a major military defeat from which it could not be expected to recover.

What was easily forgotten amidst the frightening scenes of death and destruction which filled the world's television screens and newspapers during 1982 and 1983 was that the long years of exile and struggle had also produced an impressive victory on the international front. 'Palestine' and 'the Palestinians' had become household words once again and whatever the fate of the various solutions proposed by the United States, the Soviet Union, Israel and the Arab states, it was clear that the PLO's basic demand for an independent state was supported by world public opinion and by almost all the world's governments. Only the United States and Israel still seemed determined to prevent the Palestinians from fulfilling their dream.

However the diplomatic successes, given the losses on the military front, were insufficient to achieve the Palestinians' main aim – to return home. Within the PLO the evacuation from Beirut in 1982 was followed by an uprising among Fatah's own rank and file which quickly attracted leading officers, including some close to PLO Chairman Yasser Arafat. Like the dissension which followed the civil war in Jordan in 1970 and 1971 and that in Lebanon in 1975 and 1976, this internal conflict threatened to weaken the PLO's international image and its relations with the conservative monarchies of Saudi Arabia and the Gulf. Yet the tenacity of the PLO dissidents reflected their determination to remain in the

176

one unoccupied battlefield left to the PLO guerrillas: the Beqaa Valley in eastern Lebanon.

Disenchanted with the failure of the diplomatic campaign to gain its ultimate aim − an Israeli withdrawal from the occupied territories − and with Arafat's inability to turn world sympathy into concrete action in favour of the Palestinians, the dissidents dug in and continued their attacks against the Israelis, both in the Beqaa Valley and further south, behind Israeli lines, in occupied Lebanon. There they were joined by armed cadres drawn from the Shi'a Amal, the Lebanese National Front, the Communist Party and other militias of the Lebanese left, which had successfully repelled right-wing Phalangists in the autumn of 1983. The ideology of armed struggle was once again in the forefront. Stripped of his olive branch by US and Israeli intransigence and plagued with internal strife, Arafat was left with the gun. His unwillingness to use that option against Israel after years of diplomacy threatened to undermine his own future and that of the unified PLO which he headed. Once again the resistance movement was torn between those, like the Mufti in the 1930s, and the pro-Abdullah faction in the 1950s, who advocated negotiation and a peaceful settlement, and those, like the rebels of Galilee and the hill country, and the demonstrators in Jordan, who were ready to use arms to repel the invader.

The question here is to what extent these and other more important differences within the Palestinian resistance movement reflect differences of class and class consciousness. While this study has attempted to examine some of the social differences within Palestinian society and the evolution of class interests, it is not at all clear that class consciousness as such has reflected itself in the ideology of the PLO or in the thinking of the majority of Palestinians living in exile. Other factors, such as place of origin, family ties, religion, age and education may be equally important in determining political consciousness and the direction which the various movements have taken over time. While it is obvious that another volume of equal length could be written on this question alone, it may be useful here to look at the relationship between the various political movements and class interests, if only for the sake of providing hypotheses that may guide students of the subject in the future.

Ideology and Class, 1948-74

Prior to 1967, Palestinian political activity tended to be directed into four main channels of action: (1) the movement to achieve liberal democracy in Jordan; (2) pan-Arabism and Arab nationalism; (3) the Communist Party and other Marxist organisations; and (4) Islamic reformism. While each of these movements at times received support from a variety of class elements, the articulation of political thought and action within each of these major trends tended to reflect the interests of specific classes more than those of others. Palestinians who helped to formulate the ideologies and strategies involved – as distinct from those who simply gave their support – were, consciously or unconsciously, reflecting class, as well as national, interests. Although space precludes an adequate discussion of the role of the intellectuals and intelligentsia in these movements, a brief description of the ideology, activity and membership of some of these movements may help to illustrate the way in which potential areas of class conflict have been expressed, or dampened, within the Palestinian diaspora.

The Liberals

After the Jordanian occupation of the West Bank in 1948 and the exodus of hundreds of thousands of Palestinians to Jordan, the Palestinian representatives in the Parliament in Amman sought to modify the patriarchal system of power which had been established by the Hashimite monarchy. Palestinian leaders in the Senate set the stage for the campaign in their response to King Abdullah's Speech from the Throne in April 1950 marking the formal annexation of the West Bank. Their demands included 'the supremacy of the law, the independence of the judiciary and the regulation of relations between the legislative and executive powers'. Economic reforms, including measures to reduce imports and to improve national production, as well as the establishment of a modern educational system, were also put on the agenda.[1]

By the mid-1950s they had been able to achieve considerable success on many of these issues and, in addition, to introduce a system of merit in parts of the civil administration whereby technical competence, rather than family relations, became the basis for hiring and promotion. Social legislation and conditions safeguarding some of the basic rights of the workers were also introduced along with vocational education, although trade unions remained banned. Ideological political parties were allowed to operate, although not without restrictions, and freedom of the press and of assembly were formally guaranteed despite severe opposition from the monarchy and its supporters among the East Bank tribal leaders and landed aristocracy. Later, during the government of the National Socialists led by Sulaiman Nabulsi, Palestinian representatives in the Chamber of Deputies put forward a demand for the abrogation of the Anglo-Jordanian Treaty of Alliance and the establishment of a more neutral foreign policy that would end Jordan's isolation from its neighbours and allow a closer relationship with the republican states of Egypt and Syria and with Saudi Arabia (see Chapter 4).

While many of these measures failed to survive the downfall of the Nabulsi regime, the formulation, articulation and implementation of a programme of democratic reform during the early and mid-1950s demonstrated the degree to which the new class of liberal professionals, both salaried and independent, had matured during the last years of the Mandate. The ranks of the parliamentarians included young lawyers like Anwar and Rashad Khatib, Abdul Halim Nimr and Fuad Abdul Hadi, who had been educated in British universities, as well as business-men and landowners anxious to introduce modern forms of capitalism and industrial production to the kingdom.[2] Active support for the reforms and the new legislation came from the educated middle class in the West Bank and in Amman trained in commerce and finance, accountancy, urban planning, civil administration, science and engineer-ing who hoped to obtain jobs in the civil service or in the private sector. Although the programme of reform also stressed the need to provide adequate provision for the hundreds of thousands of unskilled refugees, the reforms were primarily aimed at opening up what was essentially a tribal system to free enterprise.

By the 1960s, demands by the more radical intelligentsia drawn from the ranks of students, teachers and camp leaders (see below) for the abolition of the monarchy, the arming of the refugees and a massive programme of social reconstruction had been deflected into an indivi-dual campaign of personal advancement and economic development which encouraged consumerism and private consumption at the expense of the public interest. However because the reforms also opened new opportunities for education and for jobs in the public sector, the opposition's case for more radical change met with a divided response within the ranks of the Palestinian community. The sense of national unity within the Palestinian diaspora was weakened, as was its ability to withstand the political repression which followed the down-fall of the Nabulsi regime.

By September 1970, when Jordan erupted into civil war, the Palesti-nian community in Jordan, the largest in the diaspora, was sharply polarised along class lines to the extent that some wealthy landowners, merchants and sections of the prosperous middle class actively or passively supported the King's action against the Palestinian resistance movements. The loss of the West Bank three years earlier had also enabled the King to isolate the revolutionary wing of the PLO while, at the same time, the Marxists in movements such as the Popular Front for the Liberation of Palestine (PFLP) and the Democratic Front were unable to mobilise the support they enjoyed among the refugees within the camps in the West, as well as the East, banks of the Jordan.[3]

Although many of the reforms introduced by the liberals in the 1950s had made possible a large measure of physical security and social advancement, their success had been achieved at the cost of dividing the refugee population and of forgoing the opportunity to launch a military campaign to end the Israeli occupation of the homeland. Given a choice between revolutionary struggle and the maintenance of the monarchy and the benefits it provided, many Palestinian liberals chose the latter. While some later joined the PLO, or gave it their support, the social strains and lack of a unified ideology weakened the Palestinian resistance at the height of its power in the Arab world as a whole.

The Arab Nationalists

While the Palestinian bourgeoisie from the West Bank was busily engaged in a struggle to achieve democratic reform in Jordan, other Palestinians were at work in what were to become important movements of political change in the wider Arab world during the 1960s. Three were particularly influential: the Ba'ath Socialist Party, the Arab Nationalist Movement (ANM) and the Nasserists. All espoused pan-Arab unity, anti-imperialism and social change. But their ideologies, strategy and tactics varied considerably, as did the base of their support.

The Ba'athists. Prior to its takeover of power in Syria in 1963 (and, temporarily, in Iraq that same year) and the division of the party into two wings — one pro-Syrian, the other pro-Iraqi — the Ba'ath was one of the leading proponents of anti-imperialism in the Arab world. Founded in the early 1940s by two young schoolteachers educated in Paris, it had established branches in Lebanon and Jordan as well as in Syria and Iraq after the Second World War.[4]

In Jordan the party's commitment to unity (*al-wahdah*), liberation (*al-hurriyah*) and socialism (*al-ishtirakiyyah*) attracted the younger intelligentsia, particularly teachers, students and minor bureaucrats, and received active support from thousands of refugees drawn to the streets of Amman in support of their demand for an end to British imperialism and the termination of all projects aimed at integrating the refugees into the neighbouring Arab countries. In the 1950 election Abdullah Nawas, the Ba'athist candidate from Jerusalem, received just over 5,000 votes. Another Ba'ath nominee who also edited the party's newspaper in Jordan, Abdullah Rimawi of Ramallah, also received a large number of votes, but they were invalidated by the authorities and he, together with Nawas, was subsequently arrested and the party's newspaper banned. By 1956, however, the Ba'athist vote had risen to 34,000, enough to give them third place in the parliamentary elections behind the National Socialists and the Communists.[5] Their representatives in Parliament included a young poet from the West Bank, Kamal Nasser, who was later to become the official spokesman of the PLO in Beirut. Rimawi, by now the party's leader in Jordan, was made Minister of State for Foreign Affairs, a position which recognised the party's broad support in the country for its policy of neutralism and pan-Arabism.

The downfall of Nabulsi and the King's appeal for troops from Britain spelt an end to the Ba'ath Party's role in Jordan, just as it did for the liberals' attempts to introduce parliamentary democracy and economic reform. But unlike the liberals drawn from the wealthier families of the West Bank, the Ba'ath leaders paid a heavy price for their opposition. Scores of their supporters within the bureaucracy, schools and universities were arrested or sacked from their jobs. The leaders themselves were deported or forced into exile.

The failure of the Palestinian aristocracy loyal to the monarchy to support their compatriots during the crackdown has been discussed above (see Chapter 4). But with the Ba'ath the lack of solidarity also emanated from the younger liberal parliamentarians and the members of their allies among the National Socialist Party led by Nabulsi. When, for example, the Ba'ath insisted on boycotting the new Cabinet set up by the King and led by Dr Hussain Fakhri al-Khalidi after Nabulsi was summarily dismissed in April 1957, the National Socialists demurred and, in the end, supported Khalidi. While they later participated in a National Congress called by the Ba'ath to support the restoration of parliamentary government and an end to the British (and American) role in the country, the damage had already been done. The Congress's demands, which were presented to the King by a delegation which included Bahjat Abu Gharbiyyah of the Ba'ath and a young doctor active in the Arab Nationalist Movement (ANM), George Habash, were rejected out of hand. The constitution was suspended, martial law declared and all political parties banned.[6]

The Ba'ath's insistence on a re-alignment of Jordan's foreign policy

towards support of Arab nationalism threatened to remove the economic base of the Palestinian aristocracy and to undermine the benefits
which it received from the monarchy. In addition, the party's demand
for socialism conflicted with the liberals' hopes of enlarging the privileges accorded to the nationalist bourgeoisie and the role allotted to
private enterprise. Finally, its demand that the refugees be armed and
that they be allowed to campaign for an end to the Israeli occupation
challenged the basis upon which the kingdom, and its alliance with the
Palestinian landowners and merchants of the West Bank, had been
built. Given a choice the pro-monarchists, among both the aristocracy
and the liberals, decided that the liberation of the homeland would
have to wait while their own power in Amman was consolidated.

While the Ba'ath continued to attract Palestinians elsewhere in the
Arab world, its banishment from Jordan diminished its ability, and that
of its Palestinian members, to mobilise the refugees in the country
where they were most concentrated. During the next ten years the party
focused its activity on efforts to achieve Arab unity, first by forming
an alliance with President Nasser of Egypt and then, after the break-up
of the United Arab Republic in 1961 (which included Egypt, Syria and
North Yemen), on establishing Ba'athist rule in Syria and in Iraq. Its
Palestinian recruits were expected to wait for the achievement of this
wider unity before launching the struggle for the liberation of their
own homeland. As the rivalries between the various Ba'athist parties
proliferated and as the Ba'athist government in power in Syria began
to implement tight controls on Palestinian activity, many Palestinians
in the Ba'ath decided that it was time to put Palestine first.

Some went to Lebanon, where they joined other underground
movements formed by Palestinians; others in the army joined forces
with Ahmad Jibril, a refugee in Syria who had graduated from Britain's
Royal Military Academy at Sandhurst and had become an officer in
the Syrian army. He had set up the Palestine Liberation Front (PLF) in
1959 after briefly flirting with the Syrian National Socialist Party
and had begun to organise training for would-be guerrillas as early as
1961.[7] By February 1966, when a left-wing Ba'athist government
composed of officers and trade union leaders and committed to Third
World revolution had come to power, the PLF, together with another
unknown guerrilla movement called Fatah, was already using Syrian
territory to mount raids into Israeli-held territory through Jordan. The
new government gave them the freedom to distribute their military
bulletins to the press and to circulate their views among the refugees
in the camps. By the time the 1967 war broke out, Jibril's organisation,

later known as the Popular Front for the Liberation of Palestine-General Command (PFLP-GC), together with Fatah, was ready to join the struggle for the liberation of the homeland with arms as well as words. Among his recruits were a number of young workers and peasants from the refugee camps in Syria and northern Lebanon.

The Arab Nationalist Movement and Nasser. The declaration of martial law and the suspension of the constitution in Jordan in April 1957 also caught another pan-Arab movement in its grip. Aside from the leaders of the Ba'ath Party, Dr George Habash of the ANM, together with a new recruit – a former medical student named Nayif Hawatmah – was forced to flee along with other members of the movement. Hawatmah, 22 years old at the time and a native Jordanian born in Al Salt to a Christian Bedouin tribe, had been sentenced to death for his role in organising the opposition and had taken refuge in Iraq, where he was also arrested and later released when the Ba'ath came to power in 1963.[8] Habash re-established the movement's headquarters in Damascus, where, with the help of another recruit, a young novelist and journalist from Acre, Ghassan Kanafani, he continued publishing the organisation's newspaper, *Al-Rai (Opinion)*. It was widely read in the refugee camps of Syria and Lebanon, just as it had been in Jordan.

Another leader of the movement, Wadih Haddad, a member of a well-to-do Greek Orthodox family from Safad who had joined Habash in helping to set up a medical clinic for refugees in Amman (after completing his medical studies at the American University of Beirut), returned to Lebanon to carry on the work in the camps. Like two other of the original founders of the ANM in Beirut, Ahmad Yamani (Abu Maher) – a former trade union leader from the Upper Galilee – and Abdul Karim Hamad (Abu Adnan) – also from Upper Galilee, he later became a specialist in military affairs and intelligence. Haddad was also responsible for much of the planning of the 'special operations' which the PFLP carried out in the late 1960s and early 1970s.

The ANM had originally been founded at the American University of Beirut (AUB) in the early 1950s.[9] Like the Ba'ath it espoused pan-Arab unity and anti-imperialism and drew many of its members from the young intelligentsia of the Arab world. However, unlike the Ba'ath, it espoused social reform rather than revolutionary socialism, and, until its transformation into a Marxist party in the early 1960s, took a dim view of Communism, preferring instead – like its hero and mentor, Gamal Abdul Nasser – to emphasise the need for modernisation and nationalist unity. In addition, unlike the Ba'ath, it was led by Palestinians for whom the struggle to regain Palestine was paramount, although the movement believed that this could not be achieved without an end to imperialism and neo-colonialism in the Arab world first.

The adoption of Marxist ideology and the principles of scientific socialism in 1962 also heralded the movement's break with Nasserism which it had espoused throughout the period since its formation. The emergence of a new left-wing tendency in the movement led by Hawatmah and Qais Samarrai (Abu Leila), a young theoretician born to an Iraqi father and a Palestinian mother who had studied economics in London, also brought into question the views of some of the movement's founders whom the younger intelligentsia regarded as too 'petit bourgeois'. In 1968, after the movement's Palestinian leadership had formed the Popular Front for the Liberation of Palestine and had begun to train guerrillas for infiltration into Israeli-held territory, the wing led by Hawatmah and Abu Leila split from the main body of the Front to form the Popular Democratic Front for the Liberation of Palestine (PDFLP), later known simply as the Democratic Front or DFLP. It advocated direct action with the workers and peasants and rejected the role of a Leninist vanguard party as well as any united front with the petite bourgeoisie.[10]

The Popular Front's decision, in 1966, to adopt armed struggle as the means to liberate Palestine, did not mean that it rejected the ideology of Arab unity. In June that year Habash had paid a secret visit to Nasser to discuss the change of tactics and had agreed to wait a year, at the Egyptian president's request, before launching guerrilla raids.[11] However Nasser's defeat in the June war of 1967 and the subsequent revelations about the lack of Egyptian military preparedness had led to great disillusionment throughout the Arab world as well as among the Palestinians. Henceforth, the drive for Arab unity, and for the liberation of a Palestine that was now totally under Israeli occupation, was seen to be impossible without the active participation and political education of the Arab masses, as well as the overthrow of the conservative monarchies of Jordan, Saudi Arabia and the Gulf.

Pledged to a policy of carrying the battle to the capitals of the imperial West, as well as of those of Jordan and the Gulf, the Popular Front and the Democratic Front attracted a growing number of new recruits drawn from the generation that had grown up in the camps and whose only knowledge of Palestine was that which they had learned from their families and from the resistance movements.

However, despite its ideology, the Popular Front and its later offshoot, the DFLP, failed to attract as many workers and peasants to their ranks as did Fatah. The Popular Front, best known in the West for its spectacular hijackings of the late 1960s and early 1970s, nevertheless had a wide following in the refugee camps of Lebanon, Syria and Jordan, partly because of the conscientious social work carried out by members of the Front. The Democratic Front, despite its reverence for the workers and peasants, drew most of its cadres from the intelligentsia, particularly among Palestinian students studying abroad, and received a disproportionate share of support from the Marxist left of Europe, Japan and the United States. Unlike the Popular Front, which rejected financial assistance from Arab governments and which relied on voluntary donations from its members, the Democratic Front also drew funds from some supporters in the Gulf states who had previously donated to Fatah.[12]

The pan-Arab movements of the 1960s, unlike the liberal reform programmes launched in Jordan in the early 1950s, appealed to young middle-class Palestinians in the diaspora who had been deprived of their homes and livelihoods and to others, particularly those among the Greek Orthodox, who rejected the traditional outlook of the Sunni Muslim merchants and landlords. While their policies of anti-imperialism and of social reform also brought them active support among large numbers of the displaced peasantry, the leadership continued even after the formation of the Palestinian fronts to be drawn from the urban, educated elements for whom a rational, secular view of the world, science and theory was the prerequisite for the completion of a successful struggle to achieve national liberation.

The Palestinian fronts suffered not only from the enmity of the Arab regimes, Israel and the governments of the United States and Europe, but also from the difficulty of trying to organise a population where there were few industrial workers and where the proletariat was scattered and subjected to draconian limitations on its mobility. Furthermore, unlike Vietnam, Cuba or Algeria, the Palestinian peasantry in the diaspora did not constitute a productive base, and the lack of a secure hinterland, save for the camps in Lebanon and Syria, also limited their ability to translate Marxist ideology into mass mobilisation. When efforts to organise the peasantry and workers succeeded, as they did spectacularly in Gaza and Jordan in the 1960s, the repression was total, and the leaders of the PFLP and DFLP were forced to retreat to other Arab lands where their reception was far from welcoming.

Differences with Fatah over the role to be allocated to the Arab regimes left them vulnerable to those, both inside and outside the Palestinian resistance, who felt that the adoption of revolutionary socialism impeded the struggle for national liberation. This was particularly evident during the civil war in Jordan in 1970 and 1971, when the cadres of the PFLP bore the brunt of the fighting and the losses in men and material.[13] The installation of a more repressive regime in Damascus in 1970 also removed a base of support for those who remained on good terms with the Ba'ath but outside the officially sponsored resistance movement, Saiqa. By 1974, as we shall see, the Palestinian nationalist movement was split between those who advocated the continuation of a revolutionary struggle for total liberation and those who favoured a peaceful settlement and the pursuit of political independence in alliance with the Arab regimes.

The Communist Party

Although the Palestine Communist Party had been one of the largest and most influential in the Middle East during the days of the Mandate, it had suffered greatly during the last years of British rule due to differences among its members over the national question. After the dissolution of the Comintern in 1943, the party had split into several movements, largely recruited from among the Jewish population. Arab members joined the grouping known as the League for the National Liberation of Palestine ('Usbah al-Taharrir al-Wataniyyi) which was founded in September 1943 and which attracted recruits from the trade unions and urban proletariat as well as from the younger intelligentsia.

After the establishment of the state of Israel the League transferred its headquarters to the West Bank and, in 1949, became the Communist Party of Jordan.[14] Committed to the 'organic unity' of the Palestinian and Jordanian people, it campaigned during the 1951 parliamentary elections on a platform committed to republicanism, the abrogation of the Anglo-Jordanian Treaty and the expansion of democratic freedoms. It also called on the government to redistribute the large landed estates to the peasants and to establish state industries and development projects to provide work for the unemployed. Outlawed as early as 1948 and subject to severe harassment, it nevertheless obtained just over 10 per cent of the vote in the 1951 parliamentary elections, largely because of its strong support in Nablus. Two candidates from landowning families in the West Bank who had stood as individuals with Communist Party support, Abdul Qadir al-Salih and Qadri Tuqan, were returned and took their seats in the Chamber of Deputies.

In the 1956 elections the party campaigned with the Ba'ath Party and the National Socialists under a National Front (Jabhah al-Wataniyyah) and obtained the second-largest number of votes after the National

Socialists. Abdul Qadir al-Salih along with three other candidates who were either members of the party or supported by it — Abdul Khalil Yaghmur of Nablus, Faiq Warrad of Ramallah and Ya'qub Ziyadain of Jerusalem — were elected to the Chamber of Deputies. Al-Salih was made Minister of Agriculture in Nabulsi's Cabinet, thus marking the first time in the Arab world that the Communist Party had taken part in government.[15]

As with the liberals, the Ba'ath and the Arab Nationalists, the subsequent repression, suspension of the constitution and the banning of all political parties put an end to the party's overt activities in the kingdom. Efforts to regroup the progressive forces to face the repression by forming a National Liberation Front failed and by 1959 the party was forced to continue its work totally underground. The party's Chairman, Fuad Nasser, was exiled to Eastern Europe and scores of party members in the West Bank were arrested. (The three deputies outside the Cabinet — Yaghmur, Warrad and Ziyadain — had been arrested in April 1957 when the Nabulsi government was dismissed.) Works by George Bernard Shaw, Gorki, Pushkin and Arab philosophers and writers such as Sati al-Husri and al-Sharqawi were banned, as were those of Marx, Engels and Lenin. Jordanians and Palestinians were forbidden to distribute any literature promoting communism or neutralism, to rent accommodation to a communist or to assist party members in any other way.[16]

During the 1960s the party also suffered from its inability to come to terms with Arab nationalism and the tremendous popular appeal enjoyed by Gamal Abdul Nasser among the poorer refugees of Jordan, Lebanon, Syria, the West Bank and Gaza. Even during the 1950s at the height of its success in Jordan it had laboured under the liability of its association with the Soviet Union, which had been one of the first countries to recognise the state of Israel. Although some of the party's members in the West Bank had urged it to support plans for Arab unity and for the liberation of Palestine, the party's leaders in the Politbureau continued to regard an alliance with the nationalist bourgeoisies of the Arab world as deviationist. Demands for the establishment of a Palestinian state, in turn, were regarded as 'secessionist' and contrary to the idea of class struggle and the solidarity of the working classes internationally.[17]

As a result the party's support among the displaced peasantry and the urban proletariat of the refugees dwindled away in favour of Nasser, the Arab Nationalists and, to a lesser extent, the Ba'ath. Several members of the young intelligentsia deserted the party to help found a new monthly, *Filistinuna* (*Our Palestine*), which reflected the ideas of another underground organisation, Fatah. Distributed clandestinely in Kuwait and the refugee camps of Lebanon, it denounced Zionism as a tool of imperialism and called for armed struggle and the liberation of the homeland as a prelude to the achievement of Arab unity.[18] Only after 1970, when the Communist Party of Jordan split into two sections and was taken over by a majority who supported armed struggle and national liberation, did it begin again to gain wide support in the West Bank.[19]

In 1976, when the first free municipal elections were held in the West Bank, the party succeeded in gaining control of several important posts through its participation in the National Front which supported the Palestine Liberation Organisation and the right of Palestinian self-determination.[20] As in the 1950s, the party's support came from the urban proletariat of the West Bank towns, students, teachers, health workers and municipal employees. Its following among the peasantry in the villages and rural areas, as well as among the majority of the inhabitants of the refugee camps, remained relatively small.

Islamic Reformism

The attraction of strictly religious movements among the Palestinians has never been particularly strong. Despite the great following which the Mufti obtained in the days of the Mandate, the emphasis throughout the movement for independence since 1919 has been on a joint struggle uniting Christians and Muslims. Movements committed to secularism, democracy and liberation have obtained a far wider, and more active, following than have those which appealed solely to the Islamic sentiments of part of the population.

Nevertheless during those periods when the leadership of the nationalist movement or the various Arab parties has been discredited, the Islamic reform movements have seen their support among the Palestinians increase considerably. This was particularly true in the aftermath of the 1948 defeat and, most recently, in the early 1980s following the revolution in Iran, the growth of Muslim militancy in Egypt and the failure of the Arab governments to halt the Israeli invasion of Lebanon and the continuing Israeli settlement of the West Bank and Gaza (see below).

In 1948 the occupation of the West Bank by King Abdullah, the defeat of the Mufti's forces — the Jaish al-Jihad al-Muqaddas (see Chapter 4) — and the repression of political activity fostered the growth of support for the Muslim Brethren, the one movement that was allowed to operate in the West Bank. Originally founded in Egypt in the 1930s, the Brethren had led a bitter campaign against the monarchy of King Farouk and British intervention in the country's domestic and foreign policies. By the early 1950s it enjoyed an extremely large following in Egypt and in the Gaza Strip, particularly among the rural peasants, the urban poor and the refugees. However its attacks on leading politicians and its alleged participation in a series of massive demonstrations and bombings in Cairo and other Egyptian cities in 1952 had led the government to enact severe measures against it.[21] After the Free Officers *coup d'état* in 1952 and the rise of Nasser, the Brethren were once again subjected to severe harassment and many of their leaders were jailed following several attempted assassinations on the life of the President and other government officials.

As a result the organisation's headquarters was shifted to Jerusalem. There the Brethren set up the World Muslim Congress (Al-Mutamar al-Islami al-'Alami) which included representatives of the Brethren in other parts of the Arab world, Pakistan and Europe. The Brethren's newspaper, *Al-Jihad* (*Sacred Struggle*), began publishing in the Holy City later that year and the organisation rapidly began to attract a following among the Palestinian refugees.[22] They had already been impressed by the fighting spirit volunteers from the Brethren had displayed on the battlefront in southern Palestine and Gaza in 1948 and by the Brethren's strong support for the Arab Higher Committee and the Mufti at the time of Abdullah's occupation of the West Bank.

Palestinians who were still continuing, clandestinely, the resistance against the Israelis in Gaza, the West Bank and the border areas of Israel particularly welcomed their organisation in Jerusalem, as did others who wanted to resume the armed struggle. In the 1956 parliamentary elections the organisation obtained more than 22,500 votes even though it had refused to take part publicly in mass demonstrations that year against the Western-sponsored Baghdad Pact and the British presence in Jordan because of the participation of the Communist Party and other leftist movements.[23] Another Islamic party, the Islamic Liberation Front (Jabhah al-Tahrir al-Islami), which was particularly strong in Tulkarm, received just over 6,000 votes even though it was banned due to its avowedly republican ideology.[24]

Although the Brethren, unlike the other victors of 1956, were allowed to continue to operate in Jordan after the dismissal of Nabulsi's government, their political support among Palestinians declined markedly in subsequent years due to their refusal to take a more active position against the monarchy and the conservative Arab regimes.

However the fact that they enjoyed government support and could therefore provide access to government officials and that they had opened schools and social centres in areas neglected by the central government brought them considerable sympathy even during the height of Nasser's popularity in the Arab world.[25] By the early 1980s, when a new generation of students and teachers had joined the movement, the Brethren and their offshoots in Jordan, the West Bank and Gaza were ready to renew their campaign to achieve pan-Islamic unity and the restoration of Islamic law in the Arab world as a whole.

The PLO and Palestinian Nationalism, 1964-83

Unlike the Palestinian refugees, the Arab states in the 1950s and 1960s had relegated the liberation of Palestine to the bottom of their list of priorities. However the death in 1963 of the Palestinian representative to the Arab League, Ahmad Hilmi Pasha, confronted them with the problem of naming his successor. While almost all of the League's members were agreed that the danger of the Palestinians forcing the Arab governments into a premature war with Israel had to be avoided, none of the Arab leaders wanted to see his rival, or the Palestinians, gain sole control of the right to represent the Palestinian cause lest it undermine the legitimacy of their own regimes in the eyes of the Arab people. The manoeuvring, always present, was particularly fierce when it came to choosing Ahmad Hilmi's successor.

At an Arab League meeting called to discuss the issue in September 1963, Iraq insisted that the entire question of the 'Palestinian entity' be re-opened. Supported by Syria, where the newly installed Ba'athists were consolidating their power, Baghdad proposed that a Palestinian state be created in the West Bank of the Jordan and in Gaza.[26] Such a plan, which at last recognised Palestinian rights, would give the Ba'athist regimes in Baghdad and Damascus the unquestioned allegiance of the refugees and remove both Jordanian and Egyptian control over those parts of Palestine they still occupied.

Faced with the resulting opposition to the plan from Cairo and Amman, the Arab League decided to appoint a lawyer from a notable family in Acre, who had served as the League's Assistant Secretary-General, Ahmad Shuqairi, as Ahmad Hilmi's successor. This was done with the understanding that he would make a tour of Arab capitals to ascertain the wishes of the member states regarding the future of the Palestinian cause. Iraq then agreed to withdraw its proposal given the impossibility of implementing it without approval by Jordan and Egypt. Shuqairi, after consultations with the other Arab states, drew up a document known as the Palestinian National Charter (PNC) which became the basis for the establishment of the Palestine Liberation Organisation (PLO).[27]

The Formation of the Palestine Liberation Organisation

The Charter and the formation of the PLO were ratified in May 1964 at a meeting of the newly established Palestine National Council held in Jerusalem which was attended by 242 Palestinian representatives selected by the governments of Jordan, Syria, Lebanon, Egypt, Kuwait, Qatar and Iraq.[28] Shuqairi was elected President; three others – Hikmat al-Masri of Nablus, Haidar Abdul Shafi of Gaza and Nicholas al-Dair of Lebanon – were elected to serve as Vice-Presidents. Shuqairi was also empowered to select a new fifteen-man Executive Committee and his choices included representatives of the liberal professions and of the newly emergent bourgeoisie as well as others from the traditionally respected families of the West Bank and Gaza. Jerusalem was named as the PLO's headquarters and a Palestine National Fund (PNF), headed by the son of the founder of the Arab Bank, Abdul Majid Shoman, was set up to collect funds from the Arab governments and from the refugees, each of whom was asked to contribute a quarter of a *dinar* (about $1) per year.[29]

The following September the Arab League states, at a summit meeting held in Alexandria, agreed to establish a Palestine Liberation Army (PLA) composed of Palestinians serving in the existing Arab armies. Kuwait and Iraq each agreed to contribute £2 million sterling to the army, Saudi Arabia £1 million sterling and Libya £500,000 sterling. A lieutenant-colonel serving in the Kuwaiti army, Wagih al-Madani, was named Commander-in-Chief. By the end of the year PLA units had been established in Gaza, Syria and Iraq. Some two hundred young Palestinians were also receiving military training at a camp set up for the commandos in Gaza by Shuqairi with the assistance of Palestinian militants from the Arab Nationalist Movement.[30]

While on the surface the formation of the PLO appeared to the outside world and to Israel to herald a new era of militancy and of joint Arab-Palestinian struggle, it in fact represented an attempt by the Arab regimes to prevent the Palestinian movement from taking overt military action on its own and to use Palestinian militants to defend the interests of the Arab governments against Israel. Under the terms of the Charter the existing state boundaries were formally recognised, including Jordanian sovereignty over the West Bank, Egyptian control in Gaza and the Syrian annexation of the Himmah.[31] Rather than establishing the means whereby the Palestinians could launch an armed movement to regain their land, the establishment of the PLO in 1964 represented a move by the Arab governments to reconcile the points of view of President Nasser, King Hussein and the Ba'athists while preserving unity and the *status quo* in the face of Israeli threats to divert the waters of the Jordan Valley and to launch hostilities against Jordan, Syria and Egypt. The PLA, which even after the rise of Fatah continued to oppose the aims and tactics employed by the guerrillas, was totally under the control of its respective Arab government hosts, most of whom had no intention of letting its Commander-in-Chief enjoy real power.

Demands by Palestinians active in the various pan-Arab and leftist movements for participation in the formation of the PLO's constituent bodies were ignored and it became instead a talking shop for the Palestine notables allied to the various Arab governments. The reluctance of some of the Palestinian militants, including George Habash and the other future leaders of the PFLP and DFLP, to undertake armed struggle independently without the prior commitment of the Arab governments to a war with Israel also split the younger generation of Palestinians who had criticised the PLO from its outset and who had been particularly disillusioned at the choice of Shuqairi and other traditional notables to serve as the representatives of the Palestinian people.[32] Only after the unexpected defeat of the Arab armies in June 1967 and the Israeli occupation of the West Bank and Gaza did all the Palestinian guerrilla movements agree on the necessity of launching independent military action immediately.

Fatah Takes over the PLO

While the Palestinian bourgeoisie in Jordan concentrated on consolidating its wealth and the intelligentsia sought to further Arab unity, a group of engineers, mathematicians and teachers who had studied in Cairo and Alexandria and fought against the Israelis during their occupation of the Gaza Strip in 1956 were busy organising a new underground movement that was to emerge as Fatah after the 1967 war. Three of the original founders, Yasser Arafat (Abu'Umar), Khalil al-Wazir (Abu Jihad) and Salah Khalaf (Abou Iyad) had helped to organise the General Union of Palestinian Students in Cairo and Gaza in the early 1950s and had also worked closely with members of the Muslim Brethren which, at that time, was campaigning for the re-opening of hostilities against the Israelis in Palestine and against the British presence along the Suez Canal.

Disillusioned with the state of Egypt's fighting ability during their experiences in Gaza, the three had emigrated to the Gulf states after the Suez war where, because of their qualifications, they rapidly obtained well-paying jobs, mostly in the public sector. Their attempts to set up an underground organisation devoted solely to the recon-quest of Palestine bore fruit quickly and they were joined by a num-ber of students, teachers and civil servants, including three others who were to play a major role in the PLO and in Fatah: Farouk Kaddoumi (Abu Lutf), a petroleum engineer working in Saudi Arabia; Kamal Adwan, a teacher in Qatar (who later studied petroleum engineer-ing in Cairo); and Khalid Hassan (Abu Sa'id), the secretary of the municipality of Kuwait. Other Palestinians, such as Youssef al-Najjar (Abu Youssef) and Mohammad 'Abbas (Abu Mazin), who had already been active in helping to set up organisations similar to Fatah in Saudi Arabia and Qatar, joined the underground movement as well. Financial contributions to support the publication of *Filistinuna*, the purchase of arms and the travel expenses of the leaders were obtained from the members themselves, each of whom was pledged to give a portion of his salary. Other contributions were solicited from Palestinian businessmen and civil servants in Saudi Arabia, Kuwait, Qatar and Libya.[33]

In the autumn of 1964, while the notables selected for the PLO settled into their new-found role as clients of the Arab League govern-ments, the leaders of Fatah assembled for one of their most significant debates. The matter at hand concerned the timing of their first military moves against Israel. As Abou Iyad later revealed, not all of Fatah's leaders were in favour of action at that moment. Although Fatah's insistence on the need to liberate Palestine as a prerequisite for the achievement of Arab unity (rather than the other way around, as both the ANM and Ba'ath insisted) had gained considerable merit since the break-up of the United Arab Republic in 1961, the organisation itself was still very small given the need to preserve total secrecy at all times. Similarly, although the tremendous success of the Algerian revolution, which had culminated in independence from the French in 1962, had not only vindicated Fatah's theoretical reliance on armed struggle but also given its recruits another place, alongside Syria, in which to set up training centres, the prospect of intense Israeli reprisals against the civilian population in the refugee camps and in the neighbouring states could not be ruled out. Was it advisable to launch military action when the neighbouring states were so ill prepared and when Fatah's own cadres were still lacking in numbers and weapons?

Of the two camps, the 'adventurers' — as they were called by the Fatah commandos themselves — won the argument, not least because of the persuasive powers of Yasser Arafat and Abou Iyad, who had urged that the armed struggle be launched as soon as possible.[34] Three months later, on the night of 31 December, groups of commandos using the name of Al-'Assifa (the Tempest) to preserve Fatah's anonymity, slipped across the border from Lebanon and the West Bank and attacked several points where Israel had been attempting to divert the waters of the Jordan Valley to its own use — a *cause célèbre* against which the Arab states had been complaining in vain for two years. Although it was to be some weeks before the commandos were able to inflict serious damage on the installations, the armed struggle had been launched.[35]

The sudden defeat of the Arab armies in the June war of 1967 brought Al-'Assifa, and Fatah, to international attention. After another debate about the advisability of launching commando raids given the overwhelming superiority of the Israeli forces and the possibility of severe demoralisation among the newly occupied residents of the West Bank and Gaza (an assumption that Yasser Arafat was able to prove erroneous after a clandestine visit to the West Bank at the end of June), Fatah's operations in the occupied territory escalated rapidly.[36] Their impressive victory at Karamah in March 1968, when the guerrillas repelled a major attack on the East Bank by the Haganah, demonstrated Fatah's ability to take on a regular army despite its small numbers and brought the movement triumphant acclaim from both the Palestinian and Arab masses for whom the victory helped to assuage the humiliation of the 1967 defeat.

By June, after Fatah's leaders had decided to try to infiltrate the PLO to provide a political cover for the underground organisation and to make use of its diplomatic and military resources, Fatah was able to obtain almost half the seats on the Palestine National Council. In July the Council amended the National Charter to include Fatah's basic principle that 'armed struggle is the only way to obtain the liberation of Palestine'. Confirmation of Yahyia Hammoudah as Chairman of the PLO also favoured Fatah since he was more sympathetic to the guerrillas than Shuqairi, who had been dismissed the previous December.[37]

In February 1969 at the Fifth Session of the PNC held in Cairo, the resistance movements advocating armed struggle, which included the PFLP and Saiqa as well as Fatah, received 57 seats out of a total of

105, giving them an absolute majority. However the PFLP's decision to boycott the Cairo conference, and its insistence that the existing PLO be completely dismantled to give all the resistance movements an equal voice in the leadership of the armed struggle, together with the fact that Fatah, in addition to its 33 seats, enjoyed the sympathy of several independents elected to the PNC as well as representatives of the General Union of Palestinian Workers (GUPW), gave Fatah the decisive edge.

In subsequent elections to the Executive Committee, Yasser Arafat (who had made his first public appearance as Fatah's spokesman in Damascus in April 1968) was elected Chairman of the PLO and three other Fatah leaders — Abu Youssef, Abu Lutf and Khalid Hassan — were named to the Committee, giving Fatah control over both the Council and the Executive Committee. Despite the enlargement of the Council in subsequent sessions, the PFLP's decision to participate in the Executive Committee and the addition of representatives from the smaller guerrilla groups, Fatah retained its predominant position within the representative institutions of the PLO throughout the 1970s and early 1980s.

The Council's decision at the Fifth Session to adopt Fatah's declaration that 'the objective of the Palestinian people is to establish a democratic society in Palestine open to all Palestinians — Muslims, Christians and Jews', remained a cardinal principle of the PLO as well.[38] Fatah's belief in the priority of Palestinian nationalism and in the creation of a democratic and secular state was thus enshrined, along with the concept of armed struggle, as the basic ideology of the Palestinian resistance movement, despite the internal debates which had plagued the PLO since its foundation.

Nationalism and Class Struggle within the PLO

Fatah's original appeal, unlike that of its predecessors or rivals, was directed solely to Palestinians and its emphasis on national unity within Palestinian ranks attracted the peasants (*fellahin*) and urban elite (*madaniyyin*) alike. Arafat's own lineage, which included his close relationship (through his mother) to the Hussaini clan and his service on the 1948 battlefront in Jerusalem under Abdul Qadir al-Hussaini, gave the movement a legitimacy in the eyes of the refugees — both the impoverished and well-to-do — that few other leaders could emulate.

For the urban middle classes, Fatah's insistence on the *national* rights of the Palestinians responded both to the sense of repression and exploitation which they felt under the control of the local Arab bourgeoisies and to their hope of obtaining recognition in a state of their own. Its implicit denial of the importance of any other factor, whether class, religion or place of origin, also appealed to the Palestinian bourgeoisie of the Gulf and to the younger educated elements of the landed families who hoped to take what they saw as their rightful place in the government and administration of an independent Palestinian state.

For the peasants, Fatah's incorporation of the great symbols of Arab and Islamic history, including its heroes and legends, the idea of *jihad* (sacred struggle), of sacrifice and martyrdom as well as its choice of dress (the *kuffiyah*, for example, was familiar from the 1930s, when it had been worn by the peasant rebels of the countryside) gave it an aura of power and authority that transcended theory and rational argument. One did not need to know a foreign language or to have studied abroad to comprehend its message or to advance up the ranks of the organisation. More importantly, Fatah's primary emphasis on the idea of 'return' responded uniquely to the longings of those still in the camps who, unable to spend their time in exile amassing wealth or educational qualifications, sought immediate results. For much of the displaced peasantry, the notion of 'return' to 'the land' meant not so much the freedom to live in an independent state of their own but the simple physical restoration of their homes, livelihoods and means of production.

This promise, together with the prospect of living with one's kin and of restoring the traditional social and communal networks which had been destroyed in 1948 and 1967, was far more attractive to many of the displaced refugees than the campaign offered by the Marxist movements for liberation through class struggle in the wider Arab context. The fact that Fatah also paid its fighters a monthly wage and promised to care for the wives and children of those killed or injured also made it attractive to many young men who might otherwise have been forced by communal pressure and the need to provide for their families to eschew involvement in politics and in armed struggle.

While other resistance movements, such as Saiqa and the Arab Liberation Front, also attracted support, their close ties with Syria and Iraq respectively limited their appeal primarily to those living in either of the two host countries. In Syria, where the Palestinian community was much larger than in Iraq, many Palestinians who might otherwise have volunteered for Fatah or for one of the Popular Fronts were forced by government restrictions in the 1970s to enrol in Saiqa if they wished to serve the Palestinian cause directly. In Iraq the presence of a

Fatah office whose leader in the 1970s, Sabri al-Banna (Abu Nidal), was sentenced to death by Fatah's Central Command in 1974 for his assassination attempts on resistance leaders divided the ranks of those outside the Arab Liberation Front (ALF) who supported the independent Palestinian movements.[39] For these reasons the main opposition movements within the Palestinian resistance were formed by the PFLP and by the DFLP, both of whom, like Fatah, were seen by Palestinians as existing independently of support from a particular Arab regime.

Both Fronts drew their recruits from those Palestinians who criticised Fatah's reliance on the Arab regimes for both diplomatic and financial support, its refusal actively to support other liberation movements within the Arab world and its lack of a clear ideology which took into account the class structure of the Palestinian diaspora. One of the major differences which separated them from Fatah became evident during the civil war in Jordan. While Fatah's cadres adhered firmly to the movement's policy of 'non-interference in the internal affairs of the Arab regimes', the PFLP and DFLP called for the overthrow of King Hussein and his replacement by a revolutionary government committed to the 'people's war of liberation'.[40] Once the fighting had begun, Yasser Arafat, Salah Khalaf and other leaders of Fatah sought to act as mediators between the King and the radicals in the two Fronts before Fatah was eventually forced to respond to the crackdown with arms as well.[41]

Although relations between the two Fronts and Fatah improved after the PNC in 1973 issued a call for the 'liberation of Jordan', Fatah's policy again diverged from that of the PFLP and the DFLP after the October 1973 war on the issue of relations with King Hussein.[42] The leaders of Fatah, who had urged acceptance of a 'ministate' in the West Bank, opened discussions with the government in Amman on proposals which would allow the PLO to re-establish *feda'iyyin* bases in the country while the PFLP, which had helped to set up the 'Rejection Front', continued to call for the overthrow of the monarchy and the liberation of the Arab world from the 'reactionary' regimes as well as for the liberation of the entire area of Palestine under Zionist occupation. At the end of 1982, when the PNC was split on the response to take to the Reagan Plan, Arafat again sought to reach a *rapprochement* with the King who was seeking, in accordance with US plans, to establish an autonomous Palestinian entity in the West Bank that would be allied to, and controlled by, Jordan. Despite opposition to the talks within Fatah's own Command Council, as well as from the PFLP and Democratic Front, Arafat renewed these talks at the end of 1983 after his expulsion from Tripoli.

In Lebanon the differences between Fatah and the two Fronts regarding policy towards the Arab governments showed themselves on the battlefront during the civil war of the mid-1970s. While overt conflict between Fatah and its opponents was avoided, Fatah's attempts during the early part of the war to avert a further escalation of the war and to avoid being drawn into the conflict, which opposed the Phalangists and other forces of the Lebanese right against those of the Lebanese National Movement (LNM), left many militants of both the PFLP and the DFLP vulnerable to attack. Unlike Fatah, both these groups were closely allied with leftist movements in the LNM. They had also helped to set up the Arab Popular Front for the Support of the Palestinian People led by the head of Lebanon's Progressive Socialist Party, Kamal Jumblatt, and to defend neighbourhoods, camps and villages that housed Lebanese and Syrian Muslims as well as the Palestinian poor.[43]

After the war Fatah's attempts to work out a *modus vivendi* with the Maronite Christians and with the Phalangist leaders also provoked sharp differences within the resistance and the attempts were harshly criticised by the PFLP's leader, George Habash.[44] Differences over the attitude to be taken towards the Arab regimes also provoked an open split in the resistance after the Israeli invasion of Lebanon in 1982. While many of Fatah's leaders continued to support Arafat's diplomatic campaign to gain the backing of the Arab states for modifications in the Reagan Plan that would lead to the establishment of an autonomous 'entity' in the West Bank, the PFLP, together with substantial numbers of fighters from other organisations, sought to insist on the primacy of the armed struggle and the importance of fighting US imperialism as well as Zionism and Arab reaction. Although both the PFLP and the DFLP refrained from supporting Fatah's dissidents when they opened fire on Fatah 'loyalists' in northern and eastern Lebanon in the summer and autumn of 1983, the extent of the divisions within Fatah itself indicated the degree to which the resistance as a whole was divided over both the question of the attitude to take towards the Arab regimes and to the question of continuing the armed struggle.[45]

These two related issues, and the differences within the resistance movements surrounding them, reflected the latent divisions within the Palestinian diaspora over the role that social revolution should take within the Palestinian liberation movement in particular and the Arab world in general. The Palestinian bourgeoisie in Saudi Arabia, Kuwait, the United Arab Emirates and, to a lesser extent, in the United States and Western Europe, favoured Fatah's policy of combining diplomatic negotiations with armed struggle while avoiding interference in the internal affairs of the Arab regimes or support for opposition movements in the Arab world. Concerned solely with the creation of an independent state on those parts of Palestinian territory which could be 'liberated' from Israeli occupation, these Palestinians saw the radical movements within the resistance as a threat to their own security in their countries of refuge and to the cohesion of the liberation movement as a whole. The radical demands of the PFLP and of the DFLP for Arab revolution, for a rejection of diplomatic and financial assistance from the conservative monarchies of the Gulf and for an increased military campaign against Western interests in the Arab world threatened their own positions while at the same time, in their view, making the ultimate aim of liberating Palestine more remote.

While the two Fronts so far have responded by avoiding an outright split in the resistance and by asserting the primacy of national unity, the emergence of a new generation of both working- and middle-class Palestinians who are disillusioned with the existing leadership of the PLO and with the continuing failure of the PLO's diplomatic campaign to achieve even its most minimal demands in the face of US and Israeli intransigence could lead, at minimum, to an increase in support for the views taken by the PFLP and the DFLP regarding the need to escalate the armed struggle and to extend it to those parts of the Arab world where the existing leaderships are seen as closely allied with the West. The decline of job prospects in the Gulf states as a result of the fall in oil revenues, the imposition of severe restrictions on Palestinian immigration to the Gulf and the growing sympathy which the Palestinian bourgeoisie has for the internal opposition in some of these states could also further increase the trend towards radicalisation and towards the establishment of closer links between the resistance and the underground opposition movements which exist in parts of the Gulf as well as in Jordan, Iraq and Egypt.

Aside from the differences over policy towards the Arab regimes and the conduct of the armed struggle, the differing levels of class consciousness within the resistance are also evident in the internal organisation of the various movements and in the institutions of the PLO. Only a few examples can be given here, but they help to illustrate the degree to which the existing division of labour, which has characterised the resistance since the ascendancy of Fatah, serves to enhance the interests of certain elements within Palestinian society at the expense of others and to prevent the equal sharing of the burdens of resistance among all sectors of Palestinian society.

For the PFLP and the DFLP, the importance of mass mobilisation

and of a 'people's war' along with armed struggle, has led to the establishment of grass-roots organisations within the camps that are considerably different from those of Fatah, Saiqa and the other movements
that place less emphasis on class consciousness. Communal systems of
self-help were more common in the camps controlled by the PFLP,
for example, than in those where Fatah dominated. Fighters and camp
workers were equally expected to share the burdens of the struggle,
unlike the situation in Fatah where the fighters, who were paid a
monthly salary, were often set apart from those who worked in the
schools, clinics and workshops in a civilian capacity and who received
their wages, if any, from UNRWA, from the Palestinian Red Crescent
or from SAMED.

Similarly, while Fatah attempted to duplicate the modern systems
of health and education which had impressed many middle-class Palestinians during their studies in the West, the PFLP and the DFLP sought
to avoid rigid hierarchies of command and to establish co-operatives
in the schools, clinics and workshops that encouraged popular participation and the acquisition of skills by those who had no qualifications
or craft experience.

In part this reflected the different level of resources available to the
various resistance movements. While Fatah and the PLO institutions
could draw on their substantial revenues from Palestinians working in
the Gulf and from the sizeable contributions they received from the
Arab regimes, the PFLP and the DFLP were forced to rely far more
heavily on volunteer workers and on the local production of equipment
and supplies. PFLP clinics, for example, used more paramedics than
specialists and placed greater emphasis on preventive care and on training mobile teams of personnel than did the Palestinian Red Crescent,
which established hospitals equipped with modern operating rooms
staffed by highly trained doctors, pharmacists and laboratory technicians trained in the United States and Europe. While Fatah, from the
middle of the 1970s on, also began to rely less on 'outside experts'
and to place more emphasis on training camp residents directly, very
few camp residents, whether young or old, men or women, have
advanced up Fatah's ranks sufficiently to re-direct its social services
in a way that is better suited to the needs of those in the camps, particularly the women, children and elderly.[46]

Other major differences exist in matters of administration and finance.
While Fatah's civilian organisations – and those of the PLO which it
controls – are mainly located in the capital centres of the Arab world
and are primarily staffed by middle-class, well-educated Palestinians,

both the PFLP and the DFLP have tended to operate with smaller circles of adherents drawn from various constituencies. The PFLP, for example, has organised social and medical services for young teachers in Kuwait, for workers in Gaza and for camp residents and students in Lebanon and Jordan. The DFLP is particularly active within student organisations in the United States and Europe which include Palestinians and other Arab students as well as sympathisers drawn from progressive movements in the West. Finally, unlike Fatah, which invests a substantial share of its revenues in financial institutions which channel sums to corporations and banks in the United States and Europe, both Fronts eschew such 'capitalist' activity in favour of projects that combine the use of labour and capital in ways that will benefit the local communities directly.[47]

This is not to say, however, that the latent class conflicts evident in the different ideologies and practices of the various resistance movements are a deciding, or even primary, factor in the conduct of the resistance. The continuing oppression which all Palestinians have felt during their long years of exile and occupation, combined with the repeated dispersals many have endured in Lebanon, Jordan and the occupied territories of the West Bank and Gaza, have so far overshadowed the social divisions within Palestinian society. While class consciousness is likely to increase and to manifest itself in changes within the PLO leadership and in the way in which the resistance movements are organised, Palestinian nationalism remains the dominant ideology, consciously or unconsciously, to which most Palestinians in the diaspora adhere. Demands by Palestinians for social reforms or for revolutionary social transformation, both within Palestinian society and within the Arab world as a whole, may grow, but they are likely to grow alongside, rather than in conflict with, the desire for national liberation.

Finally it must also be noted that Palestinian consciousness, and the ideology of the various movements which make up the PLO, are also related to the state of the Arab world in general. The outbreak of fighting between the Palestinian loyalists, led by Yasser Arafat, and the dissidents, led by Abu Musa and Abu Salih, in 1983, rather than reflecting a growing class consciousness among Palestinians, instead served to demonstrate the degree to which national unity had been weakened in the wake of the defeat in Beirut and the massacre of hundreds of Palestinian men, women and children in the camps of Sabra and Chatilla in September 1982. This dissension within Fatah threatened to open the movement even more to interference by the

Arab regimes, with Arafat and the loyalists supported by Egypt, Jordan and Saudi Arabia, the dissidents by Syria and Libya and the PFLP and the DFLP by South Yemen and the various opposition movements within Lebanon and the Arab world.

While such internecine conflict within the leadership of the national movement, and particularly within its armed cadres, resembled that which had occurred during the three-year revolt in Palestine in the 1930s, in Jordan in the 1950s and in Lebanon in the early 1970s, it was doubtful that the end result would be another phase of relative passivity. A change in any of the Arab regimes could dramatically alter the balance of power within the Arab world and, consequently, within the PLO itself. Similarly, armed aggression against Syria, Lebanon or any other Arab state by Israel almost certainly would lead to an upsurge of resistance among both the Palestinians and the opposition forces within the Arab world, including the 'left' as well as the Islamic militants. Further attacks in the West Bank were also to be expected, given Israel's intransigence on the question of Jewish settlements.

Thirty-five years after the creation of the state of Israel, the Palestinians appeared bloody, but unbowed. With the skills and determination acquired in the long years of exile, their struggle to achieve a state of their own would go on, just as it had since 1920.

NOTES

Introduction

1. Penguin Books, Harmondsworth, Middlesex, 1970.
2. *The Third World* (London, 1975), p. viii.

1 Palestine under the Ottomans

1. In some areas, particularly in southern Palestine, the sheikh's position was held by a local leader bearing the title 'amir, i.e. 'prince', a remnant of Mamluke usage. However, since they generally acted in the same manner as the sheikhs, employing a similar pattern of alliances and operating within the same overall hierarchical structures, I have referred to this form of government throughout as 'sheikhal'. Interestingly in Egypt itself the strongest leader of the Mamlukes, elected by them at fixed intervals, was called 'Sheikh al-Balad', i.e. 'Sheikh of the Country'; Stanford J. Shaw, *Ottoman Egypt in the Eighteenth Century* (Cambridge, Mass., 1962), pp. 9-10; P. M. Holt, 'The Later Ottoman Empire and the Fertile Crescent' in P. M. Holt, Ann Lambton and Bernard Lewis (eds.), *Cambridge History of Islam* (2 vols., Cambridge, 1970), vol. 1, p. 378.
2. The names are thought to be derived from two mythical brothers of pre-Islamic Arabia. *Encyclopedia of Islam,* old edn. (8 vols., Leiden and London, 1913-18).
3. Anonymous, trans. and compiled by R. A. Steward MacAlister and E. W. G. Masterman, 'Occasional Papers on the Modern Inhabitants of Palestine', Palestine Exploration Fund, *Quarterly Statement* (October 1905), pp. 343-52; (January 1906), pp. 33, 42-3. In battle the two opposing sides were distinguished by their banners and costume. The colour worn by the Qais was red and the Yaman white.
4. Elizabeth A. Finn, *Palestine Peasantry, Notes on their Clans, Religion and Laws* (Edinburgh, 1923), pp. 18-21. Although most Muslims in Palestine were Sunnis, only about 10 per cent followed the Hanafi code favoured by the Ottoman Turks. The majority were adherents of the Shafa'i code, while about 10 per cent practised Hanbali rites. Fannie Fern Andrews, *The Holy Land under the Mandate* (2 vols., Boston and New York, 1931), vol. 1, p. 189.
5. Ihsan al-Nimr, *Tarikh Jabal Nablus wa-l-Balqa* (History of Jebel Nablus and the Balqa) (2 vols., Nablus, 1937 and 1961), vol. 2.

6. Nimr, vol. 2, pp. 265-8; MacAlister, 'Occasional Papers' (October 1905), p. 356.

7. MacAlister, Part 1 (1905), p. 344. A *zalat* was a silver coin of four drachms weight.

8. Shaw, p. 5; Bernard Lewis, *The Emergence of Modern Turkey* (London, 1968), pp. 442-3.

9. Samuel Bergheim, 'Land Tenure in Palestine', Palestine Exploration Fund, *Quarterly Statement* (July 1894).

10. A. Granott, *The Land System in Palestine* (London, 1952) (first Herbrew edition, *Ha-Mishtar ha-Qarq'i be-Eretz Israel,* published under the author's former name, A. Granovsky, Tel Aviv, 1949), p. 79.

11. Granott, pp. 87, 91-3.

12. 'Umar Salih Barghouthi and D. Khalil Tawtah, *Tarikh Filistin* (*History of Palestine*) (Jerusalem, 1922), pp. 265-8, cited in Nabil Badran, *Al-Ta'lim wa-l-tahdith fi-l-mujtama' al-'arabiyyi al-filistiniyyi* (*Education and Modernisation in Palestinian Arab Society*) (Beirut, 1969), p. 32.

13. Granott, pp. 81-2.

14. C.R. Conder, *Tent Work in Palestine* (2 vols., London, 1878), vol. 2, p. 328. Lawrence Oliphant put the figure as high as 200,000 *dunums* (18,000 hectares) in his *Haifa, or Life in Modern Palestine* (London, 1887), p. 292.

15. Oliphant, *Haifa,* p. 60.

16. Y. Firestone, 'Production and Trade in an Islamic Context: Sharika Contracts in the Economy of Northern Samaria 1853-1943', *International Journal of Middle East Studies,* vol. 6 (1975), p. 309; 'Arif al-'Arif, *Tarikh al-Quds* (*History of Jerusalem*) (Cairo, 1951), p. 125; Shmuel Avitsur, 'The Influence of Western Technology on the Economy of Palestine during the Nineteenth Century' in Moshe Maoz, *Studies on Palestine during the Ottoman Period* (Jerusalem, 1975), pp. 485-98.

17. Great Britain, Parliamentary Papers, Accounts and Papers, *Diplomatic Reports from HM Consuls on the Manufacturing and Commerce of their Consular Districts – Jerusalem and Jaffa* (1908); Arthur Ruppin, *Syrien als Wirtschaftsgebiet* (Berlin and Vienna, 1920), p. 61; Badran, p. 43. For more details on the growth of the citrus industry, see F. A. Klein, 'Life, Habits and Customs of the Fellahin of Palestine', Palestine Exploration Fund, *Quarterly Statement* (April 1881) and N. Verney and G. Dambmann, *Les puissances étrangères dans le Levant, en Syrie et en Palestine* (Paris, 1900).

18. Lewis, p. 177; Uriel Heyd, 'The Later Ottoman Empire in Rumelia and Anatolia', *Cambridge History of Islam,* vol. 1, pp. 376-8. See also 'Report on the State of Palestine, presented to the Rt Honourable Mr Winston Churchill, PC, MP, by the Executive Committee of the Third Arab Palestinian Congress', Jerusalem, 28 March 1921, p. 38, cited in Andrews, vol. 2, pp. 76-7.

19. Heyd, pp. 365-7.

20. Lewis, pp. 105-8, 365-7.

21. Israel Margalith, *Le Baron Edmond de Rothschild et la*

colonisation juive en Palestine 1882-1889 (Paris, 1957), pp. 141-2, cited in Nathan Weinstock, *Zionism: False Messiah*, trans. from the French and ed. Alan Adler) (London, 1979), p. 66.

22. Granott, pp. 80-1; Chaim Weizmann, *Trial and Error: An Autobiography of Chaim Weizmann* (London, 1949), p. 457; Khairiyah Qasmiyah, 'Najib Nassar and *Carmel* Newspaper', *Shuun Filistiniyyah (Palestinian Affairs)* (July 1973), p. 111. See also Oliphant, *Haifa*, and his *The Land of Gilead* (New York, 1881), p. 277.

2   The Transformation of Palestinian Society, 1876-1917

1. The name is derived from the French phrase, 'La Jeune Turquie', used by the Committee on the pamphlets they printed in Paris and Brussels where they had secretly organised themselves in the preceding decade. Sherif Arif Mardin, 'Libertarian Movements in the Ottoman Empire, 1878-1895', *Middle East Journal*, vol. 16, no. 2 (Spring 1962), p. 169. For a history of the Committee's origins, see also Mardin's *The Genesis of Young Ottoman Thought* (Princeton, 1962) and Ernest E. Ramsauer Jr., *The Young Turks: Prelude to the Revolution of 1908* (Princeton, 1957). Neville Mandel's *The Arabs and Zionism before World War One* (Berkeley, Los Angeles and London, 1976) also contains useful information on this period, although it is primarily devoted to a study of Arab resistance to Jewish colonisation from 1882 to 1914.

2. Delegates were sent from Palestine, including Sa'id Bey al-Hussaini, Ruhi Bey al-Khalidi and Hafiz Bey al-Sa'id. In 1913, a member of the Alami clan was elected, and the delegate from the Hussaini clan, Ahmad 'Arif al-Hussaini, was defeated by a rival candidate from the Nashashibis. 'Arif, *Tarikh*, pp. 120-1. See also Zeine Zeine, 'The Arab Lands', *Cambridge History of Islam*, vol. 1, pp. 586-91.

3. Heyd, pp. 360-1.

4. Carl Brockelmann, *History of the Islamic Peoples,* trans. Joel Carmichael and Moshe Perlmann (New York, 1960; 1st edn, Munich, 1939), p. 385.

5. Heyd, pp. 372-3.

6. Among the many studies of this era, Albert Hourani's *Arabic Thought in the Liberal Age* (London, 1967) remains the definitive intellectual history of the origins of Arab nationalism. George Antonius's *The Arab Awakening* (Beirut, 1955; 1st edn London, 1938) is widely regarded as the first work, in English, to explain Arab nationalism from an Arab point of view. Nikki Keddie's *Sayyid Jamal ad-Din 'al-Afghani': A Political Biography* (Berkeley, 1972) is a detailed history of reformist thought in Islam at the turn of the century. Both A. L. Tibawi's *A Modern History of Syria, Including Lebanon and Palestine* (London, 1969) and Zeine Zeine, *Arab-Turkish Relations and the Emergence of Arab Nationalism* (Beirut, 1958) contain material not found elsewhere. H. A. R. Gibb, *Modern Trends in Islam* (Chicago, 1947), although

subject to re-interpretation by those critical of the 'orientalist' approach, nevertheless combines a lucid exposition with a sense of immediacy not present in contemporary histories of the period.

7. Nimr (1961), vol. 2, p. 158.

8. Badran, p.22; *Encyclopedia of Islam* (old edition), 'Waqf'; and interview with Burhan Dajani, London, November 1981. For a detailed description of the types and amounts of *waqf* land in Palestine, see Granott, pp. 137-55; A. L. Tibawi, *The Islamic Pious Foundations in Jerusalem* (London, 1978) and 'Arif, *Tarikh*.

9. Nimr, vol. 2; B. Dajani, interview; Badran, pp. 20-1.

10. Badran, pp. 22-3; Nimr, ibid.; B. Dajani, interview.

11. Muhammad Kurd 'Ali, *Khutat al-Sham* (*The Districts of Syria*) (6 vols., Damascus, 1925-8); special section on the *awqaf*, pp. 101-30; Muhammad 'Izza Darwazah, *Al-Qadaiyyah al-filistiniyyah fi-mukhtalifi marahiliha* (*The Various Stages of the Palestinian Problem*) (Sidon, 1959), p. 51; Badran, p. 22.

12. Badran, p. 20; Granott, pp. 152-3. Claude Cahen, in 'Economy, Society, Institutions', (*Cambridge History of Islam*, vol. 2, p. 519) notes that such registration also occurred as a way to ensure that land was retained solely by the male heirs, i.e. contrary to the Islamic laws of inheritance which guaranteed the right to inherit land regardless of sex.

13. Nimr, cited in Badran, pp. 22-3; p. 33.

14. Darwazah, ibid.; Badran, ibid. See also 'Arif, *Tarikh*, for a list of the families which participated in the Supreme Muslim Council and so also in the control of the *awqaf*.

15. Badran, p. 24; Ruppin, *Syrien als Wirtschaftsgebiet*, p. 242; Granott, p. 151.

16. Badran, ibid.

17. Ibid.

18. Badran, pp. 25-6; Andrews, vol. 2, p. 198.

19. 'Umar al-Salih al-Barghouthi, 'Al-Iqta' fi filistin', *Al-'Arab*, 11 March 1933, cited in Badran, p. 32. By 1930 the number of individuals in the Barghouthi clan had risen to 3,000; the Jaiyussis and the Abdul Hadis each counted 600. For the number of villages owned by each of these clans, see p. 13.

20. 'Arif, *Tarikh*, pp. 124-5; J.-A. Jaussen, *Coutumes palestiniennes I: Naplouse et son district* (Paris, 1927), p. 135. By the time of the Mandate, there were some fifty soap factories in Jaffa and Haifa, as well as Nablus. Regarded as a luxury because it was made from olive oil, much of the annual production of about 8,000 tons was exported to Egypt, Syria and other parts of the Arab world. Hannah Solh, *Filistin wa-tajdid hayatiha* (*Palestine and the Modernisation of its Life*) (Jerusalem, 1919), p. 78; Badran, p. 47.

21. The extent of Arab investment in citrus cultivation can be gauged by the fact that of the 1,608,570 boxes of fruit exported from Jaffa in 1913, Arab growers accounted for 65 per cent, Jews 24 per cent and Germans 2.5 per cent of the total. Badran, p. 43.

22. Lewis, pp. 448-9; Cahen in *Cambridge History of Islam*, vol. 2, pp. 522-3. The use of the word 'foreign' here can be somewhat

misleading; it refers, in fact, to trade conducted between 'Dar al-Islam' and 'Dar al-harb', i.e. between the Muslim and non-Muslim states. Within the Ottoman Empire, and indeed within the Islamic world as a whole, Muslim merchants engaged in long-distance trade and the Empire as a whole prospered greatly because of this extensive commerce. See Samir Amin, *La nation arabe* (Paris, 1976).

23. A. H. Hourani, 'The Changing Face of the Fertile Crescent in the Eighteenth Century', *Studica Islamica*, vol. 13 (1957), pp. 89-122.

24. Heyd, pp. 368-9.

25. Vital Cuinet, *Syrie, Liban et Palestine: géographie administrative, statistique, descriptive et raisonée* (Paris, 1896); J. B. Barron, *Palestine: Report and General Abstracts of the Census of 1922* (Jerusalem, 1923), p. 3; James Parkes, *A History of Palestine from 135 AD to Modern Times* (London, 1949), p. 276; Mandel, p. xx.

26. Mandel, p. 20; Parkes, p. 275.

27. Parkes, p. 275.

28. Mandel, p. xxi.

29. Ruppin, p. 186.

30. By 1913 the price of land in central Jerusalem was six times as much as that located outside the city walls. In Jaffa and Haifa the ratio was even higher, often amounting to 15 or 20 times the cost of land located outside the city. Ruppin, pp. 519-20.

31. Solh, p. 97; Badran, p. 43.

32. Solh, p. 53; Badran, ibid.

33. Avitsur in Moshe Maoz (ed.), *Studies on Palestine during the Ottoman Period* (Jerusalem, 1975), pp. 485-94.

34. Ibid.; 'Arif, *Tarikh*, p. 125.

35. Heyd, p. 369; Badran, p. 35; Ruppin, p. 355.

36. Charles Issawi, 'Asymmetrical Development and Transport in Egypt, 1880-1914' in W. R. Polk and Richard L. Chambers (eds.), *Beginnings of Modernisation in the Middle East: The Nineteenth Century* (Chicago, 1969), p. 394, cited in Gabriel Baer, 'The Impact of Economic Change on Traditional Society in Nineteenth-Century Palestine', in Maoz, pp. 495-8.

37. The extensive use of foreign-owned, rather than local, companies stemmed from the pressures put on the Sultan in the wake of the financial collapse of the mid-1870s. In 1881 the Powers forced the Ottoman Treasury to agree to the establishment of a Council of the Public Debt to ensure that foreign debts, and the interest due on them, was paid according to the schedules demanded by the foreign creditors. Since the Treasury was virtually bankrupt, the debt, which amounted to some £200 million sterling in 1881, was to be met by granting the creditors exclusive rights to all the profitable sectors of the economy, whether these were located in the Turkish, European or Arab provinces. Lewis, pp. 446-8; George E. Kirk, *A Short History of the Middle East*, 7th revised edn (New York, 1964), pp. 86-96.

38. Mandel, pp. 23-5; Ronald Storrs, *Orientations* (London, 1943), p. 442; Kirk, *Short History of the Middle East*, p. 86. For the development of the Mavromatis electricity concession in Jerusalem and of the

Sursock and Baihum land reclamation scheme (later taken over by Salim al-Salam of Beirut) and their subsequent loss after the British occupation of Palestine, see Barbara J. Smith, 'British Economic Policy in Palestine towards the Development of the Jewish National Home: 1920-1929', unpublished D Phil thesis, St Antony's College, Oxford, 1978, pp. 250-7.

39. Shimon Shamir, 'The Impact of Western Ideas on Traditional Society in Ottoman Palestine' in Maoz, pp. 507-16; Abdul Wahab Kayyali, *Palestine: A Modern History* (London, 1978), pp. 32, 36-9; David Hirst, *The Gun and the Olive Branch: The Roots of Violence in the Middle East* (London, 1977), pp. 30-2; Mandel, pp. 127-8.

40. Solh, p. 77. Alfred Bonné, *State and Economics in the Middle East* (London, 1955), p. 230; Badran, p. 47.

41. Badran, p. 49.

42. Two excellent works which include descriptive material on the guilds in late Ottoman Egypt are André Raymond's 'Quartiers et mouvements populaires au Caire au XIIIème siècle' and Afaf Loutfi el Sayed's 'The Role of the 'Ulama in Egypt during the Early Nineteenth Century', both of which are available in P. M. Holt (ed.), *Political and Social Change in Modern Egypt* (London, 1968). A more general survey is contained in Gabriel Baer's 'Guilds in Middle Eastern History' in M. A. Cook (ed.), *Studies in the Economic History of the Middle East* (London, 1970) and in Cahen in *Cambridge History of Islam*, pp. 527-9.

43. Badran, p. 49.

44. Badran, pp. 49-50; Baer, 'Guilds', p. 23.

45. 'Arif, *Tarikh*, p. 124; Badran, pp. 47-8. By 1925, despite the disruption caused by the war, the total production of religious articles was valued at £70,000 sterling. Some 1,500 workers were employed in the industry in Bethlehem alone.

46. Badran, pp. 47-8.

47. 'Arif, *Tarikh*, p. 124.

48. Granott, pp. 293-4.

49. The form of landholding in Palestine was particularly liable to a division of labour in production for ploughing, sowing, the provision of water or animals, the cultivation of orchards, etc. This increased the amount of produce that could be expropriated from the peasants in the form of rent or interest. See text, Chapter 1.

50. Badran, pp. 54,57-9; Oliphant, *Life in Modern Palestine*, pp. 194-5.

51. Louis Lortet, *La Syrie d'aujourd'hui* (Paris, 1881) and Oliphant, *Life in Modern Palestine*, pp. 194-5; Badran, pp. 52-3; Granott, pp. 82-4.

52. *Al-'Arab*, 17 June 1933, cited in Badran, p. 37.

53. Weinstock, p. 75.

54. Hirst, p. 29; Granott, pp. 280, 292-5; Nevill Barbour, *Nisi Dominus: A Survey of the Palestine Controversy* (Beirut, 1969), pp. 113-4; Mandel, pp. 35-7. The latter describes a similar process, involving two Arab money-lenders from Jaffa, which resulted in the expulsion of the original owners of the land 'sold' to the Jewish settlement of Petah Tikvah in the 1880s.

55. Weinstock, p. 80. He notes that although the percentage of land sold by the peasantry amounted to 42.7 per cent in the decade 1891-1900, the total amount sold by them was relatively small compared to later sales. From 1901 to 1914, when huge purchases were made by the Jewish Colonisation Association and by other Zionist organisations, sales by the peasantry accounted for only 4.3 per cent of all the land sold. The decline in the percentage reflected an increasing opposition to Zionism on the part of the peasantry and an awareness of its political aims with regard to Palestine rather than any improvement in their own material conditions.

56. 'Arif, *Tarikh,* pp. 125-7; Badran, pp. 52-3; Granott, p. 296.

57. Weinstock, p. 55; Granott, p. 294.

58. Weinstock, pp. 63-4. 'Harrath' in *Encyclopedia of Islam.*

59. The annual income of a comfortable peasant family of seven people in 1904 was estimated to total no more than the equivalent of £P27. Weinstock, pp. 58, 62.

60. Weinstock, p. 62.

61. D. Kalayi, 'La deuxième alyah' in *Le mouvement ouvrier juif en Israël* (n.p., 1949), pp. 55-6, cited in Weinstock, p. 68.

62. Badran, p. 59.

63. Ibid., pp. 56-9. The effect of the rise of wage labour on the structure of the peasant family in Palestine urgently needs investigation as well. Few studies exist, but the indications are that one result, aside from the increasing division of labour along sexual lines, was the isolation of the women and children and an intensification of the male role in preserving the honour (*'ird*) of their womenfolk, and hence of the family as a whole. This may have stemmed from the increasing importance of children as agricultural labour and from a breakdown in the traditional patterns of endogamy, i.e. of the marriage within the village and amongst one's own kin. See Chapter 3 and Hilma Granqvist, *Marriage Conditions in a Palestinian Village* (Helsingfors, 1931).

64. Parkes, p. 279.

65. Parkes, pp. 278-9.

66. Interview with Yusif al-Bandaq, Beirut, April 1972. See also Storrs, pp. 286-7, and Barbour, pp. 95, 132.

67. A British government official reported in 1920 that 'The devastation caused by the malaria reached its climax during the recent military campaign, when moving masses of Turkish troops, almost all suffering from malaria, carried the disease from place to place . . . and infected a population already weakened by under-feeding'. *Report on the Administration of Palestine, 1920-1921,* cited in Barbour, p. 119. Typhus and meningitis were also rampant. Storrs, pp. 293-5.

68. Storrs, pp. 287, 294.

69. Parkes, p. 279. In addition to the problems of hunger and disease, heavy snowstorms hit Jerusalem, the hill country and Galilee. Fuel was in extremely short supply, most of the trees — including the olive and citrus groves — having already been felled. Storrs, pp. 302, 308.

3 The British Mandate

1. Hussain-McMahon Correspondence (14 July to 24 October 1915), Cmd. 5957, p. 5, cited in Barbour, pp. 86-7.

2. Government of Palestine, *A Survey of Palestine* (2 vols., Jerusalem, 1945); *idem, Supplement to the Survey of Palestine* (Jerusalem, 1947), p. 15.

3. Lord Balfour, Britain's Foreign Secretary at the time of the British occupation of Jerusalem, was to write at the end of the war: 'The four Great Powers are committed to Zionism, and Zionism, be it right or wrong, good or bad, is rooted in age-long tradition, in present needs and future hopes of far profounder import than the desires and prejudices of the 700,000 Arabs who now inhabit that ancient land.' E. L. Woodward and R. Butler (eds.), *Documents on British Foreign Policy, 1919-1939* (London, 1952), first series, vol. 4, p. 345.

4. The development of the motor car, and of the aeroplane, had a dramatic effect on military strategy in the years just preceding the war. A British air base in Cyprus connected to Palestine and to new all-weather roads linking the Mediterranean coast with the Arabian Gulf would eliminate the need to supply India by sea along the Cape route. In the course of the war, it became a paramount aim of British policy to secure access to the overland route and, above all, to prevent it falling into hostile hands.

5. Sami Hadawi and Robert John, *The Palestine Diary* (2 vols., Beirut, 1970), vol. 1, p. 54.

6. Ibid., p. 55. For the full text see Woodward and Butler (eds.), pp. 241-51.

7. The declaration was issued on 7 November 1918, just before the German surrender. Hadawi and John, vol. 1, pp. 97-9; Barbour, pp. 71, 87; Kirk, *Short History of the Middle East*, p. 138; David Waines, *The Unholy War: Israel and Palestine 1879-1971* (Wilmette, Ill., 1971), pp. 53-5. For Hussain's views on British intentions in Palestine, his rejection of an independent Jewish state in Palestine and of the controversial accord signed in 1919 by Hussain's son and representative in Damascus, the Amir Faisal, that 'All necessary measures should be taken to encourage and stimulate immigration of Jews into Palestine on a large scale,' see Barbour, pp. 69, 89-90, 102; Kayyali, *Palestine*, pp. 65-6; Simha Flapan, *Zionism and the Palestinians* (London and New York, 1979), pp. 37-52; and Weizmann, p. 308.

8. Doreen Ingrams, *Palestine Papers 1917-1922, Seeds of Conflict* (London, 1972), p. 73.

9. Barbour, p. 70.

10. Ibid., p. 62. See also Nicholas Bethell, *The Palestine Triangle* (London, 1980), pp. 16-17, and Lloyd George's own account in *The Truth about the Peace Treaties* (London, 1938).

11. Text in Ingrams, pp. 12-13, and Barbour, p. 61.

12. The statement has been attributed to Arthur Koestler, author of *Promise and Fulfilment: Palestine 1917-1949* (London, 1949),

and is cited in Bethell, p. 17. Bethell himself notes that the Arabs felt that 'Britain and her allies had no more right to promise the Jews a home in Palestine than, say, Iraq would have had to promise them a home in California', ibid, p. 17.

13. Stephen S. Wise and Jacob Haas, *The Great Betrayal* (New York, 1930), p. 288.

14. Palestine Royal (Peel) Commission, *Report* (Cmd. 5479, London, 1937), cited in Hadawi and John, vol. 1, p. 90.

15. Barbour, pp. 62, 97. Arab newspapers which obtained a copy from the Turks were prevented from publishing its contents by military censorship and threats of dire consequences should they fail to observe the regulations. Kayyali, *Palestine,* p. 45. The Sykes-Picot agreement was not published by the British government until 1939. Hadawi and John, vol. 1, p. 95.

16. The causes of the riots, in which more than a hundred Arabs and Jews were killed and another 451 injured, are described in the *Report of the Commission of Inquiry into the Palestine Disturbances of May 1921* (the Haycraft Report) (Cmd. 1540, London, 1921). A complete description is contained in Hirst, pp. 45-73, and Kayyali, *Palestine,* pp. 70-9. For a criticism of the treaties by Lord Grey, Foreign Secretary at the time of the Hussain-McMahon Correspondence, Lord Curzon and others, and the rejection of the Mandate by the House of Lords, see Barbour, pp. 65-9, 106-8, and Bethell, pp. 18-19, as well as Ingrams, p. 169. On attempts at *rapprochement* see Hadawi and John, vol. 1, Ch. 4; Barbour, pp. 70-2, 88-90; and Flapan, pp. 31-48.

17. Winston Churchill attempted in the White Paper of 1922 to distinguish between 'a Jewish National Home' in Palestine, with the connotations it carried of creating a Jewish state at Palestinian expense, and a 'national home *in* Palestine' (my italics) in which Arabs and Jews would live together in peace. However it was impossible to reconcile either with the Wilsonian principle of self-determination originally encouraged by the League of Nations, since the Palestinian Arabs, who constituted 93 per cent of the population, had never been consulted about the Balfour Declaration prior to its becoming a matter of policy. The text of the White Paper (Cmd. 1700) is reproduced in the *Survey,* vol. 1, pp. 87-90.

The Paper also made it clear that the provisions of the Mandate regarding Jewish settlement in Trans-Jordan would be ignored, despite vehement Zionist protests. By this time the British had installed the Amir Abdullah, the son of Sharif Hussain, in Amman, and were anxious to avoid any further friction with the Hashimites. The exemption was subsequently ratified by the League in September 1922.

18. Storrs, p. 345; Barbour, pp. 69-70.

19. Barbour, pp. 70, 124. The local Jewish populations, which spoke a Sephardic dialect, complained that the Hebrew used in the Zionist schools was virtually incomprehensible as a result of Yiddish and Slavonic accretions. Storrs, p. 367.

20. Storrs, pp. 346-8.

21. For the text of the military reports criticising the activities of the Zionist Commission written by the Chief Administrator in Palestine, Sir Louis Bols, see W. F. Boustany, *The Palestine Mandate Invalid and Impracticable* (Beirut, 1936), p. 135, reprinted in Barbour, pp 96-7.

22. *Survey*, vol. 1, p. 18. The sudden announcement of a resumption in Jewish immigration, now officially encouraged by an occupying power, was a major cause for the outbreak of demonstrations and rioting in Jaffa in May 1921, in which 13 Jews were killed. See Hirst, pp. 48-58 and Kayyali, *Palestine*, pp. 95-9.

23. Calculated from official statistics given in the *Survey*, vol. 1, p. 185. For a description of the legislation concerning immigration into Palestine see ibid., pp. 165-83. The debate on 'economic absorptive capacity' and the views of the various commissions sent by London to examine immigration policies are discussed in Barbour, pp. 109, 135-42 and 152-64. For Arab reaction to the legislation see Kayyali, *Palestine*, pp. 155-83, and Hirst, pp. 45-106.

24. *Survey*, vol. 1, p. 14.

25. Dr Arthur Ruppin, Land Settlement Officer in Palestine at the time, calculated that nine-tenths of all the land bought by Jews up to 1929 was acquired from absentee landlords. Barbour, p. 118. See also Ruppin's own work on the subject, *The Jewish Fate and Future* (London, 1940).

26. Barbour, pp. 117-18. For the Arab reaction to the sale, which produced violent protests at the time, see the memoranda of the Arab Executive reproduced in Abdul Wahab Kayyali (ed.), *Withaiq al-muqaw-wamah al-filistiniyyah al-'arabiyyah 1918-1939* (*Documents of the Palestinian Arab Resistance 1918-1939*) (Beirut, 1968), pp. 85, 217, 357-8.

27. Yehoshua Porath, *The Emergence of the Palestinian Arab National Movement* (2 vols., London, 1974 and 1977), vol. 2: *1929-1939*, p. 83; *Survey*, vol. 1, p. 299.

28. Barbour, pp. 120-2; Badran, p. 37.

29. Barbour, pp. 123, 142, 185; *Survey*, Supplement, pp. 32-3.

30. *Survey*, vol. 1, pp. 103, 244.

31. Weinstock, pp. 132-4.

32. Barbour, p. 137. According to Weinstock in *Zionism*, the accumulation of capital in Palestine during this period benefited greatly from a pact, known as the Haavara (Transfer) Agreement, signed by the Zionist Organisation with the Reich concerning the transfer of German-Jewish assets to Palestine. See pp. 135-6.

33. *Survey*, vol. 1, p. 125, and vol. 2, p. 536.

34. Government of Palestine, Department of Migration, *Annual Report* (Jerusalem, 1938).

35. For details of the Fund's leases and of Poale Zion, see Weinstock, pp. 41-50, 70-6, 132; Flapan, pp. 178-87, and Arie Bober (ed.), *The Other Israel* (New York, 1972), pp. 145-58. The net result of such a policy was that the numbers of evictions of Arab tenants increased dramatically, culminating in violent protests as early as 1908. Mandel, pp. 66-70.

36. Significantly, the issuance of labour certificates was not related to the number of either Jewish or Arab unemployed in the country, and increased immigration was often accompanied by a steady rise in the number of unemployed and in the amount of funds spent by the government for relief. Waines, pp. 76-7.

37. Weinstock, p. 135.

38. Flapan, pp. 199-208, 219-23; Barbour, pp. 138-9; Weinstock, pp. 142-5, 152-3.

39. New research conducted by Simha Flapan, the editor of the influential Jerusalem monthly, *New Outlook,* using previously unavailable material from the Zionist archives, establishes that 'the Zionist leadership . . . had made the fateful decision as early as February 1937 to stake everything on partition . . . including the concept of using the British army to effect the compulsory transfer of Arabs out of the Jewish state'. *Zionism,* p. 232. For the views of Judah Magnes, Pinchas Rutenburg, Martin Buber, A. M. Hyamson and other leading Zionists who were adamantly opposed to the creation of a separate economy, and to partition, see pp. 217-30, 267-73.

40. The Mandate had provided that 'An appropriate Jewish Agency shall be recognised as a public body for the purpose of advising and co-operating with the Administration of Palestine in such economic, social, and other matters as may affect the establishment of the Jewish National Home and the interests of the Jewish population in Palestine' (Article IV). The Agency was empowered 'to construct or operate . . . public works, services, utilities, and to develop any of the natural resources of the country, insofar as these matters are not directly undertaken by the Administration' (Article XI) and to assist the Administration in its efforts to 'encourage . . . close settlement by Jews on the land, including state land and waste lands not required for public purposes' (Article VI). *Survey,* vol. 1, pp. 4-11.

41. For details of the administrative changes, see H. St John Philby, 'Trans-Jordan', *Journal of the Royal Central Asian Society,* vol. 2, part 4, (1924), pp. 296-312.

42. In Palestine Egyptian notes and coins were used as legal tender from 1921 to 1927 when the Egyptian pound was replaced by a Palestinian unit minted in London and linked to sterling. 'Arif, *Tarikh,* p. 161.

43. Palestine Citizenship Order-in-Council, 24 July 1925, *Official Gazette,* no. 147 (16 June 1925). For the dilemmas facing Palestinians living abroad, and their subsequent loss of citizenship, see Mrs Stuart Erskine, *Palestine of the Arabs* (London, Bombay and Sydney, 1935), pp. 169-70.

44. 'Umar Djabry, 'La question économique' in 'La Syrie sous le régime du Mandat', unpublished PhD thesis, University of Toulouse, 1934, pp. 265-6; Fifth Report of the Chambers of Commerce, March 1933, in *Memorandum of the Merchants Association,* Beirut, 8 September 1933.

45. 'Palestine Citizenship Order', part 3; *Survey,* vol. 1, p. 207.

46. FO 371/3384, 18 October 1918, cited in Kayyali, *Palestine,* p. 56.

47. For details, see *Survey*, vol. 2, pp. 541-2, 853-72.

48. Government of Palestine, Department of Statistics, *Statistical Abstract of Palestine, 1937/8* (August 1938), p. 59; *idem, General Monthly Bulletin of Current Statistics* (August 1938), p. 330.

49. *Statistical Abstract of Palestine*, pp. 77, 79; Sawwaf Husni, 'Foreign Trade' in Said Himadeh (ed.), *The Economic Organisation of Palestine* (Beirut, 1938), p. 406.

50. *Survey*, vol. 1, p. 463.

51. *Statistical Abstract*, p. 78; Sawwaf, p. 410; *Survey*, vol. 1, p. 474.

52. Montague Brown, 'Agriculture' in Himadeh (ed.), p. 111. The *Survey* provides figures on land ownership by nationality only for the year 1943, when the amount of land owned by Jews totalled 1,514,247 *dunums*, or 13.6 per cent of the total arable land. Vol. 2, p. 566.

53. *Survey*, vol. 1, p. 141.

54. Calculated from population figures in the *Survey*, where the Jewish population in 1935 is given as 355,157, and from the total amounts of arable and non-arable land given in the *Survey*, vol. 2, p. 566. For a discussion of the various estimates of total arable land, see Himadeh, 'Natural Resources', in his work cited above, pp. 44-5; Granott, pp. 103-7; and Sir John Hope Simpson, *Report on Immigration, Land Settlement and Development* (Cmd. 3686, London, 1930), p. 22.

55. The estimates of the minimum holding needed to maintain subsistence are for non-irrigated land. Where irrigation was available, or where sufficient capital was provided to support dairy farming, the minimum amount needed ranged from 40 to 100 *dunums*. Cultivation of citrus on large plantations reduced the basic amount needed still further, to 15 to 20 *dunums* (assuming steady world prices for citrus), but this also led to a severe reduction in the amount of labour actually needed for such a capital-intensive crop. Simpson Report and *Survey*, vol. 2, pp. 272-9.

56. *Report of the Committee Assigned to Study the Economic Conditions of Agriculturalists in Palestine* (Johnson-Crosbie Report), (Jerusalem, 1930), p. 3, cited in the *Survey*, vol. 1, p. 364, and in Badran, p. 212. See also Doreen Warriner, *Land and Poverty in the Middle East* (London, 1948), pp. 61-2 and C. F. Strickland, *Report on the Possibility of Introducing a System of Agricultural Co-operation in Palestine* (Jerusalem, 1930). Out of a total of 22,573 households surveyed by the committee, 3,873 owned plots of more than 2 *feddans* (240 *dunums*) and 1,604 plots of 1-2 *feddans*. The number of tenants cultivating 1-2 *feddans* was 657; those cultivating plots less than 1 *feddan* numbered 8,396; another 1,103 households had tenant rights to either forests or orchards. Badran, p. 212.

57. Muhammad Tawfiq Jana, *Political Evidence Presented to the Royal Commission on Palestine* (Damascus, 1937), p. 26, cited in Badran, p. 208; 'Arif, *Tarikh,* pp. 161-3. The average net income of the peasant in 1934 was £P23.37 a year. By comparison, landowners with an average net income per year of £P250 effectively paid less tax:

only 21.5 per cent. Merchants paid a rate of about 12.5 per cent on average. In addition to tithe, peasants were also liable to the *wirku* tax on immovable property until 1935 and to the *ghanim,* or animal, tax. Until the passage of the Rural Property Tax Law in 1935, when the condition of the land was taken into account in assessing property tax, peasants in the hill country, where the land was less fertile, paid a disproportionate share of taxes relative to those, primarily the Zionist settlers, whose lands in the coastal plains were far more productive.

58. *Survey,* vol. 2, p. 246; Montague, pp. 129-30; Djabry, pp. 125-8.

59. In 1930 the tithe due was remitted by 30 per cent, in 1932 by 50 per cent and in 1933 by 25 per cent. Porath, vol. 2, p. 114. In 1931 the market price for wheat, barley and sesame was only two-thirds, or less, the price obtained in the years 1924 to 1927. A. Granovsky, *The Fiscal System of Palestine* (Jerusalem, 1935), p. 168, cited in Badran, p. 208. The average indebtedness of a *fellah* family by 1930 had reached £P27, about the same as his gross income for the year, which ranged between £P25 and £P30. *Survey,* vol. 1, p. 364.

60. Interest rates for loans to finance seed, animals and subsistence until the harvest averaged 30 per cent in the period from 1922 to 1930 according to the government committee assigned to investigate the conditions of the peasantry in 1930. Johnson-Crosbie Report; *Survey,* vol. 1, pp. 364-7.

61. The quotation is cited in George Hakim and M. Y. al-Husseini, 'Monetary and Banking System' in Himadeh (ed.), pp. 497-8.

62. The number of immigrants to Palestine rose from 9,553 in 1932 to 30,327 in 1933; 42,359 in 1934 and 61,854 in 1936. Thereafter it declined substantially, although the annual rate through 1939 was still far in excess of that which prevailed in the late 1920s. *Survey,* vol. 1, p. 185. In addition, the number of illegal immigrants, who often arrived as tourists or who were landed at remote spots along the coast, increased dramatically. For example, Moshe Shertok, head of the Political Department of the Jewish Agency, estimated that the total number of Jewish immigrants from September 1938 to September 1939 amounted to 35,000, as against the 10,000 to 15,000 reported in the government's official statistics. *Jewish Chronicle,* 3 November 1939, cited in Barbour, p. 207.

63. The total value of notes and coins in circulation rose sixfold in the period from 1930 to 1936, largely as a result of the influx of Jewish capital. Since the growth in national production was only a fraction of this, the result was a huge increase in prices for virtually all commodities except citrus fruits. Hakim and al-Husseini in Himadeh (ed.), p. 449. *Survey,* vol. 1, p. 338.

64. The Fund leased land to the new immigrants only on condition that the land was empty and that no Arab labour was hired to cultivate it. As a result peasants working on land sold to the Fund were evicted either by the Arab landowner prior to the sale, or by the Fund after it. Purchases of land by the Jewish National Fund rose dramatically in the late 1920s, and totalled 196,700 *dunums* in 1927. By 1936 the amount

had doubled to 369,800 *dunums* and accounted for about a quarter of the total land held by Jews in Palestine. Weinstock, pp. 71-2; *Survey*, vol. 1, p. 376.

65. The Arab population of Haifa grew from 18,400 in 1922 to 34,200 in 1931. By 1944 it had reached 62,500. In Jaffa the rate of increase was almost as high, rising from 27,400 in 1922 to 47,500 in 1931 and 66,200 in 1944. Overall the urban Arab population increased by 40 per cent between 1922 and 1931 to 274,640, and by 49 per cent between 1931 and 1944, to 410,000. Thus, despite a significant (24 per cent) increase in the rural population as a whole during the period from 1922 to 1931, the percentage of Arabs living in the cities rose from 19 per cent of the total (Arab) population in 1922 to 32 per cent in 1931. Badran, p. 127.

66. Barbour, p. 133; *Survey*, vol. 2, p. 696. See also Flapan, p. 216.

67. Barbour, p. 134; Weinstock, pp. 173-4, 186; Flapan, pp. 206-7.

68. Flapan, pp. 215-16. In private industry an unskilled Arab labourer in the building trades was paid 109 *mils* a day in 1939 while his Jewish counterpart received 315 *mils* a day; an Arab baker was paid 219 *mils*, a Jewish one 511; an Arab labourer in the citrus plantations received about 100 *mils* a day compared to 190 for a Jewish labourer. Numerous other examples could be cited. *Survey*, vol. 2, pp. 735-45, 776-7.

69. Flapan, pp. 215-16; *Survey*, vol. 2, pp. 735-45, 776. As late as 1945, a survey of 244 establishments employing Arab labour showed that 80 per cent worked more than 50 hours a week. In 10 per cent of the total the average was 70 hours a week or more. Government of Palestine, Department of Statistics, *Statistical Abstract, 1944/5*, p. 143, cited in Badran, p. 243. See also the testimony of George Mansour in Jana, cited in Badran, pp. 287-302.

70. Badran, pp. 230-9; Mansour, in Jana, cited in Badran, pp. 287-302.

71. Figures compiled from the Government of Palestine, Superintendent of the Census, *Census of Palestine, 1931* (2 vols., Alexandria, 1933), pp. 282-300. The 19,000 include apprentices, deliverymen and vendors as well as skilled workers, but it is impossible to say from the statistics what proportion of the total the latter represented. The total (Arab) labour force in 1931 was 212,000, of which 113,200 were agricultural labourers, fishermen, shepherds and forestry workers. Badran, p. 234. Sir John Hope Simpson, p. 132, reported in 1930 that 'There is no doubt that unemployment increased greatly among Arab workers in the manufacturing sector during this time [1922 to 1930].'

72. Mansour, in Jana, cited in Badran, pp. 287-302; Badran, p. 239.

73. Mansour, in Jana, cited in Badran, pp. 287-302; Badran, pp. 238-40.

74. Ibid. A woman working as a domestic servant earned on average £P2 a month; her son, in the same work, earned £P0.25 to £P1 a month.

75. B. Veicmanas, 'Internal Trade' in Himadeh (ed.), p. 349.

76. Ibid., pp. 349-50.

77. Sawwaf in Himadeh (ed.), p. 399.

78. Brown in Himadeh (ed.), pp, 129-33; Sawwaf in Himadeh (ed.), p. 428.

79. Brown in Himadeh (ed.), p. 130.

80. Sawwaf in Himadeh (ed.), pp. 425-31; 'Arif, *Tarikh,* pp. 208-9.

81. For examples, see the *Directory of Arab Trade, Industry, Crafts and Professions* published by the Palestine Chambers of Commerce (Jerusalem, 1938). In the sphere of agricultural imports, it was common for Arab merchants who operated chain-type grocery stores to prefer the sale of imported, brand-named goods. Once a merchant had obtained a monopoly on the import of a certain item from the foreign manufacturer, he could set the price at will and thereby obtain larger profits than he would were he to engage solely in the sale of local raw produce. Veicmanas in Himadeh (ed.), p. 362.

82. Himadeh, 'Industry' in Himadeh (ed.) p. 265.

83. Weinstock, pp. 134, 161; *Statistical Abstract, 1937/8,* p. 160.

84. Calculated from figures in the *Statistical Abstract,* ibid., and in Badran, p. 262.

85. For figures showing that very little land was sold by small-holders, see A. Bonné, *Palästina: Land und Wirtschaft* (Berlin, 1937); Emile Al-Ghawri, *Al-Muamar al-kubra: ightiyal filistin wa mahq al-'arab (The Great Conspiracy: The Assassination of Palestine and the Destruction of the Arabs)* (Cairo, 1955), p. 49, cited in Badran, pp. 260-1. See also the Government of Palestine, *Reports on Agricultural Development and Land Settlement in Palestine* by Lewis French, First Report (Jerusalem, December 1931), Supplementary Report (Jerusalem, April 1932). Porath, vol. 2, pp. 314, 325, mentions the Abdul Hadis, the Tajis and other members of the Arab Higher Committee as being among those who either sold land directly or who arranged its sale through intermediaries. For offers of land to the Zionist Executive by the Banu Sakhr and the Majalis of Trans-Jordan, and of the Amir Abdullah's lease of 70,000 *dunums* in the Ghor al-Kabd in return for annual payments from the Jewish Agency, see Porath, vol. 2, pp. 72-3.

86. Cited in Porath, vol. 2, p. 86.

87. Ibid., p. 87. For further details see Hirst, pp. 78-80; Naji 'Allush, *Al-Muqawwamah al-'arabiyyah fi Filistin, 1917-1948 (Arab Resistance in Palestine, 1917-1948)* (Beirut, 1970), pp. 91, 122; Muhammad 'Izza Darwazah, *Hawla al-harakah al-'arabiyyah al-hadithah (On the Modern Arab Movement)* (5 vols., Sidon, 1951), p. 59; and Kayyali, *Palestine,* p. 179.

88. D. Horowitz in J. B. Hobman (ed.), *Palestine's Economic Future* (London, 1946), cited in Weinstock, p. 160; Brown in Himadeh (ed.), p. 147.

89. Horowitz, cited in Weinstock, p. 160.

90. Brown in Himadeh (ed.), p. 143.

91. Until 1935, when land was taxed according to its quality in terms of fertility, rainfall, etc., the citrus grower, who reaped a far more valuable crop per *dunum,* paid the same, or less, tax than the tenant farmers or smallholding peasants. 'Arif, *Tarikh,* pp. 162-3. See also Badran, p. 273.

92. Horowitz, cited in Weinstock, p. 160; Brown in Himadeh (ed.), p. 147.

93. Badran, p. 265.

94. Brown in Himadeh (ed.), p. 142.

95. Calculated from figures shown by Brown, ibid., p. 140.

96. Claims by some of the landowners that the credit institutions they helped to set up in the mid-1930s, such as the Agricultural Bank and the Arab National Bank, were aimed at alleviating the burden of the peasantry are refuted by 'Allush and Badran (see above). The latter notes on p. 273 that the Agricultural Bank charged 18 per cent interest on loans and also quotes Ahmad Hilmi, who founded the National Bank in 1943, as saying that it was established primarily to provide an investment outlet for those who had earned substantial sums as money-lenders, brokers and middlemen of various kinds. See also Kayyali, *Palestine*, p. 176; J. C. Hurewitz, *The Struggle for Palestine* (New York, 1968; 1st edn, New York, 1950), pp. 183-4; and Hakim and al-Husseini in Himadeh (ed.), pp. 500-1.

97. Storrs, pp. 333-4.

98. For the controversy surrounding the appointment of the mayor and the role of the British in securing Hajj Amin's 'election' as Mufti, see John Marlowe, *Rebellion in Palestine* (London, 1946), pp. 69-75, and Porath, vol. 1.

99. *Survey,* vol. 2, pp. 901-2; Andrews, vol. 2, pp. 190-6, 221.

100. The Council's revenues from the tithes assessed on *waqf* land and property fell from £P28,474 in 1929 to only £P5,772 in 1931. Porath, vol. 2, p. 114. In return for a restoration of its level of revenue, the SMC agreed to submit its budget proposals to the High Commissioner for his approval, to limit its total expenditure and to adopt an accounting system approved by the government. Porath, vol. 2, pp. 115-16.

101. There were some notable exceptions to this division along clan lines, of which the most important was Musa Kazim al-Hussaini's 'defection' to the Nashashibi camp in the early 1930s. Porath, vol. 2, pp. 47-8. The Khalidis, one of the oldest sharifian families in Palestine, also split from the Nashashibis in 1935 to form a separate opposition party which drew support from some large landowners formerly loyal to the Hussainis. The Abdul Hadis supported the Istiqlal, or Independence Party, founded by 'Awni Bey Abdul Hadi in 1920. Porath, vol. 2, pp. 60, 77-8, 147-8. See also *Survey,* vol. 2, pp. 945-50; 'Arif, *Tarikh,* pp. 276-8, 216-22; Kayyali, *Palestine,* pp. 175-8; 'Allush, pp. 88-9; John Marlowe, *The Seat of Pilate* (London, 1959), pp. 102-3, and Erskine, pp. 168-78.

102. In 1938 a conference of 32 governments called by President Roosevelt to deal with the question of Jewish refugees from Europe refused to agree on a plan whereby the refugees would be absorbed in their host countries. Of the 32, only the Dominican Republic agreed to change its restrictive quotas in favour of Jewish entry. Walter Laquer, *A History of Zionism* (London, 1972), cited in Weinstock, p. 203. In 1943, when the holocaust was at its height, the United States allowed

only 4,705 Jews to enter. Boats transporting refugees were forced to turn back after reaching the foot of the Statue of Liberty. Although the quota was lifted slightly after the war, only 25,000 were admitted to the United States in the period from 1945 to 1948. Ibid., pp. 203, 220. See also R. H. S. Crossman, *Palestine Mission* (London, 1947), pp. 87-8. Britain also refused to take any substantial number of refugees, preferring instead a policy of re-integrating them in Germany, Poland and other parts of Eastern Europe. Ibid. See also Bethell, pp. 212-13, 237.

103. Barbour, p. 163. For one government official's recollection of the brutality with which the police operated, see Hugh Foot's interview with Nicholas Bethell in *The Palestine Triangle*, p. 26.

104. Barbour, p. 163.

105. Ibid., p. 161. A subsequent investigation showed that it was one of several deliveries sent to underground Zionist organisations that year. In 1937 it was estimated that enough arms and ammunition had been sent in to the Zionists to equip an army of 10,000 men. Royal Commission (Peel) Report, p. 200, cited in Barbour, ibid.

106. In December the Arab Workers' Federation petitioned the government to be allowed to demonstrate against unemployment, the Jewish boycott of Arab labour and Zionist immigration. The request was refused by the District Commissioner for Jaffa. Subsequent written protests against the awarding of government contracts to Jewish contractors who refused to employ Arab labour were also ignored. See George Mansour, 'The Arab Worker under the Palestine Mandate' in *Minutes of Evidence to the Peel Commission,* CO 134, July 1937 (Jerusalem, 1938), cited in Barbour, pp. 161-3, and also his testimony published in Jana, cited in Badran, pp. 287-302.

107. For details of al-Qassim's history, ideology and tactics, see 'Allush, pp. 113-20; Subhi Yassin, *Al-Thawrah al-'arabiyyah al-kubra fi Filistin, 1936-1939 (The Great Arab Revolution in Palestine, 1936-1939)* (Cairo, 1959), pp. 21-30; Porath, vol. 2, pp. 132-9; Hirst, pp. 75-80 and Kayyali, *Palestine*, pp. 180-2.

108. For a description of the incidents, which took place mainly in Galilee, Haifa and in the Tel Aviv/Jaffa area, see Barbour, pp. 165-6, and Porath, vol. 2, pp. 162-4. On the Legislative Assembly proposals and their rejection by the House of Lords and the House of Commons, see *Survey,* vol. 2, pp. 33-4.

109. Both are quoted in Bethell, p. 36.

110. Hirst, pp. 84-5, 89; Porath, vol. 2, pp. 248-9, 267-9; Kayyali, *Palestine,* pp. 197, 214; Marlowe, *Seat of Pilate,* p. 151. No official estimate of the number of wealthy Palestinians — landowners, merchants, brokers and notables — who fled abroad is available, but Kayyali puts the figure in the 'thousands'. *Palestine,* p. 214. Most went to Egypt, Lebanon, Iraq, Syria and Trans-Jordan, although some fled as far as Europe and North and South America. A few sent back funds to aid the counter-revolutionary forces led by the Nashashibis. Porath, vol. 2, p. 253.

111. CO 733/398/75156, cited in Porath, vol. 2, p. 269.

112. Antonius, pp. 406-7.

113. Nearly 1,000 Arabs had been killed by British troops and the police during the six-month general strike. Barbour, p. 172; Royal Commission (Peel) Report, p. 55. Altogether an estimated 5,000 Arabs died in the fighting from April 1936 to May 1939. Waines, p. 89. See also Walid Khalidi, *From Haven to Conquest* (Beirut, 1973), who estimated that the number of wounded may have exceeded 14,000.

114. *Survey,* vol. 2, p. 538; Waines, pp. 84-9; Bethell, pp. 26-7.

115. Bethell, p. 37; Hirst, pp. 104-5; Hadawi and John, *Palestine Diary,* vol. 1, p. 284. See also Christopher Sykes, *Orde Wingate* (London, 1959).

116. For details, see Porath, vol. 2, pp. 169-71; Kayyali, *Palestine,* pp. 166-71, 193-5; and 'Allush, pp. 113-24, 127-8.

117. Porath, vol. 2, pp. 212-15; Barbour, p. 171.

118. Porath, vol. 2, p. 117.

119. 'Allush, pp. 113-15; Kayyali, *Palestine,* pp. 197-206; Porath, vol. 2, pp. 137-9. See also the works by Yassin and Darwazah cited above.

120. Porath, vol. 2, p. 234, mentions in particular Hasan Shukri, the Mayor of Haifa and 'Abd al-Razzaq al-Tuqan, the Mayor of Nablus.

121. For details, see Porath, vol. 2, pp. 249-62, 268; Kayyali, *Palestine,* p. 214; Hirst, pp. 84-5, 89. Evidence also exists that both the Zionists and the British government actively supported the counter-revolutionaries with military and financial assistance. Porath, vol. 2, pp. 253-6.

122. Porath, vol. 2, pp. 250, 254-5, 257.

123. Marlowe, *Seat of Pilate,* pp. 172-3; Hirst, pp. 104-6.

124. *Memoirs* (Tel Aviv, 1974), p. 332, cited in Flapan, p. 257.

125. Cmd. 5479; see also the accompanying Government Statement of Policy (Cmd. 5513), which proposed a limit of 8,000 Jewish immigrants between August 1937 and March 1938.

126. Cmd. 6019.

127. Bethell, p. 134; Marlowe, *Seat of Pilate,* pp. 174-5; Flapan, pp. 182-3.

128. *Survey,* vol. 1, p. 134; vol. 2, pp. 585-6, 599, 874-5, 904-5.

129. Marlowe, *Seat of Pilate,* pp. 199-200.

130. Cmd. 6808; Marlowe, *Seat of Pilate,* pp. 207-8.

131. Violent resistance to British rule had increased significantly from 1944 onwards when the Irgun dropped its wartime truce and began to launch a campaign of terror and sabotage against British military installations. Although the Jewish Agency publicly disavowed the attacks, as it had disavowed the activity of the underground Haganah, recent evidence has shown that the Agency had close links with the Irgun in planning certain joint operations. Bethell, pp. 252-4; Flapan, pp. 116, 289; Hirst, p. 129.

132. R. H. S. Crossman, *Palestine Mission* (London, 1947), p. 25.

4 The Decline of the Ruling Families, 1948-1967

1. So great was the fear that the Haganah had begun to store supplies and arms in caves and various hideouts near the Dead Sea and outside Haifa. Plans were laid to assemble the elderly and young of the Yishuv near Mount Carmel and to evacuate them through Haifa while the others stayed to fight, partisan-style, from the hills. The British, having already withdrawn their headquarters from Cairo to Palestine, planned to withdraw some of their troops to the mountains of Lebanon; there they hoped to enlist the support of the Jewish irregulars and the Free French forces of General Catroux in Syria to fight a rear-guard battle against the Germans. Bethell, pp. 134-5.

2. At that time the party was thought to consist of less than two hundred members. Munib al-Madi and Sulaiman Musa, *Tarikh al-Urdun fi al-qarn al-'ishrin* (*History of Jordan in the Twentieth Century*) (Amman, 1959), p. 246. See also Philip Khoury, *The Politics of Nationalism: Syria and the French Mandate,* 3 vols., unpublished PhD thesis, Harvard University, Cambridge, Mass., 1980.

3. Aqil H. Abidi, *Jordan: A Political Study 1948-1957* (London, 1965), pp. 193-4; and Porath, vol. 2, pp. 123-7. For a history of the origins of the party and its activity in Syria during Faisal's reign, see Khoury, pp. 128-35.

4. For details of their programme, see Kayyali, *Palestine,* pp. 166-9.

5. Porath, vol. 2, pp. 124, 126.

6. Ibid., p. 165.

7. Ibid., p. 292.

8. Hurewitz, p. 183; Xavier Baron, *Les Palestiniens: un peuple* (Paris, 1977), p. 68.

9. Hurewitz, p. 183.

10. Marlowe, *Seat of Pilate,* p. 209; *Supplement,* p. 141; Hurewitz, pp. 184-5. Ahmad Hilmi had served as Director-General of *awqaf* under Hajj Amin al-Hussaini in 1925. Abidi, p. 51.

11. Hurewitz, p. 184.

12. In its first manifesto, published in 1932, the Istiqlal had attacked the ruling class for looking after its own interests before those of the nation and blamed it for the disarray within the national movement. Later they also demanded the abolition of the feudal privileges enjoyed by the larger landowners and *ashraf* and called for greater public participation in politics. Kayyali, *Palestine,* p. 167. In April 1936, at the time of the general strike, several members of the party sought to set up a unified national leadership, but they were rebuffed by both the Hussainis and the Nashashibis. Rashid al-Hajj Ibrahim, who had travelled from Haifa to Jerusalem to seek support for the proposal, told a journalist on his return to Haifa, 'Jerusalem remains the same Jerusalem, and we almost failed there . . . because of the deep-rooted family considerations and hatreds among its people, those people who lead with a truncheon and rule by inertia.' Porath, vol. 2, p. 165.

13. Hurewitz, p. 184. Both the Reform and Youth Congress parties

had supported the five-point programme announced by the Palestine Arab Party in 1935 which called for an independent Arab state in Palestine. Their leaders also supported the Hussaini faction in the Arab Higher Committee set up in 1936. Abidi, p. 195.

14. Hurewitz, p. 185; Marlowe, *Seat of Pilate*, p. 217. *Supplement*, p. 137.

15. Hurewitz, p. 187.

16. Marlowe, *Seat of Pilate*, p. 180.

17. Ibid., p. 209; 'Note to the Reader' (introduction to) Musa Alami, 'The Lesson of Palestine', *Middle East Journal*, vol. 3, no. 4 (October 1949), p. 372; *Survey*, vol. 1, p. 74.

18. *Supplement*, p. 139; Marlowe, *Seat of Pilate*, pp. 209-10.

19. Aside from those mentioned, the Committee also included Ishaq Darwish al-Hussaini (who was still in exile), Rafiq al-Tamimi, Sheikh Hasan Abu Sa'ud and Munib al-Madi. *Supplement*, pp. 139-40. Ahmad Hilmi Pasha was born in Sidon in southern Lebanon and served as a general in the Ottoman army and as a Minister of Finance in Trans-Jordan before becoming Director-General of *awqaf* in Palestine in 1925. Abidi, p. 51.

20. Flapan, pp. 326-7. Rony E. Gabbay, *A Political Study of the Arab-Jewish Conflict: The Arab Refugee Problem* (Geneva and Paris, 1959), pp. 56-7.

21. Flapan, pp. 326-7; Marlowe, *Seat of Pilate*, pp. 246-8. General Safwat had resigned on 13 May in protest at the lack of a unified command structure among the Arab states (see below). A. Mahmoud, 'King Abdullah and Palestine', unpublished PhD thesis (n.p., 1950), p. 129, cited in Flapan, p. 321.

22. From the Mufti's memoirs, *Haqaiq 'an qadaiyah Filistin* (*The Facts of the Palestinian Problem*) (Cairo, 1953), pp. 22-3, cited in Flapan, p. 330.

23. Flapan, pp. 298, 330; Gabbay, pp. 79-81. For details of the bitter hostility between the Mufti and the Commander of the Jaish al-Inqadh, see Muhammad Nimr al-Hawari, *The Secret of the Catastrophe* (n.p., 1955), cited in Gabbay, pp. 79-81; Hajj Muhammad Nimr al-Khatib, *Min athir al-nakbah* (*Aspects of the Disaster*) (Damascus, 1949); and Ahmad Shuqairi, *Arba'un 'aman fi al-hayat al-'arabiyyah wa-l-dawliyyah* (*Forty Years in the Life of the Arabs and the World*) (Beirut, 1969). Qawuqji's memoirs were published in an abridged edition in the *Journal of Palestine Studies* in two parts: vol. 1, no. 4 (Summer 1972), pp. 27-58, and vol. 2, no. 1 (Autumn 1972), pp. 3-33.

24. Flapan, p 327; 'Allush, pp. 157-62.

25. Among the volunteers was a 19-year-old Palestinian studying in Cairo, Yasser Arafat. He was joined by Salah Khalaf (Abou Iyad), who headed Fatah's security forces in the 1970s (see Chapter 7). For details of the Brethren's role in the fighting in Palestine and its support of the Mufti, see 'Arif al-'Arif, *Al-Nakbah* (*The Catastrophe*) (2 vols., Sidon, 1956), vol. 2, pp. 398-413; Flapan, pp. 321, 329, 338-40 and Abidi, pp. 196-7. See also Kamil Ismail Sharif, *Al-Ikhwan al-muslimin fi-harb*

Filistin (The Muslim Brotherhood in the Palestine War) (Cairo, 1950); and Ahmad al-Sharabati, *Min ajil Filistin (For the Sake of Palestine)* (Cairo, 1954).

26. Flapan, p. 297.

27. Flapan, pp. 320-1. See also Larry Collins and Dominique Lapierre, *O Jerusalem!* (New York, 1972), pp. 311-12.

28. John Bagot Glubb (Pasha), *A Soldier in the Desert* (London, 1958).

29. Ann Dearden, *Jordan* (London, 1958), p. 77.

30. Abidi, pp. 48-52; 'Arif, *Al-Nakbah,* vol. 3, pp. 703-4.

31. 'Issam Sakhnini, 'Damm Filistin al-wusta ila sharqiyyi al-Urdun 1948-1950' ('The Annexation of Central Palestine to East Jordan 1948-1950'), *Shuun Filistiniyyah (Palestinian Affairs),* no. 42-3 (February 1975), pp. 67-8; 'Abdullah al-Tal, *Karithat Filistin: muthakkirat 'Abdullah al-Tal (Disaster in Palestine: The Memoirs of Abdullah al-Tal)* (Cairo, 1959), p. 263. See also John Bagot Glubb (Pasha), *A Soldier with the Arabs* (London, 1957).

32. Porath, vol. 2, pp. 228-31; Flapan, pp. 253-6. See also Abdullah's letter to Abdul Hamid Said, President of the Young Muslim Men's Association in Cairo, 5 June 1938, reprinted in Abdullah's *My Memoirs Completed ('Al-Takmilah'),* trans. H. W. Glidden (London, 1978), pp. 86-9.

33. For details of Abdullah's negotiations with the British and the Israelis, see al-Tal, pp. 437-544; Sakhnini, pp. 56-7; Flapan, pp. 320-3, 332-7, 341-2; and Dearden, pp. 63-6.

34. Glubb, *A Soldier with the Arabs,* Ch. 5; Marlowe, *Seat of Pilate,* p. 247; Dearden, p. 68; Abidi, p. 56; Abdullah, p. 32. The annual subsidy, which amounted to £2.5 million sterling in 1948, rose to £7 million sterling in 1953. In addition other substantial sums were given in the form of loans and grants for military construction, training and related transport and communications projects. Dearden, p. 104. See also P. J. Vatikiotis, *Politics and the Military in Jordan: A Study of the Arab Legion, 1921-1957* (London, 1967), pp. 78-9.

35. Sakhnini, pp. 67-8; Abidi, pp. 175-6.

36. The English text of the agreement is printed in Dearden, pp. 201-8. Pleas by various Palestinian leaders from the West Bank, notably Sulaiman Tuqan and Hashim al-Jaiyussi, that a Palestinian delegation be allowed to participate in the armistice negotiations at Rhodes were rejected by the Jordanian Prime Minister, Tawfiq Abul Huda, and the agreement was signed only by the Trans-Jordanian representatives. Hazza al-Majali, *Muthakkirati (My Memoirs)* (n.p., 1960), p. 90, cited in Abidi, p. 44.

37. Abidi, p. 66.

38. Texts of the speech and of the decree are reprinted in Amin Abu al-Sha'r (ed.), *Muthakkirat al-Malik 'Abdullah bin al-Hussein (The Memoirs of King Abdullah bin al-Hussein)* (Sao Paulo, 1953). See also Abdullah, pp. 16-17, 88. On the abolition of the name 'Palestine' from all official documents and its replacement by the 'West Bank' see *Al-Jaridah al-rasmiyyah (The Official Gazette)* (Amman), no. 1012, 1 March 1950.

39. Porath, vol. 2, p. 330; Abidi, p. 53; Dearden, pp. 76-7. Shaikh Sa'ad al-Din al-'Alami was appointed Vice-President. Other members of the conference's executive committee were 'Ajaj Nuwayhid, a Druze journalist from Jerusalem and former leader of the Istiqlal Party and Dr Nur al-Din al-Ghusain, a member of a leading landowning family. Sakhnini, p. 59.

40. Estimates of the number attending vary greatly. The most authoritative source, 'Arif al-'Arif, gives a figure of 1,000 in *Al-Nakbah*, vol. 4, p. 877. Dearden (p. 79) says the number was 2,000 while Xavier Baron (p. 79) puts it at only about 500. See also George Kirk, *Survey of International Affairs: The Middle East 1945-1950* (Oxford, 1954), p. 290, and Esmond Wright, 'Abdullah's Jordan', *Middle East Journal*, vol. 5, no. 4 (Autumn 1951).

41. Sakhnini, pp. 60-2; Dearden, pp. 75-9; 'Arif, *Al-Nakbah*, vol. 4, p. 877; al-Tal, pp. 375-6.

42. Sakhnini, p. 62; Abidi, pp. 55, 57-9.

43. Text in Abidi, p. 87.

44. Text of Sasson's message in al-Tal, pp. 440-4, cited in Sakhnini, p. 64.

45. Abidi, p. 68. See also Sakhnini, pp. 67-70.

46. Sheikh Jarallah was a staunch supporter of both the Hashimites and the British. In 1921, although he topped the list of candidates chosen by the *ulama* for the title of Mufti, he was persuaded, presumably by the British, to resign, thereby making Hajj Amin's accession possible. In October 1937 he agreed to serve as the sole Muslim member of the Council when it was re-organised after its other members, including Hajj Amin, had been deported, exiled or banned from returning to the country. Abidi, p. 57; Porath, vol. 2, p. 235.

47. Abidi, p. 52.

48. Dearden, p. 167. See also Janet Abu Lughod, 'The Demographic Transformation of Palestine' in Ibrahim Abu Lughod (ed.), *The Transformation of Palestine* (Evanston, Ill., 1971).

49. 'Assistance to the Palestine Refugees: Report of the Director, UNRWA', *Official Records of the United Nations General Assembly (GAOR)*, vol. 4, Supplement No. 16 (A/1905), p. 2. See also Abidi, pp. 63-4, and Dearden, p. 173.

50. Jane Hacker, *Modern Amman: A Social Study* (Durham, 1960), p. 136. Some authors estimate that Amman's population in the early 1940s was even less. See, for example, Naseer H. Aruri and Samih Farsoun, 'Palestinian Communities and Arab Host Countries' in Khalil Nakhleh and Elia Zureik (eds.), *The Sociology of the Palestinians* (London, 1980), p. 119. For a detailed description of economic conditions in Jordan prior to the annexation, see A. Konikoff, *Trans-Jordan: An Economic Survey* (Jerusalem, 1946).

51. Royal Hashimite Kingdom of Jordan, Directorate of General Statistics, *Annual Statistics, 1951* (Amman, 1952), p. 4, cited in Jamil Hilal, *Al-Diffah al-gharbiyyah: Al-tarkib al-iqtisadiyyi wa-l-ijtima'iyyi, 1948-1974* (*The Economic and Social Structure of the West Bank, 1948-1974*) (Beirut, 1975), pp. 40-1.

52. Dearden, p. 164.

53. Europa Publications, *The Middle East 1953* (London, 1953), p. 194; and *The Middle East 1959* (London, 1959), p. 201.

54. Ali T. Dajani, *A Directory of Jordan's Industrial Firms: The Industry of Jordan, 1965* (Amman, 1965), p. 8; A. M. Goichon, 'La transformation de l'économie jordanienne', *Orient,* nos. 45 and 46 (First and Second Quarter, 1968), p. 122. Altogether the increase in cultivable land in the West Bank is estimated to have risen by more than one-third between 1948 and 1967. Hilal, p. 41.

55. For example the refugee settlement of Karameh, located 35 kilometres west of Amman in the Jordan Valley, provided a quarter of Jordan's poultry products in addition to exporting early market vegetables to other parts of the Middle East. Some indirect trade was also carried out with Israel through the sale of agricultural produce in Jerusalem. Dearden, p. 165; Baron, p. 163. Produce from Musa Alami's Arab Development Society at Jericho was exported to Saudi Arabia under a contract signed with the Arab American Company (Aramco) in Dhahran. Dearden, p. 177, and Sir Geoffrey Furlonge, *Palestine is my Country: The Story of Musa Alami* (New York and Washington, 1969), pp. 184-5. For a description of the development of terraces in the West Bank and the cultivation of tomatoes for export on these new fields, see Dearden, pp. 173-5.

56. Al-Salti, 'The Agrarian Question in Jordan', *New Times,* (Moscow), no. 35 (2 September 1964), p. 17, cited in Naseer Aruri, *Jordan: A Study in Political Development* (The Hague, 1974), p. 54; Government of Jordan, Ministry of Information, *Al-Iqtisad al-urduniyyi (The Jordanian Economy)* (Amman, 1966), p. 10.

57. Gabriel Baer, 'Land Tenure in the Hashemite Kingdom of Jordan', *Land Economics,* vol. 33, no. 3 (August 1957), p. 196. See also Doreen Warriner, *Land Reform and Development in the Middle East* (Oxford, 1962).

58. See Chapter 5 for more information on Palestinian holdings abroad.

59. Gabbay, p. 451; Dearden, p. 171.

60. Hilal, p. 40.

61. The one exception to the pattern of general neglect of the small farmer was the establishment of a programme in 1952 to encourage the terracing of new agricultural land, primarily in the East Bank. Skilled Palestinian labourers were sent across the Jordan Valley to teach Trans-Jordanians the art of constructing such terraces. For this arduous work, the farmer received a loan of JD7.5 ($21) for each *dunum* of land to be terraced. The average loan during the four-year period that the programmed existed never exceeded JD50 ($140). Dearden, p. 175.

62. Yusif al-Nimr had been sent by Sulaiman the Magnificent in the early days of the Ottoman rule of Palestine to put down a revolt by the Tamimiyyah tribe of East Jordan. Many of his descendants, and other Ottoman soldiers as well, remained in the area and together they formed the Aghwat tribe of Trans-Jordan. F. Peake, *History and Tribes of Jordan* (Miami, 1958); Peter Gubser, *Politics and Change in Al-Karak,*

Jordan (London, New York and Toronto, 1973), p. 14. Abdul Halim al-Nimr served in Parliament as a member for the East Bank from 1950 to 1954 and from 1956 to 1957. He was Minister of Finance from September 1951 to September 1952 and Minister of both Interior and Defence from October 1956 to April 1957. Abidi, pp. 216-23.

63. Dearden, pp. 98, 107. For a history of the Majali clan which had originally come to Trans-Jordan from Hebron, see Gubser, pp. 14-15. Hazza al-Majali served briefly as Prime Minister in 1955, as Minister of Agriculture from December 1950 to July 1951, as Minister of Justice from October 1954 to May 1955 and then as Minister of the Interior from May to December 1955. Salah al-Majali served as Minister of Posts, Communications and Civil Aviation twice in the 1950s. Abdul Wahab al-Majali held the post of Minister of Interior in 1965, while Ma'arik Pasha al-Majali was a member of the Chamber of Notables in 1950 and 1951. Afaullah al-Majali was a member of the Chamber of Deputies during the early 1950s as well. Abidi, pp. 216-33; Europa Publications, *The Middle East 1966* (London, 1966). Another member of the tribe, Habes al-Majali, served as Chief of Staff and Military Governor during the time of the civil war in Jordan in 1970 and 1971. Baron, pp. 245, 252; Marius Haas, *Husseins Königreich: Jordaniens Stellung im Nahen Osten* (Munich, 1975), pp. 42-6.

64. Ahmad al-Tarawnah served as Minister of Agriculture in the autumn of 1950 and from October 1952 to May 1953 in addition to serving several times in the Chamber of Deputies. Abidi, pp. 216-33. For other details of the trade carried out by the tribes of the Negev, Hebron and Trans-Jordan, see Gubser, pp. 119-25, and '1979 Independence and Army Day Supplement', *Jordan Times* (1979).

65. *The Middle East 1953*, p. 195; *The Middle East 1959*, p. 203. One dinar = \$2.80.

66. Vegetable Oil Company of Jordan, *Fourteenth Report of the Board of Directors*, cited in Aruri, *Jordan*, pp. 55-6.

67. Yitzak Oded, 'Agriculture in the West Bank', *New Outlook*, vol. 2, no. 2 (February 1968), p. 27.

68. Ibid.

69. Hilal, pp. 37-9.

70. Ibid., pp. 39, 107.

71. Quoted in Sakhnini, p. 66.

72. Between May 1949 and April 1957 the post was variously held by Raghib Bey al-Nashashibi, Khulusi al-Khairi, Sulaiman al-Tuqan, Hikmat al-Masri, Sheikh Muhammad 'Ali al-Ja'abari, Hashim al-Jaiyussi and Abdul Qadir al-Salih, all of whom were members of the landowning and/or mercantile elite which supported Hashimite rule in the West Bank. See the list of Cabinet members in Abidi, pp. 218-23.

73. For Abdullah's eagerness to draw on capable Palestinians to run his expanded kingdom, see his letter to Abdul Hamid Said, President of the Young Muslim Men's Association in Cairo, dated 5 June 1938, in Abdullah, pp. 86-9.

74. For an example of this attitude, see the 'Reply of the Chamber of Deputies' to King Abdullah's 'Speech from the Throne', 24 April

1950, announcing the formal annexation of the West Bank in which the Palestinian Deputies expressed their 'satisfaction and confidence that this unification has been brought about without any prejudice to the general Arab rights in Palestine or to the final settlement of their case'. Abdullah, pp. 16-20.

75. Abidi, p. 68.

76. Wright, p. 453.

77. Ibid., p. 454; Abidi, p. 65.

78. Abidi, pp. 57, 65. See also Abdullah, pp. 92-4. Dr Hussain Fakhri al-Khalidi succeeded to the post of Custodian and Supervisor of the Haram al-Sharif on the death of Raghib Bey al-Nashashibi in 1951. Dr Khalidi was succeeded in 1955 by Hassan al-Khatib, then Governor of Jerusalem, and the title of his post was later changed to Muhafiz (Guardian) of Jerusalem and the Holy Places. Dearden, pp. 189-92.

79. The Khatibs were a sharifian family from Jerusalem which traditionally provided the preachers for Al-Aqsa Mosque in Jerusalem, one of the holiest places in Islam. Like the Abdul Hadis they were also extensive landowners (see below) and had used the profits from their lands to give their sons a Western education. For a summary of the legal changes in Jordan in 1951, see E. Theodore Mogannam, 'Developments in the Legal System of Jordan', *Middle East Journal,* vol. 6, no. 2 (Spring 1952), pp. 194-205, and J. N. D. Anderson, 'Recent Developments in Sharia Law VIII: the Jordanian Law of Family Rights, 1951', *The Muslim World,* vol. 42, no. 3 (July 1952), pp. 190-206.

80. Tribal courts were established in Amman, Irbid, Kerak and Maan as well as in other parts of the Jordanian desert (*The Middle East 1953*). Before their powers were reduced in the early 1960s they had extensive control in East Jordan, where the Bedouin made up a large part of the population prior to the influx of the Palestinians.

81. Palestinians in the West Bank and in Jordan were granted Jordanian citizenship in December 1949. Abidi, pp. 66-7.

82. The full list is contained in Abidi, Appendix A, p. 216. The Nusaibahs had been hereditary guardians of the Holy Sepulchre and were one of the most venerated sharifian families in Palestine.

83. For a list of members from April 1950 to April 1957 see Abidi, p. 218.

84. Abidi, pp. 216-23; David Gilmour, *Dispossessed: The Ordeal of the Palestinians 1917-1980* (London, 1980), p. 122, and Wright, p. 453. Other Tuqans holding ministerial posts during the 1950s included Sulaiman (Defence and Agriculture, member of the Chamber of Notables), Jamal (Foreign Affairs) and Salah (Finance). Qadri Tuqan, as mentioned earlier, was a member of the Chamber of Deputies from April 1950 to October 1954.

85. For the lists of ambassadors, see the yearly editions of *The Middle East* (Europa Publications, London), especially the volumes dated 1953 to 1966. Other Palestinian ambassadors included Akram Zuaitar, a member of a provincial landowning family in Nablus and a leader of the Istiqlal Party during the 1936-9 revolt who also served on

the Arab Higher Committee, and Ihsan Saïd, a member of a notable family in Jaffa which was closely allied to the Nashashibis. The Salahs were an influential family from near Nablus. Abidi, pp. 196, 209. All the ambassadors were appointed by royal decree. Abidi, p. 184.

86. Shaul Mishal, *West Bank, East Bank* (New Haven, 1978), p. 106.

87. Ibid., pp. 106-7.

88. Wright, p. 453. Although training was compulsory, conscription was never introduced in Jordan for fear that it would lead to the dilution of the King's support in the Arab Legion.

89. Vatikiotis, pp. 79-81.

90. Vatikiotis, p. 112; Aruri and Farsoun, pp. 117-18. Even as late as 1972, after the civil war in Jordan had left thousands of Palestinians dead and the commandos expelled from the country, some units of the Palestine Liberation Army (which was financed by the Arab League) still remained loyal to the King. They were led by a member of the Nusaibah clan which, as we have seen, was closely associated with the Hashimite regime during the entire period of Jordanian rule in the West Bank. *Al-Nahar Arab Report*, 25 December 1972, 3 and 15 January 1973.

91. Dearden, pp. 93-4.

92. Many of the 'infiltrators' were villagers living along the border who had crossed into Israeli-held territory to reap their harvests, recover their household possessions or to search for missing relatives. Dearden, pp. 102, 132-3; 'Arif, *Al-Nakbah*, vol. 4, p. 840; Anis Sayigh, *Al-Hashimiyyun wa-l-qadaiyyah al-filistiniyyah* (*The Hashimites and the Palestinian Problem*) (Beirut, 1966), p. 258; Abidi, p. 110; Sakhnini, pp. 67-8. See also E. H. Hutchinson, *Violent Truce* (New York, 1956), pp. 20-9; Hirst, p. 179; and Fawaz Turki, *The Disinherited: Journal of a Palestinian Exile* (New York, 1972), p. 38.

Among the first to be arrested were two newspaper editors from the West Bank, Abdullah Rimawi and Kamal Nasser, who were imprisoned at a desert camp near Al-Bayr. They later stood as parliamentary candidates in the 1950 election, but were deported in August 1950 after another crackdown on dissidents. In 1951 several leading leftists were arrested, including Fuad Nasr, the Secretary-General of the Jordanian Communist Party, who was sentenced to ten years' imprisonment. Wright, pp. 453-4; Abidi, p. 73. By the spring of 1953 several hundred prisoners, mostly 'infiltrators' and dissidents, were 'languishing without trial in concentration camps', according to Dearden (p. 103).

93. Jean-Pierre Alem, 'En Jordanie: l'agonie d'un royaume', *Orient*, no. 2 (April 1957), pp. 100-15.

94. Scores of Palestinians, mostly peasants and refugees, were killed in the raids which occurred in Qibya and Nahhilin. Hirst, pp. 181-2.

95. Vatikiotis, p. 119; Dearden, pp. 106-8; Sakhnini, pp. 68-9.

96. The budget included an annual subsidy to the Arab Legion paid directly to the Legion by Britain through a special bank account in London. Dearden, pp. 91, 105; Abidi, pp. 73-4. See also Aruri and Farsoun, p. 121.

97. Aside from the budget, the Palestinians in the Chamber were also unhappy with the way the seats in the lower house were allocated. Although Palestinians were allowed half the seats on an equal basis with the Trans-Jordanian representatives, this division, while accurately reflecting the natural (pre-1948) population of the two banks, did not take into account the large number of refugees who had sought refuge in Jordan after the war. On this basis, the Palestinians should have received two-thirds of the seats in the Chamber, not half. A similar situation existed in the Cabinet as well where Trans-Jordanians held on average 60 per cent of the ministerial posts from 1949 to 1974, even though they formed less than one-third of the total population. Haas, pp. 136-7.

98. Dearden, p. 91.

99. Both won their seats in the election. Once in the Chamber they joined the opposition led by two militant Ba'athists, Abdullah Nawas and Abdullah Rimawi, two young intellectuals of middle-class origins who had been freed from prison.

100. Tawfiq Abul Huda, like his colleagues Samir al-Rifa'i and Ibrahim Hashim, was of Palestinian origin. The three had first come to Jordan in the early 1920s after the fall of Faisal's government in Damascus and served in the Trans-Jordanian government when it was part of the British Mandate. Unlike the Palestinians absorbed in the wake of the 1948 war, they were commonly regarded as Jordanians and, above all, as 'the King's men'. None took an active part in Palestinian politics nor did they retain any significant ties with the West Bank. Dearden, pp. 52-3. For details of the parliamentary debate in November, see Abidi, pp. 109-11. On the British powers to intervene in internal affairs, which included the right to station troops in the country under British command, to appoint advisers to the civil administration and to oversee the budget, see Dearden, p. 105.

101. Dearden, pp. 108-9.

102. They were encouraged in this strategy by the growing reluctance of the King's favoured prime ministers to tamper with the voting. Asked to form an interim government to supervise new elections at the end of 1955, Ibrahim Hashim, for example, resigned after only seventeen days in office. He was quoted by the West Bank deputy, Walid al-Shaka, as saying at the time: 'I swear by Almighty God that if they [the Palace] ask me to remove this object from this place to that one, I will refuse. I am growing old and have no intention of allowing myself to be burnt for the King's sake ... Why should I voluntarily commit political suicide by being implicated in the falsification of elections?' Similar sentiments were reportedly expressed about the same time by Tawfiq Abul Huda. Hashim was later killed in the streets of Baghdad during the revolution which overthrew the Hashimite throne in Iraq in 1958. N. Nashashibi, *Matha jara fi al-Sharq al-Awsat (What Happened in the Middle East)* (Beirut, 1962), cited in Aruri, p. 125.

103. Dearden, pp. 115-16.

104. Dearden, p. 95; Abidi, pp, 209-10.

105. Dearden, pp. 116-17, 128.

106. Abidi, pp. 144, 209.

107. The Baáth campaigned on a programme of pan-Arab unity, socialism and democratic reform. It was composed of members from both the West and East banks and in 1950 merged with its counterpart in Syria. Abidi, p. 201.

108. Interview with Abdul Halim al-Nimr, the Defence and Interior Minister in the Nabulsi government, 28 March 1960, cited in Abidi, pp. 203-4. See also Majali, p. 143.

109. Interview, 13 April 1974, in Haas, pp. 240, 625-8.

110. Abidi, p. 147.

111. Jordan, Chamber of Deputies Debates, *The Official Gazette,* 9 December 1956, pp. 1-5, cited in Abidi, pp. 148-9. Two days after his speech Nabulsi won a vote of confidence in the Chamber by 39 votes to 1.

112. Abidi, pp. 150-1; Dearden, pp. 126-7. The name of the Legion had been changed after King Hussein dismissed Glubb in March 1956. The British bases were located at Mafraq, Amman and Aqaba. Dearden, p. 128.

113. Abidi, p. 155.

114. Abidi, p. 153. Eisenhower declared on 24 April 1957 that he considered 'the independence and integrity of Jordan as vital'. The next day the US Sixth Fleet sailed to the Eastern Mediterranean. Abidi, p. 164.

115. For details of his various moves on this front between January and the end of March see Abidi, pp. 153-8 and Benjamin Shwadran, *Jordan: A State of Tension* (New York, 1959), pp. 346-8.

116. The order affected twenty officials, including the former Mayor of Jaffa, Yusif Haikal, who had served as ambassador to the United States and France. Abidi, p. 158.

117. The full story of the *coup* is still unknown. It is outlined in Abidi, p. 150, and in Shwadran, pp. 348-52, and discussed at length in Vatikiotis, pp. 127-34, as well as in the King's own memoirs, *Uneasy Lies the Head: An Autobiography* (London, 1962). However, as Vatikiotis notes, some accounts of the period deny that the *coup* actually took place at all. See Erskine B. Childers, *The Road to Suez* (London, 1962) and the statement by Major-General 'Ali al-Hayyari in *Al-Hayat,* 21 April 1957, cited in Abidi, p. 164.

118. Abidi, pp. 162-3; Shwadran, pp. 351-5.

119. Abidi, pp. 162-3. Shwadran, p. 356. The Palestinians included Khulusi al-Khairi (Minister of Economy), Tuqan and Anastas Hanania (Minister of Finance).

120. Shwadran, p. 356.

121. Shwadran, pp. 362, 368; Haas, p. 516. The sums were more than the entire British subsidy and as the aid was renewed and increased in successive years, Jordan became almost totally dependent on the US for its basic economic survival and for the ability to maintain its large army and security forces. A few days before receiving the grant, King Hussein had revoked Sulaiman Nabulsi's order that diplomatic relations be established with the Soviet Union.

122. The leading Baathist in the West Bank, Abdullah Rimawi, who had served as Minister of State for Foreign Affairs in the Nabulsi government, was sentenced *in absentia* to 15 years' imprisonment in September along with Abu Nuwar and the man who replaced him, Major General Ali al-Hayari. All were charged with plotting to overthrow the King. Shwadran, p. 366; Mishal, pp. 93-4; Aruri, pp. 97-8.

123. Shwadran, p. 380. For a general account of the events in the region leading up to the military interventions by the US and Britain, see Malcolm Kerr, *The Arab Cold War: Gamal Abd al-Nasser and his Rivals, 1958-1970*, 3rd edn (Oxford, London and New York, 1971), pp. 1-17.

124. Khatib, in addition to serving as Mayor of Jerusalem, also held several ambassadorial posts in the 1960s; Nusaibah was appointed to the Senate by King Hussein in 1963 and retained his seat until the 1967 war. Abdul Qadir al-Salih, the Minister of Agriculture in Nabulsi's government, went on to serve successively as Minister of Development and Reconstruction, Minister of Defence and Minister of Public Works in the 1960s. Haas, Appendix 1. On Nasser and the role of *Al-Jil al-Jadid* in post-1948 Jordan, see Sakhnini, pp. 68-9.

5 Nationalism and the Bourgeoisie

1. President Nasser, one of the Free Officers who led the *coup* against Farouk, later wrote of his experience in Palestine during the summer of 1948 that 'As staff officer of the Sixth Battalion, I soon began more than anybody to realise the bewilderment and incompetence which characterised our High Command'. 'Nasser's Memoirs of the First Palestine War', trans. Walid Khalidi, *Journal of Palestine Studies*, vol. 2, no. 2 (Winter 1973), p. 11.

2. For general histories of this period see Kennett Love, *Suez: The Twice-Fought War* (New York, 1969); Kirk, *Short History of the Middle East*; John Marlowe, *Arab Nationalism and British Imperialism: A Study in Power Politics* (London, 1961); Patrick Seale, *The Struggle for Syria* (London, 1965); Anwar Abdel-Malek, *Egypte: société militaire* (Paris, 1962); and Kerr, Ch. 1. On the Gaza raid and its aftermath see also Ghassan Kanafani, 'Letter from Gaza', trans. by the Tricontinental Society, in *Palestine: The 1936-1939 Revolt* (London, 1980); and Abou Iyad (Salah Khalaf), *Palestinien sans patrie: entretiens avec Eric Rouleau* (Paris, 1978), pp. 47-50.

3. The development of Middle Eastern oil is discussed in Stephen Longrigg, *Oil in the Middle East* (London and New York, 1954); Joe Stork, *Middle East Oil and the Energy Crisis* (London and New York, 1975); George Lenczowski, *Oil and State in the Middle East* (Ithaca, NY, 1960); Peter Odell, *Oil and World Power* (Harmondsworth, Middlesex, 1975); and Anthony Sampson, *The Seven Sisters* (London, 1975). For early production figures, see the country surveys in *The Middle East Yearbook, 1980* (London, 1981) and in *The Middle East and*

North Africa, an annual survey produced by Europa Publications, London. Saudi Arabian figures for the period 1938 to 1973 are also available in Emile A. Nakhleh, *The United States and Saudi Arabia: A Policy Analysis* (Washington, DC, 1975), p. 12.

4. On the economic development of Lebanon in the early 1950s, see Charles Issawi, 'Economic Development and Liberalism in Lebanon', *Middle East Journal,* vol. 18, no. 3 (Summer 1964); Charles W. Churchill, *The City of Beirut: A Socio-Economic Survey* (Beirut, 1954); and Samir Khalaf and Per Kongstad, *Hamra of Beirut: A Case of Rapid Urbanisation* (Leiden, 1973). On Amman, see Hacker, *passim*; United Nations Economic and Social Office in Beirut, *Studies in Social Development in the Middle East 1969,* part 2: 'Report on the Social Survey of Amman, Jordan, 1966' (New York, 1970); and the report by the International Bank for Reconstruction and Development (the World Bank) entitled *The Economic Development of Jordan* (Baltimore, 1957).

5. The 1970 figures are taken from Nabil Shaath, 'High-Level Palestinian Manpower', *Journal of Palestine Studies,* vol. 1, no. 2 (Winter 1972), p. 91. The sources for the figures, and the dates of the estimates, are provided in accompanying notes to his table. The actual total population was likely to be slightly higher than indicated since small communities settled in Australia, Canada, Britain, France, Switzerland and the Sudan, as well as in other parts of Europe and Africa, are excluded. For population figures in 1973, and their distribution geographically, see Edward Hagopian and A. B. Zahlan, 'Palestine's Arab Population: The Demography of the Palestinians', *Journal of Palestine Studies,* vol. 3, no. 4 (Summer 1974). The 1980 figures are drawn from the *Palestinian Statistical Abstract 1980* published by the Palestine National Fund's Central Bureau of Statistics (Damascus, 1980). See also May Seikaly and Pamela Ann Smith, 'Palestinians in the Gulf', *Middle East Annual Review 1982* (Saffron Walden, Essex, 1982).

6. The Committee's findings were published in the Palestine government *Survey.*

7. Of the £P39.3 million held in foreign liquid assets, £P29.2 consisted of net currency reserves, £P9.3 million of net banking reserves and £P800,000 of individual and company investments. *Survey,* vol. 2, pp. 565-6.

8. The total budget for 1944/5 amounted to £P18,196,594, of which more than £P12 million was for internal security and war-related expenditure. *Survey,* vol. 2, p. 538.

9. *Survey,* vol. 2, pp. 559, 562. Some of these shares may be included in the *Survey*'s figures on capital ownership, but it is impossible to distinguish whether any such overlap exists from the data given.

10. United Nations Conciliation Commission for Palestine (UNCCP), A/3835 (16th Progress Report, 18 June 1958) and A/3199 (15th Progress Report, 4 October 1956). See also *Haaretz,* 17 September 1956 and 17 November 1954.

11. The property held by Arabs in Palestine that came under Israeli

control has been variously estimated to have been worth from $500 million to $3 billion. Net income for that property since 1948 would raise its value to quite a considerable sum, even allowing for inflation in the past three decades. For the estimates see UN Document A/3199, 4 October 1956, p. 8. Other relevant studies include the one by Don Peretz, who estimated that some 350 of the approximately 400 Jewish settlements established after 1948 were built on refugee property and that two-thirds of the cultivated land acquired by Israel had been Palestinian-owned; *Israel and the Palestine Arabs* (Washington, DC, 1958). In addition, he writes, 'property abandoned by the Palestine Arabs was a valuable resource helping to make room for hundreds of thousands of Jews who replaced the Arab refugees. The abandoned Arab fields, orchards, vineyards, homes, shops, factories and businesses provided shelter, economic sustenance and employment for a significant percentage of the nearly 700,000 new immigrants who came to Israel between May 1948 and the end of 1951. Israel would have found it far more difficult to more than double its population during this period without access to abandoned Arab property.' 'The Palestine Arab Refugee Problem' in P. Y. Hammond and S. S. Alexander (eds.), *Political Dynamics of the Middle East* (New York, 1972), p. 281, cited in Halim Barakat, 'The Palestinian Refugees: An Uprooted Community Seeking Repatriation', *International Migration Review*, vol. 7 (Summer 1973), p. 153.

12. Hurewitz reported that at the end of the Second World War total foreign assets accumulated by the Palestinian Arabs amounted to more than $157 million, 'almost exclusively held in sterling balances' (p. 189).

13. *Review of Economic Conditions in the Middle East, 1951-52*, UN Department of Economic Affairs, Document E/2353/Add. 1, ST/CA/19/Add. 1 (New York, March 1953), pp. 113-14. The bonds were redeemed in sterling. UN Document A/3199, p. 11.

14. *Review of Economic Conditions*, p. 114.

15. *Review of Economic Conditions*, p. 114. These transfers, together with the infusion of Palestinian banknotes into Jordan, virtually doubled the money supply in Jordan almost overnight, according to the UN report.

16. UN Document A/3199, p. 8, and A/3835. See also Gabbay, pp. 522-3.

17. UN Document A/3199, p. 11; Gabbay, pp. 522-3. See also UNCCP, Document A/5545 (21st Progress Report), 8 December 1962 to 31 October 1963, p. 2.

18. *Haaretz*, 10 October 1958; Gabbay, pp. 522-3.

19. 'The Intra Bank Affair: A Reappraisal', *The Banker*, vol. 122, no. 551 (January 1972), pp. 76, 79.

20. After its formation in 1953 the company began to import edible oils for sale in Jordan in addition to selling refined olive oil produced on the Tuqan estates in the West Bank. Vegetable Oil Company of Jordan, Fourteenth Report of the Board of Directors, submitted to the UN General Assembly, 21 May 1965, cited in Aruri, pp. 55-6.

21. On the payment of the allowances, see the *Survey*, vol. 2, p. 539.

22. Each of the two firms was initially registered in Palestine with a total capital of $400,000. Hurewitz, p. 190.

23. Saba was also Managing Director of the Palestine-based Al-Mashriq Financial Investment Company Ltd and a consultant to the Arab Bank, which had several branches abroad at the time of the defeat (see text below). *Palestine Personalia* (Tel Aviv, 1947). See also 'Saba and Company: Proud of its Arab Roots', *Middle East Economic Digest*, 11 December 1981.

24. Arab Bank Ltd, *Twenty-Five Years of Service to the Arab Economy, 1930-1955* (Amman, 1956).

25. For examples of women selling their gold and jewellery (and sometimes their household goods as well) to provide for family needs, see Leila Khaled, *My People Shall Live: The Autobiography of a Revolutionary*, ed. George Hajjar (London, 1973), pp. 34-5; Abou Iyad, p. 36, and the various reports of refugees in Lebanon included in the works by Rosemary Sayigh and Nafez Nazzal. My own conversations in Lebanon with Palestinian women living both inside and outside the camps were replete with references to the sale of gold and jewellery and to the vital benefits the sale of these possessions provided during the early years of exile.

26. See Chapter 6.

27. An exception was made for travel to Syria, where Palestinians could obtain return visas for short stays. However there was no legal guarantee of this and those Palestinians who had engaged in political activity in Lebanon were often refused requests for such visas. Gabbay, pp. 206-10.

28. Ibid., pp. 215-16; Channing B. Richardson, 'The Palestinian Arab Refugee' in S. N. Fisher (ed.), *Social Forces in the Middle East* (Ithaca, NY, 1955), p. 242. For personal examples of the humiliation and destitution suffered during the first years of exile in the Strip, see Abou Iyad and Kanafani, 'Letter from Gaza', pp. 29-30. Among those allowed to stay in Egypt were the Mufti and members of his family as well as Ahmad Hilmi Pasha.

29. Gabbay, pp. 213-15.

30. Ibid., p. 217; interview with 'Issam Sakhnini, Research Centre, PLO, Beirut, 8 March 1972. See also his 'Al-Filistiniyyun fi-l Iraq' ('Palestinians in Iraq'), *Shuun Filistiniyyah (Palestinian Affairs)*, no. 13 (September 1972), pp. 90-116.

31. Gabbay, p. 217.

32. 'Kuwait', Special Survey, *Financial Times*, 26 February 1979, p. 21; Bassam Sirhan, *Al-Filistiniyyun fi-l Kuwait: nataij awaliyyah li-bahth ijtima'iyyi (The Palestinians in Kuwait: Preliminary Results of Social Research)* (Kuwait, n.d. [1978?]) and Bilal Hasan, *Al-Filistiniyyun fi-l Kuwait (The Palestinians in Kuwait)* (Beirut, 1973). See also Badr Al-Din 'Abbas al-Khususi, *Dirasat fi tarikh al-Kuwait al-ijtima'iyyi wa-l-iqtisadiyyi, 1913-1961 (Studies in the Social and Economic History of Kuwait)* (Kuwait, 1972). In the late 1970s Kuwait and other Gulf states

initiated further restrictions on immigration. Foreign companies working in the Gulf were not allowed to employ immigrant labour except under contracts which required them to 'import' labour themselves, to house their workers and to ship them home once the company's contract for a specific project had ended, Palestinians from Lebanon who sought to join their families in Kuwait and in other Gulf states during and after the Lebanese civil war of 1975-6 and after the Israeli invasions in 1978 and 1982 faced additional obstacles since the governments of the Gulf states feared that many were activists who had taken part in the fighting or who had obtained stolen or forged passports and identity cards.

33. For the exemptions affecting foreign firms, see Gabbay, p. 209, and Paul J. Klat, 'Labour Legislation in Lebanon', *Middle East Economic Papers,* Economic Research Institute, American University of Beirut, (Beirut, 1959), p. 81.

34. Khalaf and Kongstad, p. 8.

35. Gabbay, p. 215.

36. Most of the wealthier Palestinians lived in Yarmouk camp, located just outside Damascus. The camp had its own city council and mayor and was provided with schools and a hospital supervised by Palestinians. The Director of the camp was a Palestinian from Haifa related to the Abdul Hadi family of Nablus. 'Yarmouk: The Camp with a City Council', *Gulf Times,* 6 August 1981, p. 21.

37. David H. Finnie, *Desert Enterprise: The Middle East in its Local Environment* (Cambridge, Mass., 1958); David Sperling, 'The Arabian American Oil Company Goes to Lebanon', unpublished paper, Centre for Middle Eastern Studies, Harvard University, Cambridge, Mass., 1955; *Aramco World* (November 1955); Aramco, *Annual Report* (1954), p. 45, and interview with Prof. A. J. Meyer, Cambridge, Mass., December 1971. See also his *Middle Eastern Capitalism* (Cambridge, Mass., 1959).

38. Abdel Muhsin Qattan's other interests included a huge hotel, restaurant and office complex in Beirut which, like his construction firm and trading agencies, provided employment for hundreds of Palestinians. Interviews in Beirut with M.D. and M.B., May 1972, and Hikmat Nashashibi, London, February 1982.

39. Finnie, p. 175. See also Longrigg, p. 230.

40. Palestine Liberation Organisation, *Palestinian Statistical Abstract 1980* (Damascus, 1980), p. 311.

41. *Events* (London), 30 June 1978, p. 59. See also 'The Migration of a Minority', in Barbara Aswad (ed.), *Arabic Speaking Communities in American Cities* (New York, 1974), pp. 85-110. By 1981 the American-Ramallah Association in the US had an estimated 5,000 members. The Palestine Congress of North America, which included immigrants and their offspring from all parts of Palestine, represented some 40,000 Palestinians, or about 35 per cent of all those in the US in 1981. *Middle East International,* 15 January 1982.

42. Interview with Mayor Elias Freij, *Events,* 30 June 1978. Interviews with Y.B. and M.B., Beirut, 3 and 7 May 1972.

43. Ibid.; interview with S.S., Beirut, 15 January 1972.

44. *L'Orient-Le Jour* (Beirut), 13 September 1974; *The Times* (London), 6 March 1981, p. xii.

45. *The Times*, ibid.

46. Porath, vol. 2, p. 115.

47. Both Abdul Hamid Shoman and his son, Abdul Majid, married daughters of Ahmad Hilmi Pasha, a shareholder in the bank and its general manager in Jerusalem. He had been the Minister of Finance in the short-lived Arab government set up in Damascus in 1920 by the Amir Faisal and later became the representative for Palestine to the Arab League (see the preceding chapter). Interview with Burhan al-Dajani, Secretary-General, Federation of Arab Chambers of Commerce, Industry and Agriculture, London, 21 November 1981. The pro-Hussaini daily newspaper, *Al-Difa'*, was financed by Shoman and the bank in the early 1940s. Hurewitz, p. 185.

48. *The Times*, 6 March 1981; *Twenty-Five Years*. Assets of the Haifa branch were moved to Beirut and Amman after 1948; those of the Jaffa branch were transferred to Nablus and Ramallah. A new branch was opened in the Arab-occupied sector of Jerusalem, replacing the one taken over by the Israelis.

49. Middle East Commercial Information Centre, *Annuaire des sociétés libanaises par action* (Beirut, 1970), p. 19; *Financial Times*, 'Survey of Jordan', 25 May 1977. Dollar figures are converted from 1968 exchange rates.

50. *Annuaire*, pp. 1312-3.

51. Ibid., pp. 25-6, 995, 1571-2; Sa'd became Jordan's Minister of Finance in 1971 and also held substantial interests in tobacco, cigarette and shoe companies in Jordan as well as serving as a director of the Jordan Petroleum Refinery Company and Royal Jordanian Airlines. *The Middle East and North Africa 1975-6* (London, 1975), p. 890. Abul Wafa al-Dajani also served on the board of the Jordanian Electric Power Company, the Jordan National Bank and the Jordan Phosphate Mines Company, *International Who's Who of the Arab World 1978-79* (London, 1978). The Al-Mashriq Board also included Badr Sa'id al-Fahoum, a member of a prominent family from Nazareth and a distinguished Palestinian lawyer, Henry Cattan, as well as Fuad Saba, whose accountancy firm is described in the text below.

52. *Middle East Economic Digest*, 28 April 1978, p. 34. For biographical profiles of Fuad Saba and his sons, see *Palestine Personalia;* the *International Who's Who of the Arab World 1978-79*; *Middle East Economic Digest*, 11 December 1981; and Porath, vol. 2, pp. 15-17, 193, 235 and 282.

53. For a description of the bank's management policies, see the comments of Abdul Majid Shoman in *The Times*, 6 March 1981, p. xii.

54. 'The Intra Bank Affair', pp. 76, 79. Some funds to start the bank in Beirut may have been provided by Berte Malouf, the Lebanese wife of a prominent Palestinian psychiatrist who was killed by the Stern gang in 1948.

55. For details of Intra's holdings, see the *New York Times*, October

1966 to January 1967; 'The Intra Bank Affair', ibid.; *Al-Nahar Arab Report*, vol. 2, no. 45 (8 November 1971), *The Observer* (London), 27 April 1975; and Michael Field, *A Hundred Million Dollars a Day* (London, 1976), pp. 138-42.

56. Interview with M.B., Beirut, 5 July 1972; G.S., Beirut, 8 June 1972. See also William W. Miller, 'The CAT Company', unpublished MA thesis, American University of Beirut, 1955, and Andrew Lycett, 'CAT, Mothercat and Kittens', *The Middle East* (July 1980), p. 57.

57. Interview with A.H., London, 9 January 1982; Lycett, ibid.

58. Finnie, p. 175.

59. From 1955 to 1965 Aden benefited from a huge influx of foreign exchange provided by both the British troops stationed in the colony and the tourists who arrived from various ports of call. This, together with the government expenditure on infrastructure and the income provided by the refinery, added to the colony's prosperity. *The Middle East and North Africa, 1975-6*, p. 797. See also Fred Halliday, *Arabia Without Sultans* (Harmondsworth, Middlesex, 1974) and Tom Little, *South Arabia* (London, 1968).

60. Lycett, p. 57.

61. See Bustani's biography in *Who's Who in the Lebanon, 1967-68*, which was published after his death (Beirut, 1968), pp. 109-11.

62. For details of the repercussions Bustani's plan to develop the Arab world had in Europe and in the Arab states, see Nicholas Sarkis, *Le petrole et les économies arabes* (Paris, 1963), pp. 235-7. Bustani's own views on the importance of using Palestinian skills and Arab oil revenues to promote Arab economic integration are described in his own book, *Marche arabesque* (London, 1961).

63. Interviews with M.B., Y.B., G.S., E.S., L.D. and S.K., Beirut, 1972, and London, 1975 and 1976.

64. *Who's Who in the Lebanon, 1974* (Beirut, 1974).

65. Colin Smith, 'A Palestinian's Dream of Home', *The Observer*, 9 February 1975.

66. *Annuaire*, p. 1405; *Middle East Financial Directory, 1977-8* (London, 1977), pp. 149, 153, 319.

67. Kemal Sayegh, *Oil and Arab Regional Development* (New York, 1969), pp. 106-7; Sperling, p. 2; Longrigg (1968), p. 230; *Al-Jazirah al-Jadidah*, 1972 issues, trans. Arab Support Committee (Berkeley, 1973), pp. 4-5, 22.

68. Sayegh, pp. 85, 87.

69. Ibid., pp. 85, 92.

70. Finnie, pp. 156-7, 165; Longrigg (1968), pp. 211-12.

71. M. W. Khouja and P. G. Sadler, *The Economy of Kuwait: Development and Role in International Finance* (London, 1979), p. 125, and Aruri and Farsoun, p. 136.

72. Leslie Ann Mitchell in the *Financial Times*, 26 February 1979, p. 21.

73. Sayegh, pp. 19-20. See also Hanna Batatu, *The Old Social Classes and the Revolutionary Movements in Iraq* (Princeton, NJ, 1978).

74. Interviews with G.K., B.R., B.S., Beirut, 1972; Aruri and Farsoun, pp. 138-9. See also Kerr, pp. 23-4, and Tabitha Petran, *Syria: A Modern History* (London and Tonbridge, 1972), pp. 193-5.

75. Interviews with A.D., A.S., Beirut, 1972, and Cambridge, Mass., 1971; Ruth First, *Libya: The Elusive Revolution* (Harmondsworth, Middlesex, 1974), p. 172.

76. Interviews with A.D. and A.S.; First, p. 171.

77. *New York Times,* 16, 17 and 19 October 1966. At the time the withdrawals were said to have been prompted by rising interest rates for US dollars which made deposits in Intra less attractive. However subsequent events seemed to confirm that the withdrawals were also motivated by a desire on the part of Gulf investors to increase their role in Intra and to re-direct more of its investments into profitable commercial properties in the US and Europe rather than into the development of industries and trade in Lebanon and the Arab world. Interviews with E.S. and L.D., London, 1975 and 1976.

78. *New York Times,* 16, 19 and 20 October 1966; 'The Intra Bank Affair', p. 78; Field, p. 140. For Baidas's own allegations about the political 'machinations' aimed at destroying Intra's role in Lebanon, see the *New York Times,* 30 October 1966. The Central Bank's actions in preventing the collapse of the country's banking system following the Intra crash are outlined in an interview with the bank's governor at the time, Elias Sarkis (later President of Lebanon) in *The Banker,* vol. 122, no. 551 (January 1972), pp. 55-6.

79. 'The Intra Bank Affair', pp. 78-9; *New York Times,* 27 October 1966. Three US banks, Chase Manhattan, First National City Bank and Bank of America, refused to turn over deposits held by Intra in their New York branches at the time of the crash, despite a ruling by the State Superintendent of Banks in New York that such action violated the state's banking laws. *New York Times,* 19 and 20 October, 17 November 1966.

80. *International Herald Tribune,* 27 December 1972; *New York Times,* 19 November 1966, 31 August 1967; 'The Intra Bank Affair', pp. 79, 81; *Al-Nahar Arab Report,* 8 November 1971, 18 December 1972; *Daily Star* (Beirut), 21 December 1972, 25 February 1975; Field, p. 141. Intra's commercial banking activities in Lebanon were taken over by a new institution, Bank al-Mashriq, in which Morgan Guaranty of the US later obtained a controlling interest.

81. Elias Saba, who later became Deputy Prime Minister and Minister of Finance in Lebanon, felt that aside from being Palestinian, Intra also exhibited a unique capacity (at that time) to channel the oil revenues of the Gulf states into productive investment in the Arab world. This, Saba told me, may have provoked resentment on the part of some Western interests who wanted to take a more direct role in the re-cycling of 'petrodollars', as well as in some 'financial circles' in the Gulf who did not want Lebanon to become the 'Switzerland' of the Middle East. Interview, London, 1975.

82. See for example the comments by Hasib Sabbagh in an interview in *The Observer,* 9 February 1975, and the views of the Shoman

family expressed in the Arab Bank's report, *Twenty-Five Years*.

83. In the Senate appointed by the King after the 1974 Arab summit only 8 of the 30 members were of Palestinian origin. The Chamber of Deputies, in which Palestinians had been guaranteed equal representation with Trans-Jordanians, was dissolved altogether and only reconvened, after new elections, ten years later. David Hirst, 'Conflicts of Head and Heart', *Guardian* (London), 19 December 1974. See also Aruri, pp. 59-60.

6 The Fragmentation of the Peasantry

1. For an account of the causes of the exodus see Walid Khalidi, 'Why did the Palestinians Leave?', *Middle East Forum*, vol. 35, no. 7 (July 1959), pp. 21-35. Zionist accounts of the flight and claims that the refugees left of their own accord or at the behest of the Arab governments are refuted in Erskine Childers, 'The Other Exodus', *Spectator*, 12 May 1961, pp. 672-5, and in the *Progress Report of the United Nations Mediator on Palestine* (Count Bernadotte), Rhodes, September 1948 (Cmd. 7530, London, 1948).

2. The estimate was made by William St Aubin, the delegate of the League of Red Cross Societies, in his article 'Peace and Refugees in the Middle East', *Middle East Journal*, vol. 3, no. 3 (July 1949), p. 251. Additional material on the numbers and plight of the refugees is available in S. G. Thicknesse, *Arab Refugees: A Survey of Re-settlement Possibilities* (London, 1949); *Annual Report of the Secretary-General of the United Nations, 1 July 1948 to 30 June 1949*, p. 102; Fred Bruhns, 'A Study of Arab Refugee Attitudes', *Middle East Journal*, vol. 9, no. 2 (Spring 1955); and in the final report of the Economic Survey Mission which was sent to the area in 1949 by the United Nations General Assembly (A/AC 25/6, Part 1). See also the work by Jacques de Reynier, the representative of the International Red Cross at the time, entitled *A Jérusalem un drapeau flottait sur la ligne de feu* (Neuchâtel, 1950), and the history of the refugees written by John Davis (formerly Commissioner-General of the United Nations Relief and Works Agency), *The Evasion of Peace* (London, 1968). Studies written later include Avi Plascoff, *The Palestinian Refugees in Jordan, 1948-1957* (London, 1981) and Edward Buehrig, *The UN and the Palestinian Refugees* (Bloomington, 1971). Gripping and detailed accounts of the exodus by the refugees themselves are available in Nafez Nazzal, *The Palestinian Exodus from Galilee, 1948* (Beirut, 1978); Rosemary Sayigh, *Palestinians: From Peasants to Revolutionaries* (London, 1979); and in Elias Shoufani's 'The Fall of a Village', *Journal of Palestine Studies*, vol. 1, no. 3 (Summer 1972).

3. The Arab population of Palestine in 1947 is estimated to have totalled 1,303,585. Janet Abu Lughod, 'The Demographic Transformation of Palestine', in Ibrahim Abu Lughod (ed.), *The Transformation of Palestine* (Evanston, Ill., 1971), p. 155. See also Hagopian and

Zahlan, 'Palestine's Arab Population', pp. 32-73; and George Kossaifi, 'Demographic Characteristics of the Arab Palestinian People', in Nakhleh and Zureik (eds.), pp. 13-46.

4. Thicknesse, p. 102; see also Barakat, p. 150. Aside from those living in the camps or registered for rations there were 30,000 still living in caves. An estimated 8,000 refugees from the landowning and professional classes were sufficiently well off not to need relief.

5. United Nations Relief and Works Agency (UNRWA), *Registration Statistical Bulletin*, UN Document A/6013 (First Quarter, 1966), p. 27. See also Harry N. Howard, 'UNRWA, the Arab Host Countries and the Arab Refugees', *Middle East Forum*, vol. 42, no. 3 (1966), pp. 29-42.

6. By December 1967 an estimated 245,000 Palestinians had fled from the West Bank and Gaza Strip into East Jordan; 116,000 had left the Israeli-occupied area of Syria and some 61,000, including 11,000 from Gaza and 50,000 from the Sinai Peninsula, had taken refuge in Egypt. Of the total, about 145,000 were refugees who received assistance from the United Nations and who were uprooted for the second time in their lives. Davis, p. 69.

7. Hagopian and Zahlan (as reprinted and translated) in *Problèmes politiques et sociales: l'organisation de liberation de la Palestine et les Palestiniens* (Paris, 1975), pp. 6-7.

8. Annual Report of the Director-General of the United Nations Relief and Works Agency (UNRWA), cited in the *Palestinian Statistical Abstract*, p. 361.

9. The total number of refugees in southern Lebanon including both Palestinians and Lebanese was estimated to have reached 600,000 by mid-June. Many were living in vacated flats, gardens, warehouses and schools in western Beirut. Others set up tent camps in the beaches along the coast. *The Times*, 14 June 1982.

10. United Nations Resolution 194 (III), 11 December 1948, quoted in Sami Hadawi, *Bitter Harvest: Palestine 1914-1967* (New York, 1967), p. 158; Davis, p. 61.

11. *Annual Report of the Secretary-General, 16 June 1958 to 15 June 1959*, UN Document A/4132, p. 3.

12. Ibid. The words are the Secretary-General's commenting on the Mission's interim report to the General Assembly, dated 6 November 1949.

13. Resolution 302 (IV), 3 December 1949; ibid.

14. *Annual Report* (A/4132), p. 4. See also Richardson, p. 239.

15. Hadawi, p. 158.

16. For an explanation of the terminology used by UNRWA and the political connotations implied in the use of the word 're-integration', see Richardson, p. 239.

17. Hadawi, pp. 159-62.

18. For reports of the demonstrations in Jordan and elsewhere see Alem, pp. 100-15; Sulaiman al-Nabulsi, 'Palestinian Arabs in the State of Jordan', *Al-Difa'* (Jerusalem), 14 May 1953; A. R. Abdel Kader, *Le conflit judéo-arabe* (Paris, 1961), p. 302; and *Haaretz*,

15 November 1952. Other reports are contained in *Filistin,* 21 November and 17 December 1953; *Al-Hayat,* 11 December 1952; *Kul Shai,* 14 September 1953; and *Al-Sayad,* 16 June 1954.

19. Baron, pp. 120-1.

20. Baron, pp. 101-3; Abou Iyad, pp. 43-7.

21. Abidi, pp. 208-9. See also Sakhnini, 'Damm Filistin al-wusta ila sharqiyyi al-Urdun 1948-1950', pp. 73-6.

22. Abidi, pp. 201-2; see also Mishal, p. 87. Later the Islamic Liberation Party developed a novel theory whereby some aid from UNRWA and the West could be accepted in so far as it was regarded as 'jizyah', i.e. as the traditional tax paid by non-Muslims. Abidi, p. 211.

23. Gabbay, pp. 458, 529-32. *Annual Report of the Secretary-General, 1 July 1951 to 30 June 1952,* UN Document A/2141, p. 25.

24. By the end of 1965 some 74 countries had made voluntary contributions to UNRWA; however 70 per cent of the total UNRWA budget spent from May 1950 to 31 December 1965 came from the US. Britain contributed $90.5 million over the period, bringing the combined share provided by the US and Britain to about 90 per cent. Howard, 'UNRWA', p. 30. Critics of the organisation claimed that these two countries provided the major portion of the finance mainly because they were the states which were primarily interested in preserving the *status quo* in the area and in ensuring that the Palestinians were prevented from returning to their homeland. Israel's contribution over the same period amounted to less than $725,000. The Arab states contributed $14,800,000 to UNRWA in addition to providing direct relief themselves which was estimated to be worth some $64 million from 1948 to 1965. Howard, 'UNRWA'.

25. Expenditure figures are taken from UN Document A/6313, Table 5, cited in Hadawi, pp. 178-9. The *per capita* figures were calculated assuming the total number of registered refugees to be 1,308,837, as given in the *UNRWA Registration Statistical Bulletin* (First Quarter, 1966), no. 1/66.

26. UN Document A/5813, p. 5, cited in Hadawi, p. 174.

27. Ibid. For additional material on the conditions in the camps, see Bassam Sirhan, 'Palestinian Refugee Camp Life in Lebanon', *Journal of Palestine Studies,* vol. 4, no. 2 (Winter 1975), pp. 91-107; Halim Barakat and Peter Dodd, 'Two Surveys of Palestinian Refugees [in Jordan]', unpublished paper provided to the author, American University of Beirut, 1972; 'Yarmouk: The Camp with a City Council', *Gulf Times,* 6 August 1981; Lena Rifkin, 'Notes from the Occupation: Peace Treaty Sharpens Struggle on West Bank', *MERIP Reports,* vol. 9, no. 10 (December 1979), pp. 3-8; Mary Khass, 'Gaza Under Occupation', *MERIP Reports,* vol. 8, no. 2 (March 1978); and Celeste Feigener, 'Courage in Adversity', *Middle East International* (July 1976), pp. 22-5. Rosemary Sayigh's *Palestinians* also contains a wealth of detail on camp conditions in Lebanon.

28. Turki, *The Disinherited,* p. 53.

29. Article III, Published in Dearden, p. 202.

30. Dearden, pp. 132-3.

31. Hutchinson, pp. 120-1. See also Hirst, pp. 178-9.

32. The number of fighters who remained in the occupied areas or who continued to carry out armed resistance from bases in the West Bank, Gaza and the neighbouring Arab countries is difficult to estimate. The daughter of one Palestinian who fought behind the Israeli lines in 1949 and 1950 told me that they numbered 'in the hundreds', but that virtually all had been either killed, injured or forced to lay down their arms by the end of 1954. See also Sakhnini, 'Damm Filistin', pp. 67-8.

33. Hirst, p. 179.

34. See Chapter 4; A. M. Goichon, 'Les réfugiés palestiniens en Jordanie', *Espirit* (July and August/September 1964); and Peter Dodd and Halim Barakat, *River without Bridges* (Beirut, 1969).

35. Sayigh, pp. 106-7.

36. Kader, p. 303.

37. The Christians were sent to two camps specifically reserved for them: Sin al-Fil and Dbaiyyah. Both were endowed with services, such as secondary schools, not readily available in the other camps reserved for Muslims. For more information, see Sayigh, pp. 119-20.

38. Sayigh, pp. 106-7.

39. Gabbay, p. 210; Turki, pp. 40-1; Sayigh, pp. 133-5; and Sirhan, p. 105.

40. My own conversations in 1972 with Shi'a peasant women from southern Lebanon were replete with references to their astonishment when they heard from the refugees that the Lebanese army had not taken an active part in the fighting in Palestine in 1948 and that the Arab Army of Liberation, rather than protecting the villagers, had often retreated in the face of Israeli advances. See also Nazzal, pp. 20, 22-3, 40-1, 91-7, for extensive examples of the refugees' views and Kader, p. 302, and Gabbay, pp. 206-7.

41. For an account of the raids and the casualties involved, see UN Documents S/3373, A/2935, S/3378, S/3430, S/3516 and S/3638, cited in Hadawi, pp. 238-40; Hutchinson, pp. 120-1; and E. L. M. Burns, *Between the Arabs and Israelis* (New York, 1963), pp. 158, 180, 184. Commander Hutchinson served on the Israeli-Jordanian Mixed Armistice Commission from 1949 to 1954 and was succeeded by General Burns, who served from January 1955 to September 1956.

42. Gabbay, pp. 215-16.

43. Ibid., p. 216.

44. Love, pp. 61, 83, 95, cited in Hirst, pp. 199-200.

45. Howard, pp. 40-1; 'Yarmouk, the Camp with a City Council'.

46. Gabbay, p. 214.

47. Examples are found in Sayigh, Abou Iyad and Nazzal.

48. The Palestinians as a whole, including those who became self-supporting, formed almost two-thirds of Jordan's population until 1967 when the West Bank was lost to Israel. Hilal, pp. 71, 79.

49. One of the major characteristics separating the urban city dwellers from the peasantry was the latter's collective lack of access to education. Professor Mahmoud al-Ghul, a Palestinian from the village

of Beit Silwan near Jerusalem, explained the difference, as he saw it, to me during a visit to Harvard University in March 1974. 'Take my own case,' he said. 'I am, I suppose, like Walid Khalidi [a well-known Palestinian scholar from a notable Jerusalem family] in that I am educated, have the requisite degrees, have taught in England, Iraq and Syria and now here. In that sense we are doing the same work. But I am not middle class. I cannot forget my family . . . My sisters are illiterate.' Other differences stemmed from the peasantry's distinctive dialect, their identification with a specific village or region, the preservation of extended family ties and their concern about family honour (*'ird*). For other examples described by Palestinians themselves, see Sayigh, pp. 52-3. Sadiq al-'Azm, a distinguished Syrian scholar and philosopher, has analysed what he calls the 'Fahlawian Personality' in his work on the 1967 war, *Self-Criticism After the Defeat*, trans. Lewis R. Scudder Jr., in 'Arab Intellectuals and the Defeat', unpublished MA thesis, American University of Beirut, 1971, pp. 232-48.

50. The Israeli writer, Amos Elon, has described the astonishment Israeli soldiers felt on discovering the strength of these ties after they overran several refugee camps in the West Bank in June 1967: 'Upon entering a refugee camp one young soldier discovered that the inmates were still organised into and dwelled as small clans or neighbourhood units according to the town, and even the street they had lived in prior to their dispersion in 1948 . . . Beersheba, Zarnaga, Ramlah, Lod, Jaffa, Rehovoth.' *The Israelis: Founders and Sons* (New York, 1972), p. 339, cited in Barakat, p. 25. See also Sayigh, pp. 124-8; Sirhan, pp. 101-3; and Sirhan's pamphlet, *Palestinian Children: The Generation of Liberation*, Palestine Essays no. 23, Research Centre, Palestine Liberation Organisation (Beirut, 1970), pp. 13-17.

51. A figure of 28 per cent for the West Bank is also recorded in an unpublished report, 'Figures About Agriculture in the West Bank', compiled by Shehadeh Dajani in March 1980 and cited in Emile Sahliyeh, 'West Bank Industrial and Agricultural Development: The Basic Problems', *Journal of Palestine Studies*, vol. 11, no. 2 (Winter 1982), p.63.

52. UN Document A/3212, p. 23, and A/3686, p. 25; *Filistin*, 12 December 1956; Gabbay, p. 532; 'The Bridge of No Return', *Gulf Times*, 13-19 July 1980. For a description of the Bashatwah tribe see Tawfiq Canaan, 'The Saqr Bedouin of Bisan', *Journal of the Palestine Oriental Society*, vol. 16 (1936), pp. 21-32.

53. Gubser, *Politics and Change*, pp. 124-5.

54. Ibid., p. 125.

55. These funds, which were made available under UNRWA's individual grants programme from 1955 to 1957, were allocated to those refugees who could present acceptable projects to the Agency. However very few of the peasants in the camps possessed the skills and contacts such a presentation required and as a result the funds were granted mainly to the more well-to-do refugees from the cities. When the programme was discontinued in 1957 because of a lack of funds, UNRWA had spent more than $2 million on 714 individual projects, 242 of which were for agricultural schemes. Gabbay, p. 531.

56. Baron, pp. 163-4; Goichon, 'La transformation', p. 150.

57. Goichon, 'La transformation', p. 150; Salim Tamari, 'Re-peasantisation in the Jordan Valley', unpublished paper, Bir Zeit University, 1981, pp. 301, 314-15, 330-1; and UNRWA, *The East Jordan Valley: A Social and Economic Survey* (Amman, 1961), p. 166.

58. Uri Davis, *et al.*, 'Israel and the Water Resources of the West Bank', *Journal of Palestine Studies*, vol. 9, no. 2 (Winter 1980), cited in Sahliyeh, 'West Bank Development', pp. 64-5. See also Hisham Awartani, *West Bank Agriculture: A New Outlook*, Research Bulletin no. 1, Al-Najah University (Nablus, 1981); and Peter Gubser, *West Bank and Gaza Economic Development*, Middle East Problem Paper no. 20, Middle East Institute (Washington, DC, 1979), pp. 2-3.

59. Tamari, 'Re-peasantisation', and his 'From the Fruits of their Labour: the Persistence of Share Tenancy in the Palestinian Agrarian Economy', unpublished paper, Bir Zeit University, Bir Zeit, 1981, pp. 30-2.

60. Tamari, 'From the Fruits', pp. 30-2.

61. More than half the landowning farmers in the West Bank and three-quarters of those in the East Bank owned 30 *dunums* or less, an amount which was too small to provide a basic living for a refugee family. Tamari, 'Re-peasantisation', pp. 314-15. The sharecroppers, who paid an average of 30 to 66 per cent of the crop's value to the landlord, received even less. Ibid., p. 305.

62. Salim Tamari, 'Building Other People's Homes: The Palestinian Peasant's Household and Work in Israel', *Journal of Palestine Studies*, vol. 11, no. 1 (Autumn 1981). Tamari makes use of an unpublished PhD thesis written by Linda Ammons, 'West Bank Arab Villages: The Influence of National and International Politics on Village Life', Harvard University, Cambridge, Mass., 1978.

63. Khass, pp. 21-2. See also Waines, p. 159.

64. Sirhan, 'Palestinian Refugee Camp Life', pp. 99-100.

65. Sayigh, p. 114.

66. Ibid.

67. Ibid., pp. 116-17.

68. Ibid., p. 117.

69. 'Class Structure of the Palestinians', unpublished MA thesis (in Arabic), American University of Beirut, 1977, cited in Sayigh, p. 121.

70. Ibid.

71. The International Red Cross estimated in mid-June 1982 that the number of homeless in the country, including both Lebanese and Palestinians, totalled 600,000. *The Times*, 14 June 1982. Even before the 1982 invasion Israeli raids on southern Lebanon had forced thousands of Palestinian refugees to emigrate to other parts of the country or to the neighbouring states. Many of the 3,000 agricultural workers who remained in the area lost their jobs when their Lebanese landlords and employers fled abroad to escape the shelling. Caroline Tisdall, 'The People with Nowhere to Run', *Guardian*, 28 August 1979.

72. 'Young Refugees Build New Careers in Syria', *Gulf Times*, 13 August 1981, p. 7.

73. Ibid.

74. *Gulf Times*, 13-19 July 1980; UNRWA, *From Camps to Homes: Progress and Aims* (Beirut and New York, 1951) and *Aid to Arab Refugees from Palestine* (Beirut, 1954). See also Hilal, pp. 78-9.

75. Gabbay, p. 531.

76. Ibid., pp. 457-8.

77. Sirhan, 'Palestinian Refugee Camp Life', pp. 98-9; *Events* (London), 17 October 1977; and Davis, p. 65.

78. SAMED, *Sons of Martyrs for Palestine Works Society: SAMED* (Beirut, n.d. [1974?]), pp. 11-15, and the pamphlet published by the Palestine Liberation Organisation, *The Other Face of Palestinian Resistance* (London, 1980), pp. 8-10.

79. Interview with Muhammad Zaki Nashashibi, President, Palestine National Fund, London, 22 May 1980. See also *The Middle East* (August 1980) and the PLO pamphlet, *The Other Face*, p. 9.

80. *The Other Face*, pp. 5-8.

81. *Gulf Times*, 13 August 1981, p. 7.

82. Ibid.

83. Ibid.

84. Sirhan, 'Palestinian Refugee Camp Life', p. 101.

85. Ibid.

86. Fiegener, 'Courage in Adversity', pp. 24-5; Sayigh, p. 122. See also the excellent study by Hani Mundus, *Al-'Amal wa-l-'umal fi al-mukhayyamat al-filistiniyyah* (*Labour and the Workers in the Palestinian Camps*) (Beirut, 1974).

87. Some 250 Palestinian workers at the port of Beirut received compensation totalling LL1.9 million after staging an all-day sit-in at the port in 1978. They were protesting against their unemployment during the civil war and against the killing of some 14 workers during the fighting. Reuters, Beirut, 12 January 1978.

88. Goichon, 'La transformation', p. 125, and Dajani, p. 3. See also United Nations Economic and Social Office in Beirut, *Organisation and Administration of Social Welfare Programmes: A Series of Country Studies: Jordan*, UN Publication E/68/IV/6 (Beirut, 1968); and *Studies in Social Development in the Middle East*, part 2.

89. Hacker, p. 129.

90. Guy Loew, 'L'essor urbain en Jordanie orientale', *Maghreb-Mashrek*, no. 81 (July-September 1978), pp. 52-3.

91. Guy Sitbon, 'Des camps de tentes aux palais princiers', *Le Nouvel Observateur*, 17 April 1982, p. 34.

92. Aruri, p. 92. See also Mishal, *West Bank, East Bank*, and especially Hilal, pp. 78-9, 93-5.

93. Gabbay, p. 533.

94. *Gulf Times*, 13-19 July 1980. See also Elisha Efrat, 'Changes in the Settlement Pattern of the Gaza Strip, 1945-1975', *Asian Affairs*, no. 63 (1976), pp. 168-77.

95. Ann Lesch, 'Israeli Settlements in the Occupied Territories

1967-1977', *Journal of Palestine Studies,* vol. 7, no. 1 (Autumn 1977). See also Sarah Graham-Brown, 'The West Bank and Gaza: The Structural Impact of Israeli Colonisation', *MERIP Reports,* no. 74 (January 1979), pp. 9-14; and Salim Tamari, 'The Palestinians in the West Bank and Gaza: The Sociology of Dependency' in Nakhleh and Zureik (eds.). Other relevant articles include Arie Bregman, 'The Economy of the Administered Areas, 1974-75', Research Department, Bank of Israel, 1975; and Amal Samed, 'The Proletarianisation of Palestinian Women in Israel', *MERIP Reports,* no. 50 (August 1976), pp. 14-15.

96. Atallah Mansour, 'West Bank Aid', *Events* (London), 17 October 1977, and unpublished material sent to the author. See also *Al-Fajr,* 27 September to 3 October 1981; *Haaretz,* 2 August 1978; and *Al-Hamishmar,* 1 August 1978; as well as *MERIP Reports* (January 1979), no. 74, pp. 24-5.

97. Interview with Muhammad Milhelm, Mayor of Hebron, London, June 1980. See also Khass, p. 22; Graham-Brown, 'The West Bank and Gaza', p. 11.

98. Mansour, 'West Bank Aid'; Tamari, 'The Structural Impact', p. 101. See also Sheila Ryan, 'The West Bank and Gaza: Political Consequences of Occupation', *MERIP Reports* (January 1979), no. 74, p. 4; Hisham Awartani, *A Survey of Industries in the West Bank and Gaza* (Bir Zeit, 1979) and a report compiled by the Federation of Chambers of Commerce in the West Bank in 1978 which is summarised in *Al-Qabas,* 8 April 1978.

99. Finnie, pp. 102-3. See also Thomas Stauffer, 'The Industrial Worker' in S. N. Fisher (ed.), *Social Forces in the Middle East* (Ithaca, NY, 1955), pp. 83-98; 'Izz ed-Din Amin, *Kuwait's Workers: From the Pearl to Petroleum* (in Arabic) (Kuwait, 1958), cited in Willard Beling, *Pan-Arabism and Labor* (Cambridge, Mass., 1961), p. 68; Longrigg, pp. 211-12; Kemal Sayegh, *Oil and Arab Regional Development* (New York, 1969), p. 103; and Kuwait Oil Company, *The Story of Kuwait* (London, 1955).

100. Sperling, p. 2.

101. Richard Sanger, *The Arabian Peninsula* (Ithaca, NY, 1954), p. 119.

102. *Al-Jaz'irah Al-Jadidah* (*The New Peninsula*) (Journal of the People's Democratic Party of Saudi Arabia) (1972), trans. by the Arab Support Committee, Berkeley, entitled 'Struggle, Oppression and Counter-Revolution in Saudi Arabia, pp. 4-5; Sperling, p. 2; Finnie, p. 102; and Turki, p. 89.

103. Ghassan Kanafani's highly praised novel, *Men in the Sun,* although a fictional account of three Palestinian workers seeking to emigrate to Kuwait, graphically portrays the fears and emotions experienced by many Palestinian *émigrés* in the Gulf since 1948 (trans. Hilary Kilpatrick, Washington, DC and London, 1978). See also Fawaz Turki's vivid account of his experiences working for Aramco in Ras al-Tanura in the early 1960s in *The Disinherited,* pp. 85-93, and a similar account by Leila Khaled of experiences working in Kuwait in *My People Shall Live,* pp. 78-94.

104. Seikaly and Smith, 'Palestinians in the Gulf', pp. 53-5. For details of the restrictions, see also Suzannah Tarbush, 'Manpower Patterns: The Development Issue of the 1980s', in the same *Review,* pp. 46-51.

7 Nationalism and Class Struggle

1. Abdullah, pp. 18-20; Aruri and Farsoun, p. 120. See also Albert Hourani's classic study *Arabic Thought in the Liberal Age* for a more general discussion of the historical context out of which liberalism arose. Abdullah Laroui's *The Crisis of the Arab Intellectual,* trans. Dairmid Cammell (Berkeley, Los Angeles and London, 1976) provides some profound insights concerning the liberal intellectual's political role within the larger context of imperial and neo-colonialist hegemony in the Third World.

2. Aruri, p. 96.

3. The divisions within the Palestinian community were also reflected in the Jordanian army and in the Palestine Liberation Army units based in Jordan. Some Palestinian officers remained staunchly loyal to the King despite his crackdown on the guerrillas and their final expulsion from the kingdom after a series of brutal battles in the forests near Irbid in July 1971. *Al-Nahar Arab Report,* vol. 3, no. 52 (25 December 1972), pp. 3-4. Sitbon, p. 34.

4. Kerr, p. 7.

5. Abidi, p. 209; Mishal, *West Bank – East Bank,* p. 94.

6. Abidi, pp. 161-2. Subsequent evidence also indicated that Anwar Khatib, one of the leading spokesmen of the liberals, had been receiving funds from Iraq (then still under Hashimite rule) for passing information about the Baath and other opposition parties in the Cabinet to King Hussein.

7. Baron, p. 126; Abdullah Schleiffer, *The Fall of Jerusalem* (New York and London, 1972), pp. 66-7; Riad El-Rayyes and Dunia Nahas, *Guerrillas for Palestine* (London, 1976), pp. 49-51.

8. *Al-Nahar Arab Report,* 2 May 1975; Baron, pp. 121-2.

9. For a detailed history of the movement, see the PhD thesis, 'The Arab Nationalist Movement 1951-1971: From Pressure Group to Socialist Party', written by Dr Bassel Koubessi at the American University, Washington, DC, 1971. Dr Koubessi helped to found the Iraqi branch of the ANM and was a close associate of George Habash during his medical student days at AUB. He was assassinated in Paris in April 1973. Baron, p. 119.

10. Baron, pp. 129-31. The PFLP's ideology is outlined in *A Strategy for the Liberation of Palestine* (Amman, 1969). See also the various press conferences given by George Habash, notably the one given in Beirut on the occasion of the Arab summit meeting in Beirut, 25 October 1974, reprinted in the *Journal of Palestine Studies,* vol. 4, no. 2 (Winter 1975), pp. 175-7. Other documentary material is contained in

Leila S. Kadi, *Basic Political Documents of the Armed Palestinian Resistance Movement* (Beirut, 1969); interview with Khaled al-Hassan in *Palestine Lives: Interviews with Leaders of the Resistance* (Beirut, 1973); Gerard Chaliand, 'The Palestinian Resistance Movement', *Le Monde Diplomatique* (March 1969); and the newspapers published by the DFLP − *Al-Hurriyah* − and the PFLP − *Al-Hadaf* − in Beirut.

11. Baron, p. 127.

12. One Fatah official told me in Beirut in June 1972 that the Democratic Front had begun to receive funds from certain members of the royal families in the Gulf as early as 1968. However I was unable to confirm this and the Front has denied that it has received any substantial material assistance from states in the Gulf.

13. At one point relations between Fatah and the PFLP deteriorated so badly that Kamal Adwan, a member of Fatah's Central Committee, accused the Front in 1971 of acting as if it were an agent of the Jordanian regime. Adwan also criticised the PFLP for providing the Jordanians with a pretext for liquidating the resistance movement in the country, a reference, presumably, to the spectacular hijacking of four airliners by the Front in September 1970. He hinted that Fatah had considered 'settling accounts' with the PFLP when the civil war broke out. El-Rayyes and Nahas, p. 40. See also John Cooley, *Green March, Black September: The Story of the Palestinian Arabs* (London, 1973) for a detailed analysis of the differences between Fatah and the PFLP.

14. *Fiches du Monde Arabe* (*FMA*), no. 736 (31 August 1977); Aruri, pp. 96-7.

15. Abidi, pp. 209, 217.

16. *FMA*, nos. 736, 743; Aruri, pp. 96-8.

17. Naji 'Allush, 'Les communistes arabes et la Palestine', *Afrique-Asie*, no. 3 (2 May 1972), pp. 20-6; *FMA*, nos. 743, 748. See also Bassam Tibi (ed.), *Die Arabische Linke* (Frankfurt on Main, 1969).

18. Baron, p. 108; 'Issam Sakhnini, 'Al-Kiyan al-filistiniyyi 1964-74' ('The Palestinian Entity, 1967-74'), *Shuun Filistiniyyah* (*Palestinian Affairs*), no. 40 (December 1974), p. 50.

19. 'Allush, p. 23; *L'Orient-Le Jour*, 24 June 1972; *FMA*, no. 748. The majority favourable to armed struggle, led by Fuad Nasser, Faiq Warrad and 'Arabi Awad, later expelled those, like Fahmi Salfiti, Rushdi Shahin and Emilie Naffah, who had opposed the adoption of armed struggle and the formation of a separate guerrilla group, the Ansar, sponsored by the Communist Party of Jordan.

20. *Le Monde Diplomatique* (May 1976, June 1980). Interview with Mohammad Milhelm, London, 2 June 1980, and Bassam Shaka, London, August 1980. See also Salim Tamari, 'The Palestinian Demand for Independence Cannot Be Postponed Indefinitely', *MERIP Reports* (October-December 1981), on the growth of the Communist Party in the West Bank and Gaza after the elections.

21. The history of the Brethren in Egypt has been the subject of several detailed works in English, including Richard P. Mitchell, *The Society of the Muslim Brothers* (London, 1969) and Christina Phelps

Harris, *Nationalism and Revolution in Egypt: The Role of the Muslim Brotherhood* (The Hague, 1964).

22. Abidi, p. 202; *FMA,* no. 1162 (10 January 1979). See also Sharif, p. 122, and Sharabati, *Min ajil Filistin.* Sharif was a close associate of Nasser's before the *coup d'état* and later became one of the Brethren's leaders in Jordan. Al-Sharabati acted as an adviser to the organisation in Cairo. The statement by Sheikh Hasan al-Banna, the founder and Supreme Guide of the Brethren in Egypt, supporting the Arab Higher Committee and the Mufti, was made on 4 September 1948 and is noted in *Middle East Journal,* no. 3 (January 1949), p. 74.

23. Abidi, p. 209.

24. Abidi, pp. 207-9.

25. Peter Gubser reported, for example, that in the 1950s families from Gaza which settled in the al-Karak district of Jordan after the 1948 war 'were not allowed to attend the public schools. As a result many of their children went to the Muslim Brotherhood primary school and the few who wished to continue their education had to bribe their way into local secondary schools'. *Politics and Change,* p. 125.

26. Baron, p. 82.

27. Baron, pp. 85-6.

28. Kadi, p. 25.

29. Baron, pp. 85-7, 91-2.

30. Baron, pp. 87, 95-6. Hirst, p. 281.

31. *FMA,* no. 849 (11 January 1978); Baron, pp. 86-7.

32. Hirst, p. 280.

33. Baron, pp. 103-7; *FMA,* no. 677 (22 June 1977); Abou Iyad, pp. 51, 68. See also Kadi for a detailed history of Fatah's early days and biographies of its founders.

34. Abou Iyad, pp. 76-7. The others in favour of immediate action included Abu Jihad, Abu Lutf, Abu Youssef and Abu Mazin. Two separate meetings were held to debate the issue, one in Kuwait and the other in Damascus.

35. For details of the first raids see Abou Iyad, pp. 78-9, and El-Rayyes and Nahas, pp. 27-8.

36. Abou Iyad, pp. 89-91, 94.

37. Abou Iyad, pp. 108-9; Baron, pp. 158-60, 177-9.

38. Abou Iyad, p. 102; Baron, pp. 178-9; *The Middle East* (March 1979), p. 35; *Guardian,* 20 April 1981.

39. El-Rayyes and Nahas, pp. 35-6.

40. Fatah's policy of non-interference is explained in a booklet published by its Office of Information and Guidance in 1968 entitled *Dirasat wa-tajarib thawriyyah* (*Revolutionary Studies and Experience*), while the PFLP's views on the need to combat the reactionary Arab regimes is contained in its publication, *A Strategy for the Liberation of Palestine* (Amman, 1969). For the DFLP's analysis, see its pamphlet, *Historical Development of the Palestinian Struggle* (n.p., 1971).

41. For a vivid description of the events leading up to the war and Salah Khalaf's role in the events, see Abou Iyad, pp. 121-53.

42. *Documents: The Political Programme of the Palestine Liberation Organisation,* Research Centre, Palestine Liberation Organisation (Beirut, 1974), 'Prologue', p. 80.

43. Studies of the civil war are still lacking, but see David Gilmour, *Lebanon: The Fractured Country* (London, 1983) and Pierre Vallaud, *Le Liban au bout du fusil* (Paris, 1976) as well as the collection of essays produced by *Die Dritte Welt* (*Third World* magazine) entitled *Lebanese War: Historical and Social Background* (Bonn, 1977).

44. *L'Orient – Le Jour,* 18 November 1978; John Roberts, 'Palestine's PLO Embarks on a Diplomatic Offensive', *Interpress Service* (IPS), Beirut, 17 November 1978.

45. Aside from the Fatah dissidents in the Beqaa Valley, the aftermath of the Israeli invasion of Lebanon also led to a prolonged re-examination within Fatah's Executive Committee of the correctness of the movement's past approach to the Arab regimes. Salah Khalaf (Abou Iyad) said publicly in July 1983 that he felt in retrospect the principle of 'non-interference in the internal affairs of Arab regimes' had been a wrong policy to pursue. *Al-Watan Al-'Arabi,* 15 July 1983 (English translation in *The Palestine Post,* Dundee, August 1983).

46. For examples of the camp residents' views on the nature of the services provided and their criticisms of them see Sayigh, pp. 163-75.

47. Interview, Mohammad Zaki Nashashibi, President of the Palestine National Fund, London, May 1980; Helena Cobban, 'Building a State from the Rubble of Exile', *The Middle East* (November 1981).

SELECT BIBLIOGRAPHY

I Official Papers

a. Government of Palestine

Barron, J. B. *Palestine: Report and General Abstracts of the Census of 1922* (Jerusalem, 1923)

Department of Migration *Annual Report* (Jerusalem, 1938)

Department of Statistics *General Monthly Bulletin of Current Statistics* (Jerusalem, 1944-6)

Department of Statistics *Statistical Abstract of Palestine, 1937-8* (Jerusalem, August 1938)

Palestine Citizenship Order-in-Council, 24 July 1925 *Official Gazette*, no. 147 (Jerusalem, 16 June 1925)

Report of the Committee Assigned to Study the Economic Conditions of Agriculturalists in Palestine (Johnson-Crosbie Report) (Jerusalem, 1930)

Report on the Possibility of Introducing a System of Agricultural Co-operation in Palestine (by C. F. Strickland) (Jerusalem, 1930)

Reports on Agricultural Development and Land Settlement in Palestine (by Lewis French), First Report (Jerusalem, December 1931), Supplementary Report (April 1932)

Superintendent of the Census *Census of Palestine 1931* (2 vols., Alexandria, 1933)

Supplement to the Survey of Palestine (Jerusalem, 1947)

A Survey of Palestine (2 vols., Jerusalem, 1946)

b. Great Britain: Parliamentary Papers

Accounts and Papers *Diplomatic Reports on Trade and Finance; Reports from HM Consuls on the Manufacturing and Commerce of their Consular Districts – Jerusalem and Jaffa* (1905, 1908)

Report of the Commission of Inquiry into the Palestine Disturbances of May 1921 (the Haycraft Report) (Cmd. 1540, London, 1921)

Report on Immigration, Land Settlement and Development, by Sir John Hope Simpson (Cmd. 3686, London, 1930)

c. Government of Jordan

Al-Jaridah al-rasmiyyah (*The Official Gazette*) no. 1012, (Amman, 1 March 1950)

Ministry of Information *Al-Iqtisad al-urduniyyi* (*The Jordanian Economy*) (Amman, 1966)

251

d. United Nations

Department of Economic Affairs *Review of Economic Conditions in the Middle East 1951-52*, Document E/2353/Add.1, ST/CA/19/Add.1 (New York, March 1953)

Economic and Social Office in Beirut *Organisation and Administration of Social Welfare Programmes: A Series of Country Studies: Jordan*, Document E/68/IV/6 (Beirut, 1968)

— *Studies in Social Development in the Middle East 1969*, Part 2: 'Report on the Social Survey of Amman, Jordan, 1966' (New York, 1970)

Secretariat *Annual Report of the Secretary-General, 1 July 1951 to 30 June 1952*, Document A/2141

— *Annual Report of the Secretary-General, 16 June 1958 to 15 June 1959*, Document A/4132

United Nations Relief and Works Agency (UNRWA) *Aid to Arab Refugees from Palestine* (Beirut, 1954)

— 'Assistance to the Palestine Refugees: Report of the Director, UNRWA', *Official Records of the United Nations General Assembly (GAOR)*, vol. 4, Supplement no. 16, Document A/1905

— *The East Jordan Valley: A Social and Economic Survey* (Amman, 1961)

— *From Camps to Homes: Progress and Aims* (Beirut and New York, 1951)

— *Registration Statistical Bulletin* (First Quarter, 1966), Document A/6013

II Unpublished Works

Ammons, Linda 'West Bank Arab Villages: The Influence of National and International Politics on Village Life', unpublished PhD thesis, Harvard University, Cambridge, Mass., 1978

Bailey, Clinton 'The Participation of the Palestinians in the Politics of Jordan', unpublished PhD thesis, Columbia University, New York, 1966

Dajani, N. I. 'Economic Appraisal of the Yarmuk Jordan Valley Project', unpublished PhD thesis, University of Wisconsin, Madison, 1957

Djabry, 'Umar 'La Syrie sous le régime du mandat', unpublished PhD thesis, University of Toulouse, 1934

Farrell, W. Jerome 'The Distribution of Educational Benefits in Palestine (1923-1945)', (Confidential) G.P.P. 24770-200-20.3.46, Private Papers Collection, Middle East Centre, St Antony's College, Oxford University

Howard, H. N. Papers on the Problems of Arab Refugees, Record Group R659, National Archives, Washington, DC

Khoury, Philip 'The Politics of Nationalism: Syria and the French Mandate', unpublished PhD thesis, Harvard University, Cambridge, Mass., 1980

Koubessi, Dr Bassel 'The Arab Nationalist Movement 1951-1971: From Pressure Group to Socialist Party', unpublished PhD thesis, American University, Washington, DC, 1971

Miller, William W. 'The C.A.T. Company', unpublished MA thesis, American University of Beirut, Beirut, 1955

Smith, Barbara J. 'British Economic Policy in Palestine towards the Development of the Jewish National Home 1920-1929', unpublished D Phil thesis, Oxford University, 1978

Sperling, David 'The Arabian American Oil Company Goes to Lebanon', unpublished paper, Centre for Middle Eastern Studies, Harvard University, Cambridge, Mass., 1955

Taqqu, Rachel L. 'Arab Labour in Mandatory Palestine 1920-1948', unpublished PhD thesis, Columbia University, New York, 1977

III Books

a. English, French and German

Abcarius, M. F. *Palestine through the Fog of Propaganda* (London, 1946)

Abdel-Malek, Anwar *Egypte: société militaire* (Paris, 1962)

'Abdullah, Ibn Hussein *My Memoirs Completed — 'Al-Takmilah'*, trans. H. W. Glidden (London, 1978)

Abidi, Aqil H. *Jordan: A Political Study 1948-1957* (London, 1965)

Abou Iyad *see* Khalaf, Salah

Amin, Samir *La nation arabe* (Paris, 1976)

Andrews, Fannie Fern *The Holy Land under the Mandate* (2 vols., Boston and New York, 1931)

Antonius, George *The Arab Awakening* (Beirut, 1955)

Arab Bank Ltd *Twenty-Five Years of Service to the Arab Economy, 1930-1955* (Amman, 1956)

Aruri, Naseer *Jordan: A Study in Political Development* (The Hague, 1974)

Awartani, Hisham *A Survey of Industries in the West Bank and Gaza* (Bir Zeit, 1979)

Barbour, Nevill *Nisi Dominus: A Survey of the Palestine Controversy* (Beirut, 1969)

Baron, Xavier *Les Palestiniens: un peuple* (Paris, 1977)

Beling, Willard A. *Pan-Arabism and Labor* (Cambridge, Mass., 1961)

Bethell, Nicholas *The Palestine Triangle: The Struggle between the British, the Jews and the Arabs, 1935-48* (London, 1980)

Bober, Arie (ed.) *The Other Israel* (New York, 1972)

Bonné, Alfred *Palästina: Land und Wirtschaft* (Berlin, 1937)

—*State and Economics in the Middle East* (London, 1955)

Brocklemann, Carl *History of the Islamic Peoples*, trans. Joel Carmichael and Moshe Perlmann (New York, 1960)

Bullock, John *Death of a Country: The Civil War in Lebanon* (London, 1977)

Burns, E. L. M. *Between the Arabs and Israelis* (New York, 1963)

Bustani, Emile *Marche arabesque* (London, 1961)

Carré, Olivier *L'idéologie palestinienne de résistance* (Paris, 1972)

—*Septembre noir* (Brussels, 1980)

Chaliand, Gérard *La résistance palestinienne* (Paris, 1970)

Childers, Erskine B. *The Road to Suez* (London, 1962)

Churchill, Charles W. *The City of Beirut: A Socio-Economic Survey* (Beirut, 1954)

Collins, Larry and Lapierre, Dominique *O Jerusalem!* (New York, 1972)

Conder, C. R. *Tent Work in Palestine* (2 vols., Palestine Exploration Fund, London, 1878)

Cooley, John *Green March, Black September: The Story of the Palestinian Arabs* (London, 1973)

Crossman, R. H. S. *Palestine Mission* (London, 1947)

Cuinet, Vital *Syrie, Liban et Palestine: géographie administrative, statistique, descriptive et raisonée* (Paris, 1896)

Dajani, Ali T. *A Directory of Jordan's Industrial Firms: The Industry of Jordan, 1965* (Amman, 1965)

Davis, John *The Evasive Peace* (London, 1968)

Davis, Uri, Mack, A. and Davis, N.-Y. (eds.) *Israel and the Palestinians* (London, 1975)

Dearden, Ann *Jordan* (London, 1958)

Dodd, Peter and Barakat, Halim *River without Bridges* (Beirut, 1969)

Elon, Amos *The Israelis, Founders and Sons* (New York, 1972)

Encyclopedia of Islam, old ed (8 vols., Leiden and London, 1913-18)

Erskine, Mrs Stuart *Palestine of the Arabs* (London, Bombay and Sydney, 1935)

Essaleh, Salah *L'état actuel de l'économie syrienne* (Paris, 1944)

Field, Michael *A Hundred Million Dollars a Day* (London, 1976)

Finn, Elizabeth A. *Palestine Peasantry, Notes on their Clans, Religion and Laws* (Edinburgh, 1923)

Finn, James *Stirring Times* (2 vols., London, 1878)

Finnie, David H. *Desert Enterprise: The Middle East in its Local Environment* (Cambridge, Mass., 1958)

First, Ruth *Libya: The Elusive Revolution* (Harmondsworth, Middlesex, 1974)

Flapan, Simha *Zionism and the Palestinians* (London and New York, 1979)

Furlonge, Sir Geoffrey *Palestine is my Country: The Story of Musa Alami* (New York and Washington, 1969)

Gabbay, Rony, R. *A Political Study of the Arab-Jewish Conflict: The Arab Refugee Problem* (Geneva and Paris, 1959)

Gibb, H. A. R. *Modern Trends in Islam* (Chicago, 1947)

Gilmour, David *Dispossessed: The Ordeal of the Palestinians 1917-1980* (London, 1980)

Glubb (Pasha), John Bagot *A Soldier in the Desert* (London, 1958)

—*A Soldier with the Arabs* (London, 1957)

Goichon, A. M. *Jordanie réelle* (2 vols., Limoges, 1967)

Graham-Brown, Sarah *Palestinian Workers and Trade Unions* (London, 1980)
— *Palestinians and their Society 1880-1946: A Photographic Essay* (London, 1980)
Granott, A. *The Land System in Palestine* (London, 1952)
Granovsky, A. *The Fiscal System of Palestine* (Jerusalem, 1935)
Granqvist, Hilma *Marriage Conditions in a Palestinian Village* (Helsingfors, 1931)
Gubser, Peter *Politics and Change in Al-Karak, Jordan* (London, New York and Toronto, 1973)
Haas, Marius *Husseins Königreich: Jordaniens Stellung im Nahen Osten* (Munich, 1975)
Hacker, Jane M. *Modern Amman: A Social Study* (Durham, 1960)
Hadawi, Sami *Bitter Harvest: Palestine 1914-1967* (New York, 1967)
Halliday, Fred *Arabia without Sultans* (Harmondsworth, Middlesex, 1974)
Harris, Christina Phelps *Nationalism and Revolution in Egypt: The Role of the Muslim Brotherhood* (The Hague, 1964)
Himadeh, Said B. (ed.) *The Economic Organisation of Palestine* (Beirut, 1938)
Hirst, David *The Gun and the Olive Branch: The Roots of Violence in the Middle East* (London, 1977)
Holt, P. M. *Egypt and the Fertile Crescent 1516-1922: A Political History* (London, 1966)
Hopwood, Derek (ed.) *The Arabian Peninsula: Society and Politics* (London, 1972)
Hourani, Albert H. *Arabic Thought in the Liberal Age* (London, 1967)
— *Minorities in the Arab World* (London, 1947)
— *Syria and Lebanon: A Political Essay* (London, 1946)
Hurewitz, J. C. *The Struggle for Palestine* (New York, 1968)
Hussein, Ibn Talal *Uneasy Lies the Head: An Autobiography* (London, 1962)
Hutchinson, E. H. *Violent Truce* (New York, 1956)
Ingrams, Doreen *Palestine Papers 1917-1922, Seeds of Conflict* (London, 1972)
International Bank for Reconstruction and Development *The Economic Development of Jordan* (Baltimore, 1957)
International Who's Who of the Arab World 1978-79 (London, 1978)
Jabara, Abdeen and Terry, Janice (eds.) *From Nationalism to Revolution in the Arab World* (Wilmette, Ill., 1971)
Jumblatt, Kamal *Pour le Liban* (Paris, 1978)
Jaussen, J.-A. *Coutumes palestiniennes I: Naplouse et son district* (Paris, 1927)
Kader, A. R. Abdel *Le conflit judéo-arabe* (Paris, 1961)
Kadi, Leila S. (ed. and trans.) *Basic Political Documents of the Armed Palestinian Resistance Movement* (Beirut, 1969)
Kanafani, Ghassan *Men in the Sun,* trans. Hilary Kilpatrick (London and Washington, DC, 1978)

Kanafani, Ghassan *Palestine: The 1936-1939 Revolt*, trans. the Tri-continental Society (London, 1980)

Kayyali, Abdul Wahab *Palestine: A Modern History* (London, 1978)

Kazziha, Walid W. *Palestine in the Arab Dilemma* (London and New York, 1979)

Keith-Roach, E. and Luke, H. C. (eds.) *The Handbook of Palestine and Trans-Jordan* (London, 1930)

Kerr, Malcolm *The Arab Cold War: Gamal Abd al-Nasser and his Rivals, 1958-1970*, 3rd edn (Oxford, London and New York, 1971)

Khalaf, Salah (Abou Iyad) *Palestinien sans patrie: entretiens avec Eric Rouleau* (Paris, 1978)

Khalaf, Samir and Kongstad, Per *Hamra of Beirut: A Case of Rapid Urbanisation* (Leiden, 1973)

Khaled, Leila *My People Shall Live: The Autobiography of a Revolutionary*, ed. George Hajjar (London, 1973)

Khalidi, Rashid *British Policy towards Syria and Palestine 1906-1914* (London, 1980)

Khalidi, Walid (ed.) *From Haven to Conquest*, Institute of Palestine Studies (Beirut, 1973)

Khouja, M. W. and Sadler, P. G. *The Economy of Kuwait: Development and Role in International Finance* (London, 1979)

Khouri, Rami G. *The Jordan Valley: Life and Society Below Sea Level* (London and New York, 1981)

Kirk, George E. *A Short History of the Middle East*, 7th rev. edn (New York, 1964)

——*Survey of International Affairs: The Middle East 1945-1950* (Oxford, 1954)

Konikoff, A. *Trans-Jordan: An Economic Survey* (Jerusalem, 1946)

Kuwait Oil Company *The Story of Kuwait* (London, 1955)

Lackner, Helen *A House Built on Sand: A Political Economy of Saudi Arabia* (London, 1978)

Laquer, Walter *A History of Zionism* (London, 1972)

Laroui, *The Crisis of the Arab Intellectual*, trans. Diarmid Cammell (Berkeley, Los Angeles and London, 1976). First published as *La crise des intellectuels arabes* (Paris, 1969)

Lenczowski, George *Oil and State in the Middle East* (Ithaca, NY, 1960)

Le Strange, Guy *Palestine under the Moslems* (London, 1890)

Lewis, Bernard *The Emergence of Modern Turkey* (London, 1968)

Little, Tom *South Arabia* (London, 1968)

Lloyd George, David *The Truth about the Peace Treaties* (London, 1938)

Longrigg, Stephen *Oil in the Middle East* (London and New York, 1954; rev. edn, London, New York and Toronto, 1968)

Lortet, Louis *La Syrie d'aujourd'hui* (Paris, 1881)

Love, Kennett *Suez: The Twice-Fought War* (New York, 1969)

Lutfiyya, Abdulla *Baytīn: A Jordanian Village* (The Hague, 1966)

Mandel, Neville *The Arabs and Zionism before World War One* (Berkeley, Los Angeles and London, 1976)

Maoz, Moshe *Ottoman Reform in Syria and Palestine, 1840-1861* (Oxford, 1968)

— (ed.) *Studies on Palestine during the Ottoman Period* (Jerusalem, 1975)

Mardin, Sherif A. *The Genesis of Young Ottoman Thought* (Princeton, 1962)

Margalith, Israel *Le Baron Edmond de Rothschild et la colonisation juive en Palestine 1882-1889* (Paris, 1957)

Nakhleh, Emile A. *The United States and Saudi Arabia: A Policy Analysis* (Washington, DC, 1975)

Nakhleh, Khalil and Zureik, Elia (eds.) *The Sociology of the Palestinians* (London, 1980)

Nassib, Selim and Tisdall, Caroline *Beirut: Frontline Story* (London, 1983)

Nazzal, Nafez *The Palestinian Exodus from Galilee, 1948* (Beirut, 1978)

Odell, Peter *Oil and World Power* (Harmondsworth, Middlesex, 1975)

Oliphant, Lawrence *Haifa, or Life in Modern Palestine* (London, 1887)

— *The Land of Gilead* (New York, 1881)

Palestine Chambers of Commerce *Directory of Arab Trade, Industry, Crafts and Professions* (Jerusalem, 1938)

Palestine Liberation Organisation *The Other Face of Palestinian Resistance* (London, 1980)

Palestine Lives: Interviews with Leaders of the Resistance, intro. Clovis Maksoud (Beirut, 1973)

Palestine National Fund, Central Bureau of Statistics *Palestinian Statistical Abstract 1980* (Damascus, 1980)

Palestine Personalia (Tel Aviv, 1947)

Parkes, James *A History of Palestine from 135 AD to Modern Times* (London, 1949)

Peake, F. *History and Tribes of Jordan* (Miami, 1958)

Peretz, Don *Israel and the Palestine Arabs* (Washington, DC, 1958)

Petran, Tabitha *Syria: A Modern History* (London and Tonbridge, 1972)

Popular Democratic Front for the Liberation of Palestine *Historical Development of the Palestinian Struggle* (n.p., 1971)

Popular Front for the Liberation of Palestine *A Strategy for the Liberation of Palestine* (Amman, 1969)

Porath, Yehoshua *The Emergence of the Palestinian Arab National Movement* (2 vols., London, 1974 and 1977), vol. 1: *1918-1929,* vol. 2: *1929-1939*

Quandt, W., Jabber, F. and Lesch, A. M. *The Politics of Palestinian Nationalism* (Los Angeles, 1973)

Ramsauer, Ernest E., Jr. *The Young Turks: Prelude to the Revolution of 1908* (Princeton, 1957)

El-Rayyes, Riad and Nahas, Dunia *Guerrillas for Palestine* (London, 1976)

Reynier, Jacques de *A Jérusalem un drapeau flottait sur la ligne de feu* (Neuchâtel, 1950)

Ruppin, Arthur *Syrien als Wirtschaftsgebiet* (Berlin and Vienna, 1920)

Said, Edward *The Question of Palestine* (London and Henley, 1980)

Salibi, Kemal *Crossroads to Civil War: Lebanon 1958-1976* (New York, 1976)

SAMED *Sons of Martyrs for Palestine Works Society: SAMED* (Beirut, n.d. [1974?])

Sampson, Anthony *The Seven Sisters* (London, 1975)

Sanger, Richard *The Arabian Peninsula* (Ithaca, NY, 1954)

Sarkis, Nicholas *Le pétrole et les économies arabes* (Paris, 1963)

Sayegh, Kemal *Oil and Arab Regional Development* (New York, 1969)

Sayigh, Rosemary *Palestinians: From Peasants to Revolutionaries* (London, 1979)

Schechtman, Joseph B. *The Arab Refugee Problem* (New York, 1952)

Schleiffer, Abdullah *The Fall of Jerusalem* (New York and London, 1972)

Seale, Patrick *The Struggle for Syria* (London, 1965)

Sharabi, Hisham *Arab Intellectuals and the West* (Baltimore and London, 1970)

Shaw, Stanford J. *Ottoman Egypt in the Eighteenth Century* (Cambridge, Mass., 1962)

Shwadran, Benjamin *Jordan: A State of Tension* (New York, 1959)

Stork, Joe *Middle East Oil and the Energy Crisis* (London and New York, 1975)

Storrs, Ronald *Orientations* (London, 1943)

Sykes, Christopher *Orde Wingate* (London, 1959)

Thicknesse, S. G. *Arab Refugees: A Survey of Resettlement Possibilities* (London, 1949)

Tibawi, A. L. *The Islamic Pious Foundations in Jerusalem* (London, 1978)

—*A Modern History of Syria, Including Lebanon and Palestine* (London, 1969)

Tibi, Bassam (ed.) *Die Arabische Linke* (Frankfurt on Main, 1969)

Timerman, Jacobo *The Longest War* (London, 1982)

Turki, Fawaz *The Disinherited: Journal of a Palestinian Exile* (New York, 1972)

Vallaud, Pierre *Le Liban au bout du fusil* (Paris, 1976)

Vatikiotis, P. J. *Politics and the Military in Jordan: A Study of the Arab Legion, 1921-1957* (London, 1967)

Verney, N. and Dambmann, G. *Les puissances étrangères dans le Levant, en Syrie et en Palestine* (Paris, 1900)

Waines, David *The Unholy War: Israel and Palestine 1879-1971* (Wilmette, Ill., 1971)

Warriner, Doreen *Land and Poverty in the Middle East* (London, 1948)

—*Land Reform and Development in the Middle East* (Oxford, 1962)

Weinstock, Nathan *Zionism: False Messiah*, trans. and ed. Alan Adler (London, 1979). First published as *Sionisme contre Israël: Genèse de Israël 1882-1948* (Paris, 1969)

Weizmann, Chaim *Trial and Error: An Autobiography of Chaim Weizmann* (London, 1949)

Who's Who in the Lebanon, 1974 (Beirut, 1974)
Wise, Stephen S. and Haas, Jacob *The Great Betrayal* (New York, 1930)
Wolf, Eric *Peasants* (Englewood Cliffs, NJ, 1966)
Woodward, E. L. and Butler, R. (eds.) *Documents on British Foreign Policy, 1919-1939* (London, 1952), first series
Wortebet, G. M. *Syria and the Syrians* (London, 1856)
Zeine, Zeine *Arab-Turkish Relations and the Emergence of Arab Nationalism* (Beirut, 1958)

b. Arabic

Abu al-Sha'r, Amin (ed.) *Muthakkirat al-malik 'Abdullah bin al-Hussein* (*The Memoirs of King Abdullah bin al-Hussein*) (Sao Paulo, 1953)
'Allush, Naji *Al-Muqawwamah al-'arabiyyah fi Filistin, 1917-1948* (*Arab Resistance in Palestine, 1917-1948*) (Beirut, 1970)
al-'Arif, 'Arif *al-Nakbah* (*The Catastrophe*) (4 vols., Sidon, 1956)
— *Tarikh al-Quds* (*History of Jerusalem*) (Cairo, 1951)
al-'Azm, Sadiq, *Dirasah naqdiyyah li-fikr al-muqawwamah al-filistiniyyah* (*A Critical Study of the Ideology of the Palestinian Resistance*) (Beirut, 1973)
— *Al-Maqd al-dhati ba'd al-hazimah* (*Self-criticism after the Defeat*) (Beirut, 1969)
Badran, Nabil *Al-Ta'lim wa-l-tahdith fi-l-mujtama' al-'arabiyyi al-filistiniyyi* (*Education and Modernisation in Palestinian Arab Society*) (Beirut, 1969)
Barghouthi, 'Umar Salih and Tawtah, D. Khalil *Tarikh Filistin* (*History of Palestine*) (Jerusalem, 1922)
al-Dabbagh, Mustafa Murad *Biladna Filistin* (*Our Land of Palestine*) (3 vols., Beirut, 1966-71)
Darwazah, Muhammad 'Izza *Hawla al-harakah al-'arabiyyah al-hadithah* (*On the Modern Arab Movement*) (5 vols., Sidon, 1951)
— *Al-Qadaiyyah al-filistiniyyah fi-mukhtalifi marahiliha* (*The Various Stages of the Palestinian Problem*) (Sidon, 1951)
Fatah (Office of Information and Guidance) *Dirasat wa-tajarib thawriyyah* (*Revolutionary Studies and Experience*) (n.p., 1968)
al-Ghawri, Emile *Al-Muamar al-kubra: ightiyal Filistin wa mahq al-'arab* (*The Great Conspiracy: The Assassination of Palestine and the Destruction of the Arabs*) (Cairo, 1955)
Hasan, Bilal *Al-Filistiniyyun fi-l Kuwait* (*The Palestinians in Kuwait*) (Beirut, 1973)
Hilal, Jamil *Al-Diffah al-gharbiyyah: al-tarkib al-iqtisadiyyi wa-l-ijtima'iyyi, 1948-1974* (*The Economic and Social Structure of the West Bank, 1948-1974*) (Beirut, 1975)
al-Hussaini, Hajj Amin *Haqaiq 'an qadaiyah Filistin* (*The Facts of the Palestinian Problem*) (Cairo, 1953)
Kayyali, Abdul Wahab (ed.) *Withaiq al-muqawwamah al-filistiniyyah al-'arabiyyah 1918-1939* (*Documents of the Palestinian Arab Resistance 1918-1939*) (Beirut, 1968)
al-Khatib, Hajj Muhammad Nimr *Min athir al-nakbah* (*Aspects of the Disaster*) (Damascus, 1949)

al-Khususi, Badr al-Din 'Abbas *Dirasat fi-tarikh al-Kuwait al-ijtima'iyyi wa-l-iqtisadiyyi, 1913-1961 (Studies in the Social and Economic History of Kuwait)* (Kuwait, 1972)

al-Madi, Munib and Musa, Sulaiman *Tarikh al-Urdun fi al-qarn al-'ishrin (History of Jordan in the Twentieth Century)* (Amman, 1959)

al-Majali, Hazza *Muthakkirati (My Memoirs)* (n.p., 1960)

Mundus, Hani *Al-'Amal wa-l-'umal fi al-mukhayyamat al-filistiniyyah (Labour and the Workers in the Palestinian Camps)* (Beirut, 1974)

al-Nimr, Ihsan *Tarikh Jabal Nablus wa-l-Balqa (History of Jebel Nablus and the Balqa)* (2 vols., Nablus, 1937 and 1961)

Sayigh, Anis *Al-Hashimiyyun wa-l-qadaiyyah al-filistiniyyah (The Hashimites and the Palestinian Problem)* (Beirut, 1966)

Sharif, Kamil Ismail *Al-Ikhwan al-muslimin fi-harb Filistin (The Muslim Brotherhood in the Palestine War)* (Cairo, 1950)

Shuqairi, Ahmad *Arba'un 'aman fi al-hayat al-'arabiyyah wa-l-dawliyyah (Forty Years in the Life of the Arabs and the World)* (Beirut, 1969)

Sirhan, Bassam *Al-Filistiniyyun fi-l Kuwait: nataij awaliyyah li-bahth ijtima'iyyi (The Palestinians in Kuwait: Preliminary Results of Social Research)* (Kuwait, n.d. [1978?])

Solh, Hannah *Filistin wa-tajdid hayatiha (Palestine and the Modernisation of its Life)* (Jerusalem, 1919)

al-Tal, 'Abdullah *Karithat Filistin: muthakkirat 'Abdullah al-Tal (Disaster in Palestine: The Memoirs of Abdullah al-Tal)* (Cairo, 1959)

Tuma, Amil *Juzur al-qadaiyah al-filistiniyyah (The Roots of the Palestinian Problem)* (Nazareth, n.d.)

Tuqan, Subhi *'Amman* (Amman, 1950)

Yashruti, Khalid *Kitabat wa-ray fi Filistin al-thawrah (Essays and Points of View in Revolutionary Palestine)* (n.p., 1970)

Yassin, Subhi *Al-Thawrah al-'arabiyyah al-kubra fi Filistin, 1936-1939 (The Great Arab Revolution in Palestine, 1936-1939)* (Cairo, 1959)

Zuraiq, Qustantin *Ma'na al-nakbah mujaddadan (The Meaning of the Disaster Revisited)* (Beirut, 1967)

IV   Articles and Pamphlets

Abu Lughod, Janet 'The Demographic Transformation of Palestine' in Ibrahim Abu Lughod (ed.), *The Transformation of Palestine* (Evanston, Ill., 1971), pp. 139-64

Alem, Jean-Pierre 'En Jordanie: l'agonie d'un royaume', *Orient,* no. 2 (April 1957), pp. 100-5

'Allush, Naji 'Les communistes arabes et la Palestine', *Afrique-Asie,* no. 3 (2 May 1972), pp. 20-6

Anderson, J. N. D. 'Recent Developments in Sharia Law VIII: The Jordanian Law of Family Rights, 1951', *The Muslim World,* vol. 42, no. 3 (July 1952), pp. 190-206

Aruri, Naseer H. and Farsoun, Samih 'Palestinian Communities and Arab Host Countries' in Khalil Nakhleh and Elia Zureik (eds.), *The Sociology of the Palestinians* (London, 1980), pp. 112-46

Awartani, Hisham *West Bank Agriculture: A New Outlook* Research Bulletin no. 1, Al-Najah University (Nablus, 1981)

Baer, Gabriel 'Guilds in Middle Eastern History' in M. A. Cook (ed.), *Studies in the Economic History of the Middle East* (London, 1970), pp. 11-30

— 'Land Tenure in the Hashemite Kingdom of Jordan', *Land Economics,* vol. 33, no. 3 (August 1957)

Barakat, Halim 'The Palestinian Refugees: An Uprooted Community Seeking Repatriation', *International Migration Review,* vol. 7 (Summer 1973), pp. 147-61

Bergheim, Samuel 'Land Tenure in Palestine', Palestine Exploration Fund, *Quarterly Statement* (July 1894), pp. 191-9.

Bruhns, Fred 'A Study of Arab Refugee Attitudes', *Middle East Journal,* vol. 9, no. 2 (Spring 1955)

Canaan, Tawfiq 'The Saqr Bedouin of Bisan', *Journal of the Palestine Oriental Society,* vol. 16, (1936), pp. 21-32

Cobban, Helen 'Building a State from the Rubble of Exile', *The Middle East* (November 1981), pp. 24-5

Cooley, John 'Iran, the Palestinians and the Gulf', *Foreign Affairs,* vol. 57, no. 5 (Summer 1979), pp. 1017-34

Dajani, Ali 'The Manpower Boomerang hits Jordan', *ILO Information,* International Labour Office, Geneva, vol. 19, no. 4 (1978)

Dawn, C. Earnest 'The Rise of Arabism in Syria', *Middle East Journal,* vol. 16 (1962)

Efrat, Elisha 'Changes in the Settlement Pattern of the Gaza Strip, 1945-1975', *Asian Affairs,* no. 63 (1976), pp. 168-77

Firestone, Ya'akov 'Crop-Sharing Economies in Mandatory Palestine', *Middle East Studies,* vol. 2, no. 1 (January 1975), pp. 3-23, and vol. 2, no. 2 (May 1975), pp. 175-94

Ghantous, Lutfi 'Athr al-tarkib al-tabaqiyyi fi al-qadaiyah al-filistiniyyah' ('The Influence of Class Structure on the Palestinian Problem'), *Dirasat 'Arabiyyah (Arab Studies),* vol. 2, no. 1 (1965), pp. 4-22, and vol. 2, no. 2 (1965), pp. 35-53

Goichon, A. M. 'Les réfugiés palestiniens en Jordanie', *Espirit* (July and August/September 1964)

— 'La transformation de l'économie jordanienne', *Orient,* nos. 45 and 46 (First and Second Quarter, 1968)

Gubser, Peter *West Bank and Gaza Economic Development,* Middle East Problem Paper no. 20, Middle East Institute (Washington, DC, 1979)

Hagopian, Edward and Zahlan, A. B. 'Palestine's Arab Population: The Demography of the Palestinians', *Journal of Palestine Studies,* vol. 3, no. 4 (Summer 1974), pp. 32-73

Heyd, Uriel 'The Later Ottoman Empire in Rumelia and Anatolia' in P. M. Holt, Ann Lambton and Bernard Lewis (eds.), *Cambridge History of Islam* (Cambridge, 1970), vol. 1, pp. 354-73

Holt, P. M. 'The Later Ottoman Empire and the Fertile Crescent', in P. M. Holt, Ann Lambton and Bernard Lewis (eds.), *Cambridge History of Islam* (2 vols., Cambridge, 1970), vol. 1, pp. 378-80

Hourani, Albert H. 'The Changing Face of the Fertile Crescent in the Eighteenth Century', *Studica Islamica*, vol. 13 (1957), pp. 89-122

— 'Ottoman Reform and the Politics of the Notables' in William R. Polk and Richard L. Chambers (ed.), *Beginnings of Modernisation in the Middle East*, (Chicago, 1968), pp. 41-64

Howard, Harry N. 'UNRWA, the Arab Host Countries and the Arab Refugees', *Middle East Forum*, vol. 42, no. 3 (1966), pp. 29-42

Hudson, Michael C. 'Developments and Setbacks in the Palestinian Resistance Movement, 1967-1971', *Journal of Palestine Studies*, vol. 1, no. 3 (Spring, 1972), pp. 64-84

Issawi, Charles 'Economic Development and Liberalism in Lebanon', *Middle East Journal*, vol. 18, no. 3 (1964), pp. 279-92

Khalidi, Ahmad and Agha, Hussein 'The Palestinian Diaspora', *Middle East Yearbook 1980* (London, 1980), pp. 31-3

Khalidi, Walid 'The Fall of Haifa', *Middle East Forum*, vol. 34, no. 12 (December 1959)

— (trans.) 'Nasser's Memoirs of the First Palestine War', *Journal of Palestine Studies*, vol. 2, no. 2 (Winter 1973), pp. 3-32

— 'Why did the Palestinians Leave?', *Middle East Forum*, vol. 35, no. 7 (July 1959), pp. 21-35

Khass, Mary 'Gaza under Occupation', *MERIP Reports*, vol. 8 no. 2 (March 1978), pp. 20-2

Klat, Paul J. 'Labour Legislation in Lebanon', *Middle East Economic Papers*, Economic Research Institute, American University of Beirut (Beirut, 1959)

Klein, F. A. 'Life, Habits and Customs of the Fellahin of Palestine', Palestine Exploration Fund, *Quarterly Statement* (April 1881), pp. 110-18; (October 1881), pp. 297-304; (January 1883), pp. 41-8

El Kodsy, Ahmad 'Nationalism and Class Struggles in the Arab World', *Monthly Review*, vol. 22, no. 3 (July-August 1970), pp. 1-61

Kossaifi, George 'Demographic Characteristics of the Arab Palestinian People' in Khalil Nakhleh and Elia Zureik (eds.), *The Sociology of the Palestinians* (London, 1980), pp. 13-46

Loew, Guy 'L'essor urbain en Jordanie orientale', *Maghreb-Mashrek*, no. 81 (July-September 1978), pp. 52-3

MacAlister, R. A. Steward and Masterman, E. W. G., 'Occasional Papers on the Modern Inhabitants of Palestine', Palestine Exploration Fund, *Quarterly Statement* (October 1905), pp. 343-52; (January 1906), pp. 33-52

Mari, Sami Khalil 'Higher Education Among Palestinians — with Special Reference to the West Bank', in Gabriel Ben-Dor (ed.), *The Palestinians and the Middle East Conflict* (Ramat Gan, Israel, 1978), pp. 433-8

Mogannam, E. Theodore 'Developments in the Legal System of Jordan', *Middle East Journal*, vol. 6, no. 2 (Spring 1952), pp. 194-205

al-Nabulsi, Sulaiman 'Palestinian Arabs in the State of Jordan', *Al-Difa'* (Jerusalem), 14 May 1953

Oded, Yitzak 'Agriculture in the West Bank', *New Outlook*, vol. 2, no. 2 (February 1968)

Philby, H. St J. 'Trans-Jordan', *Journal of the Royal Central Asian Society*, vol. 2, part 4 (1924), pp. 296-312

Qasmiyah, Khairiyah 'Najib Nassar and *Carmel* Newspaper', *Shuun Filistiniyyah* (*Palestinian Affairs*) (July 1973)

Raymond, André 'Quartiers et mouvements populaires au Caire au XVIIIème siècle' in P. M. Holt (ed.), *Political and Social Change in Modern Egypt* (London, 1968), pp. 104-16

Richardson, Channing B. 'The Palestinian Arab Refugee' in S. N. Fisher (ed.), *Social Forces in the Middle East* (Ithaca, NY, 1955), pp. 237-51

Rifkin, Lena 'Notes from the Occupation: Peace Treaty Sharpens Struggle on West Bank', *MERIP Reports*, vol. 9, no. 10 (December 1979), pp. 3-11

Roberts, John 'Palestine's PLO Embarks on a Diplomatic Offensive', *Interpress Service* (Beirut), 17 November 1978

Rosenfeld, Henry 'From Peasantry to Wage Labour and Residual Peasantry: The Transformation of an Arab Village', in Louise Sweet (ed.) *Peoples and Cultures of the Middle East* (2 vols., Garden City, New York, 1978)

Rouleau, Eric 'Les Palestiniens au purgatoire: II – Les vaincus', *Le Monde*, 10 January 1973

—'The Wondering Palestinians', *Guardian* (weekly edition), 27 January 1973

Rubin, Trudy 'Palestinians in Beirut', *New Outlook*, vol. 18, no. 1 (January 1975), pp. 22-9

Sakhnini, 'Issam 'Damm Filistin al-wusta ila sharqiyyi al-Urdun 1948-1950' ('The Annexation of Central Palestine to East Jordan 1948-1950'), *Shuun Filistiniyyah* (*Palestinian Affairs*), no. 42-3 (February 1975), pp. 56-83

—'Al-Kiyan al-filistiniyyi 1964-74' ('The Palestinian Entity, 1964-74'), *Shuun Filistiniyyah*, no. 40 (December 1974), pp. 46-66

El Sayed, Afaf Loutfi 'The Role of the *'ulama* in Egypt during the Early Nineteenth Century' in P. M. Holt (ed.), *Political and Social Change in Modern Egypt* (London, 1968), pp. 264-80

Schlaim, A. 'The Gaza Raid, 1955', *Middle East International* (April 1978), pp. 25-8

Seikaly, May and Smith, Pamela Ann 'Palestinians in the Gulf', *Middle East Annual Review 1982* (Saffron Walden, Essex, 1982), pp. 53-5

Shaath, Nabil 'High-Level Palestinian Manpower', *Journal of Palestine Studies*, vol. 1, no. 2 (Winter 1972), pp. 80-95

Shehab, Fakhri 'Kuwait: A Super Affluent Society', *Foreign Affairs*, vol. 42 (April 1964), pp. 461-74

Shoufani, Elias 'The Fall of a Village', *Journal of Palestine Studies*, vol. 1, no. 3 (Summer 1972), pp. 108-21

Sirhan, Bassam 'Palestinian Children: The Generation of Liberation', Palestine Essays no. 23, Research Centre, Palestine Liberation Organisation (Beirut, 1970)

—'Palestinian Refugee Camp Life in Lebanon', *Journal of Palestine Studies*, vol. 4, no. 2 (Winter 1975), pp. 91-107

Sitbon, Guy 'Des camps des tentes aux palais princiers', *Le Nouvel Observateur*, 17 April 1982, pp. 33-4

Smilianskaya, I. M. 'The Disintegration of Feudal Relations in Syria and Lebanon in the Middle of the Nineteenth Century', in Charles Issawi (ed.), *The Economic History of the Middle East* (Chicago, 1966), pp. 227-47

Smith, Colin and Andrews, John 'The Palestinians', Minority Rights Group Report no. 24, new edn (London, February 1977)

St Aubin, William 'Peace and Refugees in the Middle East', *Middle East Journal*, vol. 3, no. 3 (July 1949)

Tamari, Salim 'Building Other Peoples' Homes: The Palestinian Peasant's Household and Work in Israel', *Journal of Palestine Studies*, vol. 11, no. 1 (Autumn 1981)

— 'The Palestinian Demand for Independence Cannot Be Postponed Indefinitely', *MERIP Reports* (October-December 1981), pp. 28-35

Wright, Esmond 'Abdullah's Jordan', *Middle East Journal*, vol. 5, no. 4 (Autumn 1951)

Zeine, Zeine 'The Arab Lands' in P. M. Holt, Ann Lambton and Bernard Lewis (eds.), *Cambridge History of Islam* (Cambridge, 1970), vol. 1, pp. 586-91

V Newspapers and Magazines

a. United States and Europe

Afrique-Asie
Al-'Arab (London)
Arab Report and Record
Christian Science Monitor
Die Dritte Welt
Elements
Events (London)
Financial Times
Foreign Affairs
Guardian
International Herald Tribune
Khamsin (London)
Maghreb-Mashrek
MERIP Reports
The Middle East
Middle East Economic Digest
Middle East International

Middle East Journal
Middle East Monitor
Middle East Studies
Le Monde
Le Monde Diplomatique
Monthly Review
The Muslim World (Hartford)
Al-Mustaqbal (Paris)
New York Times
Le Nouvel Observateur
The Observer
Orient
Oriente Moderno
The Palestine Post (Dundee)
Peuples Méditerranéens
Sunday Times (London)
The Times (London)

b. The Arab World and Israel

Al-Ahram (Cairo)
Al-Akhbar (Cairo)
Al-Anwar (Beirut)
Aramco World

Le Commerce du Levant
Daily Star
Al-Difa' (Jerusalem)
Dirasat 'Arabiyyah

Emirates News
Al-Fajr (Jerusalem)
Fiches du Monde Arabe (*FMA*)
Filistin (Haifa)
Gulf Times (Qatar)
Haaretz
Al-Hadaf (Beirut)
Al-Hayat (Beirut)
Al-Hurriyah (Beirut)
Jordan Times
Journal of Palestine Studies
Al-Katib al-Filistinniyyi

Mawaqif
Middle East Forum
El Moudjahid (Algiers)
Al-Nahar Arab Report
New Outlook
L'Orient-Le Jour
Al-Safir (Beirut)
Shuun Filistiniyyah
Al-Tali'ah
Al-Tariq (Beirut)
Al-Watan (Kuwait)

GLOSSARY OF ARABIC TERMS*

'abā' (p. = *'a'bay'ah*): woollen cloak worn by the Bedouin tribes of Palestine.

'ā'ilah: household; extended family.

'āmir: prince; commander.

'ard: land; (the) earth.

'ashā'ir (s. = *'ashīrah*): tribal clans.

al-'ashrāf (s. = *sharīf*): the nobility.

badāwī (p. = *badāwiyyīn*, i.e. 'Bedouin'): nomad; member of a nomadic tribe. In Palestine the Bedouin often cultivated small plots of land as well as grazing animals.

bait: house; home; residence.

biyyārāt (s. = *biyyārah*): plantations, often used for the cultivation of citrus fruits.

dār: house; home; country seat of a clan or extended family.

dīnār: Arab unit of currency. In 1950 the Jordanian *dinar* replaced the Palestine pound as the legal currency in the West Bank; at that time 1 JD was equal to £1 sterling or $2.80.

dūnum: measure of land equal to approximately 900 square metres.

durra: hard wheat originally used to make bread, but later used primarily to make macaroni.

fedā'i (p. = *fedā'iyyīn*): literally, one who sacrifices himself for a cause or country; guerrillas.

fellah (p. = *fellahīn*): peasant.

Filistīn: Palestine.

ghanim: under the Ottomans, a tax on sheep and other animals.

harrāth (p. = *harathīn*): ploughman.

hawākir (s. = *hākūrah*): small vegetable gardens, each usually tilled by a single family.

'iltizām: concession or contract; under the Ottomans, a tax concession on land.

'imām: a religious title used in Shi'a Islam; in Palestine the term refers to an informal leader of prayers.

al-'imārah: princely status; princely manners or bearing.

'iqtā': fief; feudal estate.

'iqtā'ī (p. = *'iqtā'īyyīn*): holder of a fief; feudal lord.

'ird: honour (especially family honour); respect; dignity.

---

*Because of the use of a more detailed transliteration system in this list, the spellings may differ slightly from those used in the text. The Arabic consonants ' [ain] and ' [hamza] have no equivalent in English. s. = singular; p. = plural. Long vowels are indicated as *ā, ī, ū*. An 'e' or 'ee' may replace the Arabic 'a' or 'ī' in words commonly used in English, i.e. *sheikh, fellahin, jeel*.

'izzah: honour; respect; pride.

jaish: army.

jabal: mountain.

jeel (jīl): age or epoch; generation.

jihād: a war in defence of the faith; sacred struggle; holy war.

jizyah; a poll tax imposed by the Ottomans on non-Muslims.

kūffiyah: draped cloth headdress worn by the peasantry.

khatīb: religious orator; preacher; title of the official allowed to give the Friday sermon in a mosque.

madanī (p. = *madaniyyīn*): urban dweller; a civilised person.

majlis-i 'idārah: administrative council set up by the Ottomans in the second half of the nineteenth century.

mewat: grazing land.

mīrī: Crown land.

mūftī: interpreter of Koranic law; under the Ottomans the title of the highest dignitary in Jerusalem.

mulk: landed property given by the Sultan to a military leader; freehold.

multazim: concessionaire; tax farmer; the holder of an *iltizām*.

mushā': in Palestine, a system of joint tenancy; joint or public ownership.

al-nakbah: catastrophe; disaster; term referring to the defeat of the Arabs by Israel in 1948.

qādī: judge empowered to rule on matters of Islamic law; magistrate.

al-Qais (s. = *Qaisi*): one of two major tribal confederations in Palestine.

qiyādah: leadership; the quality of leadership or command.

al-Quds: Jerusalem.

sheikh (p. = *shuyuk*): title given to the head of a clan; more commonly, a title of respect.

al-Shā'm: Syria. Under the Ottomans the term referred to the Arab provinces of the Levant, including Lebanon, Jordan and Palestine as well as Syria.

Sharī'ah: the Holy Law of Islam; canonic law.

sharīf (p. = *'ashrāf*): generally a title of nobility reserved for the descendants of the Prophet Muhammad and the great military leaders of the first Islamic conquests; in Palestine a title applied to the intellectual and religious elite.

Shī'a: A branch of Islam loyal to 'Ali, the son-in-law of the Prophet Muhammad.

simsār: broker; agent; middleman.

Sunnī: the main body of Islam, commonly regarded as orthodox.

Tanzimāt: reforms; a set of legal decrees introduced by the Ottomans in the nineteenth century.

thawrah: revolution.

'ulamā' (s. = *'alīm*): body of learned men; the clergy.

'ushr: literally, a tenth; tax (tithe) on agricultural produce imposed by the Ottomans.

walī: friend or associate; under the Ottomans the title given to a provincial governor.

waqf (p. = *'awqāf*): charitable estate donated to provide revenues for the Muslim community; land set aside in perpetuity (usually for a family and its heirs) which was regarded as inalienable.

wilāyah: province.

wirkū: land use tax imposed by the Ottomans.

wajāhah: prestige; notability.

wujahā' (s. = *wajīh*): notables; body of distinguished men.

al-Yaman (s. = *Yamani*): one of two major tribal confederations in Palestine.

za'āmah: leadership; claim or pretension of leadership.

zalat: Turkish coin used by the Ottomans.

INDEX

Note: Arabic names are alphabetised under the first name after the Arabic article, as are such names as Abu. *Noms de guerre* are generally given under the proper name.

269